THE COMIC
IMAGINATION
IN AMERICAN
LITERATURE

THE COMIC IMAGINATION IN AMERICAN LITERATURE

Edited by
Louis D. Rubin, Jr. 1923 –

RUTGERS UNIVERSITY PRESS
New Brunswick   New Jersey

"Dog Around the Block," from *The Fox of Peapack*, by E. B. White, copyright © 1930 by E. B. White, originally appeared in *The New Yorker* and is reprinted by permission of the author and Harper & Row, publishers.

"The Kangaroo," copyright © 1942 by Ogden Nash, originally appeared in *The New Yorker;* "Spring Comes to Murray Hill," copyright © 1930 by Ogden Nash, originally appeared in *The New Yorker;* "The Turtle," copyright © 1940 by Ogden Nash; and "The Duck," copyright © 1936 by The Curtis Publishing Company, are reprinted from *Verses from 1929 On*, by Ogden Nash, by permission of Little, Brown and Company.

"The Rich Man," from *The Melancholy Lute*, by Franklin P. Adams, is reprinted by permission of the estate of Franklin P. Adams.

"Bric-à-brac" and "Unfortunate Coincidence" from *The Portable Dorothy Parker*, copyright © 1926, 1954, by Dorothy Parker; and "Résumé" from *The Portable Dorothy Parker*, copyright © 1928, 1956, by Dorothy Parker are reprinted by permission of The Viking Press, Inc.

Library of Congress Cataloging in Publication Data

Rubin, Louis Decimus, 1923–
    The comic imagination in American literature.

    Based on a series of lectures prepared for the Voice of America.
    1. American wit and humor—History and criticism.
I. Voice of America (Radio program) II. Title.
PS430.R8   810'.9'17   73–7921
ISBN 0–8135–0758–8

Contents

Preface

The thirty-two papers in this book, all having to do with the comic imagination in American literature, were originally prepared for a Forum series on that topic to be broadcast to overseas audiences over the Voice of America. In 1971 I was approached by the United States Information Agency and asked to serve as coordinator for such a series. I was given the general theme; the choice of individual topics within that framework, and of those persons who would be asked to handle them, was my own, the only stipulation being that I was expected to provide an introductory and a concluding paper and to give at least one of the others. The broadcast format dictated that the papers were to be prepared so that each could be delivered in twenty-seven minutes, though no limitation of length was placed on the published version. The contributors were also given the option of either delivering the papers they had written as talks, or being interviewed on the topics discussed in the papers. As in previous such Forum series, the Voice of America planned to publish the papers for overseas distribution, and I was encouraged to arrange for U.S. publication as I saw fit. Accordingly, the Rutgers University Press was approached, and agreed to undertake book publication.

As should be obvious, given the nature of the occasion for their preparation, the papers that follow are introductory. They are designed to acquaint an audience of listeners, presumably without much detailed knowledge of American literature, with some of the themes, high points, and principal practitioners of comedy in American literature. The term "comic imagination" was construed along broader lines than might ordinarily be expected. Of course the out-and-out humorists were to be included—one could hardly do better than to secure James M. Cox to discuss Mark Twain, Gerald Weales for the *New Yorker* writers, and so on. But of at least equal importance in any portrayal of the comic imagination in American literature were those writers who, while not ordinarily considered humorists, draw deeply upon the comic impulse in their work. A novelist such as William Faulkner, for example, though perhaps best known for his great tragedies, has also written some of the finest comedy in the English language. Not only that, but as Robert D. Jacobs shows, there is, mixed in with the tragedy in such novels as *Light in August*, much that is calculated to draw laughter. And there are other writers whose work, as George Core points out about Henry James, while not the straight, side-splitting comedy of a Clemens or a Faulkner, is nonetheless deeply infused with the comic spirit. And even such "morbid" and "gloomy" writers as Nathaniel Hawthorne and Edgar Allan Poe are not without the important comic overtones which Hennig Cohen explores in his paper.

Indeed, one could go on from there, and demonstrate that there is scarcely an important American writer who does not at one time or another see the problem before him comically. Surely Jake Barnes on Robert Cohn's predilection for *The Purple Land* in Hemingway's *The Sun Also Rises* is amusing, and also Little Topsy in *Uncle Tom's Cabin*, and the amatory tactics of the salesman Drouet in Dreiser's *Sister Carrie*, and the spectacle of Tom Buchanan trying to think about the future of the Nordic race in Fitzgerald's *The Great Gatsby*, and so on. But one would have to draw the line somewhere, if the Voice of America were not to devote its Forum to comedy in American literature for years to come.

In any event, I set out to make up my list, and to select contributors accordingly. The objective was to sketch out the modes of American comedy, ranging from the journalistic and the subliterary on through the reaches of artistic achievement, to cover some of the leading practitioners of comedy, and to try to suggest some of the relationships between the comic writings of Americans and the problems—literary, philosophical, social, political, economic— of the society whose life they sought to interpret. Beyond what was possible through the selection of topics and contributors, I did not presume to instruct my colleagues as to precisely what those problems and those relationships were, since I did not pretend to have more than a very general notion about the matter myself. At first it was thought that the cause of unity of focus in these papers might be advanced by preparation of an introductory essay which could be distributed to all the participants in advance. But after I surveyed what was available in the line of commentary and theoretical formulation about American comedy, beyond Walter Blair's introduction to his anthology *Native American Humor*, I came to the swift conclusion that so little had been written on the subject (the best such book, Constance Rourke's *American Humor*, was forty years old!) that it would be both premature and presumptuous to attempt to formulate any such thematic preface and then expect the contributors to follow it. Thus the two essays that introduce and conclude this collection represent my own independent notion of what is involved, and do not in any sense serve as a blueprint for the thirty papers appearing between them in the Table of Contents. Perhaps from these papers a future scholar may be able to find the suggestions from which to develop a more definitive and all-inclusive theory of American literary comedy than is set forth here.

If one surveys the various papers that make up this volume, one notes at once that not all the contributors viewed their tasks in the same way. Some of the papers concentrate on presenting the work discussed to an audience largely unfamiliar with it, without too much interpretation, while others seek to use the work to get at the culture from which it came. Perhaps this is just as well; for this volume constitutes in effect the first full-scale symposium ever attempted on the length and breadth of the American comic imagination, and under such circumstances a variety of approaches is all to the good. The industry and prodigality of modern-day American literary scholarship being what they are, it may seem strange that so little writing has been done about so vast a subject, but such would appear to be the case. Perhaps the very tentative nature of this kind of volume, intended not so much for other American scholars as for an overseas listening audience, may serve to whet the appetites of American scholars for more and better study of the subject; if so, I, the contributors, and the publisher will be gratified.

All the same, despite the introductory function imposed upon the contributors, there are some distinguished papers here, which go deeply and imaginatively into their subjects, and are not soon to be superseded. One doubts, for example, that the basic impulse behind much nineteenth-century humor has anywhere been more keenly searched out than within the brief compass of James Cox's study of the Southwestern humorists, or that a better insight into what Ring Lardner and Sinclair Lewis were about has been provided than in C. Hugh Holman's essay, or that the relationship of the contemporary Jewish novelists to American tradition on the one hand and European Jewish humor on the other has been set forth with more authority than Allen Guttmann manages in his paper. Or that—but one must desist, or else appear to be playing favorites among a host of good papers.

In a sense, writing *about* humor and humorists is perforce an awkward business. For after all, the humor is *funny;* it is aimed at the risibilities, designed to make the reader laugh, not think. So when one sets out to think about it and to subject it to analysis, there is always the lurking suspicion that, in so doing, one is not only responding improperly, but behaving just a trifle ridiculously. One lays oneself wide open for the critic to ridicule all this solemn pontificating about funny writing. But what, after all, can one do about that? Quote generously from the humor, of course; but even that scarcely does justice to it: it was not meant to be excerpted and quoted but read in full. Now of course in point of strict logic one ought not to feel that way. One does not require the dentist to have the toothache, and the political analyst to run for office and accept free vacations in Florida, in order that they may ply their trades. Still, in a project such as this one, the unease is present, and it might just as well be admitted. In any event, I would declare that, given the limitations of the format, the contributors have all in all labored very sturdily indeed, and to good effect, and that it is to editorial incapacity rather than to authorial inadequacy that most of the defects herein deserve to be ascribed.

Speaking of which, the editor is all too conscious of certain omissions. Somehow, in the planning and assigning of thirty-odd essays on American comedy, provision was not made for presentation of the extravagances of Thomas Wolfe's Gant family, and that is most unfortunate. The local color writers would appear to have been shortchanged: very little Bret Harte or George W.

Cable. There should have been a place for William Saroyan, and for Clarence Day, and for a few of those creatures of John Steinbeck. And isn't there much humor in Walt Whitman, and considerably more in Emily Dickinson? Where is J. D. Salinger? Where is John Crowe Ransom? Where indeed? Can one view Mr. Apeneck Sweeney with entire gravity, or even J. Alfred Prufrock? And so on. The editor is to blame for this; he freely admits it, but he is to blame nonetheless.

As for imbalance, well, that is another matter. One might, for example, question the decision to devote an entire essay, even so good a one as Jay Martin's, to Ambrose Bierce, while a James Thurber or an E. B. White is discussed, though very well indeed, only to the extent of a few paragraphs. To this I would reply that within so limited a purview, I had to group and combine where I could, and that whereas Thurber and White (and Benchley and Perelman and others) might with some appropriateness be considered together as exemplary of the best performance of a single, very influential magazine, there was no way to combine a Bierce with anybody or anything else. Given sixty-four essays instead of thirty-two I could have cut down on such imbalance, though even then hardly to the satisfaction of everyone. But with only thirty-two places to be filled, and so much with which to fill them, it was necessary to use sleight of hand, and that is what I did.

The idea for this Forum on the comic imagination in American literature was first conceived by Max Grossman, then editor of the Voice of America Forum series. Midway through the proceedings Mr. Grossman retired, and was succeeded by Richard Gordon. It would be impossible for the coordinator of such a venture as this to have received greater support and understanding than that provided by both these gentlemen, and I am grateful. Karin Gleiter, a graduate student at the University of North Carolina at Chapel Hill and business manager of the *Southern Literary Journal*, provided the steadfast secretarial stability that any such catch-as-catch-can editorial venture needs. The Department of English of the University of North Carolina at Chapel Hill, in particular its then-chairman James R. Gaskin, offered ample help and encouragement.

And it was good to be part of an American Literature staff of such strength up and down the line that when at the last minute certain papers turned up undelivered, one had only to turn to one's own departmental colleagues for fill-ins. Finally, a number of the broadcast recordings of these papers were done here in Chapel Hill, where I enjoyed the full cooperation of the University's Department of Radio, Television, and Motion Pictures.

Louis D. Rubin, Jr.
University of North Carolina
at Chapel Hill

Chapel Hill, North Carolina
November 1, 1972

THE COMIC
IMAGINATION
IN AMERICAN
LITERATURE

Introduction:
"The Great American Joke"

Louis D. Rubin, Jr.

He took a pen and some paper. "Now—name of the elephant?"

"Hassan Ben Ali Selim Abdallah Mohammed Moise Alhammal Jamsetje-jeebhoy Dhuleep Sultan Ebu Bhudpoor."

"Very well. Given name?"

"Jumbo."

Mark Twain, The Stolen White Elephant

The American literary imagination has from its earliest days been at least as much comic in nature as tragic. Perhaps this is only as might be expected; for while the national experience has involved sadness, disappointment, failure and even despair, it has also involved much joy, hopefulness, accomplishment. The tragic mode, therefore, could not of itself comprehend the full experience of the American people. From the moment that the colonists at Jamestown were assailed by the arrows of hostile Indians, and one Mr. Wynckfield "had one shott cleane through his bearde, yet scaped hurte," there has been too much to smile at. The type of society that has evolved in the northern portion of the western hemisphere bears no notable resemblance either to Eden or to Utopia, of course. From the start it has been inhabited by human beings who have remained most human and therefore most fallible. Even so, if one views American history as a whole it would be very difficult to pronounce it a tragedy, or to declare that the society of man would have been better off if it had never taken place (though Mark Twain once suggested as much).

3

Yet for all that, it is remarkable how comparatively little attention has been paid to American humor, and to the comic imagination in general, by those who have chronicled and interpreted American literature. Thalia, the muse of comedy, has always been something of a wallflower in critical circles, and the attention has gone principally to Melpomene and her more glamorous celebrants of tragedy. In large part, of course, this is because in the hierarchy of letters comedy has always occupied a position below and inferior to tragedy. We have tended to equate gravity with importance. The highest accolade we give to a humorist is when we say that even so he is a "serious" writer—which is to say that although he makes us laugh, his ultimate objective is to say something more about the human condition than merely that it is amusing. This implies that comedy is "un-serious"—we thus play a verbal trick, for we use "serious" to mean both "important" and "without humor," when the truth is that there is no reason at all why something cannot be at once very important and very comic.

In any event, more time and effort have been invested in attempting to study and to understand American tragedy than American comedy, and humorous writing is customarily relegated to a subordinate role. In so doing, we have been guilty of neglecting a valuable insight into the understanding of American society. For not only have many American writers been comic writers, but the very nature of comedy would seem to make it particularly useful in studying life in the United States. When Mark Twain speaks of "the calm confidence of a Christian holding four aces," he makes a joke and notes a human incongruity of interest to historians of American Protestantism. The essence of comedy is incongruity, the perception of the ridiculous. The seventeenth-century English critic Dennis's remark, that "the design of Comedy is to amend the follies of Mankind, by exposing them," points to the value of humor in searching out the shortcomings and the liabilities of society. In a democracy, the capacity for self-criticism would seem to be an essential function of the body politic, and surely this has been one of the chief tasks of the American writer. Thus H. L. Mencken, himself a newspaperman, rebukes the American press. The brain of the average journalist, he reports, "is a mass of trivialities and puerilities; to recite it would be to make even a barber beg for mercy." From colonial times onward, we have spent a great deal of time and effort criticizing ourselves, pointing out our short-comings, exploring the incongruities and the contradictions within American society. As the novelist and poet Robert Penn Warren put it, "America was based on a big promise—a great big one: the Declaration of Independence. When you have to live with that in the house, that's quite a problem—particularly when you've got to make money and get ahead, open world markets, do all the things you have to, raise your children, and so forth. America is stuck with its self-definition put on paper in 1776, and that was just like putting a burr under the metaphysical saddle of America—you see, that saddle's going to jump now and then and it pricks." Literature has been one of the important ways whereby the American people have registered their discomfort at those pricks, and repeatedly the discomfort has been expressed in the form of humor—often enough through just such a homely metaphor as Warren used. For if we look at Warren's remark, what we will notice is that it makes use of a central motif of American humor—the contrast, the incongruity between the ideal and the real, in which a common, vernacular metaphor is used to put a somewhat abstract statement involving values—self-definition, metaphysical—into a homely context. The statement, in other words, makes its point through working an incongruity between two modes of language—the formal, literary language of traditional culture and learning, and the informal, vernacular language of everyday life.

This verbal incongruity lies at the heart of American experience. It is emblematic of the nature and the problem of democracy. On the one hand there are the ideals of freedom, equality, self-govern-ment, the conviction that ordinary people can evince the wisdom to vote wisely, and demonstrate the capacity for understanding and cherishing the highest human values through embodying them in their political and social institutions. On the other hand there is the *Congressional Record*—the daily exemplary reality of the fact that the individual citizens of a democracy are indeed ordinary people, who speak, think and act in ordinary terms, with a suspicion of abstract ideas and values. Thus Senator Simon Cameron of Penn-sylvania, after his Committee on Foreign Relations had rejected the nomination of Richard Henry Dana as U.S. Ambassador to

England, could exult because his country would not be represented
at the Court of St. James's by "another of those damned literary
fellows." The problem of democracy and culture is one of how,
in short, a democracy can reach down to include all its citizens in
its decision-making, without at the same time cheapening and vul-
garizing its highest social, cultural and ethical ideals. Who, that is,
will, in a democracy, commission the Esterhazy quartets? Confronting this problem, Thomas Jefferson called for an *aristoi*, an
aristocracy of intellect; he believed that through public education
the civilized values of truth, knowledge and culture that he cherished would be embodied and safeguarded in the democratic process
so that leadership could be produced which would not be dema-
gogic and debasing. His good friend John Adams was skeptical of
this ever coming to pass, and Adams's great-grandson, Henry
Adams, lived to chronicle and deplore a time when the workings
of political and economic democracy made heroes of the vulgar
and the greedy, and had no place in the spectrum of power, he
thought, for an Adams who by virtue of inbred inheritance still
believed in the disinterested morality, as he saw it, of the Founding
Fathers. What Henry Adams could not fathom was why the public could nominate for the presidency of the United States a Ulysses
Grant, a James A. Garfield, a James G. Blaine, and then vote for
him. He could only conclude that "the moral law had expired—
like the Constitution." "The progress of evolution from President
Washington to President Grant," he concluded, "was alone evidence enough to upset Darwin."

The problem has been part of American experience from the
start, and it is at least as crucial today as in the past. Though it is
by no means purely or uniquely American, it is nevertheless distinctively so, and if we look at American literary history we will
quickly recognize that the writers have been dealing with it all
along the way. Herman Melville's famous invocation to the muses
in *Moby-Dick* faces it squarely:

If, then, to meanest mariners, and renegades and castaways, I shall hereafter ascribe high qualities, though dark; weave round them tragic graces;
if even the most mournful, perchance the most abased, among them all, shall
at times lift himself to the exalted mounts; if I shall spread a rainbow over

his disastrous set of sun; then against all mortal spirits bear me out in it, thou just Spirit of Equality, which hast spread one royal mantle of humanity over all my kind! Bear me out in it, thou great democratic God! . . .

Melville wanted to create a tragedy along metaphysical lines, and yet he wanted to write about the Nantucket whaling fleet; his problem was how to render the everyday experience of life aboard a whaling vessel while creating a tragic protagonist, one who, in Aristotle's classic formula, could arouse pity and terror through his fall from eminence. Obviously such a protagonist, Aristotle declared, "must be one who is highly renowned and prosperous,—a personage like Oedipus, Thyestes, or other illustrious men of such families." How to give a whaling captain such heroic stature? Melville's solution was partly one of language. He separated the two elements. He used a literary, highly poetic, Shakespearean diction to chronicle Ahab, and a much more vernacular, colloquial diction to report on the activities of the crew. He made the language distance between tragic captain and motley crew serve his ultimate meaning.

In so doing, however, Melville was forced to distort and impoverish the experience of a whaling captain. He could not make (nor did he wish to make) Captain Ahab into a "typical" Nantucket whaling skipper. He had to leave out a great deal of what an ordinary whaling captain does and says and thinks. The Captain of the *Pequod* must not cuss out the cabin boy in approved Nantucket style. To achieve the magnificent tragedy of Ahab against the universe, Melville was forced to sacrifice much of what a whaling captain was *as a whaling captain*. The "realism" of *Moby-Dick* does not extend to the Captain of the *Pequod*. No one would lament the loss; *Moby-Dick* is worth whatever it cost to make it possible. But all the same, the problem remains. How does the writer evoke the civilized values—of language, religion, philosophy, culture in general—that have traditionally been used to give order and delineate meaning in society, while at the same time remaining faithful to the everyday texture of "low life" experience? How may a whaling captain grapple with the eternal verities and yet be shown doing it in the terms in which such things would confront a whaling captain, and in a mode of language that can reproduce his experi-

ence *as* a whaling captain? How many Nantucket whaling skip-
pers, upon confronting their prey, would be heard declaring "Aye,
breach your last to the sun, Moby Dick . . . thy hour and thy
harpoon are at hand"? How to make a whaling captain into a
tragic hero, in other words, without using as model the literary
image of a Shakespearean tragedy? This has been the dilemma of
the American writer from colonial times onward.

Henry James, in a famous passage about Nathaniel Hawthorne,
expressed the cultural problem quite (I will not say succinctly,
since that is no word for the style of even the early Henry James)
appropriately. Taking his cue from something that Hawthorne
himself wrote, James declared that

one might enumerate the forms of high civilization, as it exists in other
countries, which are absent from the texture of American life, until it
should be a wonder to know what was left. No State, in the European
sense of the word, and indeed barely a specific national name. No sovereign,
no court, no personal loyalty, no aristocracy, no church, no clergy, no
army, no diplomatic service, no country gentlemen, no palaces, no castles,
nor manors, nor old country-houses, nor parsonages, not thatched cottages
nor ivied ruins; no cathedrals, nor abbeys, nor little Norman churches; no
great Universities nor public schools—no Oxford, nor Eton, nor Harrow; no
literature, no novels, no museums, no pictures, no political society, no
sporting class—no Epsom nor Ascot! Some such list as that might be drawn
up of the absent things in American life—especially in the American life of
forty years ago, the effect of which, upon an English or a French imagination, would probably as a general thing be appalling.

But James does not stop there. "The American knows that a good
deal remains," he continues; "what it is that remains—that is his
secret, his joke, as one may say. It would be cruel, in this terrible
denudation, to deny him the consolation of his national gift, that
'American humor' of which of late years we have heard so much."
James's words are appropriately chosen, for so much of American
literature has focused upon just that national "joke"—by which I
take him to mean the fact that in a popular democracy the customary and characteristic institutions that have traditionally embodied
cultural, social and ethical values are missing from the scene, and
yet the values themselves, and the attitudes that derive from and
serve to maintain them, remain very much part of the national ex-

perience. This is what Robert Penn Warren meant by the "burr under the metaphysical saddle of America," which pricks whenever the saddle jumps. Out of the incongruity between mundane circumstance and heroic ideal, material fact and spiritual hunger, democratic, middle-class society and desire for cultural definition, theory of equality and fact of social and economic inequality, the Declaration of Independence and the Mann Act, the Gettysburg Address and the Gross National Product, the Battle Hymn of the Republic and the Union Trust Company, the Horatio Alger ideal and the New York Social Register—between what men would be and must be, as acted out in American experience, has come much pathos, no small amount of tragedy, and also a great deal of humor. Both the pathos and the humor have been present from the start, and the writers have been busy pointing them out. This, then, has been what has been called "the great American joke," which comedy has explored and imaged.

One of the more amusing sketches in Joseph Glover Baldwin's *The Flush Times of Alabama and Mississippi* (1853) is that entitled "Simon Suggs, Jr., Esq: A Legal Biography." Baldwin took his character's name from that given to the old scoundrel in Johnson Jones Hooper's Simon Suggs stories. Like his father, Suggs, Jr., is semiliterate and a complete rogue. The sketch opens with some correspondence between Suggs, Jr., and the promoters of a New York biographical magazine, who write to inform him that he has been honored by having been chosen to have his biographical sketch appear in public print, and asking him to furnish biographical details and a suitable daguerreotype. The letter to Suggs, Jr., is couched in the most formal and flowery of terms, but its message is in effect a suggestion that by having his biography appear in the magazine suitably worded, Suggs, Jr., will perhaps be chosen to be a judge some day. To this elaborately worded invitation—"We know from experience, that the characteristic diffidence of the profession, in many instances, shrinks from the seeming, though falsely seeming, indelicacy of an egotistical parade of one's own talents and accomplishments . . ."—Suggs, Jr., responds with misspelled alacrity: "I'm obleeged to you for your perlite say so, and so forth. I got a friend to rite it—my own ritin being mostly perfeshunal. He done it—but he rites such a cussed bad hand I cant

rede it: I reckon its all kerrect tho'." He doesn't have a daguerreotype available, but the engraving of his famous father appearing in
Hooper's *Some Adventures of Simon Suggs* will do for him if
retouched to make him look a bit younger. He then receives
another letter from the publisher, thanking him for his sketch, "the
description of a lawyer distinguished in the out-door labors of his
profession, and directing great energies to the preparation of
proof." In a postscript, however, the editor informs Suggs, Jr., that
"our delicacy caused us to omit . . . to mention what we suppose
was generally understood, viz., the fact that the cost to us of preparing engravings &c. &c., for the sketches or memoirs, is one
hundred and fifty dollars, which sum it is expected, of course, the
gentleman who is perpetuated in our work, will forward to us
before the insertion of his biography. . . ."

Suggs, Jr., now realizes what is going on, and he writes, *"Dear
Mr. Editor*—In your p.s. which seems to be the creem of your correspondents you say I can't get in your book without paying one
hundred and fifty dollars—pretty tall entrants fee!" He tells them
"I believe I will pass. I'll enter a nolly prossy q. O-n-e-h-u-n-
d-r-e-d-dollars and fifty better! Je-whellikens." He has begun "to
see the pint of many things which was very vague and ondefinit
before." And so on.

Following this exchange of correspondence, we then get the
text of the biographical sketch which was prepared by Simon
Suggs, Jr.'s friend for inclusion in the magazine. It is cast in the
elegiac, flowery tone of such self-adulatory biographical sketches,
and it makes the most of a very checkered career, putting the kind-
est construction possible on the events of that career. What is described is the story of various slick dealings by a consummate rogue
and trickster, involving much swindling, knavery, and dishonesty,
and couched throughout in the most formal and literary of tones.
The humor consists of the self-important pomposity of the literary
method of narration as it contrasts with the very undignified vernacular antics being described. To wit:

Col. Suggs also extricated a client and his sureties from a forfeited recog-
nizance, by having the defaulting defendant's obituary notice somewhat
prematurely inserted in the newspapers; the solicitor, seeing which, dis-

continued proceedings; for which service, the deceased, immediately after the adjournment of court, returned to the officer his particular acknowledgements. . . .

The sketch concludes with Simon Suggs, Jr., in Washington attempting to settle claims on behalf of the Choctaw Indians, and with the suggestion that "may the Indians live to get their dividends of the arrears paid to their agent."

Now the humor of this sketch, like that of most of the writings of the humorists of the old nineteenth-century Southern frontier, comes out of the clash of language modes. Baldwin is perhaps the most extreme of all of them in this respect. A well-educated and highly literate man, he adopts the persona of a cultivated gentleman in order to describe the wild, untutored, catch-as-catch-can doings of the old frontier regions. The tone is that of condescension, and the humor arises out of the inappropriateness of the way in which vernacular and usually crass activities are described in quite ornate and pompous language. But although the author's spokesman is a man of culture and refinement who is amused by and somewhat contemptuous of the uninhibited, semicivilized crudeness of the frontier folk, there is also an element of respect for the way that the low-life characters can get right to the point and deal directly with experience. Suggs, Jr.'s shrewdness in spotting what the invitation to submit a sketch for the magazine really involves, his failure to be taken in by the flowery language and erudite circumlocutions of the thing, are, in the context, quite admirable. Suggs, Jr., is a rogue, to be sure, as his biographical sketch admirably demonstrates, but he does not pretend to be anything other than that. The New York entrepreneur, by contrast, is every bit as dishonest. Though his magazine is supposedly designed to supply "a desideratum in American literature, namely, the commemoration and perpetuation of the names, characters, and personal and professional traits and histories of American lawyers and jurists," and though he says that Simon, Jr., has been selected for inclusion by "many of the most prominent gentlemen in public and private life, who have the honor of your acquaintance," what he is really doing is selling self-advertisements in the guise of biographical sketches. Unlike Simon, Jr., however, he pretends to be doing so "from mo-

tives purely patriotic and disinterested," in order that "through
our labors, the reputation of distinguished men of the country,
constituting its moral treasure, may be preserved for the admiration and direction of mankind, not for a day, but for all time."
Suggs, Jr., in brief, is a crude but honest rogue, and the editor of
the magazine is a civilized but hypocritical confidence man.

Here, indeed, is the elementary, basic American humorous situation—the "great American joke," and in one very obvious form.
The humor arises out of the gap between the cultural ideal and
the everyday fact, with the ideal shown to be somewhat hollow
and hypocritical, and the fact crude and disgusting.

The so-called frontier humor was admirably constituted to image
the problems of meaning and existence in a society that was very
much caught up in the process of formation. In the Old Southwest
—Georgia, West Florida, Alabama, Mississippi—of the 1820's,
1830's, and 1840's, virgin wilderness was almost overnight being
converted into farmland, and towns and cities coming into being
where the forest trails crossed. New wealth was being created, and
old fortunes either vastly augmented or lost overnight. Rich and
poor flocked into the new lands, and the social distinctions brought
from the older society of the Eastern seaboard were very much
disordered and distorted by the new circumstance. The ability to
parse a Latin verb or ride to the hounds would be less than completely useful in the fashionable parlors of Tuscaloosa, Alabama,
and Columbus, Mississippi, for some time to come. Society, in
other words, was being reordered, and former distinctions of class
and caste rearranged in accordance with the realities of wealth and
power in a changed community. Since language, education, culture
are always ultimately grounded in social position, the social confusion of an open frontier society is reflected in a confusion of language and cultural modes and attitudes. It will take several generations for the descendants of a Simon Suggs, Jr., to acquire the social polish and cultural sophistication that educational advantages
made possible by new wealth can ultimately afford them; and the
effort to chronicle the checkered career of an opportunistic rascal
in the sophisticated language appropriate to a biographical sketch
in an Eastern magazine provides the rich incongruity that Baldwin
could draw on for purposes of humor.

The clash between the ideal and the real, between value and fact, is of course not an exclusively American motif. Cervantes rang the changes on it in *Don Quixote*, and Aristophanes before him. But a society based theoretically upon the equality of all men, yet made up of human beings very unequal in individual endowment, and containing within it many striking social, economic and racial differences, is more than ordinarily blessed with such problems in human and social definition, and the incongruities are likely to be especially observable. The very conditions of a frontier society, with its absence of settled patterns and with its opportunities for freedom and individuality, are ideally suited for this kind of humor. One finds it already in flower long before the Declaration of Independence. Consider a work such as William Byrd II's *History of the Dividing Line*. An English-educated planter, trained for the law in the Middle Temple, member of the Royal Society, one accustomed to command and to receiving the deference due a wealthy planter, goes off with a surveying party to determine the boundary line between the Virginia and the North Carolina colonies. There in the Dismal Swamp he encounters rustics who are without culture, refinement, ambition, or wealth, and who moreover do not seem to feel the lack of such commodities very much. His response is to poke fun at them, to use ridicule to rebuke the failure of the vulgar fact to approximate the cultural and social ideal. So he adopts a mode of language that through its inappropriateness to the triviality of the occasion, makes the settlers appear ludicrous: they "stand leaning with both their arms upon the cornfield fence, and *gravely consider* whether they had best go and take a small heat at the hoe . . ." [italics mine]. Here again is the same clash of modes that Baldwin and the Southwestern Humorists would use to chronicle the New Men in the New Territory. In both instances the fact —the ordinary man, as he is, unregenerate and uncaring—is satirized by being described in a language mode customarily reserved for more elevated subject matter. But where in Byrd the satire is all directed at the low-life objects, in Baldwin it is not so one-sided. For though Baldwin is a Virginian and a Whig and a man of education and culture, he is enough of a democratic American to admire the independence and the practicality of his low-life characters just a little, and so he does not confine his ridicule to them. He turns the language mode, the elevated diction, back on itself. He is consciously over-elegant, overly genteel in his choice of phraseology, so that the formal diction, the language of Culture, is also being mocked. The Great American Joke thus works both ways, and the incongruity illuminates the shortcomings of both modes.

Neither Byrd's *History of the Dividing Line* nor Baldwin's *Flush Times in Alabama and Mississippi* is, strictly speaking, literature, so much as subliterature. The one is narrative history, the other humorous journalism. Neither was designed purely or primarily as full-fledged artistic statement. But the same kind of incongruity they offer, the clash of genteel and vulgar modes, has been incorporated into the comic art of many of America's best and most respected writers. A single example will suffice to illustrate. The twentieth-century novelist William Faulkner has not only written certain novels that are possibly the only genuine literary tragedy produced by an American author in this century, but he is also one of the finest comic writers in American literature. In his comic masterpiece, *The Hamlet,* Flem Snopes and a Texan bring a herd of wild Texas horses to Mississippi and offer them for sale at very low prices. They are snapped up by the inhabitants, who are then invited to claim the horses they have purchased. Before very long wild horses are being pursued all over the landscape; they jump fences, leap over people, run into houses, overturn wagons, until as nighttime comes they are scattered over miles of countryside. One hapless purchaser, felled by the stampeding Texas herd, is carried unconscious into a house by some of his friends. Afterwards they go outside:

They went out; they didn't look back. They tiptoed up the hall and crossed the veranda and descended into the moonlight. Now that they could pay attention to it, the silver air seemed to be filled with faint and sourceless sounds—shouts, thin and distant, again a brief thunder of hooves on a wooden bridge, more shouts faint and thin and earnest and clear as bells; once they even distinguished the words: "Whooey. Head him."

Once again, both language modes are at work: the heightened literary diction, drawing on the full resources of cadenced prose and metaphor, and the vivid colloquial counterthrust. The haunting, beautiful description of the pursuit over the pastoral landscape is undercut by the broad vulgar comedy of the actual fact itself—the hoodwinked farmers vainly attempting to corral their untamable purchases. But Faulkner is not satirizing his characters; the human dignity he has given them as they go about the activities that are the plot of *The Hamlet* is such that, though they are "low-life," they are not thereby debased. Thus when, with the escape of the wild horses and their pursuit, he moves into the mode of formal literary diction and metaphor to describe what happens, the effect of incongruity does not produce satire and ridicule, so much as a delightful counterpoint of modes that plays them back and forth, against and around and along with each other. The shouting *is* "faint and thin and earnest and clear as bells," even as they *do* call out "Whooey. Head him." The contrast of literary language and poetic description with vernacular fact and colloquial speech is developed into as marvelously comic a scene as any in American literature. Both elements are at work, and in their juxtaposition each delineates the other. It is a masterful intensification of the same brand of humor as that of Byrd's *Dividing Line*, Baldwin's *Flush Times*, Irving's *Knickerbocker History*, Longstreet's *Georgia Scenes*, Clemens's *Connecticut Yankee*, Hemingway's *Torrents of Spring*, Barth's *Sot-Weed Factor*, and many another work of American comedy. It is the interplay of the ornamental and the elemental, the language of culture and the language of sweat, the democratic ideal and the mulishness of fallen human nature—the Great American Joke. To quote the business partner of Thomas Wolfe's Bascom Pentland in *Of Time and the River*, "the Reverend knows words the average man aint never heard. He knows words that aint even in the dictionary. Yes, sir!—an' uses them too—all the time!"

Human Comedy in Early America

Louis B. Wright

The literature of colonial America is not notable for humor. The early settlers were a serious people struggling to establish themselves in a wilderness and they had little time for polite letters or for literature of sheer entertainment. Humorous writings intended merely to amuse are a product of a leisured and sophisticated society. Colonial America knew little about leisure, and such writers as flourished in this period were inspired by a sense of purpose other than entertainment. This does not mean, however, that there was no laughter and merriment. Now and then one sees a glint of humor in the writings of the day, occasionally in letters and informal communications.

From early in the history of American literature satire has been one of the commonest forms of humorous writing. Americans have enjoyed poking fun at pretentiousness, pomposity, and vainglory. They have used satire as an instrument of reform and have sometimes laughed out of existence shortcomings in society that provoked the scorn and ridicule of writers. Mark Twain, one of the greatest American writers, was a master of satire; for many generations before his time, however, American writers had been employing this instrument with comic effect. Most of the consciously humorous writing in colonial America was satirical.

Some of the humor of early colonial days was unconscious—commentary of the period that is funny to us but was deadly serious to the writers. The first American best seller was Michael Wig-

17

glesworth's *Day of Doom,* a grim Puritan poem describing the Last
Judgment and the plight of sinners on that day. Its vivid descriptions of hell and the punishments awaiting a large proportion of
the human race must have caused widespread hysteria. Yet to a
later generation, lacking the theological beliefs of the Puritans,
passages in this poem appear grotesquely comic, as for instance,
the lines in which God judges infants who are condemned because
of original sin, the sin of Adam's disobedience. In His mercy, the
Almighty decrees:

> I do confess yours is much less,
>   though every sin's a crime.
> A crime it is; therefore in bliss
>   you may not hope to dwell;
> But unto you I shall allow
>   the easiest room in hell.

Such passages caused shudders of terror in seventeenth-century
New England Puritans but their descendants can smile at these
antique beliefs.

Although most seventeenth-century authors had important matters to relate, the comic spirit was not always absent when they
sat down to write. Captain John Smith, explorer and colonizer of
Virginia, described in vivid and sometimes humorous detail his own
experiences and made pungent comments on associates who dis-
pleased him. In 1608 the English king, James I, sent Captain Christopher Newport to Virginia with a rich regalia for the Indian chief
Powhatan, who, King James had been told, was king of the Virginia Indians. Smith, a realist in his dealings with the Indians,
thought this act a piece of folly. In a treatise entitled *A Map of
Virginia* (1612) Smith provided a sardonic description of the episode. Newport had instructions to clothe Powhatan in a scarlet
robe of office, receive his oath of allegiance, and crown him. Smith
commented on the farce: "But a foul trouble there was to make
him kneel to receive the crown. He neither knowing the majesty
nor meaning of a crown, nor bending of the knee, endured so many
persuasions, examples, and instructions as tired them all. At last,
by leaning hard on his shoulders, he a little stooped and Newport

put the crown on his head." A salute fired by Newport's gunners scared Powhatan out of his wits, but he soon recovered his calm, Smith reported, and "then, remembering himself to congratulate their kindness, he gave his old shoes and his mantle to Captain Newport." Thus ended the crowning of an Indian. Newport carried back Powhatan's old cloak to King James, and it is preserved to this day in the Ashmolean Museum in Oxford.

The sternest of the early English colonists were the Puritans of New England, who hoped to establish a religious commonwealth where they could live unspotted from the world. Yet they were not able to keep from their territory men less solemn and less dedicated than themselves. One interloper who embarrassed them with his gaiety, frivolity, and fraternization with the Indians was Thomas Morton, who came to New England in 1622 and established himself at Merry Mount (now Braintree), not far from Plymouth where the Pilgrims had made their settlement. Morton scandalized his Puritan neighbors by setting up a Maypole and celebrating May Day with singing, dancing, and drinking "good liquor." Captain Miles Standish and a detail of soldiers from Plymouth finally arrested Morton and shipped him back to England, where he wrote a satirical account of his experiences, published in 1637 with the title, *The New English Canaan.* "The setting up of this Maypole," Morton declared, "was a lamentable spectacle to the precise separatists that lived at New Plymouth. They termed it an idol, yea they called it the Calf of Horeb [Golden Calf] and stood at defiance with the place, calling it Mount Dagon." Naming Standish, who was small of stature, "Captain Shrimp," Morton described his arrest: "He takes eight persons more to him, and like the Nine Worthies of New Canaan they embark with preparation against Merry Mount where this monster of a man (as their phrase was) had his den." To prevent bloodshed Morton surrendered, and thus "Captain Shrimp and the rest of the Nine Worthies made themselves . . . masters of mine host of Merry Mount." In our time, this comic episode was made the theme of a light opera.

One of the most vigorous and original writers among the early Puritans of New England was Nathaniel Ward, a preacher, who came to Massachusetts in 1634 and settled at the village of Agawam (now Ipswich). Disturbed over what he believed to be a tendency toward permissiveness and a willingness of some of his contemporaries to tolerate divergent religious beliefs, Ward published a satire on society in 1647 with the title *The Simple Cobbler of Agawam.* Representing himself as the cobbler, he punningly announced his intention of mending the souls of his brethren. He did this in prose that ridiculed what he considered the shortcomings of men and women. Ward leveled his criticism against tolerating any form of worship except that pleasing to his Puritan brethren. He ridiculed current fashions in manners and dress that did not comport with Puritan dignity.

Ward's vocabulary is extraordinary, and he invented words that he could apply with satirical effect. One of the liveliest passages in the book condemns the frivolity of women who yearn after the latest fashion. Ward admitted that he could approve in women

whatever Christianity or civility will allow . . . but when I hear a nugiperous gentledame inquire what dress the Queen is in this week, what the nudiustertian fashion of the court, with edge to be in all haste whatever it be, I look at her as the very gizzard of a trifle, the product of a quarter of a cipher, the epitome of nothing, fitter to be kicked if she were of a kickable substance, than either honored or humored.

This is not the language of a chivalrous gallant but of an indignant Puritan bigot bent upon reforming the world according to his own notions. He can find only hard words for fashion-seeking women who have nothing in their heads, he says, "but a few squirrels' brains to help them frisk from one ill-favored fashion to another." Ward advised his readers to take seriously his condemnation of "these ape-headed pullets which invent fool-fangles merely for fashion and novelty sake."

Ward did not confine his attacks to women, for he was equally certain that men who ran after the latest fashions also endangered their souls. Long hair he thought especially deplorable. He was certain that God would prove a severe barber unless the fashion of long hair was amended, and he cited Scripture to prove the Deity's dislike of long locks. Ward's robust ridicule delighted the orthodox, who laughed at his comic and sometimes heavy-footed descriptions of the erring. Women and their fashions are among the oldest themes of priestly satire, common in all ages and countries. Ward was merely making capital of a topic that men had always found entertaining.

Another seventeenth-century writer and satirist, George Alsop, expressed an entirely different view of life from that given by Nathaniel Ward. Unlike Ward, Alsop was anything but a Puritan and he rejoiced in the death of Oliver Cromwell and the restoration of Charles II to the English throne. In a boisterous little book entitled *A Character of the Province of Maryland* (1666), he described in prose and verse life in Maryland as he observed it. His language is vigorous but coarse, and he is not above indulging in comic obscenities. Moses Coit Tyler, historian of colonial literature, asserts that "for mirthful, grotesque, and slashing energy" only Nathaniel Ward can compare with Alsop.

Alsop had come to Maryland, apparently, under contract to serve four years as a servant to pay his fare, but this term of servitude did not bother him. He found Maryland to his liking and was glad to turn author and tell the world about his experiences. Ready to praise his own work, Alsop justified this action by declaring, "For I dwell so far from my neighbors that if I do not praise myself, nobody else will." With gusto he described the country, its inhabitants, trans-Atlantic transportation of emigrants, the Indians, and the prospects of gain from trade and agriculture in the new land. The abundance of animal life pleased him. "Herds of deer are as numerous in this province of Maryland as cuckolds can be in London," he commented; "only their horns are not so well dressed and tipped with silver." Included in the book are a few letters that Alsop wrote back to his friends.

Humor is a very perishable commodity, and not all of the comment that Alsop makes excites our laughter. What appears funny to one age may be insipid or boring to another. Nevertheless, Alsop's vigorous and comic efforts are a relief from countless pious pages written by Puritan preachers. Cotton Mather of Boston, for example, was responsible for well over four hundred titles, works for the most part of dreary piety.

Another emigrant to Maryland, Ebenezer Cook, following in Alsop's footsteps a generation later with a satirical poem entitled *The Sot-Weed Factor* (1708), a work that provided a modern novelist with a title for a burlesque work. Little is known about

Cook, but he may have been the author of a later work in verse on the overproduction of tobacco, *Sotweed Redivivus* (1730), and other minor poems.

Tobacco, called "sot-weed," provided inspiration for Cook's satire. It purports to be a narrative of an English trader's visit to Maryland. Its subtitle indicates the contents and treatment: *A Voyage to Maryland. A Satire in Which Is Described the Laws, Government, Courts, and Constitutions of the Country and Also the Buildings, Feasts, Frolics, Entertainments, and Drunken Humors of the Inhabitants of That Part of America. In Burlesque Verse.*

Cook, writing in imitation of Samuel Butler's *Hudibras*, gives a vivid, unflattering, and comic picture of Maryland. When he and his companions first land, tobacco planters swarm around them, provoking this satirical picture:

> These sotweed planters crowd the shore,
> In hue as tawny as a Moor,
> Figures so strange no god designed
> To be a part of human kind;
> But wanton nature, void of rest,
> Moulded the brittle clay in jest.
>
> .   .   .   .
>
> At last a fancy very odd
> Took me, this was the land of Nod;
> Planted at first when vagrant Cain
> His brother had unjustly slain;
>
> .   .   .   .
>
> And ever since his time, the place
> Has harbored a detested race,
> Who when they could not live at home
> For refuge to these worlds did roam.

Cook finds little good to say about the Marylanders whom he meets as he travels about the country attempting to sell goods that he brought from England. Attending a session of court, he observes that it ends in a riot followed by drunken brawls and thievery. To get rid of his stock he goes to the Eastern Shore of Maryland, where he meets a Quaker who cheats him:

To this intent, with guide before,
I tripped it to the Eastern Shore.
While riding near a sandy bay,
I met a Quaker, yea and nay;
A pious, conscientious rogue,
As e'er wore bonnet or a brogue;
Who neither swore nor kept his word,
But cheated in the fear of God;
And when his debts he would not pay,
By Light Within he ran away.

Cook ended his satire of the Marylanders by placing a curse upon the land:

May wrath divine then lay these regions waste,
Where no man's faithful and no woman's chaste.

Although Cook's biting satire, prudently published in London, may have angered some Marylanders if they read it, others would have laughed over his commentary. This was a robust age when men could make merry over their own and their neighbors' short-comings. Satire also has this quality: a reader usually applies the ridicule to others whom he knows, rarely to himself.

Writers of diaries and journals often provide insights into the life of the times that are entertaining and humorous, even though the authors themselves did not intend to be comic. For example, solemn, sedate, and ponderous Samuel Sewall of Boston, chief justice of the colony, kept a diary that is of consuming interest and is often highly amusing, even though Sewall was unconscious of the entertainment that he would provide for later readers. Feeding chickens on Indian corn, he was led to speculate on his greater need for spiritual food and solemnly drew a parallel between his chickens and himself.

Left a widower in his old age, Sewall debated with himself "whether to live a single or a married life" and concluded that marriage was preferable. Having a substantial fortune himself, he decided to seek out one of several available widows who also had property. He began courting Mrs. Dorothy Denison, who encouraged him. As his first gift Sewall probably made a poor choice, for on June 17, 1718, he gave her "Dr. Mather's Sermons very well bound; told her we were invited to a wedding. She gave me very good curds [to eat]." A week later, however, Sewall thought of something more attractive than Cotton Mather's sermons and gave Mrs. Denison some knives and forks, which he carefully noted had cost him four shillings, six pence, and followed this with a pound of raisins and almonds.

By November 1, 1718, Sewall believed he had made a conquest and noted in his *Diary:* "I told her [Mrs. Denison] 'twas time to finish our business. Asked her what I should allow her; she not speaking, I told her I was willing to give her two [hundred] and fifty pounds per annum during her life. . . . She answered she had better keep as she was. . . . She should pay dear for dwelling in Boston." Nearly a month later, on November 28, he noted in his *Diary:* "My bowels yearn towards Mrs. Denison, but I think God directs me in his Providence to desist."

After losing Mrs. Denison because of her dissatisfaction with the proposed marriage settlement, Sewall next turned his attention to another prosperous widow, Mrs. Katherine Winthrop, and describes this courtship in detail in his *Diary*. Mrs. Winthrop, a sprightly soul, fascinated the old justice and kept him as excited as a teen-aged boy. He continued to believe that a volume of piety made a suitable gift for a lady, and on October 3, 1720, noted: "Gave her Mr. Willard's *Fountain Opened* with the little print and verses, saying I hoped if we did well read that book we should meet together hereafter if we did not now. She took the book and put it in her pocket. Took leave." Three days later, however, he observed: "I gave her a piece of Mr. Belcher's cake and ginger-bread wrapped up in a clean sheet of paper." But on October 11 he sent her a letter and "Mr. Mayhew's *Sermons.*"

If pious reading could lure Mrs. Winthrop into matrimony, Judge Sewall intended to keep her supplied with sermons. Despite a barrage of pious reading, she had warmed up sufficiently to treat him with "a great deal of courtesy, wine, marmalade." On October 12 Sewall was bold enough to hold her hand, and wrote in his *Diary:* "Asked her to acquit me of rudeness if I drew off her glove. Enquiring the reason, I told her 'twas great odds between handling a dead goat and a living lady. Got it off."

But Mrs. Winthrop was not to be won easily or inexpensively. She insisted upon Sewall's buying a coach and getting a wig, both extravagances that he resisted. He had written in his *Diary* on October 12: "Told her the reason why I came every other night was lest I should drink too deep draughts of pleasure. She had talked of canary [wine]; her kisses were to me better than the best canary." Yet on October 20 romance was in difficulties. Mrs. Winthrop was arguing for a coach and he commented: "Was courteous to me but took occasion to speak pretty plainly about my keeping a coach. I said 'twould cost £100 per annum; she said 'twould cost but £40. . . . Came away somewhat late."

The upshot was that the courtship of Mrs. Winthrop ended like that of Mrs. Denison in a decisive "No" for the justice. He could not bring himself to the necessary generosity in settling a marriage portion on either of these widows. Not all his gifts of sermons, gingerbread, raisins, and almonds prevailed. On November 7, 1720, he called upon her once more but it was clear that the courtship was over. He noted: "I did not bid her draw off her glove as sometime I had done. Her dress was not as clean as sometime it had been." Two nights later, as he was going home by lantern light, he observed: "Madam Winthrop's shutters were open as I passed by." If he yearned for the widow, he did not let his loss discourage him from matrimony. By March 29, 1722, he had persuaded another widow, Mrs. Mary Gibbs, to be his third wife.

Another diary keeper contemporary with Samuel Sewall, William Byrd, second of his name, a Virginian, contributed some of the most urbane writing of the colonial period. Deliberate humor and urbanity were qualities sadly lacking in much of colonial writing, but William Byrd of Westover had both.

Byrd's father had come to Virginia sometime before 1670, acquired land, and made a fortune in the Indian trade. His son William, born in 1674, was sent to England for his education, eventually entered Middle Temple, was admitted to the bar, and became an official representative of the colony of Virginia in London on numerous occasions. In fact, Byrd spent many years in London and was as much at home in Mayfair as he was in Williamsburg. While a member of the Middle Temple he made friends with such writers as William Wycherley, William Congreve, and Nicholas Rowe, the first biographer of Shakespeare. At various times Byrd tried his hand at writing verse, light commentary, and delightful letters. He also kept a diary in shorthand in which he entered a daily record of his doings, sometimes revealing the sort of weakness for feminine charms that James Boswell later demonstrated during his early residence in London.

After Byrd finally settled down on his plantation at Westover on the James River he became one of the most influential figures in Virginia. When the colony decided to mark the disputed boundary between Virginia and North Carolina, Byrd was chosen to head the surveying party. With a delegation from North Carolina, they surveyed the boundary in the year 1728. This expedition led to Byrd's writing two versions of his experiences, the *History of the Dividing Line Betwixt Virginia and North Carolina Run in the Year of Our Lord 1728* and *The Secret History of the Line*. The latter version, probably written first, disguises the names of participants under pseudonyms and is more explicit than the other account about characteristics of the individuals, their shortcomings, and their activities.

Neither version was printed in Byrd's lifetime but manuscript copies circulated among his friends and provided entertainment for the readers. These accounts are perhaps the most sophisticated examples of prose written in the colonial period. Characterized by an amused attitude of the author toward humankind, the narratives are filled with humorous observations.

Byrd wrote other shorter prose narratives, the most important being *A Journey to the Land of Eden in the Year 1733* and *A Progress to the Mines in the Year 1732*. The latter work describes a visit he made to iron mines in Virginia operated by Alexander Spotswood, a former governor and rival of Byrd's but afterward his friend. The *Journey to the Land of Eden* tells of Byrd's inspection, with a party of friends, of lands that he had acquired on the North Carolina border.

The *History of the Dividing Line* has been frequently reprinted and is a delight to read. The most recent edition is contained in *The Prose Works of William Byrd of Westover*, published by the Harvard University Press in 1966.

Byrd's style is that of a sophisticated Englishman, and he draws upon his memories of London for figures of speech. In describing a bivouac, for example, he notes that the men lay around the campfire "like so many Knights Templars," a figure suggested by the effigies on the tombs in the Temple Church where he had walked many times while a resident in Middle Temple. Two lost horses when found were standing "as motionless as the equestrian statue at Charing Cross."

Byrd's wit did not endear the author to those who found themselves satirized. North Carolinians have long grumbled about his report on the shiftlessness of residents on the North Carolina frontier:

Surely there is no place in the world where the inhabitants live with less labor than in North Carolina. It approaches nearer to the description of Lubberland than any other, by the great felicity of the climate, the easiness of raising provisions, and the slothfulness of the people. . . . The men for their parts, just like the Indians, impose all the work upon the poor women. They make their wives rise out of their beds early in the morning, at the same time that they lie and snore till the sun has risen one-third of his course and dispersed all the unwholesome damps. Then after stretching and yawning for half an hour, they light their pipes, and, under the protection of a cloud of smoke, venture out into the open air; though if it happen to be never so little cold, they quickly return shivering to the chimney corner. When the weather is mild, they stand leaning with both their arms upon the cornfield fence and gravely consider whether they had best go and take a small heat at the hoe but generally find reasons to put it off till another time. Thus they loiter away their lives, like Solomon's sluggard, with their arms across, and at the winding up of the year scarcely have bread to eat. To speak the truth, 'tis a thorough aversion to labor that makes people file off to North Carolina, where plenty and a warm sun confirm them in their disposition to laziness for their whole lives.

Concerning Edenton, then the capital of North Carolina, Byrd observed that he believed it

the only metropolis in the Christian or Mahometan world where there is neither church, chapel, mosque, synagogue, or any other place of worship of any sect or religion whatsoever. . . . Sometimes the Society for Propagating the Gospel has had the charity to send over missionaries to this country; but, unfortunately, the priest has been too lewd for the people, or, which often happens, they too lewd for the priest. For these reasons these reverend gentlemen have always left their flocks as arrant heathen as they found them.

Byrd's report on the Indians of the frontier, and efforts to Christianize them, was negative. Like his brother-in-law Robert Beverley, who in his *The History and Present State of Virginia* (1705) had suggested miscegenation as the solution of the "Indian problem," Byrd also comments on this possibility as a way of civilizing the red men and populating the country, a view that he expressed somewhat sardonically:

For my part, I must be of the opinion . . . that there is but one way of converting these poor infidels and reclaiming them from barbarity, and that is charitably to intermarry with them, according to the modern policy of the Most Christian King in Canada and Louisiana. Had the English done this at the first settlement of the colony, the infidelity of the Indians had been worn out at this day with their dark complexions, and the country had swarmed with people more than it does with insects. It was certainly an unreasonable nicety that prevented their entering into so good-natured an alliance. All nations of men have the same natural dignity, and we all know that very bright talents may be lodged under a very dark skin. . . . Even their copper-colored complexion would admit of blanching, if not in the first, at the farthest in the second, generation. I may safely venture to say, the Indian women would have made altogether as honest wives for the first planters as the damsels they used to purchase from aboard the ships. 'Tis strange, therefore, that any good Christian should have refused a wholesome, straight bedfellow when he might have had so fair a portion with her as the merit of saving her soul.

At least one of Byrd's predecessors in Virginia did indeed marry an Indian. John Rolfe took as his wife Pocahontas, daughter of the chief Powhatan, and in 1614 wrote to Sir Thomas Dale to explain his own noble reasons: It was not "unbridled carnal affection," he declared, but "for the honor of our country, for the glory of God, for my own salvation, and for the converting to the true knowledge of God and Jesus Christ an unbelieving creature, namely Pocahontas." This letter must have created a certain amount of amusement, even among seventeenth-century readers who saw it.

Although Byrd kept a private diary in shorthand that throws an occasional comic light upon the times, he did not intend it for public consumption. Not until 1942 was the first of three portions of this document published. The most recently published portion of the three extant pieces, a diary for the most part concerned with his life in London, 1717–1721, appeared in 1958.

The diary entries reveal the qualities of an eighteenth-century Virginia gentleman. One can pick passages almost at random to show these characteristics. For instance, on October 31, 1709, he wrote:

I rose at 6 o'clock and read two chapters in Hebrew and some Greek in Lucian. I said my prayers and ate milk for breakfast. About 10 o'clock we went to court. The committee met to receive proposals for the building [of] the college [William and Mary] and Mr. Tullitt undertook it for £2,000 provided he might [get] wood off the College land and all assistants from England to come at the College's risk. We sat in court till about 4 o'clock and then I rode to Green Springs to meet my wife. I found her there and had the pleasure to learn that all was well at home, thanks be to God. There was likewise Mrs. Chiswell. I ate boiled beef for supper. We danced and were merry till about 10 o'clock. I neglected to say my prayers, but had good health, good thoughts, and good humor thanks be to God Almighty.

This is a typical entry. The daily stint of Greek and Hebrew he maintained throughout his life. A cultivated gentleman in the early eighteenth century was expected to know the classical tongues. Other items in the entry call for comment. A member of the Council of State, which sat as the highest court in the land, Byrd took his judicial duties seriously. His regret over forgetting his prayers is also worth noting. An eighteenth-century gentleman, though he might fall a victim to sins of the flesh, believed in the value of decorum and religion.

Although Byrd was anything but a Puritan, he showed an appetite for sermon reading that Samuel Sewall would have approved. For instance, on Christmas night, 1710, he noted that "In the evening I read a sermon of Mr. Norris but a quarrel which I had with my wife hindered my taking much notice of it. However we were reconciled before we went to bed, but I made the first advance. I neglected to say my prayers but not to eat some milk. I had good health, good thoughts, and indifferent good humor, thank God Almighty."

Mrs. Chiswell, whom Byrd mentioned in the entry for October 31, 1709, greatly attracted him. Two days afterward, on November 2, he wrote:

In the evening I went to Dr. [Barret's] where my wife came this afternoon. Here I found Mrs. Chiswell, my sister [in-law] Custis, and other ladies. We sat and talked till about 11 o'clock and then retired to our chambers. I played r—m [cards?] with Mrs. Chiswell and kissed her on the bed till she was angry and my wife also was uneasy about it, and cried as soon as the company was gone. I neglected to say my prayers, which I should not have done, because I ought to beg pardon for the lust I had for another man's wife. However I had good health, good thoughts, and good humor, thanks be to God Almighty.

Twenty-three years later, in *A Progress to the Mines*, Byrd told of a visit to Mr. and Mrs. Chiswell and reported that she had aged sadly.

The long suppressed part of the diary for the years 1717–1721 reveals Byrd's life in London where he was the official representative of the colony of Virginia. He enjoyed the society of the gallants who gambled nightly at the Spanish Ambassador's, even though he almost invariably lost money when he himself played. A widower at the time, Byrd spent much time pursuing heiresses and other less respectable women. On one occasion he called upon a certain lady of fashion but found her away from home. He improved the hour by seducing the maid. When her ladyship returned, he seduced her. Then he added complacently, "and ate a plum cake."

Many of Byrd's letters survive, especially from this period in London. Some of them read like familiar essays and demonstrate the writer's literary skill; they are frequently lively and satirical. Like other correspondents of the eighteenth century, Byrd delighted in letter writing and was unwilling to see his efforts disappear. Otherwise there is no explanation of his saving copies of these letters and dressing them up with fictitious names for his correspondents, some from French romances, like "Cleora," "Minionet," "Sabina," "Veramour," and similar appellations.

During a residence in London in the 1720's Byrd began keeping a notebook of useful thoughts and quotations, a collection that recently came to light in the Virginia Historical Society. In this notebook he jotted down odd bits that he thought might be useful, including jokes that he probably intended to use at an appropriate time. Some of the aphoristic comment, doubtless picked up in the give-and-take of sprightly conversation, he wanted to remember for future use. For instance, he noted: "When a man keeps a woman, though he can't properly be said to be married, yet he may be said to live in the suburbs of matrimony." Or, "Poets and mad men tell us there is no remedy for love, but experience that won't impose upon us is positive there are two very sure ones: marriage and a halter." One story that Byrd set down in his notebook was printed a few years ago by *Time* magazine with a Kentucky setting as a fresh joke. It follows: "Two gentlemen who pretended a wonderful nicety in distinguishing of wine went to a merchant and, tasting a particular pipe, one of 'em said it tasted of iron and the other of leather. And after it came to be drawn out of the cask, they found at the bottom a small key fastened with a piece of leather, which showed a very distinguishing faculty and great acuteness in the sense of tasting."

If my choice of excerpts from Byrd's diary and notebook suggest that he was a frivolous and light-minded person, I have done him a disservice. He was a hard-working diplomat and an industrious and prosperous planter, a leader in Virginia society. But he had an ironical sense of humor and at times wrote in an amused satirical vein. His writings have a modernity that makes them entertaining today without a panoply of scholarly footnotes.

If formal literature through most of the colonial period showed a dearth of humor, we must not conclude that Americans in the seventeenth and eighteenth centuries were all grim and austere. They were often earnest, diligent, and sober, but they probably enjoyed laughter as much as we do. A clue to the average man's interest in a merry joke may be found in the American almanacs intended to hang by everyman's chimney side. Almost invariably they contained comic anecdotes and humorous aphorisms. When Benjamin Franklin began to publish *Poor Richard's Almanac* with its crisp proverbs and short pointed anecdotes, he was following an old tradition. Almanacs provided a taste of earthy humor that anybody could enjoy. Franklin merely made a better selection than his predecessors.

Benjamin Franklin

Lewis Leary

In speaking about anything American, Benjamin Franklin is a good man to begin with. Years before the United States existed, he started things of which his countrymen continue to be proud, like libraries, civic clubs, volunteer fire departments, effective street lighting, and, not least, the use of humor as a practical device. For Franklin was solidly American, ingenious, practical, ambitious, and successful. His *Autobiography* testifies that his feet were on the ground, and that he did not stand still. No man of his time went so far, and few since have gone further. But because he not only started things, but also let it be known that he did, Franklin may sometimes be credited with more than he deserves. That is one reason why he stands confidently at the head of any native literary procession. Talking about himself, he produced his country's first masterwork.

Like Walt Whitman and Mark Twain and Ernest Hemingway, Franklin created a public image so attractive and palpable that it obscures the man who made it. Whatever influences of time or place or circumstance combined to produce the successful and whimsical plain-spoken homespun favorite remembered as Ben Franklin, the projection of this character was a literary exploit of the first magnitude. "He knew what he was about, this sharp little man," said D. H. Lawrence. "He set up the first dummy American." He was, said Thomas Carlyle, the father of all Yankees. He

33

was versatile, grave, and practical, using wit as a weapon and humor as a handmaid to success.

Franklin early learned canny control of an audience. "He has wit at will," said John Adams who was not always sure that he was fond of Franklin or approved of him. "He had humor that, when he pleased, was delicate and delightful. He had satire that was good-natured or caustic, Horace, Swift, or Rabelais, at his pleasure. He had talents for irony, allegory, and fable, that he could adapt with great skill to the promotion of moral and practical truth." A "jack of all trades," Melville would call him, the "master of all and mastered by none—the type and genius of his land."

Even as a boy of sixteen, Franklin gauged the temper of the "clan of honest wits" which in Boston encouraged his brother in the publication of a Yankee version of Addison's *Spectator*. With the essays which he then contributed to the *New England Courant*, literature in America may be said to have been born, with Benjamin Franklin as its single generative force. His neighbor Cotton Mather wrote more than he, and William Byrd in Virginia a few years later would write briefly as well. The Rev. Edward Taylor, secluded in the frontier town of Westfield, preserved notebooks filled with poetry which he did not allow published, though it was probably as good as any written anywhere at the time. Not ten years later, the Rev. Jonathan Edwards of Northampton would speak in Boston of theological insights which by mid-century would be set forth in beautifully mannered, precise prose. By then, Franklin had been long absent from New England, and he had taken literature with him, as if he had it in his pocket, neatly stowed, to be used as needed. Not until Ralph Waldo Emerson more than a hundred years later discovered, amid what Franklin had left behind, the materials for revelations of which Franklin could not have completely approved, was it to reappear to warm that chill region again.

The fourteen essays that were printed, one every two weeks, in the *Courant* over the signature of Silence Dogood commented on Boston manners much as essays in English periodicals commented on London manners, except that the widow Dogood was a New England countrywoman who spoke in native accent of local idiosyncracies. Her name alone—impiously suggestive of Cotton Mather's well-meaning essays—and her position in life were amusing, for Boston seemed overfilled with husbandless women, most of them respectable, but others merry widows, keepers of dram shops or waterfront boarding houses. Her given name of Silence was grotesquely inappropriate, for she loved to talk, especially about her neighbors. But in the first three essays she spoke mainly about herself, who she was and where she came from, much in the manner of an pseudonymous writer of any English periodical essays. She admitted her "natural inclination to observe and reprove the faults of others" and was eager to dedicate this excellent faculty for the good of her countrymen. At sixteen, Franklin knew what literature was for: it could mend the manners of men by pointing to their errors; it could admonish and correct, laugh lightly at human frailty, and suggest practical patterns which insured success.

Silence Dogood's first objective observations were on education, in an allegorical dream of Harvard College through whose gates only those approved by Riches might enter. There sat Learning, but on a throne so high and so difficult of access that most of her worshippers "contented themselves to sit at the foot with Madame Idleness and her maid Ignorance," waiting for someone to help them ascend. To simple Silence Dogood, college men were a useless lot, "unable to dig and ashamed to beg." She spoke for all Yankees who worked unashamedly with their hands when she reflected

on the extreme Folly of those Parents, who, blind to their children's Dulness and insensible to the Solidity of their Skulls, because they think their Purses can afford it, will needs send them to the Temple of Learning . . . where they learn little more than how to enter a Room genteely (which might as well be acquired at a Dancing-School), and from whence they return, after Abundance of Trouble and Charge, as great Blockheads as ever, only more proud and conceited.

Like any good Bostonian, young Franklin was gallant in defense of women and their rights, allowing Mistress Dogood to reply to an attack against female idleness, ignorance, folly, and pride by asking: Who is less often drunk? Who swears less? Whose work, by tradition and truth, is never done? And why should not women be proud, when men remain "such Simpletons as to humble themselves at their feet, and fill their Ears with extravagant Praises"? Whatever was wrong with women was the fault of men who denied women equal opportunities for education. Two weeks later women were talked of again, less gallantly, for the subject was their pride in clothes, especially in absurd wide skirts: "I would at least desire them," said the widow Dogood, "to consider whether they who pay no . . . Taxes, ought to take up more room on the King's highway than the Men, who yearly contribute to the Support of the Government."

Mistress Dogood also had notions of what poetry should be. She scoffed at transatlantic notions that good verse could not be written in colonial New England, and she pointed with pride to "a most Excellent Piece . . . entitled, *An Elegy upon the much lamented Death of Mrs.* Mehitebeel Kitel . . . of *Salem.*" She thought it "the most *Extraordinary* Piece that was ever wrote in New England," its language "so soft and easy," its expression "so Charming and Natural." What reader could be so callous as not to shed a tear over such lines as

> Come let us mourn, for we have lost a
> Wife, a Daughter, and a Sister,
> Who has lately taken flight, and
> greatly have we missed her,

she, who on her deathbed,

> kist her husband some little time before she expir'd,
> Then lean'd her Head the Pillow on, just out of
> Breath and tir'd.

Mark Twain a century and a half later had no less fun when he allowed Huck Finn to peruse the poem which Emmeline Grangerford had made "about a boy by the name of Stephen Dowling Botts that fell down a well and was drownded," than young Ben Franklin now had in allowing Mistress Dogood to suggest that poetry of this kind be named, in honor of its first victim, kitelic poetry, and to have her furnish a recipe for composing a New

England elegy, even to providing samples of useful rhymes, such as grieve us/leave us, flower/power, physicians/expeditions. "Then season all," she said, "with a handful or two of Melancholy Expressions such as Dreadful, Deadly, cruel cold Death, unhappy Fate, weeping Eyes," and the poem would be complete.

The longer they appeared, the more of Benjamin Franklin and the less of his mouthpiece appeared in the Dogood essays. Echoes of other ironic voices from abroad are heard in his suggestion that an insurance company be established for widows and for aged virgins over thirty, but it is the young Boston apprentice who compares the virtues of moderate drinking with the vices of drunkenness, and who painstakingly lists words and phrases from the vocabulary of tippling: *boosey, tipsey, merry, mellow, in a very good humor, almost froze*. Franklin kept his ears open for new rhythms, and his eyes open for local sights, like that of amorous sailors walking arm in arm with their doxies, or of predatory young women prowling dark streets with "pretty gestures," contributing thereby to "the health and satisfaction of those who have been fatigued with business or study" as well as to the prosperity of shoemakers.

Almost every tone that Franklin would later use was foreshadowed in these young essays, the first of their kind in the New World. When he borrowed from Addison, Swift, Defoe, or other men from abroad, Franklin scrupulously paid interest in native originality of phrase or incident. But not too much originality— nothing too much, neither in drinking nor wenching, not even in too great a departure from saying things as they had always been said. If Franklin could have had the patience or opportunity to read what T. S. Eliot was to write about how individual talent builds on tradition, he would certainly have agreed. If one were to persuade, simple practicality required that he must not seem eccentric or isolated. People respond to what is familiar. The trick was to provide the fillip which convinced without startling. For certainly, Franklin was later to submit, "an indiscrete Zeal for spreading an Opinion hurts the cause of the Zealot."

As a self-made writer, Franklin exhibits almost all the tendencies and attitudes discoverable in succeeding American writers of his kind, and he also shared opinions with others who were in most respects different. When Thoreau in *Walden* spoke of the cost of any thing being the amount of life exchanged for it, he extended what Franklin had said about avoiding any action inconsistent with health or fortune "because 'twould cost you more than 'twas worth." Emerson in asking native writers to turn attention to common things, the meal in the firkin, the milk in the pan, and the song in the street, emphasized in precept what Franklin established in practice. As much as Whittier or Whitman or Harriet Beecher Stowe, Franklin aimed at an audience of simple people, and his language, more than theirs, reached the workingman. Like Mark Twain, he knew the leavening power of humor and the effective force of the tall tale. He was as gallantly flirtatious in compliments to ladies as he was capable in concocting Rabelaisian anecdotes for masculine ears. America's first periodical essayist, he was also her first humorist, in a line that includes Washington Irving, Artemus Ward, Mr. Dooley, Will Rogers, and James Thurber. Laugh, but avoid being laughed at: "Pieces of Pleasancy and Mirth," he said, "have a secret charm in them to allay the Heats and Humours of our Spirits."

As proprietor for almost forty years after 1729 of the *Pennsylvania Gazette*, as compiler of *Poor Richard's Almanac*, and as editor after 1740 of the *General Magazine*, Franklin instructed but also delighted many contemporaries. He had great fun reporting "A Witch Trial" in which persons accused of "making their Neighbour's Sheep dance" and "causing Hogs to speak and sing Psalms" were submitted to trial by water which proved to be unsuccessful because the clothes which the witches wore "help'd to support them." In "A Meditation on a Quart Mug" humor and instruction are as subtly combined: it is not the mug which inebriates; like a newspaper, it is simply a vehicle of pleasure; what it contains may be dangerous or corrupting, but the vessel itself may remain a joy forever. Any paraphrase makes quite too plain the dry, laconic homely tone which goodnaturedly caught and captured and convinced colonial countrypeople.

As Richard Saunders, almanac-maker—the Sir Roger de Coverley of the masses—Franklin's writings found their way into many homes, often furnishing the whole content of family reading. *Poor Richard's Almanac* provided instruction for a quarter of a century after 1732 on when crops were to be planted, how business deals or love affairs were to be carried on, or illness cured; it explained how to bake cakes, cure hams, and "the best time to cut hair, trim cocks, and sow salads." To fill spaces left blank among such practical matters, Poor Richard purloined wit and wisdom from the finest storehouses of Europe, printing such pithy aphorisms as "There's more old drunkards than old doctors," "After three days men grow weary of a wench, a guest, and rainy weather," and "Keep your eyes wide open before marriage, half shut afterwards." He anticipated Longfellow in advising "Let us then be up and doing." He anticipated Thoreau in counseling, "Read much, but not many books." He had no shame in changing Francis Bacon's "Reading maketh a full man; conference a ready man; and writing an exact man" to "Reading makes a full man, meditation a profound man, discourse a clear man." He recommended plain speaking: "The learned fool writes his nonsense in better language than the unlearned," he said, "but still 'tis nonsense." How strange "that a man who has enough wit to write a satire should have the folly to publish it." Poor Richard was a practical man who scoffed at poets; "Poverty, poetry, and new titles of honour make men ridiculous," he said with proper masculine, democratic scorn. And critics?

> Bad commentators spoil the best of books,
> So God sends meat (they say), the Devil cooks.

Genial Poor Richard, however, was overshadowed by Father Abraham who was introduced in the almanac for 1758. His "The Way to Wealth" has been named an "American classic, *par excellence*," sharing with *Uncle Tom's Cabin* a century later the honor of "having passed by translation into more foreign languages than anything else," and bearing with it "the mark of our national spirit." More than seventy editions have appeared in English, more than fifty in French, eleven in German, nine in Italian; it has been put into Spanish, Dutch, Swedish, Welsh, Polish, Russian, Bohemian, Dutch Catalan, Chinese, and Greek; it has been done in phonetic writing and in Braille, to become after the *Autobiography* the best and farthest known of Franklin's writings, containing the essence of his homely, practical, and good-natured wisdom.

Franklin had spoken before of frugality in "Hints for Those

Who Would Become Rich" in the *Almanac* for 1737, and more explicitly in "Advice to a Young Tradesman" in the *Gazette* for 1748. "Remember," he had said then, "that time is money," and "the way to wealth . . . depends chiefly on two words, *industry* and *frugality:* that is, waste neither *time* nor *money*, but make the best use of both." Father Abraham now tightened such advice with terse, workaday aphorisms, knowing, he said, that "a Word to the wise is enough, and Many Words won't fill a Bushel." He reminded readers that "The sleeping Fox catches no Poultry," that "He that rises late must trot all day," that "Laziness travels so slowly that Poverty soon overtakes him," that "Diligence is the Mother of Good Luck," and that success comes to him who will "plough deep while others sleep," so that "Early to bed and early to rise" really "makes a man healthy, wealthy, and wise."

Franklin's was the voice of the man in the homespun suit, with all the world before him for his taking. He spoke to apprentices and shopkeepers and servant girls who dreamed of fine houses and carriages and reputation. In 1744 he issued, as the first novel printed in America, Samuel Richardson's popular, didactic *Pamela* which four years before had reminded admiring English readers that, yes, a working girl might make good. As a city man, Franklin noticed the fields or woods or streams or skies which surrounded Philadelphia, not to remark on their beauty, only their usefulness. Some contemporaries complained that Franklin boasted of his nostrums "for the preservation of prudence, the cure of poverty," much "as quacks boast an infallible cure for the itch." He was to them a penny-pinching philosopher, everything, Melville was to say, but a poet who saw beyond appearances. This he was indeed, and with no apologies: his nostrums worked, and he could prove that they did.

But all work and no play could make Benjamin a dull boy, and Franklin was seldom dull, even when he talked of education (less Latin and more arithmetic) or politics or playing chess. Sometimes he paused to put together convivial verses:

> The antediluvians were all very sober,
> For they had no wine and they brewed no October;

All wicked bad livers, on mischief still thinking,
For there can't be good living where there is not
good drinking.

At other times he sang the challenge of love, and its failure in competition with convivial companionship:

Fair Venus calls: her voice obey;
In beauty's arms spend night and day.
The joys of love all joys excell,
And loving's certainly doing well.

Oh! no!
Not so!
For honest folks known
Friends and the bottle shall bear the bell.

One evening when Franklin sat with friends in a tavern, someone is said to have remarked on how unfitting it was for honest married men to sing hackneyed songs in praise of some poet's mistress. Returning home, where his own Deborah undoubtedly patiently waited him, Franklin composed a more proper song for proper men to sing:

Of their Chloes and Phyllises poets may prate,
    I sing my plain country Joan,
These twelve years my wife, still the joy of my life;—
    Blest the day that I made her my own.

Not a word of her face, of her shape, of her air,
    Or of flames or of darts, you shall hear;
I beauty admire, but virtue I prize,
    That fades not in seventy year.
        .   .   .   .

Some faults have we all, and so has my Joan,
    But then, they're exceedingly small,
And now I've grown used to them, so like my own,
    I scarcely can see them at all.

Springtime fancies were perhaps responsible for the Chester-fieldian "Advice to a Young Man in the Choice of a Mistress" which Franklin produced in 1745. "I know of no medicine," he then confessed, "fit to diminish the violent inclinations you mention; and if I did, I think I would not communicate it to you. Marriage is the proper remedy," man and woman united to "make one complete being. Separate, she wants his force of body . . . ; he, her softness, sensitivity, and acute discernment. Together they are more likely to succeed"; a single man "resembles the odd half of a pair of scissors." But, he continued, if you will not marry "and persist in thinking a commerce with the sex inevitable, then . . . in all your amours you should prefer old women to young ones." Their conversation is better, and their discretion. "Because in every animal that walks upright . . . the face first grows lank and wrinkled; then the neck; then the breast and arms; the lower part continuing to the last as plump as ever: so that covering all above with a basket . . . it is impossible to know an old from a young one." And finally, older women are to be preferred because "they are so grateful."

In 1746 Franklin expanded in "Reflections on Courtship and Marriage" an argument which Silence Dogood had begun more than twenty years before when she suggested that women might become quite as sensible as men if they could be educated to reasonableness rather than spoiled by pampering and flattery. Marriage was a good thing, but beset with problems. Swift did not write more sharply in disgust than Franklin did when describing how housewives often appear at breakfast:

Downstairs they come, pulling up their ungartered, dirty stockings; slipshod, with naked heels peeping out; no stays or other decent conveniency, but all flip-flop; a sort of clout thrown about the neck without form or decency, a tumbled, discoloured mob or nightcape, half on and half off, with the frowsy hair hanging in sweaty ringlets, staring like Medusa with her serpents; shrugging up her petticoats, that are sweeping the ground and scarce tied on; hands unwashed, teeth furred, and eyes crusted—but I beg your pardon, I'll go no farther with this sluttish picture.

The *Gentleman's Magazine* of London in its issue of April, 1747, first presented "The Speech of Polly Baker," a tale which took all of Europe by storm, reprinted in a score of journals, attracting the attention of Diderot and Voltaire, and returning to America to reign triumphant, in spite of John Adams's protest against it as "an outrage to morality and decorum," as America's first popularly successful short story. Polly was an honest but unfortunate girl, prosecuted for the fifth time "at Connecticut near Boston in New England" for having born a bastard child.

I cannot conceive [she said with naïve lack of precision in choosing words], what the nature of my offense is. I have brought five fine children into the world at the risk of my life; I have maintained them well by my industry, without burdening the township, and would have done it better, if it had not been for the heavy fines . . . I have paid. Can it be a crime (in the nature of things, I mean) to add to the number of the King's subjects, in a new country that really wants people?

The worst she had done was to deprive some clergyman or justice of peace of wedding fees. Can it be supposed, she asked "that heaven is angry at my having children, when to the little done by me towards it, God has been pleased to add His divine skill and admirable workmanship in the formation of their bodies and crowned the whole by furnishing them with immortal souls? . . . If you gentlemen must be making laws, do not turn natural and useful actions into crimes by your prohibitions."

She asked them to consider her first seducer, now a magistrate like themselves. She asked them to think of the harm done to society by celibate bachelors who

by their manner of living leave unproduced (which is little better than murder) hundreds of their posterity to the thousandth generation. Is this not a greater offense against the public good than mine? Compel them, then, by law, either to marry or pay double the fine for fornication each year. What must a poor woman do, whom customs and nature forbid to solicit men, and who cannot force themselves upon husbands, when the laws take no care to provide them with any and yet severely punish them if they do their duty without them? The duty of the first and great command of nature and nature's God, increase and multiply; a duty from the steady performance of nothing has been able to deter me; for its sake I have hazarded the loss of public esteem and have frequently endured public disgrace and punishment: and therefore ought, in my humble opinion, instead of a whipping have a statue erected in my memory.

No statue was erected—though one of the magistrates who sat in judgment was so impressed that he married her, and together they had fifteen children—but Polly is affectionately remembered by admirers who discover her a cousin to Defoe's Moll Flanders, Polly Peacham of John Gay's *The Beggar's Opera*, and Richardson's Clarissa. Her American descendants from Hester Prynne to Carrie Meeber and Eula Varner have not been more lively or likable than she. After Pocahontas, Polly is the first American heroine to triumph before a European audience. She captivated as a sensible female equivalent of practical Ben Franklin, who late in life explained to Madame Brillon that an additional injunction should be added to the Ten Commandments: "*Increase and multiply* and replenish the earth," and who wondered why men who perform all manner of mischief by daylight, lying and scheming and destroying one another, "creep into corners, or cover themselves with the darkness of night, when they mean to beget, as being ashamed of a virtuous action."

Not for several literary generations was another native man of letters to write with equal vigor of doing what comes naturally. Mark Twain, who did not like Franklin (perhaps because he read only a few of his writings), would have been delighted with the older man's whoppers about American sheep with tails so heavy that carts had to be provided to support them, or his handsomely phrased denial that American streets were "pav'd with half-peck Loaves, the Houses til'd with Pancakes," and "the Fowls fly around ready to be roasted crying, Come eat me." He might have wished he had written, though secretly, Franklin's letter "To the Royal Academy of Brusselles" which recommended "some Drug wholesome and not disagreeable, to be mix'd with our common Food or Sauces, that shall render the Natural discharges of Wind from our bodies, not only inoffensive, but agreeable as Perfumes. . . . A pill of Turpentine no bigger than a pea, shall bestow . . . the pleasing Smell of Violets."

From first to last, Franklin was a lusty writer, earthy and with no nonsense about him—not Chloe but plain country Joan, not milady in silks but pretty Polly Baker, not pining and wasting with care, but action when necessary, and under control. However often these are demonstrated as traits common to the sensible eighteenth century or of an emerging, confident middle class, they were characteristics which Franklin set down and established because, in explaining himself, he explained his age. In doing so, he designed a pattern to which many of his successful countrymen would fit. Having made his fortune, the prosperous American then characteristically dedicates himself to good deeds and public service—Franklin in his mid-forties retired to do precisely that. Comfortably established, he has time to catch up on what he previously had no time for—like the languages which the older Franklin learned. He putters in his workshop over experiments and inventions. He goes abroad, as Lambert Strether or Sam Dodsworth did, to discover the riches of European cultures. He meets or corresponds with other men whose interests are like his. He discovers and encourages young men of ability, putting them through school, establishing them in business, showering them with advice, and standing as godparent for their children. Secure and with nothing to lose, he enjoys avuncular flirtations, daring compliments which a younger man could only risk if prepared to follow them through.

What separates Franklin from most people like him is that he did all this with such tumultuous energy that he leaves the best-intentioned imitators gasping. His political writings alone might have made his reputation—indeed, during his lifetime, they did. Without abandoning the urbanity learned from Addison, he assumed in attacks against England in such essays as "Rules for Reducing a Great Empire to a Small One" and "an Edict by the King of Prussia," the ironic mask of Swift and the straight-faced, outrageous exaggerations of Defoe with such skill that students of satire place him among its masters because of his "unerring eye for an opening and relentless pressing of each advantage; the ingenuity and invention he exhibits in exploring and exploiting the historical situation; his skill in controlling irony, that subtlest of satiric patterns." Molded to measures which moved his time, most of Franklin's political essays can thus be relished for their skill in rhetorical organization or their deftness with words, but they are not likely to impress a modern reader with much besides their strong virtuosity. Like yesterday's jokes, they speak clearly only when illumined by knowledge of circumstances which created them or their fortuitous relevance to some similar situation today.

Among the most shockingly successful was "On Humbling Our Rebellious Rebels," which Franklin published in the friendly London *Public Advertiser* in 1774. Pretending alarm because robust but rebellious American colonials multiplied dangerously fast as a result of early marriages and the amazing fertility of their women, he proposed that all American males be gelded. This done, after "fifty years it is possible we shall not have one rebellious subject in North America." Meanwhile a crop of home-grown tenors would be produced, thus saving the tremendous sums which must be spent each year to import tenors from Italy. "It might likewise be of service to our Levant Trade, as we could supply the Grand Signor's Seraglio and Harems of the Grandees of the Turkish Dominions with Cargoes of Eunuchs, as also with Handsome Women, for which America is as famous as Circassia."

But Franklin spoke effectively from behind several masks. In "A Parable against Persecution" he so adroitly used a biblical style that some readers mistook his words for Scripture. When describing his experiments or inventions, he was straightforward and plain, whether the subject was an arrangement of balloons strapped about his shoulders to take weight off his gouty feet or a device by which short men might remove books or packages from a high shelf. His letters—on official business, to scientific associates, in friendly discourse, or of admonition and advice—were models, each of its kind. The inexhaustible energy, curiosity, and kindness of this multiple man are nowhere better revealed than in these letters which allow glimpses behind the familiar mask of doughty Ben Franklin to the intelligence and artistry that molded its features so well.

Like many men who glimpse truths which they find it wisest not directly to express, Franklin often spoke most effectively in banter. The indirection of humor could provide a defense against responsibility. Franklin's was the comic view—the world a stage, each man a player, often ridiculous, especially when he reached beyond what he could touch. Literature was of value when useful, but was at best an avocation. Writing that searched beneath or above levels of common sense was to be expected only of women, or perhaps of men too sickly for manly competition, or of clergy-men from whom worldliness was not to be expected. Sensible men would use it as a prod or lever or, later, as a way toward wealth. It was often most expedient for them to speak from behind a pseudonymous mask, as Washington Irving and Samuel Clemens would speak.

Under Franklin's aegis, the ventriloquist writer invaded the new world. Humor such as his remained a hedge from behind which many who followed him would exploit the comic view. Dialect would become effective because it identified itself with the plain American, simple and wise, sly and forthright at the same time, himself a kind of comic mask. The cracker box, woodland stump, town meeting and camp meeting, lyceum and Chautauqua, the quiz show and panel discussion, good things all, became forums from which this plain American spoke or oracles to which he listened. He became a sturdy, likable, and dependable fellow, this plain American who is grave but seldom serious, a good man to have around in almost any emergency, just as Franklin was, who invented him.

The Satiric Mode:
The Early National Wits

Lewis P. Simpson

The origin of the American Republic has a significant relation to the slow evolution—political, economic, sociological, literary—of a nationalistic ethos among a colonial people. But it is to be discovered more immediately and directly—and no doubt to the student of literature, more dramatically and convincingly—in the revolutionary, cosmopolitan rationalism of the Western Enlightenment. Indeed in the most immediate sense the Republic was an invention of the intelligence of the Enlightenment, which has one of its great embodiments in the highly expressive and frequently powerful writings of Franklin, Jefferson, Hamilton, and Madison. Their works—not less astute than articulate, not less political than literary—offer strong testimony to the way in which literature (in that broad sense of Dr. Johnson's definition: "Learning; skill in letters") underlay every activity of the educated mind in the eighteenth century. As products of this mind, the Declaration of Independence, *The Federalist*, the Constitution of the United States itself, represent literary as well as political achievements. Their makers constituted an American literati, who, like Locke and Voltaire, assumed their citizenship in the Republic (or Commonwealth) of Letters. This universal, frontierless polity of the mind had become the intellectual and spiritual homeland of the secular class of the literary and learned that had come into being upon the decline of the old Western clerical order. It reached the height of its dominion in the age leading up to the American and French

49

Revolutions, immediately before the onset of the integral national-
ism that has marked the nineteenth and twentieth centuries.

What I am saying by preface is, I realize, arguable. But although
I cannot go into the complexities of the relationship between the
new American government and the politics of mind in the eighteenth century, I venture to assert a decided emphasis on the intellectual cosmopolitanism of the early American Republic because it
offers an approach to our understanding of the subject at hand:
the satiric mode of the period.

Essentially this approach lies in assuming a connection between
two general manners, or styles, of expression which largely constitute for us our general image of the mind of the early American
Republic. One of these—the dominant one and the one that tends
markedly to shape our impression of the intellect and spirit of the
time of Franklin and Jefferson—is the large, deliberative mode
characterizing the major documents of the genesis of the Republic.
These render the image of a mind composed and assured, sophisticated and confident; above all of a mind of comprehensive capac-
ities, capable of dealing adequately with historical conditions and
contingencies.

This image of the mind of the early American Republic was
profoundly meaningful for those who created it, and it retains its
meaning today. It is the image of the mind that proclaimed the
truth of the new Republic: that this government has been created
not by the designs and armies of kings (nor, as Hamilton said, by
"accident and force") but by the reflective act of the mind of man;
and, moreover, has been created as an example of rational government for all mankind to witness. The new American Republic is,
to be sure, to represent a new truth in history: the power of the
rational mind deliberately to fabricate a political order on the basis
of the consent of those to be governed under it; or, in other words,
on the basis of the sovereignty of the rational mind of mankind.
But when we examine carefully the implied attitudes of the makers
of the American Republic, we discover that this truth rests on the
assumption of the identity of the revolutionary mind and the educated, the lettered, mind. In other words, the makers worked on
the basis of the supposition that the mind of the new Republic they
were creating represented the mind of man; but they also operated

on the basis of the corollary assumption that the mind of man operates in and through the exclusive literacy of the Republic of Letters. In a real sense the Declaration of Independence is addressed not to "the opinions of mankind" but to those held by the community of men of letters. *The Federalist* spoke less "to the people of New York" than it did to this same world, or its microcosm in America. The voice of the Constitution is "we the people," but the Constitution implies in its austerity and solemnity of tone a limitation on the dominion of the people instituting the new government. That the sovereignty of the mind of man implies the equality of all individual minds—lettered and unlettered—may have had some theoretical basis in the primitivistic notions of the age. But equality of intellect was not really contemplated by the eighteenth-century mind, which was rooted in the concept that mind and literacy are equivalent. The Republic of Letters was an order founded in the distinction—simple, fundamental, and ancient—between the man *of* letters and the man of *no* letters. The exclusiveness of literacy was an integral implication of the very mind that conceived of a government by the consent of the governed. To the eighteenth-century mind, as illustrated by the outlook of the great historian Edward Gibbon, for example, literacy and illiteracy constituted the difference between civilization and barbarism.

And yet, it is clear, in historical perspective, that the Declaration of Independence, the Constitution, and *The Federalist* inaugurated an order of society that instead of being set in the ground of tradition—in the distinctions among men—would refer its existence constantly to "the opinions of mankind"—or to "public opinion." It would be like no political order in history before it. The radically democratic implication of the American Republic became manifest in certain historical events in the years following the Revolution. Among these were two small but widely bruited rebellions, both inspired by frontier populism: Shays's Rebellion in Massachusetts and the Whiskey Insurrection in Pennsylvania. These and other evidences of a fateful rise of the common people in America seemed all the more significant because they were placed in the context of the French Revolution and its cataclysmic aftermath. When we depart from documents of the early American Republic, which are carefully couched in the deliberative style, we find in other writings of the age—political tracts, periodical essays, poems—a very different style. We find, to be sure, that if on one side the mind of the early Republic is characterized by rhetorical composure, on the other it may accurately be described as distinguished by an apocalyptic style. The apocalyptic mind shows two aspects. On the one hand, it was a mind infused with millennialistic or utopian prospects; on the other, it was a mind charged with fears of the imminence of a doomsday of social collapse. In either case—whether in apocalyptic dream or nightmare—the American imagination responded to the idea which occupied it more and more as the new order began to move in history, that America is a great experiment—not simply a government founded on natural law but a profound experiment in the very nature of man. Apocalyptic optimism held that in America human nature was being transformed; that it was undergoing an unparalleled process of spiritual and intellectual regeneration, and this to such an extent that human nature was being freed from any traditional image of man and society. There was a kind of ecstasy in contemplating this possibility; it was exalted into ecstatic historical generalization. Thus St. Jean de Crèvecoeur's noted leading question in the early 1780's: "Who then is the American, this new man?" And Crèvecoeur's declaration: "The American is a new man, who acts on new principles; he must therefore entertain new ideas, and form new opinions." An apocalypse of reason, it would seem, was occurring in America. By the 1790's, however, it seemed to some that what might happen would be an apocalypse of unreason. Apocalyptic pessimism held that the Americans were staking everything on the disastrous premise that the generality of human beings are capable of the reflection and judgment required for democratic self-government, when in fact they constitute an ignorant multitude ruled by vanity. According to the gloomy prediction of the distinguished Massachusetts congressman, Fisher Ames, the people of a democracy inevitably yield to the flattery of demagogues. And following this, still under the compulsion of their "dearest and most delusive" belief, namely that "the power of the people is their liberty," they end up in the tyrannical grasp of the one demagogue who has managed to vanquish his rivals. Under the aspect of the Amesian pessimism, the American was not a new man but a creature of the long history of man that had unfolded since the fall. The Revolution had been fought not "to subvert an old government" but "to preserve old rights." To regard it as the commencement of a great experiment was an utter delusion. By 1805 Fisher Ames saw the Americans taking the same downhill path all democracies in history had taken: "We are sliding down into the mire of a democracy, which pollutes the morals of the citizens before it swallows up their liberties."

The satiric mode of the literature of the early Republic is related to both the millennial and the doomsday attitudes toward American history. It is employed to decry the rule of kings and praise the rule of the people, and it is used to make prophetic lamentations of the coming of a complete democratic disorder. But, we must note, the division of the satire in the age of the early Republic into opposing phases of the apocalyptic mood is subject to qualification when analyzed in terms of specific satires. For in both phases the more notable examples of satire against the authority of kings and magistrates tend to be ambivalent in conception, strategy, and tone. They run to a rather grimly apocalyptic humor, celebrating the emancipation of man from the authority of the establishment in a manner as melancholy as optimistic. Some of them are quite humorless.

Consider, for instance, such a well-known attack on the British monarchy as Philip Freneau's "George the Third's Soliloquy." Freneau was a mighty hater of kings, but in this poem the King emerges as a suffering, disturbed, uncertain ruler, and the drama of his situation is poignant. He is caught in the trap of international politics. He cries out, "A desperate game I play." He feels that he is in the possession of "fiends of darkness" and of "powers unfriendly to the human kind." Freneau, an archliberal and an active patriot in the Revolution, unquestionably intended in "George the Third's Soliloquy" to create a portrait of the monarch as an unscrupulous tyrant, and in so doing to make him an object of scorn and ridicule. But Freneau's motive under critical inspection proves to have been more complex than his intention, and we see in his effort to depict the mind of George III a complex ambiguity in his own mind toward the meaning of the Revolution. Consider a similar ambiguity in John Trumbull's treatment of his fictional magistrate M'Fingal, in his mock epic of the same name. Intended to be a pro-Revolutionary satirical attack on the Tories, this poem moves uncertainly between contempt for Squire M'Fingal and disdain of (it may be fear of) the mob that tars and feathers the Squire. The petty tyranny of M'Fingal seems minor in contrast to the tyranny of the mob that seizes him, gives him a drumhead trial, and sentences him to savage punishment.

> Forthwith the crowd proceed to deck
> With halter'd noose M'FINGAL'S neck,
> While he in peril of his soul
> Stood tied half-hanging to the pole;
> Then lifting high the ponderous jar,
> Pour'd o'er his head the smoking tar.

Consider a somewhat different kind of ambiguity in Joel Barlow's notable poem called "The Conspiracy of Kings." In it Barlow, who had gone from an early conservatism to a revolutionary position possibly to the left of Freneau, exults:

> 'Tis Reason's choice, 'tis Wisdom's final plan,
> To drop the monarch and assume the man.

Yet Barlow depicts the evil power of the institution of monarchy in such extreme terms that he virtually overwhelms the contrasting picture of the rule of reason.

> High on a moving throne, and near the van,
> The tyrant rides, the chosen scourge of man;
> Clarions and flutes and drums his way prepare,
> And shouting millions rend the troubled air;
> Millions, whose ceaseless toils the pomp sustain,
> Whose hour of stupid joy repays an age of pain.

It is uncertain whether in tone and effect—as Barlow's intended satire lapses into declamation—"The Conspiracy of Kings" convinces us that the conspiracy is the result of kings or of the people, whether there is any real chance that man will learn to obey "Reason's choice" or continue to obey his "chosen scourge."

When we turn to satires predicated on overtly reactionary views of democratic developments in America—developments real or imagined—we find uncomplicated visions of present disorder and impending catastrophe. One of the best known of the doomsday poems in the writings of the early Republic is *The Anarchiad*, a mock epic written largely by Lemuel Hopkins, one of the famous Connecticut Wits. Conceived in imitation of Charles Churchill's *The Rolliad* (with a distinct bow to Pope's *The Dunciad*), *The Anarchiad* specifically attacks Shays's Rebellion and the Whiskey Insurrection. Its general import is the coming chaos these ominous evidences of democracy in America portend.

> Lo, THE COURT FALLS: th' affrighted judges run,
> Clerks, Lawyers, Sheriffs, every mother's son.
> The stocks, the gallows lose th' expected prize,
> See the jails open, and the thieves arise.
> Thy constitution, Chaos, is restor'd;
> Law sinks before thy uncreating word;
> Thy hand unbars th' unfathom'd gulf of fate,
> And deep in darkness 'whelms the new-born state.

In the darkness that has become America, Anarch rules, awaiting the day when "tumultuous mobs," weary and desperate in the excess of their own disorder, ask for a king and heaven sends a wrathful one. In another satire of the doomsday variety, Timothy Dwight has a post-Revolutionary vision of America as the scene of rule of "the prince of darkness." This mock epic, entitled *The Triumph of Infidelity*, thoroughly loses its identity as a true mock epic in its prophecy of the damnation of the erstwhile "realms of freedom, peace, and virtue."

The ultimate doomsday satire by a writer of the early Republic was conceived not by a Timothy Dwight, strange to say, but by one of the most outspoken liberals, Joel Barlow. It would be inaccurate to say that Barlow finally returned to the conservative views of his early years. What happened was more complex and more dramatic: his experience of the power of Napoleon while he was in Europe on a journey that proved to be his last and that marked the end of his life. In Poland on a trade mission, he saw before him in reality the apocalyptic nightmare of a Fisher Ames: the devastated world left by Napoleon, the dictator who had risen to power in the aftermath of a democratic revolution. Gazing in the midst of the bitter winter at the frozen dead of Napoleon's legions scattered across the Polish landscape, Barlow was inspired to write his "Advice to a Raven in Russia." Called "perhaps the bitterest satire ever written by an American," Barlow's poem, in a diction more intense and moving than he managed to achieve in any other work, advises a scavenging raven to seek his food in warmer climes ravaged by Napoleon instead of plucking at "Mere trunks of ice, tho' limb'd like human frames." The raven will not lack for food in the Southern countries, for in Europe every country lies "reeking with its people's slain/And not a stream runs bloodless to the main."

Now it is not surprising that satire in the early Republic—even satire that ostensibly is directed toward the elevation of democracy and the castigation of kings—turns toward a nightmarish vision of democracy. Although it is a highly flexible and adaptable genre and is capable of being employed to dramatize and criticize an infinite variety of situations and all kinds and conditions of men, satire is primarily conservative in inspiration. The satirical impulse stems from the fundamental conviction that pride, greed, and all forms of sin and folly are innate in man's nature. One of the leading features of the Enlightenment is the way in which satire appears as a major counterbalance to the emphasis on reason and the emancipation of the intellect. No greater critique of man's capacity for reason exists than that we find in such leading figures of the Age of Reason as Swift, Pope, and Voltaire. In their age reason and ironic humor are complementary; reason, it is not too much to say, is controlled by irony.

What surprises us about the satire in the early American Republic is its relative, at times one may say its complete, lack of the magnificent sense of ironic humor which informs the satiric mode the Americans were most familiar with: the mode of "wit," the dominating mode of the great English satirists—Dryden, Swift, Pope, and such lesser descendants in the late eighteenth century as Charles Churchill. Why did satire in America fail to develop the ironic motive? Why did it prove to be so lacking in this function of wit? Congested with ironies, the American situation, it would seem, must have offered an exceedingly rich challenge to writers educated in the "wit ideal."

The questions I am asking are perhaps too complex to be answered beyond suggestion here. The wit ideal and the expression of wit is an integral part of the eighteenth-century conviction of the power of words rightly used to impose order and decorum on society. As practiced by the leading British satirists, wit—the sophisticated verbal play of mind on the follies and vices of man and society—is integrally connected to the ideal of the lettered mind and the discipline of letters. This discipline is the criterion of civilization, not merely in a formal sense but in the sense that the lettered mind is contained in the use of letters. Thus "true wit" is the expression of—the image of—the truly lettered mind which is at once the truly moral mind, the moral and literary foundations of civilized order being inseparable. It is this idealism that shines in Pope's famous lines in his "Essay on Criticism":

> True wit is Nature to advantage dressed,
> What oft was thought, but ne'er so well expressed;
> Something, whose truth convinced at sight we find,
> That gives us back the image of our mind.

The rendering of the image of the mind of an age—this is what we have in the great satires of the eighteenth century. These can be quite pessimistic about the prospective loss of order in the world, but their underlying implication asserts a control of disorder. True wit in *The Dunciad* gives back not ultimately the image of the mind of duncery but the image of the ironic, controlling, judging, decorous literary mind prophesying an apocalypse of duncery in Pope's age. But this will not occur if true wit prevails. And it does prevail. It prevails in the power of the literary art of Pope's sardonic, ironic humor.

But the apocalyptic mind of the early American Republic did not find a controlling center in the ironic perspective cultivated by the Popean literary mind. For the American satirist to seek the truth of wit—to discover a way to give back of the image of the American mind—was to undertake a quest into a world as yet unexplored by the literary mind, a world in which all the traditional norms and signs seemed obscured or obliterated, the world of an incipient equalitarian democracy. In America following the Revolution the literary mind increasingly experienced a severe sense of displacement. Central to an understanding of the melancholy of Freneau is his poem called "An Author's Soliloquy," which tells us a good deal about the ambivalence of his "George the Third's Soliloquy." The author speaks of his condition in America: "On these bleak climes by Fortune thrown/Where rigid reason reigns alone. . . ." And he imagines:

> Thrice happy DRYDEN who could meet
> Some rival bard on every street:
> When all were bent on writing well,
> It was some credit to excel
> While those condemn'd to stand alone
> Can only by themselves be known.

This is an early expression of the famous loneliness of the American writer. For all his community with his fellow Revolutionists, Freneau feels that he does not belong to a community of wit, to the company of lettered minds. His poem implies the whole enormous question in American literary history: under the novel conditions of American life, can there be a literary life? Can there be a democratic wit? a democratic literary mind? Under the sovereignty of the people, can there be a sovereignty of the literary mind?

If Freneau suggests these questions, he never explores them very far in his writings. The most important exploration of them in the days of the early Republic occurs in a long, rambling, satirical work in prose by Hugh Henry Brackenridge entitled *Modern Chivalry: Containing the Adventures of Captain John Farrago, and Teague O'Regan, His Servant*. Like Freneau, Brackenridge knew the feeling of literary displacement. About a year after he published the first two parts of *Modern Chivalry*, he wrote: "Nature intended me for a writer, and it has always been my ambition. How often have I sighed for the garrets of London. . . ." Like Freneau, and Barlow, Brackenridge was democratic in his inclinations. Unlike them he knew the feeling of American life as it existed on the Pennsylvania frontier. For this reason he was more pragmatic than either Freneau or Barlow. In terms we use today he was something like a middle-of-the-road democrat. He saw the power of the many and the power of the few as necessary historical polarities. Democracy could work if the people were willing to be responsible to the obligations of their sovereignty. If they will "shew their majesty, the nobility of their nature, *by their discrimination, and their sense of justice.*" Any man among the people, Brackenridge says, "might be made a despot, but this can only be by the people's destroying the essence of liberty, by pushing it to licentiousness. A despot is a spectre which rises chiefly from the marsh of *licentiousness. It was the jacobins made Bonaparte what he now is.*"

Brackenridge was writing this observation in the final part of *Modern Chivalry* at somewhere around the time Barlow was contemplating Napoleon's "tentless troops . . . marbl'd through with frost" on the icy plains of Poland. But he does not assume the inevitability of a downward progress of democracy into despotism. In *Modern Chivalry* he creates a portrayal of the ironic realities of the first stages of democracy in America. The book turns on the struggle of a man of letters, Captain Farrago, to establish literacy as the general basis for action in the democracy of the frontier. Brackenridge, who came from Scotland to America in 1753 when he was five years old, was given the advantages of a college education by his hardworking parents and was graduated from Princeton in 1771 in the same class with Freneau. When he moved out into the Pennsylvania frontier country following the Revolution, Brackenridge went into politics, only after a brief success to find himself ousted from the legislature by a bumptious, no more than half-literate constituency. The voters did not appreciate it when he decided, for the sake of good government, to reverse his position on a land bill the frontier settlers wanted to see approved. The idea of *Modern Chivalry*, which occupied Brackenridge for twenty-five years and which he began as a Hudibrastic poem called *The Modern Chevalier*, loosely resembles the concept of Cervantes's *Don Quixote*. The leading characters are Captain Farrago, a middle-aged, bookish and scribbling dweller on the Pennsylvania frontier, and his servant, Teague O'Regan. A recent immigrant from Ireland, O'Regan is the reverse of Crèvecoeur's idealized American immigrant, the new man in a new world. When Farrago decides to make a journey to Philadelphia and to take O'Regan with him, the two become involved in a long series of misadventures, all of them reflecting the political and sociological problem of the insurgent illiteracy of the growing American democracy. Aggressively ignorant, O'Regan displays a vanity that is matched, unfortunately, wherever he goes by the response of the populace. The people in every community want to elevate him. As the episodes unfold O'Regan threatens all the orders of society: the state (he is almost elected to the legislature); the church (he is almost made a minister of the gospel); letters and learning (he is almost made a member of the American Philosophical Society). Arguing that his servant is unsuited to a position requiring an educated mind, Farrago intervenes in each case. Finally he decides that O'Regan will sooner or later be in some position of importance; so he attempts to prepare him for responsibility. O'Regan becomes an exciseman, but he is tarred and feathered when he insists on actually collecting taxes. In the numerous subsequent episodes of Brackenridge's lengthy satire the author explores many instances of the fallibility of democracy. Although the thrust of the adventures of Farrago and O'Regan point toward the conviction that it is desirable to accept the sovereignty of the people as the operational ground of the American social order, Brackenridge never establishes a clear conceptual center in *Modern Chivalry*, a controlling irony as a perspective from which to view democracy. Farrago, the chief voice in the book, is a farrago of notions. At times he seems to be as foolish as his servant. But Brackenridge's large effort to assess the democratic experience as he saw it gets away from the apocalyptic compulsion. The formula of millennium or doomsday is avoided. Overall *Modern Chivalry* holds up the idea that it may be possible for men of letters to come out of men of no letters. A literary class primarily related to democracy may arise in the new Republic; a democratic wit and intellect—which Brackenridge associates closely with lawyers—may become a directing force.

However, a reader who looks at Brackenridge's satirical fable of democracy in America is constantly reminded that Brackenridge's education is still that of the eighteenth century. One may well feel that he is fumbling to devise a language in which what is happening in America can be imagined. He offers his experience of the democratic situation but can offer no effective satirical resolution of it. He cannot truly manage it. The truth of wit is not available to him. The underlying, unintentional irony of his jerry-built work is the inadequacy of the traditional literary mind to cope with its displacement in a new world that became stranger every day.

Washington Irving

Lewis Leary

Washington Irving has been called the father of American Humor, but he was not. Ebenezer Cook, for one, preceded him, Benjamin Franklin and William Byrd, John Trumbull, Philip Freneau, and many another local wit. But Irving had the better chance, greater exposure at a better time, and his influence may be thought to have been greater. By the time he died, on the eve of the American Civil War, he had had more imitators than any of these others. Some, like Charles Dickens in England and Bret Harte in California, did better than he, though many others, like barnstorming Artemus Ward and Orpheus C. Kerr, probably had not known him very much at all. For Irving stood at the headwaters of an American stream which flowed finally in many directions. Though its sources may be found in the great wits of England, from Chaucer to Addison and Goldsmith, to Hazlitt and Lamb, it was quickened by fresh native springs. It has never quite lost the delicate tinctures which Irving added to it.

The doubleness of Washington Irving, which is the doubleness of humor, most especially of American humor, is first discovered when at nineteen he contributed a series of eight letters to a newspaper edited by an older brother. Almost one hundred years before, young Benjamin Franklin had done much the same thing in a series of letters which he pretended had been written by Silence Dogood, and part of the joke then was that Mistress Dogood was not silent at all, but a talkative and opinionated woman. Young

63

Irving used a pseudonym somewhat more subtle, less universal, and more distinctively American. He signed himself Jonathan Oldstyle, Gent., joining the familiar Yankee name of Jonathan, the perspicacious country bumpkin who was a popular comic figure on the American stage, to that which suggested a dignified personage who was conservative and retrospective, suspicious of what was new, preferring rather the old style to which he was comfortably accustomed. Furthermore, Jonathan Oldstyle was a Gent., one of the gentry, a gentleman, and that was part of Irving's joke, and it had local, and somewhat new, and very American connotations, for democracy seemed to say that, all men being created equal, all men had the right and responsibility to become just as equal as anybody else.

One assumes that, like Washington Irving himself, Jonathan Oldstyle was a member of the new, self-conscious, and perhaps spurious aristocracy of wealth which sprang up in the United States after the American Revolution. It was the pretentious new society which a few years later Fitz-Greene Halleck good-naturedly satirized in *Fanny* which in rollicking octosyllabics set forth the misfortunes of the pretty daughter of a local nouveau riche who sought a husband among the older, established New York families. It was the upstart, half-democratic, half-anglophile, money-making society that Fenimore Cooper would castigate in *Home As Found*.

As a member of the first generation of his family to be born in America, and as the youngest son of an immigrant merchant father who had become wealthy enough to allow him early leisure, Irving never could quite withstand temptations toward sly, but usually ever so gentle, observations on incongruities in the life-styles and intentions of longer-settled (usually Dutch) families of Manhattan, and of gadabout new society in New York or Ballston Spa, and, especially, of upstart Yankees from New England. Even when travel and fame had taught him to be something of an aristocrat himself, secure behind the decent and respected pseudonym of Geoffrey Crayon, Gent., and admired as the genial dean of American letters whose quiet home overlooking the Hudson River near Sleepy Hollow in Tarrytown became a Mecca for admiring visitors —even then, he could not utterly withstand quizzical temptations, though he had learned cautious control and had acquired a mask behind which only the gentle twinkle of his eyes could not be hidden. No wonder that Fenimore Cooper, more securely to the manor born, disliked him. Cooper's humor, what he had of it, was blunt and boisterous and bruising, with no deception of geniality.

Jonathan Oldstyle pretended great contempt for innovation. Modern manners, modern marriages, modern modes of dress were objects of his ridicule in the letters which he contributed in 1802 and 1803 to the New York *Morning Chronicle*. His strategy was burlesque exaggeration, in the manner of Hogarth or Addison, with just enough intrusion of verisimilitude to insure a chuckle of recognition. When, for example, a bridegroom named Squire Stylish struts gravely into a room, "his ivory-headed ebony cane in one hand, and gently swaying his three-cornered beaver with the other," he is attired in a splendidly mod "suit of scarlet velvet, . . . the skirts stiffened with a yard or two of buckram; a long pig-tailed wig, well powdered, adorned his head; and stockings of deep blue silk rolled over his knees . . . ; the flaps of his vest reached to his knee-buckles, and the ends of his cravat, tied with the most precise neatness, twisted through every button hole." Nor was his bride less splendidly arrayed: her gown "of flame-coloured brocade" was flared ridiculously outward, in giant circumference, by a prodigious hoop, and it was embroidered all over with poppies and roses and gigantic yellow sunflowers.

This technique of exaggeration through caricature was as old as Theophrastus, as modern and as popular as Addison and Sterne, and, when applied to native idiosyncracies and native exploits, was to become one of the hallmarks of boisterous American frontier humor and of the slapstick buffooneries of the burlesque stage. Jonathan Oldstyle was on the right path certainly, and Irving was to move forward briefly later, exploring new and native comic possibilities. But now he looked over his shoulder backwards. There was little distinctively American, for example, in his remarks on modern marriage: they were as old as Eden, yet may seem to beleaguered husbands anywhere to be as true today as they have been every yesterday. "No longer," observes Jonathan, "does the wife tuck the napkin under her husband's chin. . . . The wife now considers herself as totally independent—will advance her own opinions, without hesitation, though directly opposite to his."

Perhaps the country people in the gallery of an American theater, described by Jonathan as pelting apples, nuts, and gingerbread on the heads of people below like thunderbolts from a plebeian heaven, may be thought of as presenting a kind of postparadigm of patriots at the Battle of Bunker Hill, a quizzical acknowledgement of the power of common people. And we may be tempted to discover democratic disapproval in Jonathan's description of a sharp-faced little Frenchman in trim white coat and small cocked hat who shook his fist at the gallery like "an irritable little animal," and to find in him local reference to emigrés, barbers, wig makers, dancing masters, and aristocrats, who swarmed to America in escape from the French Revolution, forgetting that the bumbling, irascible little Frenchman was a stock figure of stage comedy in England— as American, one might say, as roast beef or Yorkshire pudding, at best an imported commodity.

Much of Irving's humor, now and later, was borrowed from abroad. Strategies for the publication of the *Salmagundi* papers, in which Irving at twenty-four collaborated, were appropriated from Oliver Goldsmith's equally errant periodical the *Bee*. Irving was to remain a lifelong captive to the charm of Goldsmith, "the artless benevolence that beams through his works," his "whimsical, yet amiable views of human nature," his "unforced humor, blending so happily with good feeling and good sense." The Englishman's "soft-tinted style," his spontaneity and quiet humor, became and remained a tempting model.

But now in 1807 the young men who in *Salmagundi* would "instruct the young, reform the old, correct the town, and castigate the age, . . . interfering in all matters either of a public or private nature," were pert young Manhattan blades, quick with quip. They pretended genuine native distaste for neighbors who would spoil "honest American taste" with foreign "slop and fricasseed sentiment." Yet the Anthony Evergreen, Gent., and the Will Wizard, Esq., who contributed to it bore names which just as well might have been chosen by writers for a London periodical, though their associates Pindar Cockloft and Launcelot Langstaff may in their names reflect a pruriency, perhaps native, certainly jejune, which might not have issued from coffee houses by the Thames.

The subjects to which these young New Yorkers addressed themselves were often local enough: "This town," remarked

Launcelot Langstaff, is "remarkable for dogs and democrats." They were likely to look down their noses at their "queer, old rantipole city" and their whimsical new country which together supplied, they said, enough ridiculousness "to keep our risible muscles and pens going until doomsday." Theirs was an aristocratic pose: "Thank Heaven," one of them exploded in a tone not unlike that of H. L. Mencken more than a century later, "we are not, like the unhappy rulers of this enlightened land, accountable to the mob for our actions." They spoke with disdain, however, of the naïveté of visitors from England, and explained carefully how to identify a cockney among them. They laughed at young women who were too genteel to risk a walk with local gentlemen along the Battery which fronted New York harbor. They pretended enormous expectation for the New World: Noah, one insisted, had been born there, so that all the world besides was populated by migrating Americans. But their mode and their tone was mainly borrowed. Mustapha Rub-a-Dub Khan, an enlightened stranger from abroad, comments on peculiarities of people in their strange land much as Montesquieu's Persian and Goldsmith's Chinese philosophers had done.

But when two years later, at twenty-six, Washington Irving invented Diedrich Knickerbocker, a fresh new era in American literature and native humor began. *The History of New York from the Beginning of the World to the End of the Dutch Dynasty* as published in 1809 over the new pseudonym, is a boisterous comic epic which contrasts the braggadocio and limitless expectations of adventurers in the New World with the Homeric exploits of ancient Greek heroes, testing Old World ideals against the frontier requirements of the New. The wharfsides of Manhattan are compared to the "walls of Jericho, or the heaven-built battlements of Troy." Blundering Dutch heroes are measured against Achilles, the god of golden deeds. The mood is consistently mock-heroic as Diedrich Knickerbocker reveals "Many Surprising and Curious Matters," including "the Unutterable Ponderings of Walter the Doubter, the Disastrous Projects of William the Testy, and the Chivalric Achievements of Peter the Headstrong" in what he boasted was "the only Authentic History of the Times that Ever Hath Been Published."

Authentic it certainly was not, though much of it can be read as personalized political satire, directed, for the most part, against Thomas Jefferson and his threats of democratic innovation. But readers need know little of American politics to chuckle over its droll burlesque. Many of the Dutch in New York did not like it, and Irving was so mercilessly attacked that he seldom dared such unrestraint again. But reviewers in Boston found Knickerbocker's *History* the wittiest book that young America had yet produced. In London it was greeted as "an honest attempt . . . to found an American literature. . . . The umbilical cord is severed. America is at last independent." It even reached frontier western outposts, "going the rounds," reported a witness in Mackinac, from the commandant of the fort to the smallest Indian trader, contributing "to their merriment and pleasure."

And well it might, for its humor was robust and hearty. Hendrick Hudson, who had discovered the bay of Manhattan, was described as a "square, brawny old gentleman with a . . . mastiff mouth, and a broad copper nose which . . . acquired its fiery hue from the constant neighborhood of his tobacco pipe. His vessel, the *Half-Moon,* which "floated sideways, like a majestic goose," was, like the fair Dutch maidens who inspired its building, "full in the bows, with a pair of enormous catheads, a copper bottom, and withal a most prodigious poop!"

Old Governor Wouter Van Twiller was "exactly five feet six inches in height, and six feet five inches in circumference. . . . His legs, though exceeding short, were sturdy in proportion to the weight they had to sustain; so that when erect he had not a little the appearance of a robustious beer barrel standing on skids." The renowned Wouter was not often erect, however: he preferred to sit and snooze, "would absolutely shut his eyes for two hours at a time, that he might not be disturbed by external objects—and at such a time the internal commotion of his mind was evinced by certain regular guttural sounds, exuding through his nose in monstrous snoring, "which his admirers declared were merely the noise of conflict" in his powerful, ever-working mighty mind.

Like Jonathan Oldstyle, Diedrich Knickerbocker looked longingly back to better times long past. How superior were the "delectable orgies" of teatime feasting among the old Dutch settlers compared to the effetely fashionable "iced creams, jellies, or syllabubs; . . . the musty almonds, mouldy raisins, or sour oranges" daintily consumed in "the present age of refinement." In better, older times, the teatime company ate lustily until each member was glutted: properly armed with a sharp-tined fork, each would thrust dexterously at brown-fried slices of fat pork swimming in gravy, "in much the same manner," said Diedrich Knickerbocker, "as sailors harpoon porpoises at sea, or our Indians spear salmon in the lakes."

The white man's attitude toward the Indian was quizzically lampooned. Before white settlers came to the New World, the red man had

lived a most vagabond, disorderly, unrighteous life,—rambling from place to place and prodigally rioting upon the sumptuous luxuries of nature without tasking her generosity to yield them anything more; whereas it has most unquestionably been shown that heaven intended the earth should be plowed and sown and manured and laid out into cities and towns and farms and country seats and pleasure grounds and public gardens, all of which the Indians knew nothing about . . . they were careless stewards—therefore they had no right to the soil—therefore they deserve to be exterminated.

But the white man was benevolent, and did his best to ameliorate and improve the sad condition of these poor savages who were unable to ravage the land as effectively as the white man could. So the white man "introduced among them rum, gin, brandy, and other comforts of life—and it is astonishing to read how these poor savages learnt to estimate these blessings. . . . By these and a variety of other methods was the condition of these poor savages wonderfully improved; they acquired a thousand wants of which they had before been ignorant."

What voice is this that now speaks? There is in it certainly something of the bitter, transatlantic Irish wit of Jonathan Swift, but it anticipates also the caustic comic tone which Mark Twain more than half a century later would make a hallmark of American humor. Thus snuggled unobtrusively among the rich tomfooleries of Diedrich Knickerbocker's *History* appears an augury of that species of corrective comedy which catches the reader unawares: a stopper, Mark Twain might have called it, with a twist of inverted meaning that is derived, not through burlesque exaggeration like that which tells of Wouter Van Twiller's massive girth and prodigious snoring, but through understatement in mock seriousness which allows a speaker to pretend surprise when an audience finds his revelations comic.

If Washington Irving as Diedrich Knickerbocker can thus be said to have invented Mark Twain, he can also be said to be the articulate father of the burly, bluff burlesque, the extravagant mock gravity and massive irreverence of the American tall tale—as when he describes a sunbeam bouncing off the gigantic red nose of Antony the Trumpeter, acquiring from that nose such heat that it plunged "hissing hot" into the Hudson River "to kill a massive sturgeon that was sporting beside the vessel" in which the doughty Antony rode. And Diedrich's humor can be broad and mirthfully vulgar: Peter Stuyvesant, harassed in a duel, falls backward, Diedrich explains, "on his seat of honor" to land unceremoniously on a "cushion softer than velvet, which providence, or Minerva, or St. Nicholas, or some kindly cow, had benevolently prepared for his reception."

But Diedrich Knickerbocker invented more than this. From his sacrilegious pages there emerges, for the first time in full, disreputable array, the American backwoodsman, but presented as a comic rather than an heroic character, much as he remained when Fenimore Cooper introduced him as Natty Bumppo a dozen years later in *The Pioneers*, before he dehumanized a fallible human character by remaking him in later Leatherstocking Tales into more of an intrepid symbol than a man. The backwoodsman portrayed by Diedrich Knickerbocker is fallible indeed, and very human. His name is Dirk Sculler, and he deserves remembrance as the progenitor of a long and lusty lustrous line which includes, not only Leatherstocking himself and all his quick-eyed, stealthily treading, honest fictional offspring, but Huckleberry Finn's disreputable father also, and many of the valiant vagabonds who appear on horse or motorcycle, bravely rapacious, in filmed adventures today—the scout, the advance man, the skulker just beyond boundaries of approved polite behavior, but a man who overcomes mammoth and menacing hardships, finally to succeed.

Dirk Sculler was "a kind of hanger-on . . . who seemed to belong to nobody and in a manner to be self-outlawed." He was a vagabond, a poacher, an interloper: "Every garrison and country village," explained Diedrich Knickerbocker, "has one or more scapegoats of this kind, whose life is a kind of enigma, whose existence is without motive, who comes from the Lord knows where, and lives the Lord knows how." Dirk lounged about Peter Stuyvesant's frontier fort, "depending on chance for a subsistence, getting drunk whenever he could get liquor and stealing whatever he could lay his hands on." Sometimes, because of his myriad misdemeanors, he would find it advisable to disappear from the fort, often for as much as a month at a time,

skulking about the woods and swamps, with a long fowling piece on his shoulder, laying in ambush for game—or squatting himself down on the edge of a pond catching fish for hours together. . . . When he thought his crimes had been forgotten or forgiven, he would sneak back to the fort with a bundle of skins or a bunch of poultry, which perchance he had stolen, and exchange them for liquor, with which having well soaked his carcass, he would lay in the sun [in] luxurious indolence. . . . [Dirk] was the terror of all the farmyards of the country, into which he made fearful inroads; and sometimes he would make his sudden appearance at the garrison at daybreak with the whole neighborhood at his heels, like a scoundrel thief or a fox detected in his maraudings and hunted to his hole.

But, though Dirk apparently showed "total indifference . . . to the world or its concerns" and was "a fellow of few words," he nonetheless kept his "eyes and ears . . . always open," so that in the course of his prowlings he discovered a plot among the enemies of the Dutch that would mean the downfall of the garrison. So he set out overland to warn Peter Stuyvesant in New Amsterdam, from which city Dirk had "formerly been obliged to abscond precipitately in consequence of misfortune in business—that is to say, having been detected in the act of sheep stealing." Surely, there again is the voice of Mark Twain, laconic in understatement. And foreshadowings of the mighty feats of woodsmen like Paul Bunyan are discovered as gallant Dirk, "after wandering many days in the woods, toiling through swamps, fording brooks, swimming various rivers and encountering a world of hardship that would have killed any other being but an Indian, a backwoodsman or a devil, . . . at length arrived, half famished and lank as a weasel," on the western bank of the Hudson River, "where he stole a canoe and paddled

over to New Amsterdam . . . and in more words than he had
ever spoken before gave an account of the disastrous affair."

Like Faulkner's Sam Fathers, Dirk is part Indian, which explained, said Diedrich, his unusual propensities and habits. His appearance suggested that of almost any doughty woodsman in later
tales of American Western adventures: "a tall, lank fellow" was
Dirk, "swift of foot and long-winded. He was generally equipped
in a half Indian dress with belt, leggings and moccasons." And then
Diedrich Knickerbocker uses a phrase which may have long been
a commonplace in the spoken vernacular and which, since Irving
first wrote it in 1809, has passed down through many generations
of tellers of tall tales. "It is an old remark," he has Diedrich explain, "that persons of Indian mixture are half civilized, half savage
and half devil—a third half being expressly provided for their particular convenience. It is for similar reasons," he goes on, "and
probably with equal truth, that the backwoodsmen of Kentucky
are styled half man, half horse and half alligator."

As Diedrich Knickerbocker, Irving had the core of the matter
in him, inventing or bringing together several of the attitudes and
tones and modes which later and longer persevering hands would
more securely mold to familiar native patterns. Perhaps stung by
the bitterness of the reaction among New York friends against
the gay burlesque of Knickerbocker's *History*, Irving never allowed
his boisterous alter ego to speak so boisterously again. Yet almost
everything for which Irving is now most affectionately remembered is told in the perspicacious words of Diedrich Knickerbocker.
When, however, ten years later fame on both sides of the Atlantic
descended on Washington Irving, he wrote most often then, and
thereafter, in a quieter manner as Geoffrey Crayon, Gent., a gentle
man whose gentle pictures of English life in *The Sketch Book*
charmed but did not disturb. "Wit, after all," Irving had learned,
"is a mighty tart, pungent ingredient, and much too acid for most
stomachs; but honest good humor is the oil and wine of a merry
meeting."

As Geoffrey Crayon, he built and maintained the reputation of
being a remarkably placid and agreeable writer, deft and delightful,
but only an extension, said Melville, of Oliver Goldsmith. A few
critics, even then, in 1819, recognized that he had "lost something,"
one of them said, "of that natural run of style" for which his earlier

writings had been remarkable. He had "given up something of his direct, simple manner," the "words and phrases, which were strong, distinct and definite, for a genteel sort of language." His native, American speech, "sent abroad to be improved, . . . had lost too many of her home qualities." His writings now seemed to another contemporary to "resemble a family of sickly but pretty children,— tall, feeble, and delicately slender," lacking vigor.

And these critics were correct. Little of the younger Irving's robust comic verve survives in *The Sketch Book, Bracebridge Hall*, or *Tales of a Traveller*, the three collections which in the early 1820's made Geoffrey Crayon's name a familiar household word. Irving's aim now was quietly to amuse, "to keep," he said, "mankind in good humor with one another." Even in burlesque portraiture, his comic touch became less vibrant, containing few barbs which might sting or anger.

Only seldom does Geoffrey Crayon allow himself such extravagant exuberance as romps through the story of "The Bold Dragoon" in *Tales of a Traveller*, in which "an old soldier, and an Irishman to boot . . . blarnied the landlord, kissed the landlord's wife, tickled the landlord's daughter, chucked the barmaid under the chin," and then proceeded to outdrink a fat distiller. Retiring befuddled to his room, he found his furniture all dancing—"a long-backed brandy-legged chair, . . . studded all over in a coxcombical fashion with little brass nails," led "an easy chair of tarnished brocade . . . gallantly out in a ghostly minuet." A "three-legged stool danced a horn-pipe, though horribly puzzled by its supernumerary limb; while the amorous tongs seized the shovel round the waist and whirled it around in a German waltz." Everything in the room swirled and danced, except the "great clothes-press, which kept curtsying and curtsying, in a corner, like a dowager . . . too corpulent to dance." The bold dragoon, a true Irish gentleman, pitied her loneliness, and asked her to join him in a jig. But he reached toward her with such uncontrolled good will that she crashed down on top of him with a din that awakened the whole household. Sobered by his experience, the bold dragoon retired to rest. However funny, this is London music-hall slapstick of a kind which would be adapted to American vaudeville or burlesque.

But when Geoffrey Crayon called on Diedrich Knickerbocker

for assistance, as he does in each of these collections of sketches, then the tales come robustly alive. The stories of "Dolph Heyliger" and of "The Storm Ship" in *Bracebridge Hall* are both "drawn from the MSS. of the late Diedrich Knickerbocker." "The Devil and Tom Walker" in *Tales of a Traveller,* sometimes identified as Irving's third-best story, was also reported to have been found among old Diedrich's papers. The better tales of "Rip Van Winkle" and "The Legend of Sleepy Hollow" are both identified as by the late Diedrich Knickerbocker, and which of these two is Irving's best still provides matter for critical discussion. They represent the high points of his literary career, when in his late thirties Irving did better than he was ever to do again. In them, the comic spirit of Knickerbocker's *History* is briefly joined to the genial descriptive vein which thereafter Irving genially and repetitiously mined.

Blundering, affable Rip Van Winkle has survived for a century and a half as a comic paradigm of the American male. He is "one of the boys" who never grows up, a "kid with a dog," content to roam the woodlands in search of game or to "fish all day without a murmur, even though he should not be encouraged by a single nibble." Rip is "a simple good-natured man . . . a kind neighbor . . . an obedient hen-pecked husband . . . foremost at all country frolics." When things went wrong at home, he retired to the village tavern "to sit in the shade through a long summer's day, talking listlessly over village gossip." His was a sleepy little village, nestled charmingly at the foot of the Catskill mountains, a small enclave of quiet rural contentment, surrounded and protected by the lush bounty of nature. It was the small town of pre-Revolutionary America, and when Rip returns to it after a sleep of twenty years, he finds it only a little changed. Disputatious people rant in democratic jargon about the rights of man, but the old tavern, though new-named, is there, and Rip's son is there, a replica of his younger self. Human nature blunders irrepressibly on.

More than the charm of Irving's graceful style insures long life to Rip Van Winkle. Hart Crane called him America's "muse of memory," its "guardian angel of a trip to the past" who reminds readers of something that is familiar because it is not altogether gone. Much has been made of Irving's deft transfer of Old-World legend to a New-World setting, of his use of familiar elements of transatlantic popular lore as he transports Valhalla to the hills overlooking the Hudson, but these borrowed elements provide background only for what becomes a native comic legend. Rip survives as Huck Finn survives who would not be civilized either.

One of the most outrageously comic lines in "Rip Van Winkle," and one which certifies the tale as American, is slipped in without emphasis toward the close of the action, when Rip asks his daughter what had become of his wife. Mark Twain himself could not have contrived a more disorderly or more effective joining of comedy and pathos than she, in her laconic reply that her mother, Rip's wife, had died: "She broke a blood-vessel in a fit of passion at a Yankee peddler."

Yankees from New England had always been fair game to Diedrich Knickerbocker. In the *History of New York* they had been described as a "pumpkin-eating . . . notion-peddling people." But in the psalm-singing, lank and bony schoolmaster, Ichabod Crane, in "The Legend of Sleepy Hollow," the Yankee is more ruthlessly caricatured in all his Jonathan-like angularity, his awkward persistence in attempting to better himself by marrying the lush and wealthy Katrina, and his superstitious New England, Cotton Mather-bred doubts and fears. So persistent has been the memory of Ichabod that when in Faulkner's *The Hamlet* Eula Varner, also lush and wealthy, is wooed by her schoolmaster, she breaks from his arms exclaiming, "You old Ichabod Crane, you!" For Irving's Ichabod lives on, the mirror image of Rip Van Winkle. He is the busy American who plans to flee with the fair Katrina and make his fortune in the frontier west, and who finally leaves the rural village to become in New York a lawyer and then a judge, the successful, soulless American whose monstrous peccadilloes would be revealed on larger scale by Theodore Dreiser, Sinclair Lewis, and John Dos Passos. In a broad sense, he is a Yankee Flem Snopes, as impotent and predatory and hauntingly comic as Faulkner's ugly paradigm of democratic upward mobility.

Some forty years later, Mark Twain would first reach a national audience with a comic tale called "The Dandy Frightening the Squatter," in which a backwoodsman gets the best of an Eastern intruder. But, again, Irving anticipated him, for in "The Legend of Sleepy Hollow" Brom Bones, "a burly, roaring, roystering" country man, broad shouldered, bluff, and "always ready for fun or frolic," outwits Ichabod who is also an intruder from the East. Brom has been called "a Catskill Mink Fink, a ring-tailed roarer from Kinderhook," the ancestor of many brawlers and braggarts who rip and roar in later American frontier humor, in tales told of Davy Crockett or Daniel Boone, in Mark Twain's writings, and in all the dime novels and films in which the country boy outslicks the city slicker. Brom is no Dirk Sculer, no skulker on the outskirts of civilization. He is part of an emerging society, the guardian of its integrity against intrusion from without.

Perhaps we are tempted to discover too much meaning in "The Legend of Sleepy Hollow." Like "Rip Van Winkle," it is an imported tale, retailored to native requirements. But Irving's skill in caricature, in appetizing description of luscious food crowded onto Dutch tables, of dance and frolic and rich tomfoolery is genuinely his own. He never did as well again, though his sense of scene and comic character is briefly revealed in *A Tour on the Prairies;* mildly impious jibes at Yankee transcendentalism appear years later in "Mount-Joy," and "The Great Mississippi Bubble" sketches frontier life in a manner which looks timidly toward the lustier ironic realism of Mark Twain. However respectworthy these tentative reachings toward a native comic mode, Irving became increasingly a timid writer who seldom dared dangers of public disapproval. "Failure," said Melville, "is the test of greatness." Success such as Irving's, he said, is "proof that a man wisely knows his powers" and "knows them to be small." A younger Irving had opened doors which gave access to native varieties of the comic spirit. But he closed them quickly, after only brief glances. But he was there at the start, beginning more than he dared finish. Our gratitude to him must be great. Our understanding of his failures is inevitably sympathetic. For Washington Irving himself is perhaps the most representative comic figure of all, an early nineteenth-century J. Alfred Prufrock, who ventures only tentatively, then draws back, content to polish and to please. It was Melville again who warned that "there is no hope for us in these smooth, pleasing writers."

Yankee Humor

Cecil D. Eby

The principal ingredient of New England humor has always been the seriocomic figure of the "Yankee," as the rural inhabitant of that region is called. The word itself has undergone at least three quite different evolutionary stages, but always it has carried a faintly derisive implication.

The origin of "Yankee" has eluded researchers (etymologists still quarrel over its probable derivation), but the generally accepted hypothesis contends that it is an Anglicized corruption of "Jan Kees"—or "John Cheese"—a pejorative term which the original Dutch settlers of New Amsterdam (now New York) applied to Anglo-Americans living in the adjoining state of Connecticut. After the collapse of the Dutch colony and the absorption of its inhabitants into the American mainstream, the word "Yankee" lay dormant until just before the Revolutionary War. As ill feeling between the British and the Americans intensified, the British revived it as a label of ridicule for those colonials demanding separation from the mother country. (As it happened, "Yankee" conformed, in this sense, to another American word originating at about the same time, the verb "yank," which means "to wrench violently" or "to pull with a violent jerk.") It is unlikely that by this time the "John Cheese" meaning was remembered. Presumably it was a British surgeon who wrote the satirical song, "Yankee Doodle," which lampooned the absurd incompetence of the American militia as it organized to fight the well-trained and disciplined British army assigned to put down the rebellion. But to everyone's surprise, the Americans adopted "Yankee Doodle"—with all its absurd stanzas—as their first battle hymn and national anthem. Americans silenced British satire by joining in the laughter at themselves, by adding hundreds of stanzas of their own, and by turning a fictive American bumpkin named "Yankee Doodle" into a low-comedy figure unwilling to be intimidated by the formidable British lion. Thus the Yankee became the first of a long line of American antiheroes—that is, a scorned "common man" of little talent and even less sophistication who turned the tables on the "establishment"—in this case, the empery of Great Britain. The democratic note was struck and would be heard many times again in American belletristic and political writing—whether by Lincoln, Twain, Whitman, or Emerson.

It was this "Yankee" that entered and dominated the humor of New England during the first half of the nineteenth century. Subsequently the term, ever an elastic one, expanded to include other things. During the American Civil War, for example, Southerners labeled *all* Northerners "Yankees" even if they came from Western states like Ohio and Illinois. And by the First World War "Yankee" had become a blanket term throughout the world to designate *all* Americans whose behavior was less than exemplary. The pejorative quality of the word still remained, but the image of the simple New England rustic—a figure both ignorant but wise—had been erased from the word. As used here, "Yankee" refers to that prototypical New Englander who stamped his features indelibly upon the newly coined American character during the pre-Civil War period.

As a political creed in New England, democracy was accepted on theoretical grounds more thoroughly than practiced in fact. Suffrage was by no means universal, and political leaders were almost invariably drawn from families of some economic and social substance. Whereas Jefferson, a political radical of his time, called for a leadership measured solely by "virtue and talent," the principal New England spokesman, John Adams (who succeeded Washington to the presidency) adhered to the quadrivium—virtue, talent, *birth*, and *wealth*—as the four-pronged criterion of leadership. In other words, the intelligentsia of New England, who inherited from their Puritan forebears the notion of an *elect*, generally reflected an aristocratical political position. As a matter of fact, the first six American Presidents, who served from 1789 to 1828, were but continuations of the English parliamentary governing class—all of them country squires like Washington and Jefferson or middle-class gentlemen like the two Adamses.

The election of Andrew Jackson in 1828 changed all that. Jackson was a representative of the western frontier, a man of humble origin, a frightening spectre of "People's Power." He was the first of that line of "log-cabin Presidents" who deeply resented Eastern banking interests and regarded all influences from Europe— particularly those from Great Britain—as subversive and detrimental to American ideals. On the other hand, the traditionalists viewed Jackson's rise into power as the first symptoms of runaway anarchism, as an explosion in the sewer which brought forth the unleavened mass of humanity recruited from urban mobs and country-bred know-nothings. His predecessor, President John Quincy Adams, was so distressed by the victory of Jacksonian democracy that he refused to attend Jackson's inauguration in Washington, lest his presence somehow endorse the political "revolution" which, he imagined, had seized the nation like a malignant plague.

The appearance of Jackson and his entourage provided a catalyst for the development of New England humor. Here was a target ideally situated for satirical barbs and dangerous enough (as the conservatives believed) to require deflation. To attack Jackson was also to attack the excesses of the system which he stood for. And certainly he laid himself open for satirical assault with his hearty hand-shaking mannerisms and, at times, abysmal ignorance. (Once, on hearing that the French Ambassador had prefixed a request with the words "je demande . . . ," the President flew into a rage and swore that he was *damned* if any Frenchman would ever tell him what to do.) In short, the conservative faction seized upon the "common man" as rich vein of humor—but always there was political commentary lurking within it.

For this satire the prototypal "Yankee Doodle" figure was revived in order to comment upon the political carnival in

Washington, most of the humor deriving from the naïveté of the literal-minded rustic who described what he saw. The creator of this fleshed-out Yankee was an otherwise unimportant writer named Seba Smith, who edited the Portland (Maine) *Daily Courier*. The adventures of his fictional character, Major Jack Downing of Downingville, Maine, were soon being reprinted in newspapers throughout the Republic, and they were so realistically conveyed that many readers came to believe that Major Jack was a real person. The Major, who traveled to Washington in order to find political preferment, joined the President's "kitchen cabinet" as general factotum and political adviser. He kept Jackson informed of developments back in Downingville and eased the great man's burdens by ingenious devices. At receptions, for example, the Major stood behind the President and reached under his shoulder to shake hands with the endless lines of Democratic admirers, each desirous of clasping their chief's hand. If today the humor seems contrived and dated, Smith's sketches did revitalize the caricature of the Yankee and did experiment in conveying the speech and metaphor of ordinary people. Readers found that the distance between themselves and the Head of State was not excessive, and they enjoyed the fictive exposé, with its intimate glimpses into the halls of the mighty. Henceforth Americans would always regard their chief executive with a coldly skeptical eye, and for this we may blame—or praise—Seba Smith, one of our first democratic "levelers." In time, the garb of Major Downing—striped trousers, bat-wing collar, shaggy top hat—became the costume of Uncle Sam, the present national caricature. Both were Yankee rustics, emblems of the common man placed in situations a little beyond his depth but usually able to muddle through to a satisfactory solution.

From the foregoing it can be seen that humor, for the New Englander, was a serious matter. Comedy had to be put to some sort of pragmatic test, as in political satire; it could not exist by and for itself, as it did in the American South. Puritans, after all, were a dour and high-minded folk who believed that if art had to exist, then it ought to dedicate itself to the norms of instruction rather than of amusement. New England humor contains none of the violence and grotesquerie that characterized the best of

Southern humor at this period. The comic artist held his materials tightly in check. If he drew blood, he used a rapier, not a bludgeon, and demolished his enemy by wit rather than by sheer strength. These features marked the humor of James Russell Lowell, the most effective political satirist during the decades preceding the Civil War.

Though born and nurtured within the conservative tradition— his family was one of the most distinguished in New England— Lowell belonged to a generation which was beginning to rebel against established modes of thought. Antislavery movements were gathering momentum during the period in which he attended Harvard College; Unitarianism was bringing into question the religious assumptions of the older theologians; American writers like Emerson were calling for a national literature which would reflect the distinctive features of American landscape and society. During the 1840's Lowell became a leading writer in behalf of the abolition of slavery, at first as a polemicist and finally as a satirist. The outbreak of the Mexican War, which he conceived as a flagrantly immoral design by the South to acquire more slave states, provided him with an opportunity for barbed attack. Along with Thoreau's *Civil Disobedience*, Lowell's *The Biglow Papers* voiced opposition to the policies of the federal government which were dragging the country as a whole into an unnecessary war.

The Biglow Papers follow the *Downing Sketches* in utilizing the New England dialect (although Lowell's philological studies were more scientific and extensive than Smith's) but introduce a greater variety of character types and a more biting satire than Seba Smith ever dreamed of. Chief among these characters was Hosea Biglow, intended by Lowell to symbolize New England's "homely common-sense heated up by conscience." The initial paper contains an antiwar poem by Hosea, who has just returned to his tiny village of Jaalam, Massachusetts, from a visit to Boston, where he had seen a recruiting sergeant "a struttin round as popler as a hen with 1 chicking, with 2 fellers a drummin and fifin arter him like all nater." He becomes infuriated by the sergeant's attempt to recruit him for the army and launches his homely attack:

They may talk o' Freedom's airy
  Till they're pupple in the face,—
It's a grand gret cemetary
  Fer the barthrights of our race;
They jest want this Californy
  So's to lug new slave-states in
To abuse ye, an' to scorn ye,
  An' to plunder ye like sin.

The language is strong (in one stanza he calls the American flag "a leetle rotten") and the tone is uncompromising and wrathful. Though not a learned man, Hosea has a keen and practical Yankee intelligence that permits him to reject pious appeals to high patriotism. The war is wrong—and he will not serve.

But obviously the Mexican War, like any other war, drew great numbers of human cattle eager to rally behind the recruiting sergeant's drum. To characterize one of this sort, Lowell created Birdofredum Sawin (or "Bird-of-Freedom Soaring"), a fellow villager of Hosea Biglow, who embodied what the writer called "that half-conscious unmorality" found in the American mainstream. Sawin joined the army and marched off to fight in Mexico, where he found not glory but mutilation. He lost an eye, a leg, and his left arm; he baked by day and froze by night. An unprincipled rogue, Sawin decides that he is fit for nothing useful in life except to campaign for the Presidency using his missing parts as evidence that he has dutifully served his country. In a letter announcing his candidacy he writes:

Ef, wile you're 'lectioneerin' round, some curus chaps should beg
To know my views o' state affairs, jest answer WOODEN LEG!
Ef they aint settisfied with thet, an' kin' o' pry an' doubt
An' ax fer sutthin' deffynit, jest say ONE EYE PUT OUT!

The Biglow Papers established an antiwar tradition in American literature that, in its day, was intensely radical and mordant. In his later career James Russell Lowell became minister to Spain and to England and his voice grew more and more conservative. His best work built upon the framework of vernacular speech and

Yankee characterization which Seba Smith had laid down during the Age of Jackson.

The greatest difference in political coloration between Smith and Lowell lay in the latter's essential faith that the common man possessed a reservoir of good, plain common sense and the conviction that he could be encouraged to use it. Hosea Biglow, after all, functioned as counterballast for Birdofredum Sawin. Democratic government presupposed that the average man had a capacity for making the right choice, for spotting the fraudulent, for enlisting in the good cause. Later Abraham Lincoln, that super-Yankee whose satirical gibes once reduced a political opponent to tears in a public debate, affirmed this faith in democratic process during his Clinton, Illinois speech: "You can fool all the people part of the time and part of the people all the time, but not all the people all the time." Here was an economy of speech and practical turn of mind that any good New Englander would have endorsed heartily.

As the approaching Civil War cast its shadow across the United States during the 1850's, political humor in New England—as in the South—became more bitter and strident. The tradition of common sense appeared to have failed, for there was no reason why the sectional differences could not have been patched up. The old stereotype of Yankee did not flourish in a milieu of passionate intensities. Even the accepted feature of "Yankee-ness" began to dim. In the South, for example, all Northerners—whether of urban or rural origins, whether from New England or Minnesota—were grouped together as "damn-Yankees." It was not a time for humor or for fine discrimination. Lowell himself revived the *Biglow Papers* in order to inject a grain of common sense into the controversy. But it was too late, both for the country and for Lowell. His humor was no longer biting—it was bitter.

After the Civil War the figure of the rustic Yankee purveying good sense from his stronghold in the provinces became almost anachronistic. The center of political gravity had shifted to the cities and the day of the independent yeoman farmer was over. Rural New England produced, in the work of Sarah Orne Jewett, Mary Wilkins Freeman, and George Savary Wasson, many fine short stories which embodied the prewar Yankee sensibilities; but always these stories featured the region in a state of declining population and prosperity. Invariably the central characters are aging or ancient folk (for the young people had fled to the cities) whose "Yankee-ness" primarily consists in stoically adhering to the old customs and habits of their grandparents and resisting new-fangled ways. Political humor absolutely disappears for the simple good reason that New England had become politically powerless with the rapid development of the American West. As might be expected, the best political humor of the postwar period was found in the cities where cartoonists like Thomas Nast and verbal satirists like Peter Finley Dunne found targets in the rampaging municipal corruption that characterized the period.

Today the original Yankee subculture has largely disappeared except in obscure byways of New England. Yankee Doodle now looks, dresses, and thinks like other Americans, and the dominant strains of contemporary humor belong to other subgroupings like the Afro-Americans and the Jewish Americans. Yet the rural New Englander retains his sparseness of speech, his unwillingness to waste words, his dry wit. The last true Yankee politician to occupy the White House, President Calvin Coolidge, was famous for his taciturnity. According to one story a lady seated next to him at dinner interrupted the Coolidgian silence by saying to him, "I have a bet that I can get you to say three words." "You lose," Coolidge replied. Major Jack Downing would have enjoyed this *riposte* by a fellow Yankee.

A Comic Mode of the Romantic Imagination: Poe, Hawthorne, Melville

Hennig Cohen

The romantic age in America was, first of all, an age of innocence —optimistic, enterprising, bright with visions of progress and the main chance. The horizon stretched to the Pacific and beyond that to India. Emerson preaching his sermons on self-reliance, Whitman chanting his songs of the open road, Longfellow moralizing in a stately fashion on living in the present and thereby leaving footprints on the sands of time, were possessed of that vision which might be called comic. Fortunately for the history of American humor, there were others who viewed the same scene in a less optimistic light. Poe, Hawthorne, and Melville were not dazzled by the promise of the New World or the notion that mankind is perfectible. In an innocent age they had achieved a dark knowledge. It is in itself a sardonic joke, a comment on the blurred line between comedy and tragedy, that they produced some of the most interesting comic writing, albeit of a peculiar kind, of the romantic period.

The common reader knows Poe best for his tales of terror and madness—for "The Fall of the House of Usher," "The Black Cat," "The Cask of Amontillado." He knows Hawthorne's *The Scarlet Letter* and Melville's *Moby-Dick* as American tragedies. The universe of these works is pessimistic, egocentric, guilt-ridden, and circumscribed by a profound sense of limitation. Yet it is these very qualities that led the author in the direction of comedy. For without a comic dimension their end point was some form of escapism or annihilation. Because comedy restores balance and order and sanity and possibility, their tragic insights made its countervailing force all the more compelling.

Comic satire is a traditional means of restoration, and Poe, Hawthorne, and Melville satirized manners, politics, the literary marketplace, the business world, technology, and ideas that contributed to self-deception and self-esteem. Comedy also permits a playfulness that reminds man he is still something of a child. Hawthorne wrote stories for children, but on occasion, for weighty purposes, he would adopt the pose of children's author and write in a bantering, playful way. All three enjoyed the play of wit and the joke for its own sake. Poe and Melville were playful in still another sense. They played with their readers, toying with them and pushing them about, sometimes not so gently, often making them the butt of their jokes. One might argue that in the instance of Poe, despite his job work and his declarations that he composed rationally, many of his compositions evidence the romantic imagination at play. In contrast to this lighter quality, comedy has an earthy side, a certain grossness that recalls man's animal nature. Hawthorne was never gross. In Poe's words, his was a "most delicate humor." But Poe himself has a cat story (of which more anon) worthy of Mark Twain, and Melville's descriptions of whales include extravagances that would have delighted Rabelais. Finally, comedy provides a means whereby the tragic writer can divert his reader when the pity and terror become unbearable, and allay the reader's sense of frustration when the logic of his story, as, for example, in Melville's "Bartleby," does not permit mitigation or resolution.

So Hawthorne's sober Surveyor of Customs for the Port of Salem, a man who cherished what he called "ancient customs," chanced one rainy afternoon to survey casually a pile of dusty documents in the attic of the customhouse. Among them he found "a small package done up in yellow paper," the private notes of an "ancient Surveyor," his predecessor of a century before, and "a certain affair of fine red cloth, much worn and faded." These discoveries he imparts to the reader. But first, with his customary touches of grave humor, he introduces the reader to life in the customhouse and to the quaint political customs that prevail there.

Melville's whaleship, the *Pequod*, carries comic ballast on its fated voyage, and Ishmael, who escaped alone to tell the story, tells it with many a comic flourish. As for Poe, he wrote sketches in which he labored mightily for humorous effect. In fact, a common problem with Poe is determining when his intention *is* serious, for even in his grimmest tales he sets off comic squibs.

When we attempt to classify the humor of Poe, Hawthorne, and Melville, we find it can be divided roughly into two sometimes overlapping groups, one in which humor is secondary or covert and another in which it is primary. In the former group, comedy is present within a larger context that is tragic, or if not that, then pathetic, horrific or splenetic. Hence we become curious, not so much in regard to the nature and variety of the comic devices as their function and effect. The latter group consists of overtly comic writing—individual tales, parts of novels, perhaps whole novels (e.g., Hawthorne's *The House of the Seven Gables* and Melville's *The Confidence-Man*). Typically, works within this group are characterized by their topicality, their relationship to the popular culture, and their folkloristic roots.

The presence of the comic where we do not expect to find it makes it more potent than it would otherwise be, and Hawthorne, with a light touch, can achieve a forceful effect. His first published story, "The Hollow of the Three Hills," one of his favorites and justly so, is a case in point. The situation is banal. A woman has deserted her parents, husband, and child with whom her "fate was intimately bound." She seeks information about them through a witch, and comes to realize that she has destroyed them and in so doing destroyed herself. The "hollow" that is the setting for this tale, is a symbolic landscape—circular, enclosing, sloping downward to a pool of "putrid waters." It is sexually suggestive, hinting at the nature of the lady's offense, and sterile and decayed, foreshadowing her retribution. Stunted pines that fringe the hillsides dwindle away to brown grass and then rotted tree stumps by the pool. The season is autumn and the time is sundown, and while the hilltops are still bright, the light has begun to fade within the hollow. Thus the setting is appropriate to the dark ritual which the guilty woman and the witch will perform, and symbolic of the woman's realization of her guilt. It is also one of Hawthorne's "neutral territories," spaces that lie "somewhere between the real world and fairy-land," the geography of which he details in "The Custom-House" sketch introducing *The Scarlet Letter.*

In addition the setting exists in a time zone that is extraordinary: "In those strange times," the opening sentence tells us, "when fantastic dreams and madmen's reveries were realized among the actual circumstances of life . . . ." The word "realized" is crucial; for what Hawthorne suggests is that fantasies have become realities. Yet "realized" does not merely mean made real or brought into being. It also denotes grasping the meaning of the experience undergone, whether real or imagined.

What Hawthorne has achieved in his setting is a delicate balance between "actual circumstances" and "fantastic dreams," not so much as a stated quality of the "strange old times," or something so simple as a *donnée,* which of course it is, but as a condition created by his double meaning of the word "realized"—brought into being both in fact and in the imagination. These two meanings, which coexist in the same word, are the foundations for the symmetrical form he will construct. It is important to observe that "fantastic dreams" and "actual circumstances," fact and imagination, are antithetical. In a feat of Hegelian witchcraft, Hawthorne has synthesized them. An urge to place opposites in confrontation for the sake of conciliation, symmetry, qualification, or to enjoy the resounding crash, was characteristic of the Romantics. And in this story, at least a light touch of comedy exists as an opposing element.

The opposing principals in the story, "a lady, graceful and fair of feature, though pale and troubled" and "an ancient and meanly-dressed woman, of ill-favored aspect," sinner and witch, confront each other by prior arrangement. The sinner represents the fact of guilt, its "actual circumstances." The witch is associated with its imaginative reality, the "fantastic dreams" that she can induce and what they signify. They come together in the hollow of the three hills to conjure up three dream-visions: heart-broken parents, husband driven mad by grief and shame, child borne to the grave. The dream-visions are the sinner's realization, in Hawthorne's twofold sense, of the results of her sin. The formal balance of the story is enhanced by a ritual of black magic that precedes each dream-vision, an inversion of Christian ritual and in implied opposition to it, and by implied contrast between the sinner's former and present condition.

The heart of the story, then, is a model of balance, but in no way comic. However, this symmetrical structure is enclosed in a comic frame. The first and last words are those of the witch. She initiates the dialogue: " 'Here is our pleasant meeting come to pass,' said the old crone. . . ." And, as the lady, overcome by the dream-visions "lifted not her head," the old woman pronounces the final words: " 'Here has been a sweet hour's sport!' said the withered crone, chuckling to herself"—Hawthorne for once sparing us the dampening effect of a moral.

Slight comedy indeed. Our witch plays with words and is capable of amusing herself as she goes about her work. She looks forward to the amiable prankster of a witch in Hawthorne's "Feathertop" who makes a scarecrow come alive, and by way of contrast, the story suggests another witches' meeting in the forest, that of "Young Goodman Brown." The final notes of "Young Goodman Brown" are heavy-handed ambiguity and unmitigated gloom. "Had Goodman Brown fallen asleep in the forest and only dreamed a wild dream of a witch-meeting?" the reader is asked. No such question occurs in "A Hollow of the Three Hills," for here "fantastic dreams" and "actual circumstances" are both "realized," and the witch with her saving grace of comedy is a witch we can believe in.

Poe's "The Cask of Amontillado" and "Hop-Frog" are tales of revenge so horrendous that comic elements are scarcely expected to be found in them and certainly not expected to play an important part. In "The Cask of Amontillado," the narrator, Montresor, confesses that fifty years before he had buried alive, by masoning him into the walls of the family vault, one Fortunato, who had insulted him. "Hop-Frog" is about a court fool of that name, a crippled dwarf, who has been savaged by a jocular king and his sycophantic courtiers and in return contrives to burn them all alive. Within these revenge tales, Poe creates a comic resonance that is unmistakable. Their ambience is festive and Dionysian. The setting of "The Cask of Amontillado" is the carnival season. Fortunato wears motley, the costume of a jester. He is a connoisseur of wines, and he has been drinking. Montresor greets him, punning, as he will continue to do: "My dear Fortunato, you are luckily met." Similar wordplay occurs in "Hop-Frog" in which the narrator begins by informing us that he had never known "any one so keenly alive to a joke as the king was. He seemed to live only for joking." The king, in due course, will *die* as a result of some lively joking: a joke invented by Hop-Frog, his master of revels, as the climax of a masquerade, a joke played because the king had amused himself by forcing Hop-Frog, who had no stomach for it, to drink wine and has dashed a cup of wine in the face of Hop-Frog's exquisite little consort.

There is irony in Montresor's greeting of the unlucky Fortunato, but its depth cannot be known until the end of the tale. At its outset, the salutation appears more witty than ironical, and it suggests that whatever else Montresor may be, he has a sense of humor and the capacity for making a joke. The opening sentence of "Hop-Frog" is likewise a signal that what follows will be in some fashion comic, though by disappointing the reader's expectations regarding the nature of the comedy, Poe plays a joke on him. The vengeful Montresor plays a hideous joke on Fortunato, who wears caps and bells, but Fortunato has the last laugh. His ghost remains to haunt Montresor's conscience. The lowly, simian Hop-Frog (he "resembled . . . a small monkey") tricks the king and his courtiers into costuming themselves as chained orangutans, a prank to frighten the guests at a masked ball. (Says Hop-Frog: "the masqueraders will take you for real beasts. . . .") Thus Hop-Frog makes them his apes, reversing roles, and at the same time presents the king and the courtiers in a guise that befits their bestial natures. Thereupon, he hoists them on high and sets fire to their flammable garments, turning them into a living, blazing chandelier— for their enlightenment, and ours.

Like the *lex talionis*, in a primitive sense a ritual of revenge is restorative. But Poe has attempted something more complicated. He has qualified an horrific revenge by placing it in a comic ambience, a juxtaposition which also establishes a condition of comic incongruity. Then, though he takes the device of revenge seriously even while pushing it in the direction of an excess that approaches the parodic, he is willing to consider the idea that revenge is a joke, a *practical* joke, the business of jesters. By way of re-enforcement, he is sportive, making the details of the revenge occasions for lesser jokes: "Come, drink! the wine will brighten your wits," the king commands the abstemious Hop-Frog. It does. "I shall not die of a cough," replies Fortunato when Montresor enquires with seeming solicitude of his health. He does not. Horror shares the throne with the Lord of Misrule and thereby rules more effectively.

The actors in Poe's revenge tragedies are not tragic heroes. They are grotesques—characters distorted and extreme in an emphasis on their own individuality. Furthermore, they are comic grotesques, virtually theatrical stereotypes. Fortunato is a jester, Montresor a practical joker. The monkeyish Hop-Frog is a court fool, the apish king is given to "practical jokes." Their grotesqueness attracts the reader's interest, but because it is unnatural and dehumanizing it does not gain his sympathy. Montresor is twisted by the idea of revenge that dominates him and becomes its embodiment. Fortunato is in every respect his equivalent. The deformed Hop-Frog and the bestial king are alike in an animality that makes them something other than human. An idea that walks like a man can be ludicrous and abhorrent; likewise a man who walks like an ape. Both are impure and unnatural. Hence we can detach ourselves from the fireworks at the end because comic as well as horrific elements are involved.

"There is a wisdom that is woe; but there is woe that is madness," Melville wrote in *Moby-Dick*. To be wise is to be aware of the great dark, Melville is saying, but it is unwise to see things too darkly. There must be balance. So when he described the "fallen" world of *The Encantadas* or Galápagos Islands, and the creatures that live there, he is at pains to mention both the bright and the dark. The islands are a burned-out place, resembling "heaps of cinders," the world as it might look "after a penal conflagration." They are enchanted in the sense that they are bewitched. Disowned by "man and wolf alike," they are populated by tortoises, lizards, sea fowl, outlaws, and an occasional castaway. Having depicted the "Plutonian" character of the islands, Melville asks this question: "In view of the description given, may one be gay upon the Encantadas?" And he answers that "the isles are not perhaps unmitigated gloom" (n.b. the "not perhaps") and points out that the tortoise, its most remarkable inhabitant, "dark and melancholy as

it is upon its back, still possesses a bright side." Melville's qualifi-
cations in this famous passage on the tortoise are numerous and
his logic is slippery with wit. It is the underside that is bright; but
Melville repeats that the tortoise, which he associates with "the
identical tortoise whereon the Hindoo plants this total universe,"
is "both black and bright" as the world itself comprises both tragic
and comic.

Melville concludes his *Encantadas* sketches with a description
of a neglected cemetery and a somber account of a young naval
officer, killed in a duel, who is buried there. But the pathos of his
tone shifts quickly, and the book ends with the quotation of "a doggerel epitaph" inscribed on a marker by "some good-natured fore-
castle poet." It reads:

> O, Brother Jack, as you pass by,
> As you are now, so once was I.
> Just so game, and just so gay,
> But now, alack, they've stopped my pay.
> No more I peep out of my blinkers,
> Here I be—tucked in with clinkers.

The source of the "doggerel epitaph" is Captain David Porter's
*Journal of a Cruise Made to the Pacific Ocean in the U.S. Frigate
Essex . . .* (1815):

> Gentle reader, as you pass by,
> As you are now, so once was I;
> As now my body is in dust,
> I hope in heaven my soul to rest.

Melville's adaptation of this rather well-known folk verse differs
notably from the poetic epigraphs, in the main derived from
Spenser and highly literary and portentous, that precede each of
the ten Encantadas sketches. He has transformed a pious commonplace into graveyard humor. His mode of address establishes a human relationship rather than a polite relationship with the chance
reader of the inscription. The language is more personal, colloquial
and earthy. The beat jogs along at a faster pace and the rhyme of

the final couplet substantiates its facetious, vernacular quality. But Melville is consistent in his view of the Encantadas as a fallen world. In contrast to his source, he expresses no hope of heavenly rest even though his tonalities assert that the graveyard of his cinder heap is not perhaps unmitigated gloom.

Not only did Poe, Hawthorne, and Melville use comic effects to temper their predominantly tragic view. They also appreciated the ridiculous for its own sake. But their attraction to the comic was their sense of man's limitation and a concern for the spiritual, especially poignant in an age of enterprise and materialism. Their comic writing, often close to popular culture and folklore, found substance in the wildly speculative business operations of the expansive economy, the popular appeal of Yankee inventiveness, and the manners of a society in which sham and empty rituals assumed importance. On these subjects they made grim jokes.

Poe's "The Man That Was Used Up" is a retelling of an old folktale or joke, usually bawdy, about a lover who is disappointed to discover that the object of his affections is a bundle of cosmetic and prosthetic contrivances. LeSage in *The Devil Upon Two Sticks* (1725) provides literary analogues. He has Asmodeus describe "an amorous dotard, just come from making love. He has already laid down his eye, false whiskers, and peruke which hid his bald pate; and waits for his man to take off his wooden arm and leg" and an "old coquette" who "is a machine, in the adjusting of which the ablest mechanics have been exhausted. Her breasts and hips are artificial; and not long since she dropped her rump at church, in the midst of the sermon." Poe adapts this joke to his tale of a persistent quest to ascertain the true nature and history of "that truly fine-looking fellow, Brevet Brigadier General John A. B. C. Smith," a public man of remarkable parts. Poe's narrator is impressed by the general's handsome physique, noble bearing, resonant voice, and reserved manner but puzzled by a "rectangular precision, attend his every movement" and curious about the "mysterious circumstances" surrounding his military exploits.

The narrator's quest begins at a public meeting, continues at a church, theater, card party, reception and social call, occasions which Poe uses to poke fun at preachers, actors, socialites and bluestockings. Everyone appears to esteem the general and to be well-informed about him, but in each instance the narrator's inquiries are frustrated by interruptions. Exasperated, he calls on the general. He is conducted into the general's chambers by a servant, sees "a large and exceedingly odd-looking bundle of something . . . on the floor," and kicks it aside. To his dismay, the bundle addresses him in a squeaky voice:

> "God bless me, my dear fellow . . . what—what—what—why, what *is* the matter? I really believe you don't know me at all."
> "No—no—*no!* . . . know you—know you—know you—*don't* know you at all!" [the narrator expostulates in horror].

The servant explains that the bundle is General Smith in *déshabillé* and then begins the procedure of putting him together—cork leg, artificial arm, shoulders, bosom, wig, teeth, false eye and palate—while the general explains that he lost these members in a bloody fight with the Bugaboo and Kickapoo Indians, and lauds the ingenuity of the artisans who made the substitutes. The "matter" of which the general is comprised is essentially artificial. He is a mechanical man. But as the punning on the word "know" indicates, the narrator is in quest of knowledge that lies beneath appearances, and his systematic search reveals that the general doesn't really exist. The general is without substance, an idea, the projection of the artificialities of his society.

The structure of the story is equally artificial, a tissue of puns and significant names and a sequence of social set pieces in which the narrator is seen pursuing his quest. Each set piece pivots rather mechanically on a play on the word "man" used in a way which prevents the narrator from obtaining the information he desires. Thus, after the "public meeting," while a companion is explaining that the general has performed "*prodigies* of valor . . . you know, he's the man—" the general (the mechanical man) interrupts to introduce himself, with the words, "Man alive, how do you do?" and converses with seeming pointlessness about "the rapid march of mechanical invention."

Mechanical inventions are the general's pet subject, and while he is being patched together he gives the narrator the names and addresses of the ingenious Yankees who made his various appliances. A number of them have been identified from advertisements in contemporary newspapers, and a model for the general has been found in Colonel Richard M. Johnson, a badly wounded hero of the Indian wars who was elected Vice-President in Van Buren's administration but was so unpopular that he was not renominated. Poe has his fun with these topical allusions, and it is not easy for us to share in it, but his mechanical man as the emblem of an age that places excessive value on technological progress and social appearances remains very much alive. Actually, he has an uncanny topicality, for ours is an age in which politicians and generals are fabricated by artful image-makers and our scientists are proficient in the replacement of human parts with transplanted organs and bits of plastic and wire.

Hawthorne's "Mrs. Bullfrog" is another treatment of the mechanical man, this time an artificial woman, and hence closer to the old joke. A finicky bachelor marries impulsively. On his wedding trip the stage coach overturns, and the jolt removes his bride's wig and false teeth along with her good temper and smashes a bottle of what she had claimed was toilet water but smells suspiciously like gin. But Mrs. Bullfrog recovers quickly. She puts herself together again, explaining:

"Mr. Bullfrog . . . let me advise you to overcome this foolish weakness, and prove yourself, to the best of your ability, as good a husband as I will be a wife. You have discovered, perhaps, some little imperfections in your bride. Well, what did you expect? Women are not angels. If they were, they would go to heaven for husbands. . . ."

And she adds that the dowry she brings him is real enough. Mr. Bullfrog is accommodating. He pronounces himself "fortunate" and accepts his bride "with an overwhelming gush of tenderness." Presumably, they live happily ever after. But the reader is made to see the sham beneath the appearance in both of them.

We have here a comic version of "The Birthmark," Hawthorne's justifiably better-known tale of the scientist so dedicated to perfection that he kills his wife in an attempt to remove the tiny birthmark that mars her almost perfect beauty. "Mrs. Bullfrog" also belongs to the folk tradition of the "loathly lady" who becomes beautiful in the eyes of her husband when he proves worthy of her, and as such she is a poor relation of the shape-shifting hag in the Wife of Bath's tale. She is also probably the namesake of the transformed Frog-Prince in the Grimm fairy tale. Although comic, Hawthorne is sermonizing as usual, presenting a parable on the realities beneath the surface of an idealized marriage, but the story made him uneasy and he confided in his notebook, "as to Mrs. Bullfrog, I give her up to the severest reprehension."

If "Mrs. Bullfrog" is, for Hawthorne, cynical and a little gross, another tale of a mechanical man, "Feathertop" (named for his frizzy, foppish wig and his empty pumpkin head), is in no way reprehensible. For this delicately poised story, Hawthorne adopts the pose of children's author, retelling a tale he had "heard on my grandmother's knee." Mother Rigby, a witch who loves her work as much as her colleague in "The Hollow of the Three Hills," needs a scarecrow for her cornpatch. She decides not to make a hobgoblin "ugly enough to frighten the minister himself" but to "keep within the bounds of every-day business just for variety sake." Pleased with her handiwork, she makes the scarecrow come alive "for the joke's sake" by placing a lighted pipe in his mouth and commanding him "To puff away . . . your life depends on it." So the scarecrow puffs away "for dear life." Like General Smith, Feathertop cuts a fine figure in society though he moves about with a certain stiffness of gait, and Hawthorne observes in an authorial aside that his appearance arouses a sense of "ghastliness and awe . . . the effect of anything completely and consummately artificial, in human shape." The witch has a score to settle with the local magistrate, so she dispatches Feathertop to pay court to his daughter, Pretty Polly, a somewhat artificial young lady herself, given to admiring her countenance in the mirror. But Feathertop sees his reflection in the mirror, too, returns to the witch, and deliberately allows his pipe to die out. Because her artificial man had "too much heart to bustle for his own advantage in such an empty and heartless world," the witch puts him in the cornpatch to scare crows.

For Pretty Polly and the townspeople, impressed by his fine appearance, the scarecrow is a projection of their own superficiality, and Hawthorne capitalizes on his opportunities for satire.

The scarecrow's self-understanding and his decision to "exist no longer" softens the comic tone, but the focus of the story is on the witch, not the scarecrow, and she remains splendidly consistent. Like her counterpart in "The Hollow of the Three Hills," she frames and controls the story, but the comedy resides not so much in the playfulness of the language and the social satire as in the reversal of what we expect from folk tradition a witch to be.

Melville's *White-Jacket,* a novel based on his service in the United States Navy, is appropriately subtitled *The World in a Man-of-War.* Although its implications are cosmic, it is topical in its concern for improving the lot of seamen, and Melville creates a gallery of grotesques to document naval abuses. His masterpiece is the Surgeon of the Fleet, Cadwallader Cuticle, M.D. Dr. Cuticle is so devoted to his science that he is heartlessly mechanical. In a comic foreshadowing of the court-martial in *Billy Budd*, he assembles a panel of surgeons for consultation and then disregards the advice he receives while expressing regret at the necessity for a cruel operation. Science prevails with Dr. Cuticle as the law prevails in *Billy Budd*. The grisly episode that follows derives from an old medical joke. Dr. Cuticle performs a brilliant operation but he kills his patient.

Dr. Cuticle's appearance is in keeping with his spiritual desiccation. He is "withered, shrunken, one-eyed, toothless, hairless" and he wears a glass eye, false teeth and a wig; in short, he is a mechanical man. His pride and joy are his pathological specimens and an articulated human skeleton. Cuticle, like Ahab, is a distortion of an ideal and the result is dehumanization, but Ahab is portrayed in depth and complexity and emerges as a tragic figure. Cuticle is sketched in sharp, quick strokes and is a comic caricature.

The folktale about the disappointed lover, the popular image of the ingenious Yankee mechanic and the sense of the awful and ridiculous that Hawthorne, anticipating Bergson, felt in "anything completely and consummately artificial, in human shape" contributed to the motif of the mechanical man. As employed by Poe, Hawthorne and Melville, it served as a means of indicating the absurdity, to the point of dehumanization, of outward appearances not sustained by inner substance, in particular, apparent progress unaccompanied by a parallel spiritual development. Another em-

blem of the age, the Yankee trader, likewise the scion of folklore
and popular culture, performed a similar function.

The mechanical man is an abstraction; the emblem itself is un-
substantial. The Yankee trader—peddler, salesman, diddler, confidence man—was gross flesh and blood. Perhaps this is why Hawthorne confided his delight in the spiel of an auctioneer at a New
England fair to his notebooks rather than making a story out of it:

Bunches of lead pencils, steel pens; pound cakes of shaving soap, gilt finger
rings, bracelets, clasps, and other jewelry, cards of pearl buttons or steel—
"there is some steel about them, gentlemen; for my brother stole 'em, and I
bore him out in it," . . . and saying to the boys who climbed upon his
cart—"Fall down, roll down, tumble down—only get down"—and everything
in the queer humorous recitative, in which he sold his articles. Sometimes
he pretended that a person had bid, either by word or wink, and raised a
laugh thus. Never losing his self-possession, nor getting out of humor;—
when a man asked whether a bill was good "No!! Do you suppose I'd give
you good money."

Poe, who longed for a dreamland "Out of Space—out of Time,"
had sufficient appreciation of the vernacular to enjoy the backwoods humor of Longstreet's *Georgia Scenes* (1835). "Seldom—
perhaps never in our lives—have we laughed as immoderately over
any book," he wrote in a review for the *Southern Literary Mes-
senger*. The humor of *Georgia Scenes* is crude and earthy: gander-
pullings, fights real and mock, and a horse trade sharp enough to
please Poe's diddler.

Poe's "Diddling" is an anatomy of sharp business practices followed by a series of "modern instances." It culminates in a "rather
elaborate diddle." An apparently "respectable 'man of business' "
advertises for bonded clerks, requiring "testimonials of morality"
and "a deposit of fifty dollars," preference given to the "piously
inclined." The diddler collects the deposits and vanishes, leaving
behind "young gentlemen . . . less piously inclined than before."
"The Business Man" follows the career of a methodical man of
business. His ventures, more or less successful, include the "Eye
Sore" trade (buy property next to a handsome building under
construction, erect a pigsty on it and dispose of it for a profit),
Mud-Dabbing (soil a premise so as to be hired to clean it up) and
Organ-Grinding (crank out noisy discord in order to be paid to

move on). The pinnacle of his success is "in the Cat-Growing way." Because of a superfluity, a bounty is offered on cats. The premium is four pence per cat tail, the tail being legally established at three inches. The business man purchases breeding stock. He finds that by careful feeding he can achieve six inch tails, the equivalent of two tails per cat, and by the application of an unguent, he can produce three crops of cat tails a year. Poe's interest in felines has also been recorded in "The Black Cat," an animal whose keeper treated it with less consideration.

Clearly, the urbane Poe was not as far removed from the tradition of frontier humor as it would at first seem. He differed mainly in that the city was his setting. His cat story is reminiscent of an episode in which Davy Crockett, short of funds in a grog shop, hoodwinks the bartender into accepting coonskins for drinks. He obtains an unlimited supply of whisky by stealing back the coonskins and trading them again.

Melville's *The Confidence-Man* is a novel about the greatest trickster of them all. Complex in its conception and language, rich in material drawn from the popular culture, folklore and literature, it presents a sequence of encounters between a con man in various guises and the victims he manipulates through their greed and their trust. It is a mordant comedy, so corrosive and ambiguous as to verge on the tragic. Thus Melville carried a comic mode of the romantic imagination to its logical conclusion.

Humor of the Old Southwest

James M. Cox

First of all, there is the South. And the South is, as everyone must confess but very few remember to think about, beneath the North on all globes and wall maps. Even to go South in the mind is to go toward sin as well as sun. The Southerner is seen in the dominant Northern imagination as a little more poor, more ignorant, more lazy, more lawless, more violent, and more sensual than the Northerner. He is, after all, a figure of the lower regions, located, as he is, nearer to the equatorial belt which girdles the world.

If the location of the South on wall maps and globes poses one interesting possibility, the Old Southwest poses another. For what was the Southwest before the Civil War is now the Southeast. This is not at all true of the Old Northwest, which was made up of Ohio and Michigan. No one in his right mind would speak to-day of a Buckeye or a Wolverine as a Northeasterner. Another look at the map is instructive. Not only is the South beneath the North; it is also much to the west of it. It is well to remember that Atlanta is as far west as Detroit, just as it is well to know that Virginia's almost six-hundred-mile baseline piercing to Cumberland Gap reaches as far west as Toledo, Ohio.

There is, of course, an historical reason for our blurred sense of the original region. The Old Southwest, during the thirty years before the Civil War—the period when the Southwestern humorists flourished—was in the process of becoming the South, for the sectional strife which steadily intensified from 1830 until 1860 was reorganizing the country on a North-South rather than an East-West axis. After the Civil War, the Solid South became a decisive region in the national mind. Once that happened, Northern Americans and even many Southerners all but forgot how far west the South is of New England.

But at the beginning of the nineteenth century, the region was truly the Southwest. As West, it was wilder than the Northeast; and as South it was already involved in the whole long loss to the North which culminated in bloody Civil War. There was, then, from the beginning in the Southwest, something wild and something lost. It was bad enough to feel the cultural impoverishment of America in general. Hawthorne felt it in New England and set about recovering for his countrymen the shadow of a colonial past. Yet starkly impoverished as New England was in relation to England, Hawthorne, Emerson, Melville, Thoreau, and Whitman were making a national literature for their country between 1830 and 1860. Seen against that literature, the literature of the South is pale indeed. Poe alone—the Bostonian somehow fallen into the South—stands out. And even he stands out as writer rather than as Southerner. He is most Southern not in attaching himself to landscape as the New Englanders were doing, but in disclosing himself as displaced person. He is the Artist as Rebel; and he is most rebellious in constantly threatening to divorce truth from beauty, morality from aesthetics, and cause from effect. His perversity, his demonism, his disease, his audacious demoralization of literature all conspire to place him conspicuously against the New England tradition, causing him to seem, in the Northern imagination, something of a fraud, as if all the traditions he inherited were somehow at the point of disintegrating into his possession. Yet whatever vulgarity the practitioners of high literature might ascribe to him, his power is there. Scorn it, belittle it, lament it, exclude it, and it runs underground to be embraced as a great original imaginative current by a Baudelaire.

Aside from Poe, only the humorists of the Old Southwest are truly dominant in our early literature. Set against the Northern humorists, they are clearly more interesting. Washington Irving, the true humorist of the North, is surely a match for them, but

Irving steadily moved away from his pseudonymous identity to settle at Sunnyside and become a writer of higher literature. He had left behind him "The Legend of Sleepy Hollow" and "Rip Van Winkle," both of which have about them something of the wild and humorous fantasy exposed through the elegant style of Geoffrey Crayon, *Gentleman,* and it is small wonder that "The Legend of Sleepy Hollow" was imported by Southern humorists, disguised in one form or another, and retold along "native" lines. The process was inevitable; it was just what Irving himself had done to German stories he had read.

Aside from Irving, the greatest of the Northern humorists was Seba Smith, who graduated from Bowdoin seven years before Hawthorne received his degree there. Smith invented Jack Downing as a correspondent for his paper, and through the rural vernacular of his invention he was able to make fun of politics and politicians, particularly of the Democratic Party and Andrew Jackson. Smith's down-east vernacular was impressive; it had an acute shrewdness, a folksy plainness, and, above all, a garrulous loquaciousness which nonetheless suggested the terseness of the stage Yankee. By persistently relating Jack Downing to the subjects of politics and history, Smith directed his folk morality upon the affairs of state. Yet for all his exposure of politicians, Jack Downing's deeper social morality and essential rural quaintness remain intact. James Russell Lowell does much the same thing with Hosea Biglow. By turning to verse, Lowell gains an even greater pithiness and homely flavor for his conventional morality. James Whitcomb Riley was much later to achieve a similar effect with his poems of Hoosier life.

How different are the humorists of the Old Southwest. If Poe differs from the major Northern writers in his divorce of beauty from morality, Southwestern humor differs from Yankee humor in its threat to divorce pleasure from morality. There is of course enormous risk in such a divorce, for unless the imagination makes up in invention, surprise, and extension of language *by virtue of* the diminution of moral pressure the result is likely to be little more than joke-book and almanac humor.

The Southwestern humorists took that risk. To be sure, they did not take it abruptly or always decisively, but they took it.

There were many of them—too many to discuss in detail in such brief space—but the work of Augustus Baldwin Longstreet, Johnson Jones Hooper, Joseph Glover Baldwin, Thomas Bangs Thorpe, Henry Clay Lewis, and George Washington Harris reveals the problems they encountered and the achievements they wrought. But a few more words about these writers as a group are in order.

First of all, they were determined to appear as gentlemen. Second, they tended to be professional men and political conservatives. Third, they were willing to be seen, just as they were willing to present themselves, as gentlemen first and writers second. Many of them sent their work to William T. Porter, a Vermonter, who edited a New York sporting magazine called *Spirit of the Times*, and Porter, one of the great editors of the nineteenth century, had the good sense to call for more and more of it. By and large, the writers received little or no pay for their work, and many never even collected their pieces, though Porter himself eventually made a fine anthology of them. Finally, their work generally took the form of sketches in which the polite language of the literate gentleman was made to surround and contain a frontier dialect.

Now the bifurcation between gentleman and yokel was not new; it was old as the hills and utterly inevitable in humor and comedy. The major contribution of Southwest humor lay in putting enormous imaginative pressure on both the gentleman and the bumpkin. The gentleman became more and more foppish and effete as the frontiersman threatened more and more to take over the narrative. The result was a language which, in the hands of the best of these writers, became a means of discovering a New World humor.

The problem as well as the possibility of Southwest humor is evident in the extraordinary work of Augustus Baldwin Longstreet, whose *Georgia Scenes* really ushered in the whole movement. Published in 1835, the same year in which Hawthorne's "Young Goodman Brown" and "The Haunted Mind" appeared, Longstreet made his way not into the moral wilderness of New England but into the comic and violent wilderness of the South. His "Georgia Theatrics," the brief but brilliant overture for the collection of sketches, is a refined clerical gentleman's recollection of having gone into the "Dark Corner" of Lincoln, a county which, he says, was a shade darker than the rest of the country. Moving through the green glade of Nature, he hears ahead of him the most violent and profane language of men in mortal combat.

Yes I kin, and am able to do it! Boo-oo-oo! Oh, wake snakes, and walk your chalks! Brimstone and —— fire! Don't hold me, Nick Stoval! The fight's made up, and lets go at it. —— my soul if I don't jump down his throat, and gallop every chitterling out of him before you can say "quit!"

Hurrying toward the drama, the gentleman first hears one of the combatants scream in pain as his eye is torn out; then he hears the victor's cry of exultation. Appalled at the violence, he rushes through the undergrowth to the central scene, where he accosts the victor who is just rising from the fray. The youth replies to the morally vexed gentleman, "You needn't kick before you're spurr'd. There a'nt nobody there, nor ha'nt been nother. I was just seein' how I could 'a' *fout*." So saying, the embarrassed youth leaves the refined moralist with the truth. There has been no real victim. Instead, there are only the prints of the lone actor's thumbs where they had been plunged into the earth as he imaginarily gouged out his opponent's eyes.

This opening sketch seems to me an extraordinary transcendence of the convention it employs. Although it discloses the crude and violent imagination of the uncouth swain, it just as distinctly reveals the refined narrator's impulse to disapprove of the violence. To see that far into the sketch, and it takes blindness indeed not to see that far (though anyone disposed to feel superiority to the South is likely to be so blind) is to see that the refined moralist makes his judgment on the fight before he sees that it was imaginary. If the youth is embarrassed to be "caught" in his private theatricals, the old man has wanted the drama to be real so that he can enact his superior disapproval of the violence he is hurrying to see.

That sketch alone reveals the rare superiority of Longstreet's grasp of his subject. He realizes at once that the refined moralist and the violent youth are intricately related to each other. They truly depend on and indirectly inform each other. The youth's embarrassment should be the moralist's for having leapt to a conclusion. Evading that blush, the moralist can but record the experience in language self-gratulatory and overrefined. Unless we see the joke of the sketch and see that the joke is just as much on the moralist as it is on the violent youth—just as much, but no more—we are likely to emerge with interpretations which, emphasizing how the sketch reveals the violence of the Southern mind, miss that half of the joke which exposes the moralist's need of crudity and violence in order to achieve his moral superiority.

Good though Longstreet was in that opening sketch, he was not always so good. And his weakness came from leaning too much toward refinement, politeness, and culture. At his best, as in "The Fight" and "The Horse Swap," Longstreet establishes situations in which the violence and picturesqueness recoil through the enclosing structure and expose it for the polite frame it truly is. Thus, Ransy Sniffle—the name itself is but one more stroke of Longstreet's genius—in "The Fight" is truly a progenitor of Faulkner's Snopeses. The grotesque, cowardly and depraved poor white who eggs two men into a fight, he is not so far different from the effete style which counterpoints the story, for it too needs the contrasting violence of Ransy and his fight to amuse it. Still and all, the imaginative energy, the almost gloating delight, which the frame style assumes in delineating Ransy's depraved appearance, betrays an aggression in the story which the humor in it cannot quite discharge. In "The Horse Swap," surely one of Longstreet's finest sketches, the grotesque and sensitive sore, concealed beneath the saddle blanket, enables one confidence man to edge out another, for its goading pain makes the hopeless old nag prance about like a thoroughbred. Yet the very disclosure of that raw and sensitive wound is intended to appall as much as to amuse the reader. In making this visibly shocking disclosure *as* the humorous climax of his sketch, the refined gentleman averts his eyes, as it were, in the very act of completing his joke. Though Longstreet at his best was able to show his clerical gentlemen and poor whites in a humorous act of transcendent cooperation, he nonetheless has a moral as well as an aesthetic disposition to withdraw from his humor. That is why the edge he seeks is always in danger of being outside rather than inside his world. Even so, his achievements and limitations define the possibilities of Southwestern hu-

mor. First of all, there is Longstreet's own path, following the
border between refinement and vernacular yet keeping an edge
of refined perspective between it and the vernacular and using
that edge to barter for literary audience approval.

Longstreet's greatest successor along that path was Johnson
Jones Hooper. Pursuing the essential lines of Longstreet's form,
Hooper nonetheless made a significant change. He discovered for
himself a central character who could make successive forays into
Southwestern dialect and experience. Hooper's discovery gave his
work both unity and direction, for, once committed to his character, Simon Suggs, Hooper couldn't withdraw into the weak posi-
tions of moral and aesthetic security which fatally attracted Longstreet. True, Hooper incurred risks of his own, chief among them
the repetition compulsion lying at the heart of all humor. Thus,
anyone reading *The Adventures of Simon Suggs* is bound to feel
the author's mechanistic compulsion to send Suggs off into one
more picaresque foray.

For Suggs is, after all, the old picaro reborn as the frontier confidence man. By developing a mock-eloquent and refined perspective, Hooper can, like Longstreet, release Suggs all the more
forcibly as an energy and a language. By exposing frontier amorality in Suggs's central maxim, "It is good to be shifty in a new
country," Hooper gains the moral edge for his humorous maneuvers. Indeed, the amorality which compels Suggs to prey upon
the foolish, the ignorant and the futile releases him as a kind of
fierce, predatory, wild man, whose language possesses the imaginative energy to dilate the refined language into fancier and
fancier forms of mock eloquence.

In order for Suggs's repeated depredations to remain in humorous perspective, Hooper has to distort and demean his lower-class
world so that it can receive Suggs's raids without offense to a
civilized audience. Thus, in "The Captain Attends a Camp-Meet-
ing" (which Mark Twain drew on so heavily in *Huckleberry
Finn*), the whole evangelistic revival world is exposed as a kind
of moral and sexual chaos, devoid of any redeeming intellectual
or moral tone. Suggs's wildness and meanness constitute a warning for what could be released in the vernacular. Indeed, the very
meanness is partly required by the moral frame which would con-

tain him, for unless Suggs shows meanness, then the moral impulse in Hooper's enveloping frame cannot be activated.

Now one way out of the difficulty is to increase the imaginative investment in the framing literary language, thereby increasing the distance between the narration and the humorous character. Longstreet himself had managed such a maneuver in the sketches depicting Ned Brace, an irrepressible lying prankster. But it remained for Joseph Glover Baldwin in his *Flush Times of Alabama and Mississippi* to retreat almost totally into eloquent frame. If Longstreet's Ned Brace had cavorted in language as well as in act, Baldwin's Ovid Bolus, Esq., is all but completely materialized in the mock-eloquent narration. Although such a move makes any reader of *Flush Times* long for the colorful accents of Simon Suggs, Baldwin nonetheless repossesses a geniality which Longstreet and especially Hooper had been at the threshold of losing. Because he looks down on his subjects from a greater height, Baldwin can be more indulgent. As a result, *Flush Times* has a geniality of spirit which looks forward to Mark Twain's *Roughing It*. It is not really surprising that Baldwin himself made his way to California not as an outlaw, but as a judge bringing law and order into the territory.

Despite its recovery of geniality, Baldwin's refined perspective really loses more than it gains. For the future and ultimate power of Southwestern humor lay in discovering through dialect the direct experience of the frontier. The most dramatic example of that direct experience was the bear hunt. First emphasized by Davy Crockett, the bear hunt in one form or another had become the subject of innumerable stories. It remained for Thomas Bangs Thorpe, a Northerner who came to Louisiana, to realize the full possibilities of the bear hunt in one triumphant sketch, "The Big Bear of Arkansas." Retaining only the bare essentials of the frame, Thorpe practically turned over his entire sketch to the vernacular, making his bear hunter stand in the same relation to the bear that the refined gentleman stands in relation to the bear hunter. The bear embodies for the hunter the very wildness that the hunter embodies for the gentleman. If the bear hunter lives off and preys on the bear, so by economic implication does the refined frame live off and prey on the energy of the vernacular. That is why the frontiersman, once he has in effect taken over the sketch, pours his imaginative energy into releasing the bear as monster, as god of the wilderness, as sought-for mate, as dream—yet grounded in vernacular realism. This is not all; if it were, we would have no more than "poetic" vernacular and vivid metaphors. The height of Thorpe's imagination rests in embedding a joke so near the heart of his wild, free narrative that many critics have missed it. Thus, the bear hunter, after chasing the bear for years, is surprised by the bear during his morning defecation. Watch Thorpe make his frontier language all but conceal and circumlocute the "snapper" of his joke:

I then told my neighbors, that on Monday morning—naming the day—I would start THAT BEAR, and bring him home with me, or they might divide my settlement among them, the owner having disappeared.

Well, stranger, on the morning previous to the great day of my hunting expedition, I went into the woods near my house, taking my gun and Bowie knife along, just *from habit,* and there sitting down, also from habit, what should I see, getting over my fence, but that bear! Yes, the old varmint was within a hundred yards of me, and the way he walked over *that fence*—stranger; he loomed up like a *black mist,* he seemed so large, and he walked right towards me.

I raised myself, took deliberate aim, and fired. Instantly the varmint wheeled, gave a yell, and *walked through* the fence, as easy as a falling tree would through a cobweb.

I started after, but was tripped up by my inexpressibles, which, either from habit or the excitement of the moment, were about my heels, and before I had really gathered myself up, I heard the old varmint groaning, like a thousand sinners, in a thicket near by, and, by the time I reached him, he was a corpse.

There you have the most novel imagination of America linked up with the oldest joke in the world—the joke of being caught with one's britches down. Yet what ought to be embarrassment is converted into the very height of the tall tale happy ending.

That joke must have almost killed Thorpe, for in most of his work he withdrew into the moral superiority of the refined perspective. Thus he reduces Mike Fink to a kind of brutal killer as he rather tiresomely moralizes his narrative. He wants to show that he can't quite stand Mike Fink. It is not surprising that, with the approach of Civil War, he retreated North into the somber perspective of antislavery. Yet in his one sketch he had, in the form of the tall tale, achieved a reconciliation of the wild and the genial which no one before him had secured.

If Thorpe withdrew from Louisiana, young Henry Clay Lewis, who came there from South Carolina, did not. Indeed, Lewis refused to be intimidated by the meanness implicit in Southwestern humor. Whereas Longstreet, Hooper, and Thorpe attempted to keep their moral edge, Lewis threatened to drop it even as he kept the refined frame. Instead of having a lawyer or clergyman as his refined narrator, Lewis, who was himself a doctor, brought forth an older physician to recall his adventures as a young doctor. The old narrator is at once indulging and amusing himself with jokes savage enough to make many readers uncomfortable. Lewis brings Negroes as well as frontiersmen into the foreground of his sketches. His "Cupping on the Sternum" is surely one of the finest pieces of humor in all Southwestern writing, yet just as surely it could hardly be assigned to a modern college audience without embarrassment. A kind of extreme version of almanac humor, it yet has the grace and the relentlessness of high sophistication as the old doctor recalls his youthful mistake in treating a Negro woman. His mistake, though grotesque in the extreme, is inescapably funny, a final horrendous joke which many and many a civilized person could never publicly acknowledge he had privately laughed at. There would of course be many others who could not laugh at the joke even privately, but surely they would have as big a problem as those who laughed at it too easily in public.

Lewis did not stop there. His "A Tight Race Considerin'" brilliantly plots a joke in such a way as to achieve the kind of elaboration of "The Miller's Tale," without ever losing character portrayal and vernacular realism. In such a tale, all the language and style of the past are brought together to be exposed with maximum authority. Lewis also did his own version of the bear hunt; *his* bear hunter, who has lost his leg to a bear, finally conquers a bear by beating it to death with his wooden leg! The best part of it all is that he is telling his story to the doctor who had made the leg. No lover of *Moby Dick* should be without a consciousness of Lewis's humorous vision of Ahab's vengeance. Even to begin to appreciate Lewis's work is to know what American literature may have suffered with his death by drowning when he was only twenty-five.

Finally there is George Washington Harris, creator of Sut Lovingood. Harris drove himself deeper into frontier vernacular than any of his predecessors—so deep that his speaker, Sut Lovingood, embodies in their extremity all the amorality, savagery, meanness, and drunkenness of his progenitors in Southwest humor. But Sut is new. His dialect is practically a new language, for it is a deviation so remarkable that a reader must literally reconstruct his own language as well as Sut's if he is to understand it. Once the process of reconstruction begins, rich and wonderful possibilities of humor literally explode upon the page. Through it all, the figure of Sut Lovingood comes more and more to stand out as a new man himself. All but amoral, Sut seems to be the very principle of life and pleasure and chaos, all concentrated into his deviant language. He is, by his own definition, a "Nat'ral Born Durn'd Fool," and, aggressive though he is, his language reverberates with retaliation against centuries of repression. His very name, Lovingood, signifies the profundity of his relation to the world of sexual love. There is no better illustration of his potentiality as Sexual Lord of Misrule than his performance at "Sicily Burns's Wedding." There, he takes vengeance on the bride who has tricked him in an earlier sketch (Harris's whole rich world vibrates along lines of practical jokes as displacement for vengeance) by tormenting a bull with hornets ("insex" Sut calls them). The chaos which that bull visits upon the wedding party speaks worlds about the whole sexual principle so fragilely held in check by social institutions.

I could go on and on about Sut, but it is best to define Harris's master joke, which is, I take it, the pursuit of illiteracy with a language so sophisticated that only the most urbane audience could read it. That joke is, as all great humor must be, on Harris as well as on the reader. For if the reader has to be extraordinarily sensitive to the uttermost reaches of language to read the voice of the illiterate Sut, Harris himself was beginning to imagine for himself not a broad public for his jokes but an elite readership that would probably have surprised even him. Either that, or a large trained audience which he had somehow educated.

Whatever the case, the Civil War came and the humor of the

Old Southwest disappeared beneath the powerful but sobering vision of *Uncle Tom's Cabin*, just as "Dixie" was to be momentarily trampled beneath the martial rhythms of "The Battle Hymn of the Republic" (that song, also written by a woman, which is to this day sung by "peace" marchers—a fact that had better be a last joke for someone).

All these humorists might have been forgotten had not Mark Twain, whose whole genius was rooted in the tradition, made his way into the dominant culture and, by placating the moral sense in an absolutely disarming way, released more humor for more people than the old "gentlemen" would have believed possible. If Mark Twain's achievement is likely to be what sends us back to them, when we get there we begin to know how strong his origins truly were.

Oliver Wendell Holmes

Lewis Leary

Oliver Wendell Holmes probably possessed more minor literary virtues than any writer of his generation. He was a pert, bubbling little man, hardly more than five feet tall, famous for his conversation and his ebullient wit. He was popular as a lecturer, sought after as an entertainingly felicitous after-dinner speaker, and widely admired as a writer of deft light verse. His essays were read and admired by almost every literary compatriot. His novels, now almost forgotten, were filled with good talk and wittily turned character sketches, all strung upon plots only loosely knitted together. For Oliver Wendell Holmes was a miniaturist in literature, better at the small thing, intricately wrought, than on a larger canvas.

By vocation he was a physican, and a good one, who occupied the chair—which he preferred to call the settee—of anatomy at Harvard University for many years, and he was responsible for many medical reforms, but he is remembered for other things: his quick wit, the effervescent contagion of his good-natured raillery. Indeed his humor seems to have interfered with his professional career. Patients were disconcerted by a doctor who greeted them with such a cheerfully, disconcerting remark as "the smallest of fevers are gratefully accepted." He should have remembered, he once said, that Shakespeare's long-faced Hamlet was more universally admired than his clowns. People did not always realize, he said, that "laughter and tears are meant to turn the wheels of the same machinery." The difference is that "one is wind-power, and the other water-power; that is all."

Like most humorists, Dr. Holmes was at root an exceptionally serious man, expert in determining what, to his way of thinking, was important, and what was not. The son of a particularly fundamentalist clergyman father who thought him too harum-scarum ever to amount to anything at all, young Oliver Holmes felt strongly the generation gap between them. He seems to have thought himself more to reflect qualities of his mother's prosperous mercantile family, the Wendells, than the rigid puritanicalism of the clerical Holmeses. Born and educated at Cambridge, and then a student of medicine in Paris, he became the very model of the proper modern young Bostonian, glib, aristocratic, and convinced that birth and breeding provided license to instruct, however lightly, and to condemn. Boisterous nineteenth-century America seemed endemic with diseases which might respond to the astringent medication of his wit.

Few men of his time or place were more personally popular, for his humor, even when corrective, was seldom caustic. His wit livened meetings of the famous Saturday Club where most of the literary greats of New England gathered for weekly meetings. He spent many summers vacationing in the Berkshires, a neighbor of Herman Melville and Nathaniel Hawthorne and Catherine Sedgwick at whose fictional sentimentalities he made good-natured masculine fun. They picnicked together, and the men talked over brandy and cigars, and later, when Herman Melville was ill, Dr. Holmes was called in to prescribe the rest and relaxation which the tightly-strung novelist so badly needed.

One of the most charming scenes recorded in American literary history is that of a picnic arranged to celebrate the recent marriage of James T. Fields, the Boston publisher of most of the men who contributed to the early nineteenth-century flowering of New England. Fields was a portly man who made it a point publicly to lament his avoirdupois. It was characteristic of Holmes playfully to suggest to the publisher that if he paid higher royalties to his authors, of whom Holmes was of course one, they might be able to eat more and he less, thus controlling his rotundity. The picnic was a triumph for the effervescent Dr. Holmes. When a brief shower came, he improvised umbrellas for the ladies out of branches and leaves. While Melville morosely sat aside in gloomy contemplation, the little doctor darted here and there, keeping all the company in good humor, filling silver goblets with champagne, and managing the while to maintain a running conversation which probed lightly, among other things, into the question of whether Englishmen were superior to Americans. One can visualize the scene which suggests so much—is virtually a paradigm—of these two men, Melville and Holmes, the one withdrawn into himself and into who knows what thoughts of what depth, the other flitting brightly, the life of the party.

For Holmes did flit lightly over surfaces. His laughter was a pleasant protection against the vagaries of mad reformers, misguided clergymen, and poets like Walt Whitman and Edgar Allen Poe, both of whom seemed to most proper Bostonians undisciplined in taste and lacking in judgment. Though Dr. Holmes admired much in Ralph Waldo Emerson, and in some respects echoed in lighter vein some of his more prominent ideas, he did make playful fun of what he called the more "cobwebby" notions of the Transcendentalists. Reformers of any kind were victims, he said, of "inflammation of the conscience." He insisted that

The ludicrous has its place in the universe; it is not a human invention, but one of the Divine ideas, illustrated in the practical jokes of kittens and monkeys long before Aristophanes and Shakespeare. How curious it is that we always consider solemnity and the absence of all gay surpluses and encounter of wits as essential to the idea of the future life of those whom we thus deprive of half their faculties and then call *blessed!*

He disliked any disputatious men who argued too much or who talked fuzzily or who took themselves too seriously. He distrusted, not only Transcendentalism, but any -ism which tied man's mind to certainty. Most of all, he disliked the rugged self-assurance of the Calvinism in which he had been reared in his father's house in Cambridge. Like Emerson, he was suspicious of all man-made logical schemes, especially the harsh logic of Puritanism which pretended, he thought, that rigidity was substitution for truth. Since boyhood in his father's parsonage, Holmes had rebelled against the certainties of Puritan Calvinism. To demonstrate that it was out of date and that other strange notions like the efficacy of homeopathic medicine were out of date also, he wrote what is probably his best-remembered poem, "The Deacon's Masterpiece," which tells of "the wonderful one-hoss shay,/That was built in such a logical way" that it lasted without a sign of decay for one hundred years with everyone thinking it as strong and durable as it ever had been, until suddenly "it went to pieces all at once,–/All at once, and nothing first,–/Just as bubbles do when they burst."

But much of Holmes's humor is so topical that, unlike his one-horse shay, it failed even to outlive its century. As one of the many who found and proved provincial Boston to be the hub of America's universe, he named himself and his favorite literary companions the Brahmins of New England, men of discrete learning and taste like his fellow members of the Saturday Club, Henry Wadsworth Longfellow and James Russell Lowell, who were carefully correct as poets and who, like him, were or would be professors at Harvard University. Holmes, however, sprang to national attention earlier than most of the others of his generation. He was still a student in 1830, when aroused by discovery that the historic naval vessel, the frigate *Constitution*, famed for its part in the sea battles of the War of 1812, was threatened with destruction as obsolete, he dashed off verses on "Old Ironsides" which swept immediately through all the country, to become, as they have remained, a favorite recitation piece. How many through many generations remember having gestured magnificently on declaiming its stirring opening lines:

> Ay, tear her tattered ensign down!
> Long has it waved on high. . . .

But for years Dr. Holmes's best fame was local, among the towns of New England where he lectured, usually on literature, to augment his professor's small salary, or at banquets where he was inevitably called on for witty lines to commemorate such popular events as the arrival of Charles Dickens in Boston or the anniversary of the landing of the Pilgrim Fathers. He was always good for a chuckle, as when he solemnly pronounced at the inauguration of a college president that

> No iron gate, no spiked and panelled door,
> Can keep out death, the postman, or a bore.

Bores he disliked exceedingly, and he seems never to have been one himself. And he looked quizzically on people who wrote too much, who had an itch for scribbling without thought.

> If all the trees in all the woods were men
> And each and every blade of grass a pen;
> If every leaf on every shrub and tree
> Turned to a sheet of foolscap; every sea
> Were changed to ink, and all life's living tribes
> Had nothing else to do but act as scribes,
> And for ten thousand ages, day and night,
> The human race should write, and write, and write,
> Til all the pens and paper were used up,
> And the huge inkstand were an empty cup,
> Still would the scribblers clustering round its brink
> Call for more pens, more paper, and more ink.

Whatever his local reputation, it was not however until he was almost fifty that Holmes achieved lasting national prominence. It came to him in 1857, when his friend James Russell Lowell planned to establish a new magazine and was unable to come up with a suitable name for it. So he came to the inventive Dr. Holmes who suggested that it be called the *Atlantic Monthly*. Holmes promised to contribute to it, which he did as a favorite among its readers for the next thirty years, first with a series of essays which he called "The Autocrat of the Breakfast Table," followed by another series called "The Professor at the Breakfast Table," then a third, "The Poet at the Breakfast Table," and topped off, when he was past eighty, with a fourth called "Over the Teacups." In these essays the genial irascibility of Oliver Wendell Holmes found most effective and most exuberant expression. They were conversation pieces in which people sitting around a table engaged in sprightly good talk. If it tended often to become a monologue in which the Autocrat, the Professor, the Poet, or the aging Dr. Holmes himself monopolized most of the conversation, so much the better. Almost everything he said was worth a chortle or a gasp.

Most of these essays are colored with rambling, quiet humor, often reciting an incident, much as Mark Twain later would, with apparent great seriousness, with the humorous point, what Mark Twain would call the "nub," concealed until just the right moment, so that, when recognized, it would draw, in Holmes's writing, a quiet chuckle from the reader, never a boisterous guffaw. There was little boisterous in Holmes's quiet fun. Like Thoreau, he often approached what he thought to be a truth indirectly. For, he said,

> Every person's feelings have a front-door and a side-door by which they may be entered. The front-door is on the street. Some keep it always open; some keep it latched; some locked; some bolted,—with a chain that will let you peep in, but not get in; and some nail it up, so that nothing can pass its threshold. This front-door leads into a passage which opens into an ante-room and this into the interior apartments. The side-door opens at once into the sacred chambers.

But, he continued, be careful to whom you entrust a key to your side-door:

> If nature or accident has put one of these keys into the hands of a person who has the torturing instinct, I can solemnly pronounce the words that Justice utters over its doomed victim,—*The Lord have mercy on your soul!* You will probably go mad after a certain time,—or, if you are a man, run off and die with your head on a curb-stone, in Melbourne, or San Francisco, —or, if you are a woman, quarrel and break your heart, or, turn into a pale, jointed petrification that moves about as if it were alive, or play some real life-tragedy or other.

It is easy, that is, to avoid people who approach directly, but those —like poets or humorists—who insinuate themselves and their thoughts indirectly, to make you think or feel, these are the enemy, the torturers.

At other times he is more direct, dwelling on commonplaces of almost everyone's experience.

> Don't you know how hard it is for some people to get out of a room after their visit is over? They want to be off, and you want them off, but they don't know how to manage it. One would think they had been

built into your parlor or study, and were waiting to be launched. I have contrived a sort of ceremonial inclined plane for such visitors, which being lubricated with certain smooth phrases, I back them down, metaphorically speaking, stern-foremost into their "native element," the great ocean of out-of-doors.

Then, somewhat deviously, he turns in analogue to the subject of literature, of bad poetry which lingers on as tenaciously as do unwanted guests: "Well, now," he went on,

there are some poems as hard to get rid of as these rural visitors. They come in glibly, use up all the serviceable rhymes, *say, ray, beauty, duty, eyes, skies, other, brother, mountain, fountain,* and the like; and so they go on until you think that it's time for a wind-up, and the wind-up doesn't come on any terms. So they lie about until you get sick of them, and end by thrusting some cold scrap of a final couplet upon them, and turning them out of doors.

This is quiet Yankee humor, nourished on understatement, innuendo, and gracious prose. It does not translate easily in time or space. Sometimes it was gently, but, oh, so gently, ribald, and when it was Holmes, like the early Mark Twain, was careful to put it into the mouth of someone else, as when he suggested:

All thought, my friend, the Professor, says, is of the nature of an excretion. . . . A man instinctively tries to get rid of his thought in conversation or in print as soon as it is matured; but it is hard to get at as it lies embedded, a mere potentiality, the germ of a germ, in his intellect.

But a healthy man will get rid of his thoughts, not only to avoid intellectual indigestion, but in self-protection and as a service to his fellow men. "Every real thought," he reminded his readers at another time, "knocks the wind out of somebody."

And knock the wind out of people Holmes did, but genially with quietly familiar entrance through the side-door as a welcome friend whose scolding was as well-meaning as well-phrased. People in New England still occasionally chuckle over the sometimes innocuously naughty strictures of these essays. But the verse which he occasionally included among them seems generally to have proved more memorable than the prose. Holmes himself thought that "The Chambered Nautilus" with which he ended the *Autocrat* series in 1858 to be quite the best thing he ever wrote, and many people in his time and ours have agreed with him, especially about the last stanza which begins, "Build thee more stately mansions, O my soul." And the "Sun-Day Hymn" with which he concluded the *Professor* series is a favorite also, as in it the man of science succumbs to the man of faith who recognizes the "Lord of all being throned afar," whose "glory flames from every star."

Not many of Dr. Holmes's lines survive, but the few which do are cherished. His verse was to great poetry, he once said, what the tinkling of the triangle is to the combined harmony of the orchestra; but to tinkle the triangle, he went on, "was some accomplishment, especially when it sounded so long and so clearly in so many years." He wrote,

> Not for glory, not for pelf
> Not, to be sure, to please myself,
> Not for any meaner ends,—
> Always "by request of friends."

For he was best as an occasional poet, expertly correct in metre and in rhyme, whose light verse could be counted on to grace any anniversary or ceremonious event. He dexterously skirts pathos when he compares Herman Melville's aging grandfather to "The Last Leaf" which clings lonely to barren bough, as

> now he walks the streets,
> And he looks on all he meets
>   Sad and wan.
> And he shakes his feeble head,
> That it seems as if he said,
>   "They are gone."

> The mossy marbles rest
> On the lips that he has prest
>   In their bloom,
> And the names he loved to hear

> Have been carved for many a year
>> On the tomb.
>
> My grandmamma has said—
> Poor lady she is dead
>> Long ago—
> That he had a Roman nose
> And his cheek was like a rose
>> In the snow.
>
> But now his nose is thin,
> And it rests upon his chin
>> Like a staff,
> And a crook is in his back,
> And a melancholy crack
>> In his laugh.

But the little doctor satirizes old Major Melville in a kindly fashion, recognizing the mortality of all men:

> I know it is a sin
> For me to sit and grin
>> At him here;
> But the old three-cornered hat,
> And the breeches, and all that,
>> Are so queer!
>
> And if I should live to be
> The last leaf upon the tree
>> In the spring.
> Let them smile, as I do now,
> At the old forsaken bough
>> Where I cling.

For like all true humorists Holmes recognized in the absurdities in actions or appearances of other people, absurdities which he found also in himself. Not for him the statement "What fools these mortals be," but "What fools *we* mortals be."

He had great fun laughing at the absurdity of a maiden aunt, perhaps real, perhaps pretended, who went to ridiculous lengths to confine her increasing waistline:

>   My aunt! my dear unmarried aunt!
>   Long years have o'er her flown;
>   Yet still she strains the aching clasp
>   That binds her virgin zone;
>   I know it hurts her,—though she looks
>   As cheerful as she can;
>   Her waist is ampler than her life,
>   For life is but a span.
>
>   .   .   .   .
>
>   They braced my aunt against a board,
>   To make her straight and tall;
>   They laced her up, they starved her down,
>   To make her light and small;
>   They pinched her feet, they singed her hair,
>   They screwed it up with pins;—
>   Oh, never mortal suffered more
>   In penance for her sins.

And yet, for all this primping and squeezing,

>   Alas! nor chariot nor barouche,
>   Nor bandit cavalcade,
>   Tore from the trembling father's arms
>   His all-accomplished maid.
>   For her how happy it had been!
>   And Heaven had spared to me
>   To see one sad, ungathered rose
>   On my ancestral tree.

There was something buoyantly boyish about Oliver Wendell Holmes, something of quick alertness that never tires to maturity. Henry James the senior once told him that he seemed to him to be the most continuously alive man that he ever had known. At the thirtieth reunion of his Harvard class, Holmes prepared verses on "The Boys," saying

> Yes, we're the boys,—always playing with tongue or
>   with pen,—
> And I sometimes have asked,—Shall we ever be men?
> Shall we always be youthful, and laughing, and gay,
> Till the last dear companion drops smiling away.

Holmes did keep youthful and laughing and gay to the end. His humor was in many respects different from that of his contemporaries. It derived more from the jovial spirit of the coffee houses in Augustan England, or of convivial, aristocratic clubmen of any time, or from the epigrammatic wit of Horace at his frolicsome best than from the boisterous American frontier. It played more often on words than on vulgar risibilities. It was often bookishly intellectual. Though genial, it was perhaps at root snobbish, well-dressed, well-mannered, excellently contrived to delight a cultivated mind. He preferred, he said, above all others "the man who inherits family traditions and the cumulative humanities of at least four generations." He was fond beyond almost all besides of good talk, conversations which moved quickly, wittily over a variety of subjects. "What are the great faults of ordinary conversation among us?" he once asked. And he answered himself by explaining that "Want of ideas, want of words, want of manners are the principal ones." But in conversation, he especially disliked contentiousness. "Talking," he explained, "is like playing the harp; there is as much in laying the hand on the strings to stop the vibrations as in twanging them to bring out their music."

He preferred to toy with ideas and to toy with words, teasing them to more expressive meaning. Though himself an irredeemable punster, he pretended great distaste for the pun; people who pun should be punished. "Let me lay down the law on the subject," he said. "Life and language are alike sacred. Homicide and *verbicide*—that is, violent treatment of a word with fatal results to its legitimate meaning, which is its life—are alike forbidden." And then he proceeded in his argument, he who disliked argument, with one of the

most telling and outrageous puns of all: Manslaughter, he explained
is what homicide is about; man's laughter (which is spelled exactly
the same) is the end of verbicide. He pretended dislike of people
who might ask whether the deluge through which Noah is said to
have piloted his Ark—whether this *deluge* was not a *deal huger*
than any other flood. "People who make puns," he said, "are like
wanton boys who put coppers on the railroad tracks. They amuse
themselves and other children, but their little trick may upset a
freight train of conversation for the sake of a battered witticism."

Yet it may be that Oliver Wendell Holmes's epigrammatic witticisms, so like those of Benjamin Franklin's "Poor Richard," will
most surely survive. "Sin," he explained, "has many tools, but a lie
is the handle that fits them all." Or again: "Habit is a labor saving
device which enables man to get along with less fuel." He was
sure that "We are all tattooed in our cradles with the beliefs of
our tribes," that "We are all sentenced to capital punishment for
the crime of living." With age, he rejoiced that "To be seventy
years young is sometimes more cheerful and hopeful than to be
forty years old." He was sure that "stupidity often saves a man
from going mad," and that "The young man knows the rules, but
the old man knows the exceptions."

As a physician, he observed that "Among the gentlemen that I
have known, few, if any, are ruined by drinking. My few drunken
acquaintances were generally ruined before they became drunkards.
The habit of drinking is often a vice, no doubt, sometimes a misfortune, . . . but oftenest a punishment." As a man whose writings were greatly admired, but most often only by a small coterie
of like-minded friends, he could muse on "How small a matter
literature is to the great, seething, toiling, struggling, love-making,
bread-winning, child-rearing, death-waiting men and women who
fill this huge, palpitating world of ours." As a lecturer who livened
his own talk with sprightly and entertaining learning, he could nonetheless assert that "All lecturers, all professors, all schoolmasters,
have ruts and grooves in their minds into which their conversation
is always sliding."

Unlike his Boston friend James Russell Lowell who sometimes
frolicked in good, robust, common vernacular, and unlike Mark

Twain and the Southwestern humorists, Dr. Holmes's drolleries were most often most effectively dressed in sophisticated, learned, polite, even "literary" language. But he could accommodate himself when he had to, as he did in talking about "the wonderful one-hoss shay," to the language of the people. To call attention to the forthcoming publication of *The Autocrat of the Breakfast Table* as a book, he prepared an imaginary interview with the Autocrat's landlady who supposed that "Folks will be curious about them that has wrote in the papers." She described the Autocrat, who of course was Holmes himself:

This gentleman warn't no great gentleman to look at. Being of a very moderate dimension,—five foot five *he* said, but five foot four more likely, and I've heard him say he didn't weigh much over a hundred and twenty pound. He was light complected, rather than darksome, and was one of them smooth-faced people that kept their baird and whiskers cut close, just as if they'd be very troublesome if they let them grow,—instead of laying their face in the grass, as my poor husband that's dead and gone used to say. He was a well-behaved gentleman at table, only . . . he had a way of turning up his nose when he didn't like what folks said.

And he was a talkative little man:

Many's the time I've seen that gentleman keeping two or three of them [the other boarders] settin' round the breakfast table after the rest had swallered their meals and after the things were cleared off. . . . And there that little man would set, . . . a-talkin' and a-talkin'.

Dr. Holmes did talk on and on, brimful of wit and contagious good humor. Late in life he produced what he called "medicated novels," to demonstrate that a physician could probe springs of human conduct better than a clergyman. *Elsie Venner*, the first and best of them, attacked the doctrine of original sin, but, like *The Guardian Angel* and *A Moral Antipathy* which followed, it is today of hardly more than passing interest because of its early foreshadowing of some of the psychological methods of Sigmund Freud. For Dr. Holmes was not at his best in serious and extended writings which required argument. He spoke most effectively with quips, which entered, as he had said, the side-door of his readers' minds.

James Russell Lowell hit him off well in *A Fable for Critics*,
where he wrote of Holmes as

> matchless among you for wit;
> A Leyden-jar always full-charged, from which flit
> The electrical tingles of hit after hit.
>
> .   .   .   .
>
> His are just the fine hands to weave you a lyric
> Full of fancy, fun, feeling, or spiced with satyric
> In so kindly a measure, that nobody knows
> What to do but e'en join in the laugh, friends and foes.

So light and bright and good-natured was his humor that he made
no enemies. His wit more often traveled delightfully over surfaces
than penetrated to depths. His pinwheel mind darted exuberantly,
hovering over serious thought as if afraid to alight. It was a native
trait perhaps, the kind of comic coloration often taken on in self-
defense, the rapier wit which pierces quickly to put an adversary
off guard. He is closer to Washington Irving, whom he admired,
than to Mark Twain, who puzzled and troubled him. But, if not
in the main channel of American humor, Oliver Wendell Holmes
at least bubbles brightly through tributary streams which continue
occasionally to refresh. He would, I think, have liked it that way.

The Misspellers

Brom Weber

One of the chief distinctions creditable to American literary humor is the achievement of Charles Farrar Browne, a mid-nineteenth-century humorist. Browne, or Artemus Ward as he was popularly known, became the first American writer to earn a truly national reputation during his lifetime. He accomplished this feat in the 1860's, at the start of the American Civil War, when one might expect that national turmoil was too discomposing to permit any humorous writer to be read widely or at all.

Emerson, Whitman, Longfellow, Holmes, Melville, Lowell, Whittier, Hawthorne, and other important contemporaries of Ward had already published some of their major writings by 1860. Nevertheless, it was Ward, rather than any of these men, who was read enthusiastically from the Atlantic to the Pacific, who attracted large audiences in a Western village or an Eastern city when he appeared on the lecture platform. Again, it was Artemus Ward, rather than any other mid-nineteenth-century writer, who wrote so perceptively and freshly about national life that he became an acknowledged favorite of war-time President Abraham Lincoln. An irrepressible humorist, Lincoln appreciated Ward's insight and candor even when applied somewhat astringently to Lincoln and politics. It was no accident, apparently, that in 1862 Lincoln insisted upon reading Ward's "High-Handed Outrage at Utica" at a meeting of his cabinet officers prior to reading them the final draft of the Emancipation Proclamation.

Oddly, only rarely in the present-day worlds of academic literary studies and literary journalism does one find more than cursory or derogatory reference to Artemus Ward. It must seem wildly perverse, therefore, for anyone to confess—as I now do—that he has been reading Artemus Ward and other literary humorists of the Civil War period with a good deal of laughter and admiration. After their deaths, such popular humorists generally tend to be forgotten by cultures which are uneasy about the propriety of humor, value the ostensibly serious over the unabashedly comic, and change so rapidly that they forget the artistry and enduring substance of past humor and respond only to humor-incorporating topics and phrases of the immediate moment. These are characteristics of American culture.

But Ward and his fellow humorists also have been singled out for historical oblivion on additional grounds. They are charged with having been popular funny men whose prime comic stock in trade was butchery of the English language by means of gross misspellings and other crude linguistic shenanigans. Furthermore, so traditional literary history puts the matter, these shameless clowns—deprecatingly termed "misspellers"—leaped onto previously dignified lecture platforms and theater stages, turning them into low vaudeville shambles. There, with continued apish gesture and mechanical jokery, these vulgar "phunny phellows" amused audiences who had a great need of instructive discourse and moral uplift, at very least of the kind of respectable, serious humor purveyed by Mark Twain in the East once he outgrew the debasing influences of lower-class childhood in Missouri and young manhood in the Far West.

At the height of his fame in 1906, as though to make atonement for his former association with Artemus Ward and others long derogated not only as misspellers but also as mere "literary comedians," elderly Mark Twain summed up the quintessential negation of the Civil War humorists. First describing as a "mortuary volume" *Mark Twain's Library of Humor*, a collection of American comic writing he had helped edit in 1888 and in which the misspellers were prominent, Twain went on to explain:

Why have they perished? Because they were merely humorists. Humorists of the "mere" sort cannot survive. Humor is only a fragrance, a decoration.

Often it is merely an odd trick of speech and of spelling, as in the case of Ward and Billings and Nasby . . . and presently the fashion passes and the fame along with it. . . . Humor must not professedly teach, and it must not professedly preach, but it must do both if it would live forever.

Then, perhaps recalling that his career as a nationally distinguished humorist had been generously initiated by Artemus Ward, certainly more aware than anyone of how greatly indebted he was to the manner and substance of the misspellers, Twain added with ironic magnanimity: "By forever, I mean thirty years. With all its preaching [humor] is not likely to outlive so long a term as that."

Twain was as completely wrong about the longevity of his own writings as he was about the essential durability and art of the Civil War humorists. Throughout his life, he remained haunted by a sense of despair induced by the ignominious role assigned to humor by the governing pundits of nineteenth-century American culture. Believing that humor was intrinsically superficial and ephemeral, assigning insufficient weight to its playfulness, thematic range, and imaginative power, they insisted that to merit respect it must be enhanced with ideas and postures reflecting their own conceptions of truth, goodness, and significance. Doubting his deepest, often contrary impulses, poor Twain also doubted the misspellers and anyone else who had independently gone on to write humor. Twain's self-disparagement reminds one of the equally unwarranted self-condemnation expressed by S. J. Perelman, truly a master of modern humor, who has dismissed his works as mere feuilletons, lightweight space fillers in newspapers and magazines.

When Mark Twain asserted that the humor of Artemus Ward, Josh Billings, and Petroleum V. Nasby was "merely an odd trick of speech and of spelling," he was referring to their humorous exploitation of variations from standard grammar, pronunciation, and vocabulary. The humorists were not equally concerned with varying all established linguistic form, meaning, order, and sound, but all managed to misspell. It was this similarity which united them in the minds of some readers and critics as misspellers and, because of its inescapably prominent visibility in their writing, was regarded as the preponderant, if not the sole element of their humor. That it was a crucial misunderstanding becomes clear after a reading of more than several pieces by each of the misspellers. Actually, almost all of the misspellers wrote humor in satisfactory standard English before, during, and after the heyday of misspelling in the 1860s. More important, they were distinctively different one from the other, demonstrated a considerable degree of literary sophistication, and taught and exhorted their audiences with commendable substantive seriousness.

Isolated from its context in a literary work, pure misspelling is indeed an elementary literary technique. Its visual incongruity stimulates a reader's amusement, but it requires little more skill from a writer than an ability to rearrange the order of letters in a word and to further complicate the orthographic rearrangement by eliminating some letters and adding new ones. Such rearrangement, though deliberate, is only a little more artistically significant than the misspelling unconsciously perpetrated by a child or adult who, either illiterate or unfamiliar with a language, incorrectly spells out words he may pronounce correctly or be able to recognize in print.

The Civil War misspellers, on the other hand, were prepared and had been encouraged to do more than misspell. Literate and sensitive, in some cases exposed to a few years of higher education and in others self-educated while working as journalists or at other occupations, they were familiar with English and American literature of their own and earlier periods. All were aware that linguistic variation and distortion functioned prominently in the literary humor of great as well as minor writers. Not all may have been as conscious as the Southern journalist George William Bagby of the traditional link between misspelling and dialect when, commenting in 1878 on the style of his popular "Mozis Addums" letters, he said that "never [having] attempted anything in what is called 'Dialect,' but, having a natural turn for bad spelling, [I] thought I would try my hand." Like Bagby, however, the misspellers understood that the range of their humor would be extended by an infusion of the dialectal speech of their neighbors and associates. Along with it would come not merely the vivid phrasing, vocabulary, and imagery of a host of nonwriters, but also their vital accumulation of lore, experience, and perspective not usually tapped by conventionally written literature.

Emphasizing dialect, the misspellers stepped forth in an audacious comic role for which the outstanding precedent was Seba Smith's Jack Downing. Each Civil War misspeller invented a literary mask who spoke wholly in his own unique nonstandard language. Charles Farrar Browne's dialectal mask was Artemus Ward, David Ross Locke's was Petroleum Vesuvius Nasby, Henry Ward Shaw's was Josh Billings, and Charles Henry Smith's was Bill Arp. Shakespeare, Smollett, Thackeray, and Dickens in England and Nathaniel Ward, Hugh Henry Brackenridge, Royall Tyler, Augustus B. Longstreet, William Tappan Thompson, and James Russell Lowell in the United States had already presented comic characters who spoke an incongruously fractured English and were semiliterate, illiterate, or mentally muddled. But these had been surrounded by other characters who spoke English with facility and by authorial statements also in standard English, literary techniques which made readers understand that the author was socially and otherwise superior to dialect speakers. Thus, unlike the Civil War misspellers, these earlier dialect writers escaped the contempt, snobbism, or ridicule generated by the traditional association of dialect—as a deviation from standard linguistic norms—with inadequate education, low social status, alien origin, and intellectual deficiency. It was this animus, of course, when softened by philanthropic concern or romantic sentiment, that also aroused complacent amusement at dialect and made it a source of comedy.

The Civil War humorists' determination to express themselves wholly in dialect required them to cope with a special linguistic problem that partial dialect writers had been able to overlook. Only a phonetic alphabet is able to render all the nuances of English speech sounds, whether dialectal or nondialectal. The nonphonetic literary alphabet, which all writers use, can reproduce speech to a limited extent, but only if a writer is willing to engage in misspelling. Literary dialect is essentially a literary convention which merely approximates and suggests true dialect. Large-scale efforts to create phonetically accurate pronunciations with the literary alphabet have resulted in works, like those of the humorist George Washington Harris, which are so overcluttered with strange misspellings, so visually and mentally impenetrable, that most readers' powers of understanding are frustrated and their attention diverted.

To resolve the problem of dialect, accordingly, writers of literary dialect have found it artistically desirable to rely much more upon quasi-phonetic misspellings than upon genuinely phonetic misspellings. This quasi-phonetic misspelling, or eye dialect as it is termed by linguists, represents standard pronunciation rather than dialectal pronunciation. Accordingly, eye dialect effectively serves as a visual signal to the reader of deviation from standard language, yet can be understood without difficulty. Furthermore, any discomfort occasioned by the visual disorder of misspelling can be reduced if works containing eye dialect are kept brief.

The Civil War misspellers displayed sound artistic judgment in depending upon eye dialect as a major stylistic technique. Though there has never been any standard American language, standard regional languages have existed. These hold in common sufficient identical linguistic elements to make interregional communication possible. The brief sketches, letters, and aphorisms of Ward, Nasby, and Billings in the Northern linguistic regions and of Arp in the Southern could thus be widely read and appreciated upon their initial appearance in newspapers and magazines. Their audience continued to increase after reprinting in other journalistic outlets and in subsequent book collections.

The disturbance of language represented by misspelling humor was a tangible and profound expression of the psychosocial shock suffered by the American people during the Civil War. A humorous disordering of language was also stimulated by World Wars I and II. At times like these, humor has an opportunity to be much more openly deviant and controversial, over a broader spectrum of concerns, than more sedate forms of expression. Whether conscious of this or not, the Civil War misspellers took advantage of their fortunate freedom to deviate from sociocultural norms of many kinds by bursting forth into an exuberant and often savage riot that went far beyond misspelling. In this development Artemus Ward was most assiduous and inventive, setting the pace for his contemporaries.

The youthful experience of Ward's creator, Charles Farrar Browne, predisposed him to a career centered on language. He had been born in 1834 in Waterford, Maine, a small agricultural town which his father served in various political offices while earning a living as farmer and land surveyor. Some of Browne's intellectual independence was probably initiated by his father's liberal Congregationalism and his mother's religious free thought. At his father's death, the thirteen-year-old boy began working as typesetter and printer for newspapers in New Hampshire and Maine. Before long he joined a Boston printing firm which published a humorous journal, *The Carpet-Bag*.

Talented printers in the early nineteenth century frequently turned to journalism. Young Browne easily made this transition. During a short term of newspaper employment in Norway, Maine, he had attended an academy where he wrote pieces for student assemblies and participated in debating and dramatics. But it was from *The Carpet-Bag*, which featured the writings of some of the best humorists of the day, that Browne received his formative literary training. Edited by Benjamin P. Shillaber, famous for the comic malapropisms of his Mrs. Partington character, the magazine opened its pages to all styles and forms of humor, from the amiably amusing and ludicrous to the sharply critical and satirical. Furthermore, it welcomed unknown writers such as Mark Twain, whose first known published piece appeared in 1852, as well as Charles Farrar Browne, who contributed at least eleven items to its pages.

When *The Carpet-Bag* ceased publication early in 1853, Browne wandered west as a journeyman printer, then combined printing and writing for various Ohio newspapers. By 1857, he had become a news reporter and commentator on the local scene for the Cleveland *Plain Dealer*. Browne's rise to fame thereafter was meteoric. His journalistic wit and skill brought him an appointment as associate editor of the *Plain Dealer*. The first of his humorous Artemus Ward letters appeared in 1858 and two years later he gave the first of his comic lectures. Soon Browne was writing regularly for *Vanity Fair*, a New York comic weekly which aimed to be the American version of London's distinguished *Punch*. In 1861 he moved to New York, where he joined the editorial staff of *Vanity Fair*. A year later, in 1862, he became the magazine's managing editor and his first book, *Artemus Ward: His Travels*, was published. It appeared in an initial edition of 40,000 copies, then as now an impressive amount for the first printing of any book and a clue to its publisher's certainty of a large sale. Browne died five years later in England, where he had been contributing regularly to *Punch* and entertaining great crowds at his lectures. Internationally famous, much quoted and reprinted, he was only thirty-three years old at his death.

Perhaps because Browne died young, he never abandoned the clear, assured, optimistic vision of literary humor he once advanced:

Humorous writers have always done the most toward helping virtue on its pilgrimage, and the truth has found more aid from them than from all the grave polemists and solid writers that have ever spoken or written. It was always so, and men have borne battle for the right, with its grave truth fully in mind, with an artillery of wit, that has silenced the heavy batteries of formal discussion. They have helped the truth along without encumbering it with themselves. They have put it boldly forward and stood behind it and hurled their fiery javelins at their opponents till they have either fled ingloriously or been entirely silenced. Rabelais—vile fellow as he was and revolting to modern propriety and taste—did immense work for the reform that began contemporaneously with him; and from Rabelais down, the shaft of ridicule has done more than the cloth-yard arrows of solid argument in defending the truth. Those who bolster up error and hate the truth are still men and slow; men with no warm blood; men who hate levity and the ebullitions of wit; who deprecate a joke of any kind, and run mad at a pun. . . . They can fire point-blank charges, but the warfare of flying artillery annoys them. They can't wheel and charge and fire, and the attack in flank and rear by the light troops drives them to cover.

Professionally and personally, Browne was always ready to have some fun. One suspects that in the passage quoted he deliberately parodied the detested turgid rhetoric and platitudinous solemnity which he found to excess in all levels of American speech and writing. Without question, however, the high moral purpose, and the tenacity, intelligence, courage, and vivacity necessary to sustain it, that he ascribed to humor at its best were meant to be self-characterizing.

Extremely versatile and energetic though he was, Browne's comic genius reached its peak in two distinct yet related forms of expression. The first was his guise as the vulgar Artemus Ward, a shrewd, wandering showman who wrote fascinating, semiliterate letters about his adventures. Then there was the second Artemus Ward, a polished, educated gentleman who lectured in fine standard English on subjects of cultural and social importance. Both were humbugs, masters of fraud and hoax, but only the first Ward owned up to it frankly and discerned it in others. The second Ward, sincere, well-intentioned, and good-natured, revealed himself unintentionally, with apparent unawareness, when the sheer ludicrous incompetence of his platform performance undermined every one of his claims to authority. Neither of the two Wards was a fully individualized character, nor did either appear to have risen from or to be rooted in any precisely delineated cultural history or geographic location. Transcending time and space as it were, both of Browne's alter egos—one a commoner and the other a member of the elite—delivered a comic-caustic panorama unmasking the relation of appearance to reality, of practice to ideals, and of aspiration to possibility in mid-nineteenth-century democratic America.

Browne's carefree bachelor existence—he was for a time a member of a New York bohemian group to which Walt Whitman also belonged—did not hinder him from developing into a conscious artist. The early Artemus Ward letters written during his Cleveland newspaper days, for example, were carefully reviewed prior to collection in book form in 1862. Midwestern names and other localizing details were deleted, thus increasing potential national appeal. Having learned to value economy, Browne combined some letters and condensed others, effectively highlighting the linguistic audacities, absurd situations, and other humorous elements retained. Meticulous discipline also governed the making of his lectures. Apparently spontaneous and haphazard, seemingly marred by forgetfulness, inappropriate pauses, verbal ineptitude, free-association rambling, and other embarrassments, Ward's platform performance was carefully planned and timed. The deadpan earnestness of his effort to communicate, and the chaos that resulted, were so beautifully intermingled that his audience often did not know whether to respond with pity, contempt, or amusement.

An Artemus Ward performance burlesqued the lecturers—philosophers, politicians, ministers, travelers, generals, professors—who had for years zealously traveled about the country, and with serious mien, dispensed wisdom, edification, and inspiration to a population beset by tempestuous political crises and rapid social changes, now engulfed in a Civil War which none of that vast flood of words had foreseen in all its horror nor been able to prevent. A newspaper account of a Ward lecture delivered at Salt Lake City in 1864 aptly summarized the humorist's critique of high culture and its lecturers. Browne, said the reporter, "revels in the idea that he out-humbugs all humbugs the world ever saw," citing as illustrations of the latter Aristotle, Cicero, and two of Browne's august contemporaries, orator-statesman Edward Everett and philosopher Ralph Waldo Emerson.

All Browne's humor adds up centrally to "an appeal for reason, for balance, for common sense," words that conjure up images of eighteenth-century America and of men like Jefferson who founded the republic. Burlesque lecturer Artemus Ward dramatized the absence of those ideals in the elite of mid-nineteenth-century America. But it is the other Ward, exhibitor of waxwork figures and circus animals, whose blithe letters and sketches portray in detail how abysmally little reason, balance, and common sense Browne discovered in the nation as a whole.

There is something initially inappropriate about having as one's moral and intellectual guide a gross old rogue who boasts at one and the same time of his moral virtue and his lack of principle, who is mercenary, deceptive, opportunistic, and more than a trifle immoderate. Soon, however, his non sequiturs, puns, neologisms, misquotations, clichés, double entendres, wrenched syntax, and dialect have set us to laughing. And then we are impressed by the clarity with which Artemus Ward perceives words, gestures, clothing, people, and objects, the relentlessly literal examination to which he subjects what he perceives, and the bluntness with which he expresses his judgments. At last we understand. Only an amiable, ingratiating dissembler, one blessed with outrageous impudence, gentle spirit, and a scoundrel's insight, could move so freely everywhere, from Lincoln's White House to a Shaker community in upstate New York, and could so brilliantly illuminate the core of truth concealed beneath a misleading surface.

Scarcely an aspect of American life at the mid-nineteenth-century mark escaped Artemus Ward's scrutiny and comment. The results are elating, but painful as well. Ward found duplicity, obsession, greed, egotism, violence, and irrationalism everywhere, in politics, business, reform, and religion, in town and country, in men and women. Despite his joviality, his gibes at political chicanery, war profiteering, draft dodging, and social radicalism were bitterly resented. Anger was roused most fiercely by his restrained support of the Union cause.

Like many other Northerners, Browne had felt that slavery was an insufficient cause for internecine conflict between North and South; he had even proposed that the Confederacy be permitted to secede. He was slow to exhibit concern for the full human rights of Negroes, though his personal relations with them were warm. His postwar travels in the defeated South, where he fraternized with the former enemy, alienated many Northerners. It appears that he left the United States for England in 1866 not only because the English acclaimed him a great American writer, but also because he had been criticized with righteous severity at home and his professional career seriously damaged.

Our extensive consideration of Charles Farrar Browne and his Artemus Ward has prevented us from exploring other fine American literary humorists who turned to misspelling and related verbal play during the Civil War. As recently as a decade ago, such an approach would have been condemned as irresponsible. It would have been argued that the creators of such lively alter egos as Bill Arp, Petroleum Vesuvius Nasby, and Josh Billings belong in a group with Browne. The underlying assumption would have been that all the misspellers were extremely minor writers and essentially similar, therefore too unimportant to be dealt with separately. However, the criticism and scholarship devoted to the misspellers in the past ten years have destroyed the validity of the assumption in all its parts. The Civil War misspellers were uniquely individual writers. Their misspelling, which mistakenly led to their grouping, varies in each case in accordance with such diversifying factors as the kind and amount of regional dialect each man used. It has been my hope that a revelation of the rich complexity available in one distinguished misspeller will encourage lovers of literary humor to turn with high anticipation to the works of the other misspellers.

Mark Twain:
The Height of Humor

James M. Cox

Let me begin with a fantasy. Imagine Hal Holbrook coming to a college campus to appear before a packed academic audience who have paid five dollars per person to see his inimitable impersonation of Mark Twain. Imagine a goodly number of deans, professors, seriously cultured adults, and even a college president or two in the audience. Now imagine Holbrook, in a fit of inspiration, bursting naked before the rapt and waiting audience in one wild, brief, wheeling fling across the stage. And then, after such a reenactment of the King's part in the Royal Nonesuch, imagine Holbrook appearing briefly in the role of the Duke to announce that the evening's entertainment was concluded.

Whatever the response of the spectators to such a caper, of one thing we could be sure. Few among the audience would find the event as funny as it is when encountered in Huck Finn's narrative. There, the reader sees the hopeless and ignorant townspeople duped by the two old rascals. And Mark Twain's whole strategy in his masterpiece is to maneuver *his* audience, which is to say his readers, into a position of comfortable self-approval—a position which insulates them from the naked aggressions of the original joke. If that insulation is destroyed, then the very security upon which humor depends is threatened and the humor itself is sharply curtailed. Yet unless such a threat is somehow present, the humor will become more and more safe and the humorist will become more and more predictable. We will know what to expect and

139

the humorist will correspondingly offer us his routine, his act. The more audience and actor accept such a state of affairs the less our laughter can come from the depths of ourselves in those repeated, rhythmic seizures which shake us to our foundations as they render us literally helpless.

Now what we want—or, more accurately, what we have—in such a state of laughter is an extraordinarily pleasurable release of repressed energy. In order for that release to be pleasurable there must be a measure of safety, a measure of the self-approving insulation which assures us that the joke will somehow inevitably *be* a joke, thus making the expectation of laughter inevitable. But in order for a release to take place at all, there must also be a sense of something escaping, some generative force which either pre-exists the joke or is created by it. Thus, if the humorist becomes too safe, the wildness of incongruity, absurdity, madness, repression are diminished and the energy of humor is reduced. If, on the other hand, the wildness threatens the safety, then anxiety begins to displace security and the pleasure of humor is lost.

Keeping forever within these boundaries requires adroitness enough of the humorist. But there is a further burden. The humorist necessarily occupies a lower position in the hierarchy of aesthetic values. It is no accident that we feel laughter rising from the stomach. Nor is it surprising that those who wish to praise humor are at pains to elevate it from its low estate. Thus discussions of humor, even as they acknowledge the inescapable low laughter of humor, often seek shifty prepositional displacements in an effort to get to the tragedy beneath humor, the vision beyond it, the true joy above it, or, most of all, the seriousness behind it. All these maneuvers, though understandable, are nonetheless evasive efforts to escape the reality of humor—that "low," "common" form which we know is somehow high and marvelous yet which somehow escapes us the moment we try to "elevate" it into "high" literature.

To be both outrageous and safe, then, and to be forever doomed to "low" literature—these are the burden and the glory of the humorist's art. And no writer in the English language, unless it was Chaucer at the very beginning, carried the burdens and achieved the glory of humor with more purity and power than

Mark Twain. I say purity because Mark Twain accepted the *identity* of humorist his whole life long. After all, his very name, Mark Twain, was the pseudonym which forever assured his audiences and forever reminded him that he was fatally a humorist. He was, of course, also Samuel Langhorne Clemens, as an assurance that he was a respected and respectable family man, a social man, even a successful author who had lifted himself out of some impoverished past. But he was dominantly Mark Twain. That was his performing name as well as his pen name—and it was as performer and writer that Samuel Clemens prevailed. It was, in brief, as Mark Twain that he prevailed.

As Mark Twain, Samuel Clemens was a humorist, which means that he was in the lower orders of art. He was also an American, which meant in terms of the English language, which, alas, is what Americans speak, that he was also in the lower orders of English literature. Indeed, humor, which, like the novel, represented a "lower" order of imagination, provided an ideal direction for the American imagination to pursue. Conversely, just as the novel and America were rising in power, so was humor. Thus, what had been a term from the old physiology to refer to the bodily fluids which supposedly governed character and personality, had by the eighteenth century come to mean a genial quality of mind. The amiable humorist thus gradually but inevitably became a fixture on the literary scene. By the mid-nineteenth century, humor, though by no means the highest form of consciousness, was nonetheless seen as a distinct value, and humorous literature was providing points of departure for novelists as great as Dickens and Thackeray. Given such a frame of reference, Samuel Clemens was not going against the deeper grain of history by turning toward humorous narrative to express himself.

But Samuel Clemens was no ordinary American; he was a Southern American. He was in fact an out-and-out criminal—the only one of our major writers who was incontrovertibly an outlaw, a fact either forgotten, distorted, or repressed by much literary criticism. For Samuel Clemens first joined the Confederate army, thereby becoming a traitor to his country. After about two weeks as a rebel soldier, he "resigned" from the army, as he was later to refer to his desertion. Thus guilty of the two capital crimes of treason and desertion, he went west with his brother, Orion Clemens, who, in return for his abolitionist activity, had been appointed Secretary of the Nevada Territory by Lincoln. There in Virginia City, while the Civil War raged in the East, Samuel Clemens, after failing to find silver, discovered Mark Twain and fortune. Yet even as he released himself into humorous narrative, Mark Twain—or was it Samuel Clemens?—continued to be a troublemaker. He left Virginia City for San Francisco because a Southern joke he made connecting the American Sanitary Society (forerunner of the American Red Cross) with miscegenative activity brought him to the verge of a duel with a rival reporter. And he left San Francisco for Tuolumne County, or so he later contended, because his continual journalistic slurs upon the police force put him in jeopardy with the forces of law and order. There in Tuolumne County, in Jim Gillis's cabin on Jackass Hill, Mark Twain heard the tale of the jumping frog which his own great retelling would carry to the distant East. To visit Virginia City today where Samuel Clemens discovered Mark Twain, to look from that ghost town across the desolate landscape of Nevada, and to go to the Jim Gillis cabin in Tuolumne County—which is happily in a worse state of repair than it must have been when Mark Twain was there in 1865—is to be reminded of how deeply Mark Twain is related to *nothing*. To be sure there was a great low tradition of Southwestern humor behind him, which he knew through and through; there was journalistic reporting which he had mastered beyond any author before him; there were the Bible and English literature which he knew better than most academic critics could dream he knew them; there was even the French language, in which young Sam Clemens had kept a notebook when he was seventeen years old, as if in promise of what a great master of language he would eventually be; there were the prior pseudonyms—Thomas Jefferson Snodgrass, Quintus Curtius Snodgrass, W. Epaminondas Adrastus Blab, Sergeant Fathom, and Josh—which Samuel Clemens had tried out in earlier humorous efforts; above all, there was the experience of being a printer, a steamboat pilot on the great Mississippi, a soldier, a miner, and a star reporter.

And yet between the knowledge and experience of Samuel Clemens and the humor of Mark Twain there is a gap, a vacuum, across which the very current of humor leaps. That vacuum has to do with desolation, nihilism, and the ultimate recognition that behind morals and religion there is nothing in the universe. The glory of humor is to convert that awareness into overt pleasure— to excite God's creatures, as Mark Twain said in an early letter to his brother (already betraying full skepticism that the creatures were God's), to laughter. From that experience and that vacuum, Mark Twain, the very genius of Samuel Clemens began, during the era of Reconstruction following upon the Civil War, his own reconstruction, not of the present but of the past.

It was surely no accident that, once he followed his fame East, he emerged into the foreground of the literary world as the reporter of the first organized pleasure trip from the New World to the Old. As an interloper among the touring pilgrims, he made excruciating efforts to be reverent like them in the halls of art and religion. Yet the very ease with which, in *The Innocents Abroad*, he moved from broad joking to stately reverence, was bound to evoke skepticism in the wary reader. For amid the earnestness and gravity of style and countenance, there was always the old outlaw who had to remind his hearers and readers in one way or another that he was a version of the highwayman—bilking his audience with jokes, luring them with travel narratives, fooling them with outrageous stretchers, and reducing them to helpless laughter.

But there was one joke which Mark Twain could never get out from under—the joke of being a humorist. Helpless before that fatality, he tries to be serious; he wishes he were serious; he earnestly seeks instruction in the art of being serious, and becomes such a master impersonator of seriousness that it is impossible to tell whether he is or is not serious. Yet either his own demonic impulse to humor thwarts and betrays him at the crucial moment of an attempted flight into high literature, or his unappreciative audience, convinced that he is all humor, bursts into a guffaw in the midst of his highest seriousness. Thus if he does not bring himself down, he is brought down. That eternal helplessness is a shadow of the master humorist's power to reduce his audiences to laughter.

The rare perfection of this performing personality and the

even rarer capacity to translate the performance into writing carried Mark Twain forward in his career. The dynamic relation between the two aspects of his personality—between pained moralist and irresponsible humorist, between philosopher and fool, between respectable adult and dreaming child, between experience and innocence—made Mark Twain much more than an amiable humorist. There was always present in him the sensibility of the poet, the scorn of the satirist, and the outrage of the offended moralist. To discharge these pent-up emotions, the humor had to be broad and primitively clear. Mark Twain's transformation of the savagery, the humiliation, and the wrongs of experience as they came across the gap of nothingness into the extended incongruities and digressions of narrative humor gave his style triumphant casualness, epic garrulity, and, above all, masterful clarity.

The triumph of Mark Twain's art is, as everybody knows, *Adventures of Huckleberry Finn*. And the first thing to emphasize about the book is that it is for everyone—for children, for young adults, for the middle-aged, and for the old. And the further we live into its meaning the deeper and more pervasive its humor becomes. Its capacity to meet us throughout our lives makes it a book for everybody, whether educated or uneducated, rich or poor, sophisticated or plain, and reminds us that Mark Twain was, for all his expressed attitudes to the contrary, one of the most democratic writers in the world.

That profound democracy of expression, surely the first and last truth about Mark Twain's humorous genius, brings us irrevocably to the language, the character, and the action of his masterpiece. By letting the "low" vernacular thrust him aside, Mark Twain was able, at the height of his career, to imply conventional language without overtly using it as a frame for dialect. This vernacular or "bad" language is the perfect expression of the action of the book—the story of a "bad" boy doing the "bad" deed of freeing a slave in the Old South. This triply reinforced vision secures the total audience approval which constantly transforms what Huck thinks are bad actions into good ones.

The process of inversion is nothing less than the moral sentiment sustaining the action of the book, and it eventuates in the powerful wish that Huck and Jim be forever free—the very wish that the closing ten chapters of the novel frustrate. In those chapters, Tom Sawyer, knowing that Jim is already free, returns to stage manage the action of freeing Jim from slavery. Tom's theatricality has brought him forever under moral fire, just as the chapters which Tom dominates have brought Mark Twain under critical fire. Yet if Tom is secretly relying on his knowledge that Jim is legally free, surely every reader is equally relying on *his* knowledge that Jim is free. That security of the moral sentiment makes the reader as safe as, to borrow a line from Mark Twain, a Christian holding four aces. The reader who scapegoats Tom and Mark Twain is usually evading the moment when the novel turned against the moral sentiment.

That moment occurs when Huck utters what everyone knows is his grandest line: "All right then, I'll *go* to hell." Just there, the moral sentiment drowns Huck in applause and sends him to the heart of heaven. Yet in five minutes of reading time, Huck is in hell all right—the only hell there is in this novel which makes fun of all superstitious hereafters. That hell is none other than adult society. The very accent and rhythm of the line reveal Huck in the act of beginning to play Tom Sawyer, for his positive negation proclaims the fact that he is acting on principle.

That principle is in reality his Northern or inner conscience displacing his Southern or social conscience. His Southern conscience had put him in flight from his society; his Northern conscience welcomes him into ours. And both societies are hell. Why else would we feel so glad that Huck ultimately rejects civilization? His rejection is the radically nihilistic action which his doubly negative grammar and his ignorance of tense distinctions have led him toward. Yet if the book is nihilistic—and surely it is—it is also humorous, and continues to be acted out under the reader's indulgence, affection, and approval.

With Huck's fatal choice, Mark Twain had reached, though he could hardly afford to know how completely he had reached, the limits of his humor: that point at which humor's necessity to gain indulgent and affectionate approval mortally threatened the very identity and character of his humor. Yet even here the form of his masterpiece saved him. Even as Huck chooses the Northern conscience, he does it partly because it is the easiest thing to do in a tight place. Later when Huck lights out for the territory, he leaves civilization not because it is a sham but because it is cramped and smothery. He goes to the West not as an apostle of freedom but as a boy to play. Tom and the adult reader are the ones who have all the principle. This is not all. The ending leaves all adult readers still in the throes of the moral sentiment, if not in approval of the action, in a state of greater self-approval than at any point in the novel—complacently superior to the author's "failure" and obtusely scornful of their own sentimental surrogate, Tom Sawyer. If it is not a perfect ending, it is as good as one can easily imagine for this complete novel of Reconstruction which brought not the Old South but an entirely new South back into the union. In the process the book converted the tragic issue of slavery—the issue which had split the nation apart—into the very sentiment which would so please the mind as to veil the novel's radical disclosure that the adult conscience is the true tyranny of civilization. The book shows that under the sign of the conscience civilized man gains the self-approval to justify the atrocities of adult civilization. And thus man's cruelty is finally his pleasure. That disclosure nakedly seen would be no joke.

It is just that bleak vision which Mark Twain faced for the rest of his life. It was not that he wanted to reform man and do away with conscience; he knew that man could not be reformed. Man would go on killing and maiming his fellow men, always with a serious face, as if the whole business were not really a pleasure. And he would go on mouthing principles and worshipping the Christian God who was enabling the white man to subjugate the savage peoples of the world. Always man would be a slave to the ruthless Moral Sense; always he would lie the old adult lie—the lie by means of which he conceals from himself the truth that cruelty is his deepest pleasure.

The late Mark Twain is full of this vision—so full, I think, that his humor is simplified and weakened. It is true that, when we look at what we have been doing in Asia for the past ten years, Mark Twain's vision may not be so simple-minded as many have thought it. Well before the turn of the twentieth century he could see that white, Christian, capitalistic, technological America which had crushed the agrarian South in the name of freedom could become involved in its own version of colonialism. *A Connecticut Yankee in King Arthur's Court* raises the spectre of such a venture even as it seems to praise Yankee principles and technology. Less inclined to apologize for civilization than a writer so deep and dark as Conrad, Mark Twain was also less able to assimilate his outrage, scorn, and indignation at the complacency of Western man.

There are those, such as Maxwell Geismar, who thrill to Mark Twain's savagery and feel that the incapacity of academic criticism to deal with this prophetic side of Mark Twain amounts to a kind of implicit censorship. Now there is no question that Mark Twain realized that in the American anti-slavery conscience which emerged into the foreground at the end of the Civil War lay the seeds of economic exploitation, imperial expansion, technological threat, and unconditional surrender, which have characterized much of our twentieth-century foreign policy. Certainly our involvement in and conduct of the Viet Nam war would hold few surprises for the man who wrote "To the Person Sitting in Darkness" or "In Defense of General Funston."

Yet it seems to me that *Huckleberry Finn* will remain the height of Mark Twain's achievement just as it is surely the height of his humor. In that book he discovered in a language as rich as that of any writer we have had—and a language somehow more American than that of any writer we have had—the profound destructiveness of conscience and moral intention. True, he had accepted conscience and civilization as, alas, inevitable. So would Conrad; so would Freud. Mark Twain knew as well as Wordsworth that the boy will grow into the man. For Wordsworth the single adult value that compensates for that great loss is poetry itself; for Mark Twain the value is surely humor.

Anyone who thinks that humor is harmless, or that it is the coward's way out, should remember that *Huckleberry Finn* is the only one of our canonical "great" books that has been subjected to censorship. When it appeared, and was banned by the Concord Public Library, Mark Twain roundly applauded in his confident belief that the action would sell thirty-five thousand copies. Today, the book is again being removed from reading lists in city campuses so as not to offend minority groups. We may be sure that *The Scarlet Letter, Moby Dick, Walden,* even *Leaves of Grass* will not be accorded such a fate. Who has not laughed at the Concord Public Library's censorship? Yet who is really laughing at our own censorship? Who even wishes to mention the fact? Academic criticism used to be fond of patronizing Mark Twain for his sedulous obedience to the sexual conventions of the nineteenth century. Yet now when we can use all the four-letter words, it turns out that *Huckleberry Finn* is an embarrassment after all. Mark Twain, who always contended that the truth could not be told, would surely see the joke. If we are to have a sense of humor we had better see it too, and see that it is on us, for how can we have a sense of humor unless we can take a joke as well as tell one? Mark Twain knew that, like the dear old King doing the Royal Nonesuch in *Huckleberry Finn,* man was a naked fraud. And yet he also knew that, like Huckleberry Finn, you couldn't help laughing at him. Huckleberry Finn didn't laugh often. It took the most complete and ancient joke to break him up. That was why when he saw the inimitable Royal Nonesuch he observed that it would have made a cow laugh to see the old idiot cavorting up the world's great stage before a completely "sold" audience. And so, the image of a naked King which reduces us to a wail of pain in *King Lear*, finally reduces us to helpless laughter in *Huckleberry Finn.* So reduced, we are at the height of humor.

The Minstrel Mode

Blyden Jackson

The late James Weldon Johnson, famed Negro author, is among those who remind us that American minstrelsy did have its origin among the slaves of America's Old South. "Every plantation," in Johnson's words, "had its talented band that could crack Negro jokes, and sing and dance to the accompaniment of the banjo and the bones," so that, again in Johnson's words, "when the wealthy plantation-owner wished to entertain and amuse his guests, he needed only to call for his troupe of black minstrels." Yet Johnson's words do not quite do for us what they should. There were wealthy plantations in the Old South, but never as many as it is easy to suppose. For most of the Old South, like most of Old America, was a frontier. Crude virtues flourished in it. Nor did it cater much to social distance. Its black and white bondsmen, its sturdy yeomen, its new proprietors, as well as its riffraff of every color and description, lived in an atmosphere of easy familiarity. It was in their vulgar fellowship, rather than in the ceremonials of an upper class, that the Negro was first truly marked for his role as an American humorist, the role he played in the minstrel mode.

One should not wonder, then, when Constance Rourke, a closer student of the origins of American humor than James Weldon Johnson, expresses interest in the Negro in the South and the "new Southwest" of Old America. At that early time, of course, Alabama, Mississippi, Louisiana, Arkansas, and even backwoods Kentucky and Tennessee, could be west, southwest and new. In all such

149

sections of Old America land was still being cleared. Towns were still being founded. The great highways were still the rivers. Negroes sang and danced on those rivers as they toiled on boats or "labored" around the docks or were being carried in coffles from one auction to another. They sang and danced elsewhere, too, in field and village and in the burgeoning raw cities, like Cincinnati, Louisville, Nashville, and Natchez, or, way down near the river's end, New Orleans. From the 1840's and the 1850's Constance Rourke descries a comic trio, the Yankee, the backwoodsman and the Negro. She deposes that the three tended to merge into a single generic figure of which the long-tail'd blue, the costume worn both by Uncle Sam and the blackface minstrel, tended to become, as she points out, a lasting symbol. It was, indeed, as if the Yankee, the backwoodsman, and the Negro were a godsend to people starved not only for the arts of life, but also for the art of living. Each comic figure added a dimension of social nuance, a humanizing influence, to an often otherwise brutelike existence.

This is not to say that there were no plantation minstrels who were black and actually did live on plantations and did perform at a master's whim. Indeed, we still have, hanging in an old mansion in Williamsburg, Virginia, an unsigned painting, dating from around 1790, which shows, as Negro historian of the drama Loften Mitchell describes it, "a group of Negroes near a cabin, watching a banjo player, a drummer and dancers." The painting is entitled "The Old Plant" and clearly is intended to represent black slaves at leisure on a big plantation. These are clearly also slaves who could, if summoned, heed a master's bidding and entertain his guests. But this painting depicts them near one of their own cabins. It emphasizes their private folk behavior. And thus this painting does imply the true genesis of blackface minstrelsy and the American minstrel mode in a genuine folk figure and folk situation.

All over early America, as America moved westward from the Atlantic Coast to the banks of the Mississippi and from there onward to America's Pacific slope, this dark-skinned folk figure was much in evidence. It was not only that he was ubiquitous. He was also, even in a society that called itself democratic and prided, even preened, itself on its egalitarianism, somehow separate.

As he was unique, so was his situation. And, since he was so separate, he could be watched almost as if he were a trophy under glass. Moreover, a certain fascination did attach to watching him. He did have his gifts and his traits, his fiddling, his banjo playing, his tambourine and bones, his melodies, his fables, his tall tales, his dancing that blackface minstrelsy would later characterize as heelology, his general style of life. Constance Rourke quotes a traveler of 1795. "The blacks," said this traveler, "are the great humorists of the nation." They were, indeed, great humorists, and in their humor they were often real, or incipient, minstrels.

The second element in the minstrel mode that requires consideration is impersonation. Apparently the first impersonation of a Negro on an American stage occurred in 1769, before America became a nation, when an English actor, one Lewis Hallam, in the Englishman Isaac Bickerstaff's comic opera, *The Padlock,* played a drunken Negro on a New York stage. A real Negro, it seems, played the role of Sambo in Murdoch's drama, *Triumph of Love,* at the Chestnut Street Theatre in Philadelphia in 1795. Four years later white Gottlieb Graupner, born in Hanover, Germany, and a claimant to the distinction of being the "father of American orchestral music," at the Federal Theater in Boston, to close the second act of a play, sang a song, "The Negro Boy." He was encored repeatedly. Other stage personalities, almost all of them white, in the early years of the nineteenth century, did Negro bits of one kind or another. But probably the first impersonation of the Negro which led directly to blackface minstrelsy must be credited to a young white man named Thomas Dartmouth Rice.

Rice was born in 1808 in New York City. (Few star blackface impersonators were not born in the North.) Trained to be a wood carver, Rice soon gravitated toward the one vocational world in which he had a permanent interest, the world of the theater. The end of his 'teens found him working the towns of what was then the American West. A sort of theatrical handyman, he served as a stage carpenter, a lamplighter, and an actor in supernumerary roles. Either in Cincinnati or, more probably, Louisville his path crossed that of a Negro hostler with a hunched-up right shoulder and a rheumatic left leg, stiff at the knee. From this Negro Rice borrowed both the curious dance of a man handicapped

by an infirmity, yet still adroit of movement, and the famous
chorus, to which a rash of verses would eventually be improvised:

> First on de heel tap, den on de toe,
> Ebery time I wheel about I jump Jim Crow.
> Wheel about and turn about and do jis so,
> And every time I wheel about I jump Jim Crow.

So it was that Thomas Dartmouth Rice, in blackface, became "Jim
Crow," or "Daddy" Rice, and for the better part of twenty years,
although he was to die paralytic and impoverished, the sensation
of America and England. Late in 1832 he "jumped Jim Crow" at
the Bowery Theatre in New York City. His ecstatic audience
recalled him twenty times. In Washington he is said to have brought
the four-year-old Joseph Jefferson, who would grow up to become
one of the eminent actors of the century, on to the stage with
him, in blackface and a large sack, to plump the tiny tot out, and
then to come down toward the footlights, singing:

> Ladies and Gentlemen, I'd have you for to know
> That I've got a little darkey here that jumps Jim Crow.

In 1836 he took London by storm. Later, he was altogether as
enormous a hit in Dublin. Perhaps no individual ever matched him
as a "single" in Negro impersonation. And Rice, upon occasion,
did appear in true blackface minstrel shows. Even so, however,
the honor of initiating the true blackface minstrel show is usually
accorded to Dan Emmett, composer of the well-known song
"Dixie," and to three other white men, "Billy" Whitlock, banjoist,
Frank Bower, expert on the bone castanets, and "Dick" Pelham,
owner of a tambourine. Either late in 1842 or early in 1843, as
the Virginia Minstrels, this quartet played in New York City the
performance out of which the minstrel show was born.

Blackface minstrelsy, as a form of organized theater, lasted a
long time. Not until 1928 did the Al G. Field company, the final
survivor of hundreds of minstrel troupes, ring down the curtain
that rang out the end of professional minstrel shows. It may be
difficult now, in the days of technological theater, to realize how

successful the living theater of blackface minstrelsy once was. In the years of their prime—which would be at their very peak in the 1850's and the 1860's—the minstrel shows waxed truly like a green bay tree. They virtually took over as their particular bonanza the big towns, where they for years monopolized the best houses. One company, Bryant's Minstrels, actually played, except for an interruption of nine months in San Francisco, continuously in New York for sixteen years, nine of those years at one spot, Mechanics Hall. Nor was this company by any means the only minstrel group to stay in one town or one theater for a run of an astounding length. Moreover, there was a time when the minstrel companies, merely in trying to accede to an authentic popular demand, gave, and were long forced to continue to give, three performances a day. They could be found, too, in small towns, in villages and every hinterland. They played on the East Coast, on the West Coast, in middle America, North and South, overseas in Europe, as far afield as Hawaii and Australia, and we have at least one account of a band of Hindi minstrels playing and singing in blackface in nineteenth-century India. The minstrel show, it is true, did begin as an impersonation of the Southern Negro. But it acquired, in addition, a set form. It had a first part, a second part, and, sometimes, even, a third part. It was in the first part that the performers sat, on stage, in a semicircle with the interlocutor, who played it white and straight, in the middle, and Mr. Tambo and Mr. Bones, with their proper instruments, at either end. The first part ended with a walk-around and hoedown. The second part was called the olio and was really a variety show in which a medley of acts was presented. It was especially in the olio, which tended to absorb the occasional third part, that the connection of the minstrel show with black impersonation first grew thin and often finally in essence disappeared. The legitimate aspirations of blackface minstrelsy may be said to have resided in the impersonation of the Negro and the burlesquing of his character. The burlesquing was important and as legitimate as the impersonation. But the exhibition of virtuosity, any virtuosity, and the inclination of showmen, once they had an audience, to put on what they regarded as their own best show, supplanted genuine burlesque in blackface minstrelsy with spectacle and stunts.

From their earliest days, for obvious reasons, the minstrel shows had indulged themselves in street parades. Those parades grew larger and larger, fancier and fancier, gaudier and gaudier. So, too, and not only in the olio, did the companies. By 1880 Haverly's Mastodons carried a hundred members, with elaborate stage settings, through America into England, and beyond. But then another company appeared with, of course, one hundred and ten members, including "two bands of fourteen musicians each, a sextette of saxophone players, two drum corps of eight each, two drum majors and a quartette of mounted buglers." Meanwhile, Haverly's Mastodons by the time they arrived, in 1884, at the Drury Lane Theatre in London had expanded to eighteen end men with the traditional tambourines and bones and an additional half-dozen star end men who were presented to the audience in relays. And by this date, and later, one might well expect to see in blackface minstrelsy, for they had all appeared there with, indeed, increasing regularity, bicycle riders, club and hoop manipulators, yodelers, expert whistlers, acrobats, jugglers, contortionists, Chang, the Chinese giant, and other sideshow freaks, arias and episodes from opera, given straight or otherwise, a travesty on Sarah Bernhardt known as Sarah Heartburn, animal acts, drill teams, bird and animal imitators, pantomimists and whole plays, sometimes as farces, but (alas!) sometimes as serious attempts at serious art. As early, indeed, as 1845, Monsieur Cassimir, "the Great French Drummer," had regaled New Orleanians with an imitation on his drum of a whole battle in the Mexican war, including not only the firing of small arms and cannon, but all of the other sounds of the contending armies. As late as 1928, moreover, Al G. Field's company enacted its first part before a skyscraper background in a roof-garden setting. Not even the witty could excuse such a tableau as a cotton field in the clouds. For gradually and monumentally from blackface minstrelsy the Negro and the Negro's true agrarian world had been expunged. The humor had gone with them. The shows had been converted into extravaganzas, little, if any, different from expensive vaudeville. Once the minstrel songs had been Negro songs dealing with Negro figures: Jim Crow, Zip Coon, Dan Tucker. But, through the years, Dan Tucker had turned white. Zip Coon had sunk into oblivion beneath "Turkey in the Straw." And what was left of both had suffered the same fate as what was left of Jim Crow. It had surrendered to the version of the Negro which had come to constitute the third large element in the minstrel mode.

There was, it is certainly true, never a time, even in early Jamestown, when white Americans did not harbor some special feelings toward people who were black. Thomas Jefferson, for example, is not infrequently cited for his philosophic opposition to slavery. And there can be little doubt but that when Jefferson spoke of freedom for all he meant exactly what he said. Nevertheless, extending justice to Negroes did not also mean to Jefferson the identification of Negroes with Anglo-Saxons. White people, thought Jefferson, were more beautiful than black, more elegantly symmetrical of form. The blacks, however, seemed to him to require less sleep. They were wanting in forethought and much inferior in reason and in imagination. The love of blacks, moreover, in Jefferson's view, was "more an eager desire, than a delicate mixture of sentiment and sensation," and Negroes, as he saw them, could not grieve long, nor really be expected to reflect. Apostle of the Enlightenment that Jefferson was, he does, even so, seem conditioned to do his thinking about Negroes along racistic lines. It is hardly probable, therefore, that the first whites who impersonated Negroes were not at least a little racistic, too. Nevertheless, the animus against Negroes, within America does seem to bear some correlation to the imperial spirit of the Plantation South. The more cotton the South grew, both before and after the Civil War, the more it insisted upon an image of the Negro that would fit the Negro for the place in a Plantocracy where he belonged. Matters were not quite that simple all over America. But they were almost. The pressure of color caste affected not only Negroes. It affected also their representation. And nowhere was their representation a readier tool for racism than in blackface minstrelsy. The little darkey that jumped Jim Crow became every Negro—every Negro in real life as well as on the stage.

And so the minstrel mode, in its worst element, invaded American life, in the very process reversing a relationship, so that, instead of life dictating to art, art dictated to life. By the days between World War I and World War II, when Al Jolson, in blackface, was singing to his mammy and some Negro actresses were playing that mammy in the movies or on stage, the racistic element in the minstrel mode had become, on stage or off, a prescribed cult. It had conquered and, outlasting blackface minstrelsy as such, had put the stamp of its own minstrel mode on virtually every approach of average Americans to Negroes and Negro life.

It could not last and has not. Negroes themselves, using their own accesses to the minstrel mode, long ago began to undermine it. One has but to turn back forty years to the character of Jimboy, Negro vagrant in Langston Hughes' novel, *Not Without Laughter*, to suspect that Negro artists have been deliberately contemptuous of the old orthodoxies in the conventional American minstrel mode. Jimboy himself is a minstrel, a black wanderer who prowls America in search of a decent job, his guitar as his traveling companion, and he sings the blues. W. C. Handy, emerging out of rural Alabama, was to become, after his real life in Memphis and his real pilgrimage to New York, the recognized "Father of the Blues." Both the real W. C. Handy and the unreal Jimboy speak to us of what Charles Keil has called, in his book, *Urban Blues*, "an expressive male role within urban lower-class Negro culture—that of the contemporary bluesman." Thus, when Ralph Ellison, in *Invisible Man*, has Tod Clifton "drop out of history"—that is, cease to be his true black self—and so permits Clifton to peddle Sambo, a dancing doll manipulated as a puppet, to street crowds in downtown, white Manhattan, the episode constitutes a perfect metaphor for the racism in the minstrel mode of blackface minstrelsy. Jimboy and W. C. Handy are, on the other hand, while not perfect metaphors for a countermovement to this racism, at least important signposts. For undoubtedly in very actual life the Negro who was once in America's rural South has migrated to the city like, incidentally, both Handy and Jimboy. Undoubtedly, moreover, that Negro has created his own sense of himself. Undoubtedly, finally, he has found, and deputized, his own interpreter of this sense, and that interpreter—Ray Charles, B. B. King, and other artists of their kind and tone—is a bluesman, a black minstrel made by blacks, and, indeed, the latest strain in an American minstrel mode that was always Negro in its origins and largely Negro in its context but now at last bids fair, with jazzmen and the blues, against the background of an urban scene, to be more Negroid in its creative soul.

Comedy and Reality in Local Color Fiction, 1865–1900

Arlin Turner

In an introduction to a collection of *The World's Wit and Humor* (1904), Joel Chandler Harris wrote:

There seems never to have been a day in our history when the American view of things generally was not charged or trimmed with humor. . . . In the light of his own humor, the American stands forth as the conqueror of circumstance, who has created for himself the most appalling responsibilities, which he undertakes and carries out with a wink and a nod, whistling a hymn or a ragtime tune, to show that he is neither weary nor downhearted.

The creator of Uncle Remus could speak with authority of his own about American humor, and he might have quoted other authorities from early in the previous century. He could have mentioned an essay in the *Democratic Review* for September, 1845, when the humor of Hawthorne and Poe and Simms was discussed; or an essay on a later generation of humorists in *Harper's Magazine* for April, 1890; or an article entitled "A Century of American Humor" in *Munsey's Magazine* for July, 1901; or one by William Peterfield Trent entitled "A Retrospect of American Humor," published in the *Century Magazine* for November, 1901. Looking back over the preceding century, Trent characterized the humor that he thought distinctly American:

It is, on the whole, a broad humor that frequently does not disdain the aid of bad spelling and bad puns. It deals in incongruities of expression; it accentuates oddities; it sets the commonplace in ridiculous relief; it bur-

157

lesques pretensions; it laughs at domestic, social, and political mishaps, when they are not too serious; it makes game of foibles and minor vices; it delights to shock the prim, but sedulously avoids all real grossness; it sometimes approximates sheer though innocuous mendacity.

Across the ocean, Thomas Carlyle had spoken in 1840 of a "broad Brobdignag grin of true humor" such as might be caught "out of the American backwoods." Others in England besides Carlyle had read examples of frontier humor reprinted in *Bentley's Magazine* and in an anthology entitled *Traits of American Humor*, in which Judge T. C. Haliburton, creator of Sam Slick, had characterized three regions of American humor: that of the middle states, like the English, "at once manly and hearty, and though embellished by fancy, not exaggerated"; that of the West, like the Irish, "extravagant, reckless, rollicking, and kind hearted"; and that of the Yankees, like the Scottish, "sly, cold, quaint, practical, sarcastic."

It was the humor of the West, Carlyle's "broad Brobdignag grin of true humor," that received most attention, though often uncomfortable attention on both sides of the Atlantic. This was the humor that William Gilmore Simms, reflecting his kinship with the great Elizabethans he so warmly admired, found ideal reading for the steamboat or the railway car. Simms added, in deference to the formal literary tastes of Charleston, that such humorous books would of course not be brought into the house when the traveler reached home. This was the humor that the *North American Review* lamented in the same voice it lamented the common schools; "Common Schools make us a nation of readers. But common schools, alas! do little to inculcate taste or discrimination in the choice of reading. The mass of the community has a coarse digestion. . . . It likes horse-laughs." When Nathaniel Hawthorne visited Washington in 1862, he wrote in an essay for the *Atlantic Monthly* about the "delectable stories" for which President Lincoln was "so celebrated." "A good many of them are afloat upon the common talk of Washington," he remarked, "and certainly are the aptest, pithiest, and funniest little things imaginable; though, to be sure, they smack of the frontier freedom, and would not always bear repetition in the drawing-room, or on the immaculate pages of the Atlantic." Even this reference to the Lincoln stories was struck from the copy that went into the *Atlantic Monthly;* it is preserved because it was restored to the essay later, along with the remainder of Hawthorne's sketch of Lincoln.

During the 1840's and 1850's this earthy, extravagant humor appeared in the escapades of Henry Clay Lewis's Louisiana Swamp Doctor, Johnson Jones Hooper's Simon Suggs, and George Washington Harris's Sut Lovingood. These characters had descendants a generation later in David Ross Locke's Petroleum Vesuvius Nasby, for example, and Mark Twain's King and Duke in *Huckleberry Finn.* But such crude, raucous characters had been relegated all along to subliterary writings, and in the decades following the Civil War were hardly more acceptable in polite letters. Since the 1840's, the less abrasive comedy of Irving, Hawthorne, Lowell, Holmes, and Simms had been discussed in the magazines and had appeared in anthologies of American humor. It was such a genial fireside humor that prevailed in the second half of the nineteenth century and especially set the tone of the local color fiction of the time.

The antebellum humor—no less in A. B. Longstreet's rural Georgia that in Seba Smith's Downingville, Down East in Maine— had a strong ingredient of the local. After the war, soldiers from New England who had served in New Orleans, or soldiers from Alabama who had served in Pennsylvania or had been imprisoned in Ohio—or the families of soldiers—were primed to read about regions and peoples they had never known existed before the war. Publishers, editors, and authors kept these readers in mind. They kept in mind also the goal of reuniting the divided country and consequently strove to encourage understanding and sympathy. Suffering and bitterness remained, to be sure; Jefferson Davis, Albert Taylor Bledsoe, and others continued to debate the issues and the events of the war. But the fiction writers seemed ready to consider the hostilities closed and to distribute loyalty and bravery and generosity among both Yankees and Confederates. As a rule the local colorists dealt not with generals and politicians, but with the common folk, who were most appealing when they were most isolated in their remote communities. Hence the plots were likely to turn on elemental, if not primitive, considerations; and a story set in a remote section among distinctive people might be especially attractive—and most attractive, Bret Harte was to discover, when the characters thought and acted at the level of commonplace, homely morality.

In the decades after the Civil War, the stream of humor from the prewar years took two courses, producing in the one comedy independent of place and in the other exploitation of the local. Artemus Ward, Petroleum Vesuvius Nasby, and others aimed at a wide audience through national magazines and newspaper columns and the lecture platform. Without the local context in which the earlier humorous characters had existed—James Russell Lowell's Hosea Biglow, Down East, for example, or Johnson Jones Hooper's Simon Suggs, in Alabama—these humorists turned to national topics, mainly political, and developed a battery of humorous devices that had little kinship with real characters or actual speech. Artemus Ward's trickery of language and spelling was appropriate to his antics among the Mormons or his visit to the Tower of London. He followed his own prescription for a new school of humorists: "Let them seek to embody the wit and humor of all parts of the country. . . . Let them form a nucleus which will draw to itself all the waggery and wit of America."

But the comedy that had been recognized at least since 1830 as native American had not been simply waggery and wit. It had displayed the rich variety, "the incongruities of the new world," in the words of F. L. Pattee in 1915 "—the picturesque gathering of peoples like the Puritans, the Indians, the cavaliers, the Dutch, the negroes and the later immigrants; the makeshifts of the frontier, the vastness and the richness of the land, the leveling effects of democracy, the freedom of life, and the independence of spirit." The low characters and the horselaughs that earlier had been banished from polite letters had begun to gain status at the middle of the century from the books and the platform readings of Charles Dickens. In keeping with the mood of reconciliation fostered in the postwar literature, moreover, the characters were drawn with greater humanity and greater sympathy. The peculiar, the odd, the unexpected continued to be exploited for comic effect, but there was a changed tone, deriving in part from a Dickensian view of human nature and in part from a greater awareness and tolerance of local particularities.

The writers acknowledged an obligation to record local scenes, characters, and manners with accuracy befitting social historians. Writing in an era of literary realism, in varying degrees they sought to augment the literal truthfulness of their stories and novels by close attention to actuality and exactness of details. They had in mind readers they assumed to be eager to know the characters being described, in their particular local setting and in all aspects of their lives. William Dean Howells noted in 1872 the vogue of fiction portraying the diverse regions of the country and added, "Gradually, but pretty surely, the whole varied field of American life is coming into view in American fiction." Joel Chandler Harris more than once urged the importance of the local in literature. In an editorial for the Atlanta *Constitution* of January 25, 1880, not long before the first collection of his Uncle Remus stories appeared, he declared that "no enduring work of the imagination has ever been produced save by a mind in which the provincial instinct was the controlling influence." Later, in the Chicago *Current*, he offered American authors further limitations: "I think, moreover, that no novel or story can be genuinely American, unless it deals with the *common people*, that is, the *country people*."

Dialect became for these purveyors of the local an important aid to individual characterization and to the portrayal of communities. Irving, Poe, Hawthorne, and Melville made little use of dialect speech. Any attempt on their pages to indicate that a Negro or an Indian or an Irishman or a Dutchman had a distinctive speech was likely to be casual and to suggest whim on the part of the author rather than care. The humorists of the same period saw more need to give their characters appropriate speech; but most of them showed little concern for either accuracy or completeness in representing the dialect. James Russell Lowell and George Washington Harris were two notable exceptions. Lowell was a careful student of New England speech, as he made clear in his introduction to the Second Series of *The Biglow Papers*, and was equally careful in representing that speech in his satiric portraits. Harris had an acute ear for the language spoken in the mountains of eastern Tennessee, and he took such pains to record the speech of his illiterate mountaineer, Sut Lovingood, that he produced some of the most forbidding dialect recorded in our literature.

When George W. Cable began in the early 1870's writing the stories of Creole New Orleans that appeared in *Scribner's Monthly* and were collected in 1879 in the volume *Old Creole Days*, he carried his reverence for accuracy over into his recording of local speech. He knew French as a second native language, and he mastered the various levels of Creole patois that mingled on the *banquettes*, the sidewalks, of the old city. He had ample testimony from his friends Mark Twain and Howells and those who wrote him from the offices of his New York publishers that the speech of his Creole characters fascinated them. They spoke nothing but Creole, they wrote him, and they inserted Creole phrases in their letters. Mark Twain liked to read aloud the speech of the ancient Creole, the title character in the story "Jean-ah Poquelin." Howells took special delight in the Creole mother and daughter in Cable's first novel, *The Grandissimes*, as did also the Scottish author James M. Barrie.

From the outset, however, the difficulties inherent in the dialect were apparent. Edward King, who had heard Cable read his own stories aloud in New Orleans, secured the acceptance of the first story for *Scribner's Monthly* by reading it to the editor and thus reducing the obstacle of the written dialect. More than one of Cable's friends, reading his early stories, thought he lost narrative effectiveness in his pursuit of literal accuracy in all respects, including the dialect. In attempting to show the French Creole's pronunciation of the long vowel *a* and the consonant *r*, to cite the most bothersome instances, he laid a burden on his readers that brought protests from them—and from his editors in turn. His response was to reduce the dialect in later stories and in reprinting his first novel, *The Grandissimes*, in 1883, three years after its first publication, to simplify the speech of the Creole characters. He had comparable difficulties with the speech of a Negro from the remote backwoods, the Italian, the German, and especially the Irish segments of the New Orleans population who appeared in his fiction. With more experience, he learned to rely less on full transcription of dialect and more on occasional words, phrases, pronunciations, and locutions to suggest rather than delineate the dialect being spoken.

The literary use of dialect had been complicated by the misspellers, such as Artemus Ward, who admitted any degree of trickery and stunting in language for comic effects. Before writing his first story, Cable had decided against misspelling and had been pleased that Mark Twain had reached the same conclusion. While the literary comedians, as they are plausibly called, continued to manipulate language as itself the material of comedy, the fiction writers who gave first allegiance to the real and the local sought means of representing dialect speech as accurately and fully as possible without sacrificing readability. Grace King and Kate Chopin, chief among those who followed Cable in writing about the French of Louisiana, could profit directly from his experimentation. One of the earliest to delineate the plantation Negroes was Irwin Russell, who knew them from boyhood in Port Gibson, Mississippi, and had been reproducing their speech, in both verse and prose, several years before he died in 1879 at the age of twenty-six. Joel Chandler Harris and Thomas Nelson Page praised without reserve the work Russell had done in fields they cultivated later, saying that he "woke the first echo" and that if he had lived, they "would have taken back seats." To the novice in reading it, the speech of Harris's Uncle Remus is difficult, but the simplicity of the tales and the recurrence of a relatively few expressions enable the reader to gain a feeling for the dialect and some facility in reading it in a surprisingly short time. Apparently Thomas Nelson Page's first story, "Marse Chan," was held out of print by the editor of the *Century Magazine* four years after its acceptance for fear the readers would rebel against a story written entirely in the dialect of a plantation Negro.

Among the dialects of the local colorists, none created such difficulties for the readers as the dialects of the French in Louisiana and the ex-slaves of the South. The rural and small-town New Englanders of Harriet Beecher Stowe and Sarah Orne Jewett speak a dialect greatly leveled out from that of Lowell's Hosea Biglow. The Pike dialect that Bret Harte knew in the West and Mark Twain used as early as "The Jumping Frog of Calaveras County" was less a dialect than an illiterate modification of commonplace speech. There has been no tendency to challenge Mark Twain's statement that *Huckleberry Finn* contains "the Missouri negro dialect; the extremest form of the backwoods Southwestern dialect; the ordinary 'Pike County' dialect; and four modified varieties of this last"; nor his further statement that he possessed "personal familiarity with these several forms of speech." Recognizing speech to be an important indicator of character, whether actual or fictional, Mark Twain wanted to gain in his own fictional writings all he could from this aid to character delineation. And like the others writing tales and novels depicting distinctive peoples in singular localities, he realized the contribution that dialect would make all along the spectrum of humor, from genial comedy to extravagant buffoonery.

As is true of all humorous portraits, the comic effects achieved in local color fiction depend heavily on the relation of the author to his characters, that is, to the subjects he undertakes to picture in their special localities. We are accustomed to saying of Irwin Russell that he knew from close observation the plantation Negroes whose speech and songs and beliefs he recorded in his poems; of Joel Chandler Harris that on the middle Georgia plantation where he lived from the age of twelve he knew models for his fictional characters; of Kate Chopin that while she lived in Natchitoches, Louisiana, she knew the Cajuns she afterward portrayed, for example, in the stories collected in *Bayou Folk;* of Sarah Orne Jewett that on trips with her father, a physician, to visit his rural patients she observed such people as appear in her works; of Mary Noailles Murfree that she went with her family to spend each summer in the mountain region she recreates in her novels and stories. The most we can say of Bret Harte is that he visited the mining camps he portrayed.

It cannot be said that these and others of the local colorists belong to the people they write about. They are in varying degrees outsiders assembling materials for literary use and writing mainly for readers who know nothing of the regions and peoples being presented. That is to say that the laughing in local color fiction is normally *at* rather than *with* the characters. The distinctive peoples who appear in this fiction have rarely been among its readers. When they have been (as were some of the New Orleans Creoles reading Cable's stories), they have been as a rule less than pleased with the fictional portraits of themselves and their ancestors. Understandably they have been most critical of the comedy the authors find in their speech, manners, and other personal traits. But the essential nature of local color writing is involved here, and it would not be easy to argue that the only legitimate portrait is a self-portrait.

Rural Humor of the Late Nineteenth Century

C. Carroll Hollis

When all of the information on book and magazine publishing, lecture tours, newspaper columns, and bar and barbershop gossip is put on computers, it will be apparent that in the last quarter of the nineteenth century the form of cultural communication of greatest popularity was humor. More people read or listened to humorists than to historical romancers, oral or printed sermons, sentimental tales, western stories, drama, domestic novels, local color stories, or Horatio Alger's dime novels. But why this great attention to laughter? And what has happened to the humorists who answered so abundantly the nation's need for laughter?

It is not my task to answer these questions completely, for I wish to speak only of rural humor, which is but a part, if the largest part, of the humor of the period. But what we find out about the rural humor will provide a good part of the larger answer to the role of humor in American life. From the end of the Civil War to the beginning of the Spanish American War in 1898, American life was outwardly peaceful, not even the Indian skirmishes being of sufficient significance to give a name to the period. But if outwardly peaceful in the sense that drafts, military economy, and war patriotism did not dominate the country's attention, it was nevertheless a time of seething social change.

Note the different tags social and cultural historians use to focus on some part or other of this period. The Age of Inventions, often known as the age of the tinkerers, when there were more patents than for any period before or since, when Bell, Edison, Ford, the Wright brothers were perfecting the experiments that were to change the life of the new century so drastically. The Bible Belt, a term relating to fundamentalism in religion, with the great popular revivalists Moody and Sankey, the choir practice, the ladies' aid societies, with the concomitant opposition of the town atheist, Bob Ingersoll, and apologists for Darwin. The Age of Expansion, with the final settling of the West, the *laissez faire* economics, the cattle baron and the cowboy, the expanding railroads and expanding railroad scandals. The Genteel Tradition, with its "ideality" of the arts, the overprotection of women from the realities of life, Comstock and the Watch and Ward Society, the heyday of the historical romance with *Ben Hur, When Knighthood Was in Flower*, and *To Have and to Hold*, the sentimental falsification of childhood in *Little Women, Little Lord Fauntleroy*, and *Little Shepherd of Kingdom Come*. The Gilded Age, of Mark Twain's novel of the speculative instinct at work, but with its new moneyed aristocracy, the excessive display of excessive wealth, the Gibson girl fashions, the spectacular rise and fall of great fortunes. The Melting Pot Mistake, with the sudden influx of those from Eastern or Southern Europe with strange (therefore un-American) customs, names, religious practices, the Yellow Peril in the Far West, the Scandinavians in the farm states, the Irish on the railroads, the Jews in the cities, the Poles in the coal mines. The Muckrakers, with their exposé of the big city bosses, the patent medicine racket, the Standard Oil monopoly, the Wall Street swindlers, the beef trust. The New South, with its corresponding Tragic Era for blacks, the KKK, the carpetbagger, the poor white, the Lost Cause syndrome. The Robber Barons, with Rockefellers, Carnegies, Goulds, and Morgans, and their opposition in the Molly Maguires, the Knights of Labor, Eugene Debs, and the Haymarket Riot. And finally the Rise of the City, with its new industrialism, the sweat shops, the tenements, the skyscraper.

Of these various elements of American social life, it is only this last that needs further explanation for the understanding of rural humor, but it should be remembered that practically every item in the above paragraph becomes the subject for the humor of the period. But as to the rise of the city it is important to remember that only in 1900 had America ceased to be predominantly an agricultural and rural nation. And even in those final decades of the century the bulk of the native-born residents of the booming cities had come from farms or little towns. Consequently rural humor is the basis of native American humor from the very beginning with the Farmers' Almanacs to Will Rogers. The great substratum of American rural humor is so broad in fact that much of it has remained at the folk level, anonymous, pervasive, and indigenous to its region (Yankee or Down-East humor, the Old Southwest, the tall tale of the frontier, the gold rush humor of the Far West). What has happened is that those who have capitalized on, or who have otherwise exploited, rural humor have enormous resources in the society about them. The rural humorists in the last part of the nineteenth century had little more to do than to focus an inherited attitude and technique on some one or more of the new inventions, fads, changes, scandals, or developments in the fast-moving national evolution.

Accordingly, there is a vast anonymity in this humor. It was not that these writers imitated each other but they all imitated—or, better, mirrored and reflected—a common native attitude. If one removes such identifying features as place names, characters' names, and dialect, it would be almost impossible to reassemble a mixed-up table of contents for any of the numerous anthologies of American humor published in this period. One could identify regional humorists, to be sure, and also Marietta Holley, Harriet Spofford, and Frances Whitcher from the twenty or so men who sold as widely, but within these groups the distinctions are minimal.

If we limit the group of rural humorists between 1875 and 1900 to those whose sales were over 500,000 there are still twenty-five or so, and it would be futile for the purposes of this series to talk about each of them. Rather I wish to consider them as a group, identifying only those works as are cited, and treating their humorous efforts in terms of their common attitudes, technique, audience, subject matter, and permanent contribution. Many humorists who adopted the misspelling devices for extra comic effect were also rural humorists (Artemus Ward, Josh Billings, Petroleum Vesuvius Nasby, Orpheus C. Kerr), but they are receiving separate treatment elsewhere in this series and so will be omitted here. Similarly,

Mark Twain and Joel Chandler Harris share many of the characteristics of rural humor, but here too their separate treatment pre-
cludes consideration in this discussion.

Other commentators in this series will have sufficiently defined
humor so that we need here only to direct our attention to the
group of writers who spoke from a realistic country background,
using the humorous devices of exaggeration, malapropisms, euphemism, misquotation, mixed metaphor, anticlimax, and understatement, to an audience composed of rural, village, or small-town
people, or if in the city those of rural background and conviction.
Their subject matter varies as widely as the list of characteristics
of the period mentioned at the beginning of this discussion. Indeed,
one way of knowing the key elements in this or any other period in
American life is to notice what the humorists pick to laugh at or
ridicule. After considering these common attitudes, audiences, and
subjects treated, I would like to assess the contribution of the humorists and to indicate what has happened to them in literary history, for they have all long since vanished from our libraries and
standard reading lists.

The humorist who does no more than tell a joke does not have a
sufficiently involved and committed concern with his subject or his
audience to be remembered at all. One of the crushing disappointments to any young reader is to go from one anecdote to another,
page after page, in *Joe Miller's Joke Book* or any similar collection,
looking for the uproarious, witty, clever, subtle, or broad story
that will tickle the funny bone or bring the shout of laughter. To
the reflective student this may be a useful disappointment, for he
soon realizes that the humor of the skeleton joke is more in the
teller than the words, in the oral and not the printed rendition.
What then is needed is something more than the gag, the absurd
situation, the unexpected reversal, the clever pun, the heights or
depths of human folly, or to say this another way, these must be
presented in a form that brings out the humorous significance to the
reader.

One way of doing so was to establish a *persona*, a country or
small-town character through whom the humor was presented. Not
all, but many of the rural humorists did adopt this approach. So,

Marietta Holley is long forgotten in her own name but as Samantha, Josiah Allen's wife, became a household word for her homely kitchen philosophizing about men and manners in ubiquitous Jonesville. New Hampshire lawyer and later judge, Henry Augustus Shute, became Plupy, a young rural adolescent, so he could tell of the hilarious adventures of his friends Beany and Pewt in *The Real Diary of a Real Boy*. Charles Heber Clark, who came from the Maryland countryside to be a Philadelphia newspaper reporter, adopted the name Max Adeler for his best selling *Out of the Hurly Burly or Life in an Odd Corner*, in which he guides the villagers through the self-revelation of their multiple human weaknesses.

Like Clark (or Adeler) many of the rural humorists were journalists and wrote from their awareness of what people were interested in. Sometimes their success as humorists led to the dropping of newspaper connections, as did the best known of the group, Edgar W. Nye. Best known as Bill Nye, he was born in Maine, grew up in Wisconsin, and went to Wyoming Territory when he was twenty-five to edit the Laramie *Boomerang*. He read his funny sketches first to a local and then to increasingly distant audiences, printed these humorous skits in book after book, so that his total sales were well over five million. Sometimes, with those who maintained the journalistic connection, the humorist was known by his newspaper, as James Bailey, the "Danbury *News* Man," or Robert Burdette, the "Burlington *Hawkeye* Man," who delivered his famous sketch "The Rise and Fall of the Moustache" to five thousand audiences all over the country.

If the humorist did not establish solely for himself a *persona* through whom he made his observations on American life, he might establish one or more characters to whom, as successive adventures took place, readers could look with familiarity and expectation. Thus George Wilbur Peck created his mischievous monster, known as Peck's Bad Boy, who played one savage practical joke after another on his gullible papa. The cruelty of his character did not hurt his creator's own advancement, for Peck went on to become mayor of Milwaukee and then governor of the state. Charles B. Lewis remained only a Detroit *Free Press* reporter, but under the print shop pseudonym M. Quad he created the Bowsers, the long-suffering, patient, all-knowing wife, with her support of the impetuous, excitable, hot-tempered, conceited Mr. Bowser, with his long series of domestic follies.

Through such *personae* or established characters the rural humorists surveyed the institutions and concerns of American people to show the disparity between what people thought some institution was supposed to perform and what actually took place, to point out folly of exaggerated concern with some part of life to the neglect of other equally important parts, to ridicule the silly sentimentality of the period. Beyond the eight humorists mentioned above, there are some twenty more of comparable reputation in their day. In addition there were some forty or fifty others of local fame or short-lived popularity whose names can only be recovered by exploring the magazines and papers of that time or examining the many multivolumed collections of American Wit and Humor that are found on every publisher's list in the last years of the century. These scores of less important humorists fail less in technique, for the tricks of the humorist's trade were easy to emulate, than in attitude. Critics will differ in the number and character of the best fifty or so rural humorists, but I wish to use as my standard for the selection of the top twenty that quality of detached critical intelligence that has always marked the world's great humorists. There is no Chaucer, no Rabelais, no Cervantes, and no Molière, Fielding, Goethe, or Byron in the American group, except for Mark Twain. But if these writers are not Mark Twains they are with him in their amused, tolerant, yet critical concern with the quality of American life.

In all areas and places in American society, whether high or low, rich or poor, college-trained or self-educated, city or country, there have always been enough citizens of native shrewdness, homely common sense, and realistic awareness to keep the country from being threatened by the excesses which the national freedom permits. Jefferson put his confidence for the nation's health in the farmer, diversified tradesmen, and the small property owner, even as he feared the city with its crowding mass, or *canaille* as he called it. Cooper in his sober indictment, *An American Democrat*, his unhumorous satire, *The Monikins*, his dramatic disaster, *Upside Down, or Philosophy in Petticoats* (the only time it was ever reprinted for popular consumption was in an American Humor anthology of 1894) gave warning of democratic dangers. So did foreign visitors as Alexis de Tocqueville, Mrs. Frances Trollope, Harriet Martineau, Count Gurowski, or Charles Dickens. Whether the farmers and small-town citizens were as self-disciplined and wise as Jefferson and others believed is hard to prove, but it is obvious that because they were isolated on farms or scattered in small groups they did not, because they could not physically do so whether tempted or not, react *en masse* to some demagogue, or religious fanatic, or bank scandal, or new invention, fad, disease, or cure.

Although Jefferson seems not to have had much of a sense of humor, that limitation had little to do with his confidence in the safety of a rural society. But a far more significant safety valve than he realized was a native humor that provided psychological protection for its participants (both joker and audience) from the desperate loneliness of frontier living, from the crop disasters or natural disasters, from the assorted dangers of epidemics, raids, feuds, and foreclosures. When humor was not present or could not be fostered in time to laugh fanaticism away, national disgraces did occur from the witchcraft trials in Salem of 1692 to the McCarthy trials of 1952. But all through the nineteenth century the country-side was thought to be and perhaps was the nursery of American virtues, the anchor in national storms, the beacon light of freedom and opportunity to the oppressed of the Old World. Although there seems to be a fair amount of wishful thinking in much of this patriotic picture, there was a period between the Civil War and the Spanish American War when one of the best preservers of national sanity was found in rural humor.

The critical intelligence that I find in these country humorists is best seen through a cumulation of examples, a demonstration impossible here. Yet the deduction such a list would reveal is the faculty or power the humorist has for seeing life as it is, his understanding of his own and his neighbor's relation to it, his ability to focus his consciousness on these social relationships with detachment and without rancor or prejudice or fear. These qualities are potentially in all citizens but exist in daily life (or are developed) among the balanced, healthy, level-headed, shrewd, and wise people who set the tone of the times without realizing it—and these make up the humorist's audience. All humorists accept the idea of original sin, although few would accept its doctrinal and institutional exemplifications. As man, so society is subject to social sins none of which is original except in the peculiarities of their particular manifestations in time, place, and circumstance. The critical function which the rural humorists performed was to awaken that audience to the follies and sins of the time (and to be awakened to your folly is to be cured of it) by the healing gift of laughter.

Being serious about humor is one of the great follies of the academician, and I see that I have already apotheosized these forgotten humorists in a fashion to amuse them could they be aware of it. Charles Farrar Browne (Artemus Ward), something of a philosopher among American native humorists, once said of his fellows: ". . . they have always done the most toward helping virtue on its pilgrimage, and the truth has found more aid from them than from all the grave polemists and solid writers that have ever spoken or written. . . . They have helped the truth along *without encumbering it with themselves*." In the underlining I follow Albert Jay Nock who quotes this passage, for it captures the final qualities of the rural humorists we have been discussing. As we move away from this tradition we move into the powerful personal writing of the private genius. I mean no discredit to Melville and Whitman, or James and Dickinson, or Howells and Lanier, or Crane and Norris, for of course no one would wish to be without the poems and novels they wrote in this period. But it is true that we study the works of these eight unique and special persons through the knowledge we have of the artists themselves. By contrast, the eight humorists mentioned earlier are as transparently anonymous as the audience they wrote for. In accepting the truth of Melville's *Clarel* and *Billy Budd*, we accept it with Melville's personal shaping, his distortions, emphases, passions. And so for the other artists, and more power to them.

But the humorists absent themselves to serve as mirrors of the assorted foibles of their day. I do not claim for them any conscious abnegation in deference to a higher than personal goal. They were craftsmen and craftswomen with undisguised money-making incentives, and this motive applies to all hundred or so I have examined, including the score I think most effective. The difference is that the twenty or so had the critical intelligence to perform for their generation the critical function I have noted above.

Thus Thomas Bailey Aldrich in his *Story of a Bad Boy* writes a sweet tale and semiautobiography that many admired but few believed. And so G. W. Peck corrected the archness of Aldrich's characterization by presenting *Peck's Bad Boy*, who was as excessive in his badness as his counterpart was in virtue. Similarly Frances Hodgson Burnett's *Little Lord Fauntleroy* was so excessively refined, with name to match, that Henry Shute's *Real Boy*, Plupy, and his companions Beany and Pewt, were needed to restore the balance. Again the Wright brothers tinkered and dreamed and got their machine up for a few seconds to collapse with a crash, although they finally accomplished what hundreds of other tinkerers had tried and failed. So John Godfrey Saxe reminded his age of the continued applicability of the Greek myth in his comic poem "Icarus," and J. T. Trowbridge improved the tale, the verse, and the comic moral in his "Darius Green and His Flying Machine."

But it is futile to set up these parallels, for the list would be so long as to defeat its purpose. Indeed in going through Marshall Wilder's 1907 ten-volume collection, *The Wit and Humor of America,* I find almost every folly, danger, prepossession, freak, new departure, and disaster that threatened American sanity was met with a rejoinder by one of the rural humorists. The only disturbance in our social evolution that they failed to meet was the union crisis in the labor versus management battles that marked the period. Perhaps because of their own rural background, as well as that of their audiences, they were not able to grasp the issue, for I find no treatment in rural humor of the essential correctness of the union position on organization, child labor, workman's compensation, shorter hours, all matters that we now take for granted. But except for this important oversight, and a few less important ones, it is surprising how widespread was the humorists' net. I doubt that they were all successful in freeing the nation from its errors any more than Mark Twain could stop the Philippine take-over with "The War Prayer" and "To the Person Sitting in Darkness," but in all cases it reminded those who were worried about our growing imperialism of the errors of the time so that they could more readily restore sanity when the fever of that particular act had subsided.

So much of what Mark Twain did was done also by Bill Nye and many other rural humorists. Why is it then that Clemens is remembered and Nye and the others forgotten? The question contains its own answer, for it is just because we have singled out Mark Twain (and justifiably so) to represent the dazzling best in native American humor that his less accomplished or less artistic contemporaries have faded to comparative shade. But there is more to the discrepancy in reputation than this, for indeed Clemens does assert his personality, his rage at injustice, his hatred of hypocrisy, his scorn of the gullible grubs who were asking to be gulled. Less personal in most of his work than any of the other eight novelists or poets mentioned above, he is also much more personal than any of the humorists mentioned, or indeed than any humorist in American letters of any period or classification.

A still further reason for the loss of readers for these humorists is the form of the humor itself and the manner of its publication. The very concern with contemporary life imposed a circumscribed set of subjects. Samantha's acid jabs at Josiah Allen's unreasoned insistence on male superiority was written in 1872, almost fifty years before the Nineteenth Amendment gave women the right to vote and a century before the equal rights laws of our time. Accordingly, one of the best sections in her first book is now of interest to historians, not citizens. Not only are the subjects that were most interesting to the humorist's initial audience of little interest to later generations, but they are also hurt by the nature of their publication. This impediment applies in fact to some of Mark Twain's work, although the volumes for which he is best known have escaped.

What I mean is that almost all of the humorists wrote sketches, essays, anecdotes, or what we sometimes call short short stories. Much of the original appeal of these humorists was that they wrote or spoke in short units for oral presentation or for a newspaper column. The great popularity of the sketches led to solid cover publication of collections of the small units, one item following another in rapid order. I happen to have four volumes of Bill Nye's before me, and I find in the *Red Book* he has seventy selections in 389 pages, in *Guest at Ludlow* there are twenty-eight items in 262 pages, for *Bill Nye and Boomerang* there are 114 in 286 pages, and *Baled Hay*, with absurdly small print, 138 selections in the 320-page book. The average of four pages per essay or sketch is typical not only of Nye's work but of most of the others, which would make a full column in a newspaper or a page of a standard-sized magazine. But note that we would read the rest of the newspaper or magazine also, and perhaps another skit or two of a different humorist written in a different pattern, and be otherwise involved in many other activities before we picked up the next Nye humorous essay. James Redpath and Major Pond, who managed most of these humorists on their national speaking tours, found out very early that the best arrangement to guarantee enthusiastic audience response was to have a mixed program, so Mark Twain and George Washington Cable appeared together. Bill Nye's most successful tour was when he shared the stage with James Whitcomb Riley. All I am getting at here is that with all the humor, skill, and critical perception at Nye's command (and I use him as typical of the group), and with the most sympathetic and expectant audience any humorist could ask for, still it is almost impossible to read one of his books all the way through. One could read the first and the second with responsive chuckles, but the third would seem less funny, for the fourth one would have to concentrate to keep the mind from wandering, for the fifth one might falter but proceed, with occasional skimming, by the sixth one would know what was going to happen as soon as one determined the subject matter, by the seventh, if one got that far, the formula would be so patently obvious that one would put the book aside with a sigh of disappointment.

All art has pattern, design, formula, but as the oldest principle in aesthetics assures us it cannot be, must not be, obvious, *artis est celare artem*. Only two writers who relate to the rural humorists but are not of them seem to have escaped the general neglect of the group, Joel Chandler Harris and Mark Twain. The special quality of *Uncle Remus* has made Harris's work something of a children's classic, and thus in a quite different category from the humorists treated here. Mark Twain escaped this fatal impediment by writing longer sketches and stories, providing continuity between them (as in *Roughing It*), but even so there is a notable failing of interest in some of the late volumes that are little more than collections of anecdotal sketches. The individual story is fine by itself, but when one reads a number of them *seriatim* the problem noted above appears even with our greatest humorist. But, of course, it is the Mark Twain of the novels that we remember best, in large measure because our interest grows with each page. But all the other rural humorists, by the very facility of their skill in exploiting the short sketch for humorous purposes, limited their audience to their own contemporaries.

If, then, these humorists had only such an audience, and if their writing is not of the lasting skill of Mark Twain, and if their subjects are dated beyond recall, are they worthy of attention at all? As America became more urban, educated, sophisticated, it is perfectly true that their reputations vanished. With the turn of the century, the farm, the country town, the simple trades were scorned rather than remembered fondly. With Edgar Lee Masters' *Spoon River Anthology*, Sherwood Anderson's *Winesburg, Ohio*, Sinclair Lewis's *Main Street*, H. L. Mencken's regular "American Credo" section in each month's *American Mercury*, the rural and village background of American life lost its champions. There were new humorists, to be sure, but they adjusted to new national needs and new media—to the comic strip and cartoons, to movie, radio, and television, to *Vanity Fair, Ballyhoo, College Humor, Esquire, New Yorker, Playboy*, and *Mad Comics*.

What then is the permanent contribution of these writers? Chiefly, and almost only, in their guarding and preserving of our national sanity. When we consider how fragile a civilization is, how especially fragile it is in a democracy where freedom permits the growth and expression of antidemocratic ideas and programs, we realize how necessary it is to encourage anything that will help the nation maintain its balance, flexibility, and inner control through the good will of its citizens. What works in the political sphere applies equally to the social and cultural spheres and to all other areas of our national existence. For some forty years the rural humorists served the nation well in alerting their audiences to the assorted follies, perversions, dangers about them. This service was not as seriously intended or as patriotically motivated as my statement may indicate, for these writers wrote for money, not medals. But admitting so much does not detract from their service, it only makes them professionals. Their contribution, then, was more journalistic than literary. If we owe them any debt, it is one of gratitude for what they were able to do for their time, not for ours. But if we cannot read them with any great glee or zest, we can wish that we had their counterparts. In our own tortured time, when our democratic civilization seems even more shaky than it did a century ago, we could certainly use the same sort of treatment they gave theirs.

Henry James and the Comedy of the New England Conscience

George Core

Henry James is one of the few great novelists the United States has produced, one of the handful of American writers of the first rank who have an undeniable place in world literature. The chief reason that the greater part of James's fiction has stood the test of time and that it will continue to speak directly and convincingly to readers hinges on his brilliance as a comic writer. Indeed this is the most general thing that one can say about him. I would qualify this statement by adding that James is an ironic comedian, but at the same time insist that it will not do to see him as writing chiefly in a mode other than comedy. On occasion, it is true, James wrote sustained tragicomedy and even tragedy; yet the comic note is often sounded in these novels—in *The American* and *The Golden Bowl* as well as *The Portrait of a Lady* and *The Wings of the Dove*.

In saying that Henry James is a comic writer I mean that his vision of life is comic in the largest sense—which implies, among other aspects, that his view is ultimately serious, not simply humorous. This author presents man in an essentially sympathetic light, accepting human life with all its defects, with all its shortcomings and vices. In many respects James's fiction constitutes an *encomium moriae*, a praise and celebration of man's folly. The typically Jamesian resolution accordingly is acceptance, not rejection; and here we see the crucial difference between comedy and satire, between comedy and tragedy.

T. S. Eliot once observed that "the books of Henry James form a complete whole. One must read all of them, for one must grasp, if anything, both the unity and the progression." I have chosen *The Europeans* (1878), *The Bostonians* (1886), and *The Ambassadors* (1903) to illustrate the truth of Eliot's generalization—not only to demonstrate the unity and the progression to be found in these novels but at the same time to indicate the developing subtlety and complex richness of James's comedy. All three fictions are comedies which deal in great part with the pretense and delusion that occur within an ordered society, and all turn on matters of great importance to the New England conscience.

The Europeans is a tour de force which has variously been described as a comic pastoral, an allegory, and a dramatic poem; but everyone agrees that the novel is a comedy. It is also highly dramatic, as F. R. Leavis pointed out long ago. The pastoral element inheres chiefly in James's use of setting—the deliberate distancing and diminution employed to describe the small community inhabited by the Wentworths and Actons, seven miles outside the Boston of "thirty years since." The village has an Arcadian quality, and its chief feature is "an ancient house, ancient in the sense of being eighty years old." The Wentworths tell Felix Young that George Washington is rumored to have stayed in it, and they think of it as a venerable mansion; but Felix describes the house to his sister, the baroness, as looking "as if it had been built last night—a kind of three-story bungalow . . . a magnified Nuremburg toy." Such gentle satire operates throughout the novel, but not always, by any means, to the advantage of the Europeans. As Richard Poirier remarks, "The comedy in the novel is the result of a dramatic confrontation not of Europe and America but of misconceptions about both of them."

The pastoral conventions of *The Europeans* indicate that James incorporated certain elements of the romance into the action and setting, and indeed it has something in common with Hawthorne's *The Blithedale Romance*, as does *The Bostonians*. But for all its legend from the *Arabian Nights* and its use of the sleeping beauty theme, not to mention the celebration of the earlier and simpler life of New England in pre–Civil War America, *The Europeans* is finally a comedy of manners whose action depends on dramatic scenes, even as its tone is established by the prevalent wit evidenced by both the omniscient author and his leading characters. There are several recurrent patterns of imagery, but the dramatic metaphor is dominant, as is so often true of James's fiction. At the end we read:

"Is the play over, Eugenia?" asked Felix.
". . . I have spoken my part."
"With great applause!" said her brother.

Felix himself completes the drama by marrying Gertrude Wentworth and carrying her off to Europe. (Marriage is, of course, a typical comic resolution.) Gertrude, in her hardness and coldness, has something of Olive Chancellor's fierce New England independence. This is but one link with *The Bostonians*, a novel which is also a satirical comedy, but one which is far more ironical and profound.

This novel's ironic tonality separates it from the gentle wit of *The Europeans*, as does the fact that it is a peculiarly American novel. (*The Europeans* and *The Ambassadors* present opposite but complementary versions of the international theme.) James himself said that he "wished to write a very *American* tale, a tale characteristic of our social conditions." It was to be "as local, as American, as possible, and as full of Boston." *The Bostonians* thus is one of James's few major fictions that does not treat the international theme. It also is set apart from *The Europeans* and *The Ambassadors* by an almost strenuous insistence on public and political matters, an insistence which appears elsewhere in James as strongly only in *The Princess Casamassima*.

William James's famous objections to *The Bostonians* are well known, especially his criticism about the novel's most winning character, Miss Birdseye (whom he and others took for a replica of Hawthorne's sister-in-law, Elizabeth Peabody); but his later praise of the novel has almost been forgotten. William wrote to Henry after reading *The Bostonians* in book form, saying: "It is superlatively well done, provided one admits that method of doing such a thing at all. Really the *datum* seems to me to belong to the region of fancy, but the treatment of that of the most elaborate realism." His brother agreed, responding: "I had the sense of knowing terribly little about the kind of life I had attempted to describe—and felt a constant pressure to make the picture substantial by thinking it out—by pencilling and 'shading.' " The author's illustrative penciling gives the novel its thickness and weight as both a social document and a comedy of manners. The agitation on behalf of women's rights might best—and perhaps only—be treated in a comic vein; and that element is what James used to reveal his subject in a fiction which runs from intellectual humor to savage and even morbid satire that is distinctly unhumorous.

On the surface the movement for reform that James chooses for the central action appears trivial (although it has a quickening aspect for readers now); but as Lionel Trilling has said, "A movement of sexual revolution is to be understood as a question which a culture puts to itself, and right down to its very roots. It is a question about what it means to be a man and what it means to be a woman." The ensuing comedy is ultimately very serious, as is all great comedy; but it does not deal with the final question which comedy of the highest order almost invariably involves—the matter of redemption. Even so *The Bostonians* presents an astonishing anatomy of the New England mind—more particularly the New England conscience—and in this sense it has much in common with *The Ambassadors*.

Eliot said that "the society of Boston was and is quite uncivilized but refined beyond the point of civilization." James makes that point abundantly clear in *The Bostonians*, and one can easily understand why he once remarked: "Boston is absolutely nothing to me—I don't even dislike it." (Needless to say, Bostonians did not feel the same way—hence the cries of outrage in Boston when the novel was published.) The overrefinement of this city—its decadence—is apparent on nearly every page of the novel, especially in the portraits of Mrs. Farrinder, Mrs. Luna, and her sister Olive. Only in such a society could men like the faith healer Selah Tarrant and the gossip columnist Matthias Pardon be taken seriously: each man is an amoral parasite living off the ideas and resources of others.

Boston society is brilliantly conveyed through James's depiction of its members, each of whom lives in considerable isolation: the "society is but little organized to allow for variousness and complexity, and the social atoms seem to have a centrifugal tendency."

We are struck by the uncomfortable nature of individual relations within this world whose psychological tenor has been incisively described by Elizabeth Hardwick as a "confused scene, slightly mad with neurotic repressions, provincialism, and earnestness without intellectual seriousness." Since everyone in *The Bostonians* is seen from the outside and since only Olive Chancellor and Basil Ransom are complex characters, the novel's principal impact comes from this picture of its world. Boston is presented both sympathetically and satirically: one view is balanced against the other. We are never left in doubt, however, that the author himself thinks it is a society that is hollow at the center: Boston believes so thoroughly in itself that nothing else matters.

Woollett, Massachusetts—a provincial copy of this society—thoroughly fetters Lambert Strether until he escapes it at considerable cost. The world of Mrs. Newsome, the Pococks, and Waywarsh in *The Ambassadors* is an unmistakable duplicate of the city in *The Bostonians*, and we come away from both novels keenly understanding what Henry Adams meant in saying of the same city: "A simpler manner of life and thought could hardly exist, short of cave-dwelling." In *The Bostonians* James lovingly and ruthlessly exposes the bogus traditionalism of Brahmin society, its fraudulent social and intellectual grace; and he does it, ironically enough, through an unreconstructed Southerner. Basil Ransom tells Olive Chancellor that they are living in "an age of unspeakable shams," when she announces it is "an age of conscience." He continues: "The whole generation is womanized; the masculine tone is passing out of the world; it's a feminine, a nervous, hysterical, chattering, canting age, an age of hollow phrases and false delicacy and exaggerated solicitudes and coddled sensibilities, which if we don't soon look out, will usher in the reign of mediocrity." This is the judgment the novel makes—and makes concretely.

James accomplishes this moving satire in what is almost a tour de force; and despite the fact that the line of action is often obscured and then almost obviously propped up and set again in motion, the pace of the novel is swift. It is the satirical thrust that keeps us reading with increasing interest: the satire which invests every character in the novel and which is prevalent in the ironical tone from beginning to end. The force of the comedy enables the author to transcend the immediate donnée of *The Bostonians*, and the novel also goes beyond mere invective directed toward the suffragettes and, indeed, beyond the most corrosive form of satire, irony; for Olive emerges as a suffering pathetic individual whose plight is by no means a matter for healthy laughter. She therefore differs sharply from Mrs. Farrinder (her professional rival in the reform business) and from Miss Birdseye who "never . . . had the smallest sense of the real" and who was "heroic" and "sublime."

What we should recognize, then, is that this comedy of manners is devoted far more to an adumbration of the outer world of actuality than it is concerned with the impact experience makes upon the consciousness of the leading characters. Given the moral tenor of the times and his own predilections, James could not have investigated Miss Chancellor more thoroughly: he was content to stop with the political and moral implications of his themes—and content not to peer deeply into the dark psychology of Olive.

Although none of the characters in *The Bostonians* moves us in the way that the protagonists of James's best-known novels do— Isabel Archer or Merton Densher or Lambert Strether or even Christopher Newman—the gallery of characters is one of his most impressive since the portraits collectively add up to a detailed and satisfying depiction of a complex society. *The Bostonians*, as Mr. Leavis has observed, has "an overt richness of life such as is not commonly associated with [James]." He notes this by way of clinching another point: "This play of contrasts—thin refinement against confident vulgarity, fastidiousness against expansive publicity, restrictive scruple against charlatanism in tropical luxuriance— runs all through James's rendering of the New England aspect of American civilization." These facets of Boston society are revealed in and through its citizenry, and it is instructive to notice the pairings. Mrs. Luna is as blatantly sexual and aggressively social as her sister Olive is cold, retiring, and unfeminine; Mrs. Burrage, the social denizen of New York City, has the confident unfeeling drive of the female socialite, and she is contrasted to the calculating feminist, Mrs. Farrinder; Verena Tarrant is pursued by Mrs. Burrage's emasculate son and by the effeminate Matthias Pardon, who represents the vulgarity of the press instead of the crassness of New York money. A technique related to his pairing of opposites involves the spectrum of reformers that James presents. Miss Birdseye is the archetypal figure of the "heroic" age before the Civil War; her place is taken by a regular mob of reformers—all as professional as she is amateurish—the woman who seeks social status (Mrs. Farrinder), the woman who would compete with man through a profession (Dr. Prance), the intellectual woman who has social position and wealth and who wants to put herself and her resources to use in the Cause (Olive).

One is reminded of Jonson, Dickens, and Thackeray; and there is no reason for the modern reader to bridle at this comedy (which is often a comedy of humors). Written differently, *The Bostonians* might simply be a psychological novel or a political novel; but it would by no means be as comprehensive in its depiction of the outer world nor as comic. The inclusiveness of this novel—which directly results from the way its world is at once created and measured by a sane and humorous standard of conduct—defines its essence. James masterfully holds a complex of attitudes in solution. The precipitate involves the way that morals are played false by manners: in this case the particular texture emerges through the author's far-ranging observations of Boston society, a world in which value is chiefly public and political, for all but Ransom who has "a fund of cynicism" and who would "reform the reformers."

Nowhere else in the fiction of Henry James is the humor so broad and the comedy so comprehensive. There is every degree of mixed sympathy and satire, best seen in Miss Birdseye, that "battered, immemorial monument" of a past era, who dies revered and loved by her three disciples but apparently forgotten by everyone else after a life of unselfish service to Causes. "It was a lovely death; Doctor Prance intimated that she had never seen any that she thought more seasonable." It is typical of James's control that this hilarious observation can immediately follow Olive's wild outburst when she senses her defeat by Ransom and knows Verena will defect: "I shall see nothing but shame and ruin!" she cries. This, too, is humorous, but it is also pathetic. The rich inclusiveness and subtle modulation of effect are operative throughout the action.

The technique of pictorial representation of background and (especially) character—and the interrelation of the two elements—is precisely what is required for a comic novel that deals with a society instead of its individual members. The same is true of *The Europeans*. The typical character is revealed through his relation to society: for instance Mrs. Farrinder, the professional reformer and social climber, is "a copious, handsome woman, in whom angularity had been corrected by the air of success. . . . You could contest neither the measurements nor the nobleness, and had to feel that Mrs. Farrinder imposed herself. There was a lithographic smoothness about her and a mixture of the American matron and public character."

Henry James promised his brother William that he would write another novel by way of recompense to Miss Peabody and the other (presumably) outraged and offended Brahmins of Beacon Hill and the Back Bay. He said it would be entitled *The Other Bostonians*. But that novel was never written—at least under that title. What I would suggest is that *The Ambassadors* in some respects is the novel Henry proposed to William but that it was written in the same irreverent vein as its predecessor—and not in a contrite mood.

In *The Ambassadors* as in *The Europeans* and *The Bostonians* James employs his characteristic tactic of presenting the values of a culture through a stranger's reaction to it: in the first instance the alien observer is Felix Young (and, to a lesser extent, his sister the baroness); in the second, Basil Ransom, the Mississippian; and in the third, Lewis Lambert Strether. James moves from a detailed consideration of the outer world in the first two novels to an even greater specificity of the inner world of personal impression in the last. The shift from suburban Boston in the 1840's to urban Boston in the 1880's to Paris in the early 1900's is also worthy of our attention.

At the end of *The Ambassadors* we are not left with a view of Paris, but of course *The Bostonians* finally conveys a comic view of Boston rather than a moral view of the lives of Olive Chancellor, Verena Tarrant, and Basil Ransom. The emphasis is on the image of the curious and decadent society which forcibly emerges, on a culture strangled by its inarticulate need for reform (any reform but reform of its essential nature). The experience of Lambert Strether is an entirely different matter as James explores it. Here we see the New England conscience of one man—not the collective conscience of a society in the throes of reform. Austin Warren has shrewdly pointed out that "what occurs to Strether in his three or four months in Europe could be called either the development of conscience into consciousness—or the change from the view of conscience as identical with its early presuppositions and mandates to the view that conscience is educable." But the matter is not quite this simple, since Strether is finally dreadfully right, as Mr. Warren adds.

It is a critical commonplace that the steadily gathering impressions of Strether form the heart of *The Ambassadors*. Through this method James presents the "thickened motif and accumulated character" of his "man of imagination." In one of the most famous passages in the preface to the novel, the author goes on to describe his protagonist and the situation in which he is hopelessly embroiled: "The actual man's note, from the first of our seeing it struck, is the note of discrimination, just as his drama is to become, under stress, the drama of discrimination." In the course of the action Strether becomes a much more discerning and hence a more discriminating person than he has been heretofore in his Puritan complacency; and as the register of his consciousness becomes more acute, he understands more fully what passes before him; and therefore the comedy grows more obvious and revealing.

As I understand the action of the novel in *The Ambassadors*, James answers a question he posed in a neglected passage in the Prefaces: "A picture of life founded on the mere reserves and omissions and suppressions of life, what sort of a performance—for beauty, for interest, for tone—could that hope to be?" Lambert Strether moves from this sort of existence, a typical New England life—seen earlier in the Wentworths and Olive Chancellor and reinforced here by Mrs. Newsome—to a full appreciation of life through his dual role as "hero and historian."

The purpose of Strether's "heroic" quest to Paris is to rescue Chadwick Newsome, whom his mother, sister, and brother-in-law (together with Strether himself) presume is the victim of an unfortunate love affair. There is little or no evidence for such a presumption, but the powerful force of the New England mind is here at work, as James makes clear. At first the action involves Strether's efforts to prove this case and to return Chad to the fold so that he may be restored to Woollett, married to Mamie Pocock, and installed as chief of advertising for his late father's firm (which specializes in a vulgar but profitable business). Such is his assignment and charge from Mrs. Newsome, the stuffy grand dame of Woollett.

The reader soon suspects that Chad is not worth rescuing, and despite Strether's strenuous efforts to prove to himself that Chad is, it is plain that the miraculous transformation which has been effected involves only Chad's sensible appearance and behavior—in short his manners. Chad has greyed considerably since Strether knew him, and this is the obvious sign of his new maturity. He has become a man of the world who moves easily in Paris expatriate society and who is rapidly becoming an expatriate himself. Beneath his veneer of civilization lies a still boyish charm: Chad is not a cynic.

Madame de Vionnet is given sole credit for effecting Chad Newsome's change, and Strether concludes as much after talking with Little Bilham, a struggling artist who rooms with Chad, and with Miss Barrace, an older woman who is an habitué of Paris society. Madame de Vionnet is herself a member of this society— and a very adroit practitioner of its social graces. As the estranged wife of an impossible nobleman she is presented as a woman who has often been sinned against. It is her graciousness and, to a lesser extent, her helplessness which appeal to Strether; and he soon becomes her passionate advocate so that, by the end of the novel, he can say to Chad: "You'll be a brute, you know—you'll be guilty of the last infamy—if you ever forsake her." This we agree to, knowing that Chad has already been a brute and that he will indeed forsake her. Marie de Vionnet deserves better than she has gotten or will get, but she is not the great lady that she is made out to be.

I must confess to never having liked either Chad or Madame de Vionnet. Most critics have erroneously accepted at face value Strether's growing interest and affection for Chad and his obvious admiration and infatuation for Madame de Vionnet. But this valuation is not shared by Maria Gostrey, the character who most closely represents the author's point of view; and Strether finally (and grudgingly) admits to being wrong, especially in Chad's case. I raise this point because the comedy of *The Ambassadors* turns in large part upon Strether's ignorance of the real nature of Chad and Marie.

Madame de Vionnet is not a comic figure, nor is she treated satirically; but Chad Newsome has the sort of pomposity and unimaginative aplomb which should make us look at him warily and smile occasionally. When Strether says at the end, "I remember you, you know, as you were," and Chad responds, "An awful ass, wasn't I?", the clear meaning of the conversation is that the tense is present and future as well as past. Chad goes on to tell his friend that he is going to study the advertising business: "It really does the thing, you know." Strether replies: "Affects, you mean, the sale of the object advertised?" We now understand that Chadwick Newsome has been advertised throughout the course of the novel, retailed first by the Woollett crowd and then by his Parisian friends at radically differing values. His true value Lambert Strether finally perceives. Chad will always be callow in the moral and intellectual sense, no matter how perfect his manners or how flawless the cut of his coat.

The minor characters in *The Ambassadors* are of course all presented satirically. The satire ranges from delicate humor to withering irony, and the irony directed toward Jim and Sarah Pocock is acid and hilarious (yet not so strong as that of *The Bostonians*). There is not only the matter of the name (which Strether "sturdily confesses" to Maria Gostrey) but also the fact that Sarah is the reincarnation of her overbearing mother (with much bluster added) and that her husband is a crude and vulgar comic. His introduction is superbly drawn, and it reminds us of *The Bostonians:* "Small and fat and constantly facetious, straw-coloured and destitute of marks, he would have been practically indistinguishable had n't his constant preference for light-grey clothes, for white hats, for very big cigars and very little stories, done what it could for his identity." We are confronted by an early version of Sinclair Lewis's Babbitt who hails from Woollett, Massachusetts; and when Pocock comfortably remarks, "Why I want to come right out here and live myself. And I want to live while I am here too," we know him to be a perfect American tourist. He and Waymarsh complement one another beautifully.

Of Chad's friends in Paris none is so comical as the Pococks, but

Miss Barrace is humorously drawn. We see her (as everything) through Strether: "He envied Miss Barrace at any rate her power of not being. She seemed, with little cries and protests and quick recognitions, movements like the darts of some high-feathered free-pecking bird, to stand before life as before some full shop-window." She is the least complicated and difficult of the women that Strether is surrounded and caught by. Mrs. Newsome is the most formidable of these females who dominate the action (even though she isn't physically present) as women do in *The Bostonians* and many other Jamesian fictions. Mrs. Newsome represents the triumph of the female will in New England, precisely what Basil Ransom feared.

When Sarah, Mrs. Newsome's daughter and alter ego, arrives, Strether is put at a considerable disadvantage, and things rapidly worsen. He has already been thoroughly disarmed by the fact that Chad obviously does not need saving—that, indeed, he has profited considerably by his stay on the continent. Strether's quest by this time has become far more involved than he could ever have imagined, and yet at the same time he is thoroughly enjoying himself for the first occasion in his life, and he is beginning not only to perceive the irony of the situation but also the humor. Strether can now see the hilarity of his original mission as he set off in moral armor as a fifty-five-year-old knight to rescue a twenty-eight-year-old squire trapped in the Castle Perilous (Paris).

The stage is set for a series of Jamesian comic adventures and misadventures. These depend largely on the new character alignments that occur in consequence of the Pococks' descent on Paris. As James points out in his outline, "Contrast and oppositions naturally here play straight up. . . . Everyone and everything, but Strether and Mrs. Pocock in especial, with everything brought to a head by *her*—there is no lack of stuff." The humor goes beyond the individual character types and revolves around, and flows out of, the shifting alignments.

Two occurrences happen at this point, one following hard upon the heels of the other. First Strether learns that Jeanne de Vionnet is engaged to be married—and not to Chadwick Newsome, Esq. This of course explodes Strether's theory that Chad and Jeanne are in love, that Jeanne's mother has accomplished Chad's renovation for her daughter's sake, that Chad is involved in a wholly innocent affair, etc. Strether now realizes that he has been led astray by little Bilham, Miss Barrace, and even Maria Gostrey, as well as by his own readiness to trust in the best and most obvious appearances. Then Waymarsh and Sarah Pocock have something of an affair—a flirtation—while Jim Pocock "becomes a humorous, surreptitious backer of his brother-in-law." Waymarsh is a traitor to Strether as Pocock is to his wife and mother-in-law. The Pococks leave for Switzerland with Waymarsh in tow, after Sarah charges Strether with disloyalty and promises dire consequences. The most humorous aspect of this encounter is Strether's diplomatic suggestion to Sarah that his old companion Waymarsh has improved while under her protection.

The novel now moves rapidly to its beautifully dramatic culmination when Strether sees Chad and Marie boating together and stumbles upon them obviously enjoying an overnight holiday. In the meditative vigil which follows he fully understands all the implications involved, but the next day "he had seemed to wince at the amount of comedy involved; whereas in his present posture he could only ask himself how he should enjoy any attempt from [her] to take the comedy back."

The drama has comically ended and, with it, Lambert Strether's hopes for a safe berth with Mrs. Newsome through marriage. Through his habitual detachment and double view of himself Strether masters whatever disillusionments the experience holds. The comic resolution enables Strether (and the reader) to master the disillusionment which comes from having been caught between the conflicting values of two societies—the one narrow and biased to the point of stupidity, the other polished and elegant and shrewd but dishonest. Having for the first time lived fully, Strether liberates himself at the end not only through laughter (which is chiefly directed at himself) but also through disengagement. He retreats from Paris in good order. Strether's New England conscience has undergone as thorough an education as Chad's provincial manner. Conscience is by no means defeated: it triumphs over consciousness. Each has been responsible for Strether's undoing at various stages: excessive conscience initially and then excessive consciousness. The comedy has steadily turned around this observer and hero who is too moral and too intelligent for either society in which he finds himself. (In this respect he has not a little in common with Basil Ransom.)

What I have done is to sketch the developing comedy of *The Ambassadors* as it involves action and character and to suggest that the curve of Lambert Strether's developing consciousness follows the line of the comic movement until the two elements intersect during the great recognition scene in Book 11. The comedy embodies far more than the dramatic situation: it extends into language and metaphor and is ultimately part and parcel of a whole way of looking at the world. The comic view of this novel entails the moral aspect of experience, as is almost inevitable in James: the judgment made in the novel is not the injunction that one should live life all he can (a point which is undercut by Jim Pocock's pronouncement on the subject), but that it is better to give than to receive. That, it goes without saying, is precisely what Lambert Strether does, and that is the meaning of his concluding words. It is, moreover, the way in which his problem of conscience is solved, after he sees that Chad Newsome's life is as empty as his own has been.

We are not left with an aftertaste of the didactic: the comedy is far more subtle than that. Nor does the satire bite too deeply, as it occasionally does in *The Bostonians*. In that novel human interests are sometimes sacrificed to irony, just as human qualities are sometimes undercut by the stylized wit of *The Europeans*. The irony of *The Ambassadors* is dissolved by its comedy, even as the moral dimension is subordinated to the comic vision.

In the course of *The Bostonians*, as we have seen, the author moves beyond a satirical presentation of individual characters to a broadly comic view of a society which is less open and fluid and therefore more restricted and repressive than the society of *The Ambassadors* (but no less interesting). A brilliant image of the outer world in all its sham and folly emerges, and one is reminded of Hogarth and Pope. The neoclassical vigor, directness, and common sense that the novel rests upon make it one of James's most satisfying performances, even though it is neglected today. But *The Ambassadors*, for all its cerebral and attenuated humor, is a greater work (although, at first reading, a far more tedious one), and it merits J. I. M. Stewart's praise as "the finest novel of high comedy in the language." The outer world in it—seen chiefly in the bright image of Paris—is of relatively little significance: what we are concerned with is "thickened motive and accumulated character," as James himself put it. These dimensions of human experience provide the authenticity of life as we know it, which in the case of Ambassador Strether is always comic. The perfect concluding touch comes in the triumph of the *enlightened* New England conscience. Although Felix Young could have never foreseen the possibility, it was inevitable that his creator would turn finally from England and Europe to New England and the United States.

Ambrose Bierce

Jay Martin

Ambrose Bierce was born in 1842 in the backwoods settlement of Horse Creek Cave in Meigs County, Ohio, the tenth child of parents whom he later characterized as "unwashed savages." His childhood and adolescence were unhappy. He told Walter Neale that his first real love affair occurred at the age of fifteen, with "a woman of broad culture . . . well past seventy . . . [but] still physically attractive, even at her great age." At the age of nineteen, he was the second man in his county to enlist in the Ninth Indiana Volunteer Infantry, and the only American writer of importance to fight in the Union Army. While directing the advance of his brigade's skirmish line against an intrenched Confederate force at Kenesaw Mountain, Bierce, his commander reported, "was shot in the head by a musket ball which caused a very dangerous and complicated wound, the ball remaining within the head from which it was removed sometime afterwards." He returned from battle to learn that the young girl he wanted to marry was no longer interested in him.

In these far from humorous facts lies the background to Bierce's humor. For what his youth formed in him was a particular understanding of the world. In *The Phenomenological Approach to Psychiatry*, J. H. Van den Berg argues that "man seldom sees objects, things as such, he sees *significations* which things assume for him." For Ambrose Bierce, it was not simply that by the end of the war he had learned to suspect such cherished nineteenth-century genteel

195

ideals as the sanctity of the family, the pastoral associations which surrounded childhood, the belief in the purity of womanhood, or the assumption that war was noble and conducted by commanders untouched by vainglory or personal ambition. It was not simply that he had learned to despise social ideals of any sort, and to have "a conscience uncorrupted by religion, a judgment undimmed by politics and patriotism, a heart untainted by friendships and sentiments unsoured by animosities." More than this, the world, as he perceived it, took on a threatening aspect; like the musket ball, it attacked his head, his reason. The terrain of reality which he plotted—he was a topographic officer—he saw filled with traps. Where others saw a handsome prospect, he saw danger lurking and always assumed that beneath pleasing appearances was a threatening reality. He was convinced, in short, that reality was delusory. By emphasizing mind he attempted to preserve mind, always threatened by physical obliteration or mental deception; he defended the mind, and in doing so, took as his major theme the *growth of reflection*, the compulsion to scrutinize and observe.

This might have been a tragic theme, for reflection leads to a deeper and deeper penetration of delusion and at last to the conviction that all is delusion—that, ultimately, as Bierce said in a late letter, "nothing matters." Reality, Bierce did conclude in *The Devil's Dictionary*, was "the dream of a mad philosopher," the logical product of irrational minds, and therefore absurd—"the nucleus of a vacuum." But he treated this conviction comically, and employed humor to expose the absurdities of his deluded contemporaries and the institutions delusions created and perpetuated. In short, he preserved his own mind by ridiculing the crazed world that questioned his sense and sensibility.

His humor, this is to say, was destructive, essentially a counterattack. In his *Vorschule der Asthetik*, the philosopher Jean Paul has distinguished four constituents of humor, all of which are present in Bierce's writings. Humor, he says, obliterates distinctions, tending to identify the great and small, the pathetic and ludicrous, the beautiful and the horrible. Associated with this characteristic is that of "inverse effect": what seems to be good is damnable, or vice-versa. Both are often made convincing by what Jean Paul calls "humoristic subjectivity," which draws the reader into the subjective vision of the author through direct address. Finally, there is the humor of the grotesque and deformed. As an instrument of mind, humor, then, overturns forms, makes codes unstable, and questions the truth of accepted conventions. This aspect of humor is crucial for an understanding of Bierce's writing. In an important essay, "To Train a Writer," Bierce himself set down the knowledge which a humorous writer should possess. In addition to acquaintance with rhetoric and classical literature, Bierce said, "it would be needful that he know and have an ever-present consciousness that this is a world of fools and rogues, blind with superstition, tormented with envy, consumed with vanity, selfish, false, cruel, cursed with illusions—frothing mad! . . . He must be a sinner and in turn a saint, a hero, a wretch." Bierce was the chief product of his own school, and his humor the consequence of his education.

Certainly, Bierce's humor resembles that of other American writers. Poe's emphasis on the grotesque, Melville's inclination to treat conventions ambivalently, Twain's tendency to take a burlesque or "satanic" view of society, and, in the twentieth century, H. L. Mencken's satires on the "booboisie," or Nathanael West's and Henry Miller's very different attacks upon convention—with all of these writers Bierce has affinities. More largely, he shares with them all a sense of the growing abyss in America between the ideal symmetry of intelligence and the riotous chaos of a materialist and self-deceiving social life—a theme which not only humorists, but other American writers, chiefly Henry James and Scott Fitzgerald, pursued. Perhaps most important of all, with regard to the American-ness of his humor, Bierce early made the pragmatist's discovery that truth was instrumental, and did not consist in a set of principles. "Time was," Bierce wrote, ". . . when the moral character of every thought and word and deed was determined by reference to a set of infinitely precious 'principles'—infallible criteria—moral solvents . . . warranted . . . to disclose the gold in every proposition submitted to its tenets: I have no longer the advantage of their service, but must judge everything on its own merits—each case as it comes up." In almost every case his judgment was—*guilty*.

But Bierce was also, perhaps, the only American comic writer who deliberately attempted to write in a major tradition of European humor. He took his basic moral values from the example of antiquity. "To say of a man that he is like his contemporaries is to say that he is a scoundrel without excuse," Bierce observed. "The virtues are accessible to all. Athens was vicious, yet Socrates was virtuous. Rome was corrupt, but Marcus Aurelius was not corrupt. To offset Nero the gods gave Seneca." Bierce was convinced that the feather of truth in the midst of delusion was permanent and culture-free. Certainly, this was his assumption when he commented to Nellie Sickler in 1901: "The only originality that you or any modern can hope for is originality of expression—style. No one can think a new thought (that is worth thinking) or feel a new emotion." That conviction led him to give careful study to style. His first literary mentor, James Watkins, a veteran of New York and London journalism, had instructed him in 1868 to read Voltaire, Swift, and Thackeray's sketches in *Punch*. Not long after, Bierce sailed for London, where he came under the influence of Tom Hood the younger and wrote columns for the humorous weeklies *Fun* and *Figaro*. Bierce's contemporaries were aware of his conscious attempts to place himself in classic satiric traditions, and frequently compared him to Rabelais, Heine, Swift, and Pope. Perhaps in the end it is most just to say, as Watkins observed to Bierce in 1874, that with the methods of the great satirists and epigrammatists Bierce fused "real" "American thought" and so produced "the net result of its processes phrased with . . . wit and point and epigram."

But ultimately, Bierce is uniquely himself, a writer his contemporaries and subsequent critics have found difficult to classify. Unlike other Americans, his basic comic mode consisted in attack. Invective, a kind of secular curse, is probably the oldest form of satiric writing and consists, in its essence, of a direct assault whose purpose is to obliterate its object through abuse. Bierce described himself and his philosophy of criticism in an *Examiner* column of 1889: "Knaves and vulgarians, imposters, sycophants, the various unworthy and the specifically detestable, no sooner draw his eye than he is on them with bitter abuse." One of those knaves who caught his eye was the English wit Oscar Wilde. After remarking "the limpid and spiritless vacuity of this intellectual jellyfish," Bierce continues:

And so, with a knowledge that would equip an idiot to dispute with a cast-iron dog, an eloquence to qualify him for the duties of caller on a hog-ranch and an imagination adequate to the conception of a tom-cat, when fired by contemplation of a fiddle-string, this consummate and starlike youth, missing everywhere his heaven-appointed functions and offices, wanders about, posing as a statue of himself, and, like the sun-smitten image of Memnon, emitting meaningless murmurs in the blaze of women's eyes.

Even more primitive in its fury is his invective against a local "hoodlum":

Chuck him overboard! Let him suffocate in slimes and stenches, the riddances of sewers and the wash of slums. Give his carcass to the crabs utterly, and let the restless shrimp embed its body in his eye-socket, or wave its delicate antennae from his pale nostril. Let globes and tangles of eels replace his bowels, and the muscular squid lay coils of clammy tentacle about the legs of him. Over with him!

Invective always lurked about the edges of whatever comic forms Bierce employed and might break out at any time. His own conclusion about his temperament was apt: "I am not a poet, but an abuser."

Very far from savage invective is the civilized wit of the epigram, a form which Bierce also practiced frequently. The influence on Bierce of La Rochefoucauld's *Maximes* was reinforced by the convention in western humor of "familiar sayings," a mode which ultimately derived in America from Protestant proverbialism and was practiced by John Phoenix, Josh Billings, and Bill Nye. Mark Twain's epigraphs for *Pudd'nhead Wilson's New Calendar* are similar to, but generally less good than Bierce's definitions in *The Devil's Dictionary* or the epigrams which may be found, glowing with congealed fury, all through Bierce's work. Bierce defined *Alone* as "in bad company"; *Positive* as "mistaken at the top of one's voice"; a *Bride* as "a woman with a fine prospect of happiness behind her"; a *Handkerchief* as "a small square of silk or linen used at funerals to conceal a lack of tears"; *Love* as "a temporary insanity curable by marriage"; and *Year* as "a period of 365 disappointments." His writing so often glittered with such epigrams that in twelve volumes of collected work he could afford to omit such quips as these: "To forgive is to err, to be human is divine"; "If

men and women could read one another's secret thoughts we might
shorten our vocabulary by the length of the word 'virtue,' " and
"for the study of the good and the bad in woman, two women are
a needless expense." Obviously, though very different in form, invective and the epigram have in Bierce's writing the same function—
to attack, to expose, and thus to destroy folly. Bierce answered a
critic in 1868 by asserting: "We lash the Evil-disposed only and
commend the Good alone"; but he discerned little good and toward
evil was unsparing: "In a civilization, in which everything should
work as it ought, a man after committing an essentially mean act
would make his will, bid his weeping creditors a long farewell, pick
up a handsaw, and go out and disembowel himself by rasping it
transversely across his abdomen."

The satiric tendency in Bierce is clearly in the vituperative tradition of Archilochus and Juvenal, and contrasts strikingly with the
more genial tone of the Horatian wit which characterized American humor until the second half of the twentieth century. Aware
of the conflict between the two traditions, Bierce mocked a re-
viewer who criticized him for indelicate humor:

O, certainly [humor] should be "delicate." Every man of correct literary
taste will tell you it should be "delicate"; and so will every scoundrel who
fears it. . . . A man who is exposed to satire must not be made unhappy—O
dear, no! He must find it very good reading. . . . Don't mangle the man,
like that coarse Juvenal, and that horrid Swift, but touch him up neatly,
like Horace or a modern magazinist.

But during Bierce's career, American comic forms and conventions
operated entirely in the spirit of Horace. The tall tale, the humorous anecdote, literary burlesque, the literary hoax, the deadpan
comedy of western oral narrative, parody, and the comic debate
were wit forms which had prevailed in eighteenth century English
and American literature and were, in the post-Civil-War period,
Americanized by Mark Twain, Artemus Ward, and Bret Harte.
Such forms all tend to show a *distance* between the writer and the
object of his satire, a self-effacement of the author usually achieved
through the use of a naive narrator, and a general acceptance of the
fact that, after all, human error is inevitable and understandable.

Ambrose Bierce never acknowledged—and, in fact, explicitly

denied—that error could be tolerated. But he was, of necessity, a writer for newspapers and popular magazines, and was confined by the conventions of literary journalism to forms which were familiar to his audience. Thus, at the heart of his work is a deep, unmediated conflict between his urge to attack, to utterly destroy the object of his humor, and the assumptions of the forms available to him, that wit should function as a gentle corrective of error. While his tone is always exacerbated and personal, defending the integrity of the head and assailing the excesses of the heart, the comic forms which he perforce used allowed for the heart's folly or the head's defeats. This is to say that there is a conflict in Bierce's work between attitudes which should produce wit and forms which must offer humor. "Nearly all Americans are humorous," he said; "if any are born witty heaven help them to emigrate! . . . Humor is tolerant, tender; its ridicule caresses. Wit stabs, begs pardon—and turns the weapon in the wound." This conflict creates the primary tension in Bierce's style: the war between, on the one hand, his language—a language so savage that it is almost out of control, in which invective leads to vituperation and vituperation to frenzy; and, on the other hand, the forms he employs, whose tendency is to blunt, to efface, and to tolerate weakness. Indeed, the inert geniality of his forms becomes, itself, a prod which drives his diction to still greater fury, his images into more grotesque deformations. At times, he is willing, almost impelled, to allow his language to destroy the very forms which seek to hold them in check. For this reason, Bierce was never able to work in long forms. He hated the novel, and spoke of the work of Howells and James as "the offspring of mental incapacity wet-nursed by a conspiracy." But Bierce was incapable of controlling his language in the long, loose novel form. Even his longest stories are seldom more than a few pages, and his *Fantastic Fables* usually but a few lines long. All of his work is held together by the will, which knows that any opportunity for disruption, any flaw in the iron control, any lapse in logic, will allow the savage power of his language to break through the walls of form for a rampage of vituperative devastation.

Bierce's war with language has a direct and striking effect on the nature of action in his fiction. Even the characters in it are remarkably sparing in speech; in many of his tales no character speaks a single word. In "The Affair at Coulter's Notch," for instance, Captain Coulter obeys orders to bomb enemy forces near a plantation house without remonstrance, even though, as we later discover, the house is his own, and he knows he will kill his family inside it. In "The Coup de Grâce," Downing Madwell kills a wounded friend out of mercy, is seen doing so by an officer, and is led off to execution, without speaking. "A Son of the Gods" is a war story in which, as Bierce himself writes, "Not a word is spoken." In "One of the Missing," Jerome Searing dies of stroke through self-induced hysteria without uttering a sound. The painful apotheosis of this method occurs in "Chickamauga," where a child who turns out to be a deaf mute sees the aftermath of a battle which he cannot hear. At the end, finding the body of his mother, blown apart by a shell, he stands, "motionless, with quivering lips." Bierce silences words, as if language itself, released from the mind, could be emitted only as a scream.

This war of savage language against genial forms, of structural restraint against colloquial looseness, marks all of Bierce's writing and distinguishes him from his humorous contemporaries. He deals with their subjects and employs their forms, but the differences are apparent. His ridicule is unmitigated and thorough. He begins with Adam and Eve:

> Little's the good to sit and grieve
> Because the serpent tempted Eve.
> Better to wipe your eyes and take
> A club and go out and kill a snake.
>
> But if you prefer, as I suspect,
> To philosophize, why, then, reflect:
> If the cunning rascal on the limb
> Hadn't tempted her, she'd have tempted him.

He turns to civilization, conscious that the defects which produced the Fall are enlarged in institutions. Local government:

Somebody has attempted to rob the safe in the office of the City and County Treasurer. This is rushing matters; the impatient scoundrel ought to try his hand at being a Supervisor first. From Supervisor to thief the transaction is natural and easy.

Social morality:

Tombstone, Arizona, is said to have Three-score liquor saloons and only one Bible, yet the run on the sixty Saloons is greater than the struggle to get at the one Bible.

He perceived a society which, indeed, had written a new Bible, whose commandments Bierce mockingly records in "The New Decalogue":

> Have but one God: thy knees were sore
> If bent in prayer to three or four.
>
> Adore no images save those
> The coinage of thy country shows.
>
> Take not the name in vain. Direct
> Thy swearing unto some effect.
>
> Thy hand from Sunday work be held—
> Work not at all unless compelled.
>
> Honor thy parents, and perchance
> Their wills thy fortunes may advance.
>
> Kill not—death liberates thy foe
> From persecution's constant woe.
>
> Kiss not thy neighbor's wife. Of course
> There's no objection to divorce.
>
> To steal were folly, for 'tis plain
> In cheating there is greater gain.
>
> Bear not false witness. Shake your head
> And say that you have "heard it said."
>
> Who stays to covert ne'er will catch
> An opportunity to snatch.

Of social institutions, Bierce writes—

> Concerning marriage:
>   Of two kinds of temporary insanity, one ends in suicide,
>   the other in marriage.

> Concerning commerce and religion:
>   I saw the devil. He was working free—
>   A customs-house he builded by the sea.
>   "Why do you do this?" The devil raised his head:
>   "Of churches I have built enough," he said.

Bierce attacked individuals as fiercely as institutions. Of a powerful railroad entrepreneur he remarked:

[Collis P.] Huntington is not altogether bad. Though severe he is merciful. He tempers invective with falsehood. He says ugly things of his enemy, but he has the tenderness to be careful that they are mostly lies. . . . Mr. Huntington's ignorance is chronic and incurable. The number of things he does not know is undiminished by Time: the accuracy with which he does not know them is unaffected by reflection.

All about him, in short, Bierce saw and castigated evil. Yet, he was convinced that real improvement in man or his institutions was impossible. Human beings, quite simply, found happiness in evil; impossible to correct, they are merely "worthy of extermination." It was his considered opinion, he told Nellie Sickler not long before his death, that "you cannot make the world better—nobody can. In the 'business of uplift' by conscious and associated effort, the uplifters are simply pulled down to the level of the thing that they are raising." Bierce attacked evil not to correct it, but to protect himself against it, as if only his accurate observation of evil—his exposure of irrationality—could save his mind from it. This omnivorous growth in Bierce of observation and reflection paralyzed his sense of correction and contented him with the preservation of his mind's symmetry.

In his representation of family life he is at his most violent. He had suffered deeply both as a child and as a parent, and in a series of sketches called *The Parenticide Club*, he imitates in overt action the kind of psychic tensions in family life that alienist psychoanalysts would later describe. Again, this is to say, Bierce thrust through the delusions of civilization to expose the irrational hatreds which even such sacred institutions of civilization as the family were created to control and conceal. "My Favorite Murder" begins: "Having murdered my mother under circumstances of singular atrocity, I was arrested and put upon my trial, which lasted seven years." "Oil of Dog" is the next tale: and begins with this jocular introduction: "My name is Boffer Bings. I was born of honest parents in one of the humbler walks of life, my father being a manufacturer of dog oil and my mother having a small studio in the shadow of the village church, where she disposed of unwelcome babes. In my boyhood I was trained to habits of industry; I not only assisted my father in procuring dogs for his vats, but was frequently employed by my mother to carry away the debris of her work in the studio." Equally as casual is the narrator of "An Imperfect Conflagration": "Early one June morning in 1872, I murdered my father—an act which made a deep impression on me at the time."

By inversely mingling innocence with crime, the beautiful with the horrible, the reputable with the profane, Bierce saw all aspects of the world as reprehensible, insanely grotesque. The only imaginable relief from such a deformed world was in the symmetry of death. Bierce anticipated André Breton and other surrealists when he remarked to a friend as they overlooked a midwinter fair: "Wouldn't it be fun to turn loose a machine gun into that crowd?" After a disordered childhood and adolescence Bierce had learned his principles of personal order through his military experience, in which, for the soldier, life is perfectly symmetrical—its aims are well defined and are to be achieved by clarity and precision of action. Symmetry and death, the two dominant features of a soldier's experience, he thus came to associate, while social life, as he perceived it, was marked by the continuous danger of asymmetry and self-deception, a death in life. Bierce needed to live his death in order to control his life. His last piece of humor, not inappropriately, then, consisted in his suicidal disappearance at the age of seventy-two into Revolutionary Mexico, where no subsequent trace of his end has ever been found.

Humor, Chicago Style

Bernard Duffey

For the first fifty years after its settlement in the early 1830's, the city of Chicago grew in population, diversity, and wealth at an almost explosive rate. Tens of thousands of inhabitants and hundreds of square miles of the flat, low-lying shore of Lake Michigan and of the prairie land stretching to the west were added to its span. By the 1880's its population had reached the figure of a million persons. The damage wrought by the great fire of 1871 had been repaired, and Chicago was embarked upon a second half century of development that now had the prosperous achievements of its first fifty years from which to spring.

The second half century was to reflect prosperity. The privately founded Newberry and Crerar Libraries, and the establishment of the Chicago Public Library, brought the city's first sizable collection of books. Its theaters multiplied in number and variety. The Chicago Art Institute came into being. The Chicago Symphony Orchestra took firm root, and the University of Chicago was established and endowed in the 1890's. The city was beginning to look a little more like a metropolitan center and a little less like a vast railway junction. Two or three decades of a growing interest in writing constituted the so-called Chicago literary renaissance that culminated in the 1920's with the work of Theodore Dreiser, Sherwood Anderson, and Carl Sandburg. Downtown building construction inaugurated the era of the steel-frame skyscraper, and the architectural designs of Louis Sullivan added distinctive accomplishment to the city's central section. The building of elevated railway lines to run in a large circle around the city's heart gave that center its own characteristic name, the "Loop." The newly rich class that had subsidized the city's institutions built expensive houses along the near north shore, still, however, close to the Loop; and other substantial residential sections lay to the west and the south. A somewhat later generation profited from the architectural genius of Frank Lloyd Wright. Black migrants to Chicago brought their own culture and its jazz music with them from the Southern states and later altered it into a jazz form that came to be known as "Chicago style."

It was this second half century that also saw the rise of humor writing in Chicago newspapers, a form of metropolitan wit and sophistication reflecting the newly found character of the city. The newspaper in Chicago had thriven with the town, and (notable especially in the founding of *The Chicago Daily News* in the later seventies) had begun to seek a more ambitious identity for itself. Earlier papers had most often been crudely written and crudely printed compilations of local commercial news and violently partisan politics. Melville Stone, however, the founder of the *Daily News*, was to envision both a more broadly interested and a more sophisticated audience, and one, he hoped, that would bring greater response to advertising and greater income to his newspaper enterprise. In a world without movies, radio, or television, a growingly leisured class was largely dependent on the popular theater or the lighter products of book publication for professional entertainment. The newspaper might expect to share in this, as yet, only slightly developed market.

It is not surprising that Chicago humor should have been highly topical and so have reflected the specific events and the characteristic tone that colored the days of its writing. It may be dated from the advent of Eugene Field's column, "Sharps and Flats," in the *Daily News* in 1883 and continued through Peter Finley Dunne's contributions to the rival *Chicago Evening Post* beginning in 1892. George Ade's "Fables in Slang" were added to the morning edition of the *Daily News* in 1896, and Ring Lardner, after the turn of century, emerged from sports writing to his humorously sardonic tales of popular aspiration and behavior. Keith Preston's sophisti-

cated contributions to the *Tribune* and later to the *Daily News* got
underway in the early 1920's and ended with his death in 1927.
Though other figures might well be mentioned, these five—Eugene
Field, Peter Finley Dunne, George Ade, Ring Lardner, and Keith
Preston—will suffice to illustrate the movement of humor, Chicago
style, from the mid-1880's through the 1920's.

Eugene Field was the original and pioneering Chicago figure. He
had been born in 1850. His apprenticeship was served as a wandering newspaper writer. His earliest success came to him when, as
editor of *The Denver Tribune*, he contributed to the paper a series
of sardonic squibs, still low-browed and heavy-handed in their joking. Field's earliest humor had much of the crudity, or even the
cruelty, associated with Western life, an almost cynical kind of
joking that made a travesty of any pretensions toward superiority,
innocence, or even common honesty and sense. Malignity and folly
seemed more real. He collected his paragraphs in 1882 and published them in a little book he called *The Tribune Primer* that went
on through numerous reprintings during the later century. Despite
its elemental style, or because of it, the book commanded a substantial audience.

In 1887, four years after his arrival in Chicago, he published another collection reflecting something of this early humor of disenchantment, but one also that showed a more sophisticated attitude
and a new subject—Chicago's aspiration toward metropolitan culture. Still ironic, and making capital out of anything suggesting
pretense, Field entitled the book *Culture's Garland*, and added an
elaborate subtitle: "The Gradual Rise of Literature, Art, Music,
and Society in Chicago, and other Western Ganglia." The humor
for the contemporary reader lay in the absurdity, in 1887, of taking
Chicago culture seriously, and Field underscored the idea by the
double meaning of culture's "gradual" rise in the mushrooming
western town and its association with the anatomical and even
pathological sounding "ganglia," a word meaning either nerve
centers or tumors. Julian Hawthorne, son of Nathaniel Hawthorne
and himself a writer of popular romance, provided an introduction
for the book and included an effort to define Field's style in a newly
fledged literary context. The newspaper jokesmith was given a
more elaborate setting:

Humor—whatever it used to mean in Ben Jonson's days—now means something more than the comic eccentricity of an individual. It means the arch smile, half quizzical and half tender, that glimmers upon the countenance of human nature when contemplating its own follies and perversions.

The humorist would be a jokesmith still, but his jokes would touch the failings of humanity, even if only lightly and without Juvenalian rigor.

"Capt. Ben Wingate," Field noted, "has named his new barge the Felicia Hemans, and the same departed for Saginaw last evening with a cargo of shingles." The style was that of the brief commercial notice. The fun came in associating the name of a popular sentimental poetess with a barge-load of shingles. The appeal was subtle to the extent that the reader would feel himself superior enough to Mrs. Hemans's verse to be amused by its sudden workaday demotion. When the New England poet, James Russell Lowell, visited Chicago, it was rumored that the dinners given him during his stay totalled $40,000 in cost: "Yet," Field remarked, "there are carping critics who say that Chicago is not a great literary center," and did not add that Lowell's welcome had more to do with his diplomatic and political importance than with literature. He pretended to puzzle himself as to whether Chicago's society would be "more deeply interested in the circus which is exhibiting on the lake front this week than in the compilation of Sapphic fragments published in London." Field's style was mild and understated, one that was little calculated to challenge Chicago aspirations very seriously; but it enjoyed making lightly superior fun of them, and including the reader, along with the humorist himself, among their enlightened critics.

Where Field spoke for a somewhat sophisticated taste, and as an amateur of the literary life and its pleasures, Peter Finley Dunne would turn to a different milieu and to a more vividly dramatic imagination. He began in the *Post* in 1892 as a commentator on local politics, and to give his opinions more flavor, put them into the mouth of one Colonel McNeery, the loquacious and witty proprietor of an actual Dearborn Street saloon frequented by the city's newspapermen. McNeery objected to the use of his name as a cover for Dunne's opinions, and as a result the writer recast his spokesman as Martin Dooley, operator of a small drinking establishment on Archer Avenue in the heart of the city's Irish section. Mr. Dooley, of th' Archey road, as he called it, was given the authentic speech of the first generation Irish-American, the people among whom Dunne had been born in 1867 and who at the turn of century were a great comedy resort of popular entertainment.

Dunne did much more, however, than create one more stage Irishman. Mr. Dooley was full of sharp opinion on the matters of the day. He often mastered his situation, but sometimes was mastered by it. He had his limits, which sometimes he recognized and sometimes ignored, and he was blessed with a wit that could be introspective as well as editorial. "Though I'd make a map fr'm mimry, an' gossip iv any other man,—f'r mesilf, I'm still uncharted," he confessed. Like any journalistic character, Mr. Dooley had his better days and his worse, but if one were to make a selection of the best in Dunne, as Elmer Ellis has done in his volume, *Mr. Dooley at His Best*, the selection would show abundant creative freedom and dramatic reality.

From his own state of confirmed bachelorhood, Mr. Dooley noted that the ugly man had to marry early to disprove the testimony of his looks. "But its diff'rent with us comely bachelors," he added. "Bein' very beautiful, we can afford to be haughty an' peevish . . . The best lookin' iv us niver get marri'd at all." He was astonished at the changes of modernity. Referring to the Chicago meat-packing industry—"A cow goes lowin' softly in to Armour's an' comes out glue, beef, gelatine, fertylizer, celooloid, joolry, sofy cushions, hair restorer, washin' sody, soap, lithrachoor an' bed springs." "I can go fr'm Chicago to New York in twinty hours," he noted, "but I don't have to, thank the Lord." Referring to a pious and rich capitalist of the day, Mr. Hennessy once asked, "What do you think iv the man down in Pennsylvanya who said the Lord and him is partners in a coal mine?" "Has he divided th' profits?" asked Mr. Dooley, making his skeptical point. He satirized American jingoism in the Spanish-American War. " 'We're a gr-reat people,' said Mr. Hennessy earnestly. 'We ar-re,' said Mr. Dooley, 'We ar-re that. An' th' best iv it is, we know we ar-re.' " When peace came, Mr. Hennessy exulted that the war was over.

" 'On'y part iv it,' cautioned Mr. Dooley. 'Th' part that ye see in
th' pitcher pa-apers is over, but the tax collector will continyoo
his part iv th' war with rilintless fury.' " Out of the controversy
following the American seizure of the Philippines, some feared
that the U.S. Constitution would not apply to conquered territory,
and Mr. Dooley was dour. " 'There's wan thing I'm sure about,'
he said. 'What's that?' asked Hennessy. 'That is,' said Mr. Dooley,
'no matter whether the Constitution follows the flag or not, the
Supreme Court follows the illiction returns.' " Mr. Hennessy was
worried about educating his children. "If ye had a boy wud ye
sind him to colledge?" he asked. " 'Well,' said Mr. Dooley, 'at th'
age whin a boy is fit to be in colledge, I wudden't have him around
th' house,' " and perhaps he put his finger on a mainspring of higher
education.

George Ade, Dunne's rival and colleague, characterized the
Dooley articles:

Dunne's newspaper stories showed a careful and precise use of words, and
his witticisms were crystal clear and models of brevity . . . The "Dooley"
stories were caustic and witty editorials. . . .

Though the remark touched only one side of Mr. Dooley, it
suggested the direction Ade's own work would take. Like Dunne,
he resorted to a comic kind of speech, the slang burgeoning in
the big cities and spreading itself into general American usage,
and for his most popular writing, called "Fables in Slang," he
turned to the same comic mode that Eugene Field had used long
before in *The Tribune Primer*, that of a mock style imitating the
heavily emphatic kind of language used to teach school children
to read and, in Ade's case, patterned also on the fable, the moral
tale that often was included in a primer's contents.

But for Ade, the fable would always be ironic. For example, he
told the story of an unpopular clergyman who found a way to
success in his profession and called the tale, "The Fable of the
Preacher Who Flew his Kite but Not Because He Wished to
Do So." The preacher began by speaking to his congregation
earnestly and quietly, hoping to convince their understanding, but
they had little use for his style. "They could Understand everything he said and they began to think he was Common," too

ordinary to be respected. So he changed his ways and in his next sermon began "with a Text that didn't mean anything, read from either Direction." He fabricated nonsensical but grandiose poetry from an imagined Icelandic bard and ran on through a long list of fictitious but exotic sounding authorities. He let his voice range from shouts to whispers and resorted to the most learned sounding words he knew. The result was a huge success, ". . . everyone said that the Sermon was Superfine and Dandy. The only thing that worried the congregation was the fear that if it wished to retain such a Whale it might have to Boost his Salary." The clergyman drew his own conclusions about his flock's simplemindedness, and Ade rounded off the whole fable with its sardonic moral: "Give the People what They Think they Want."

George Ade's humor, like Field's early work, was a humor of disenchantment. All was vanity, though it was not so vain that Ade could not make an enormously profitable career out of it. More important, however, was Ade's sensing of the brand of humor that was especially to flourish as the twentieth century wore on. The city was moving toward an ever larger, busier, and tougher quality of life. Its increase in size reflected the increasing drive for success, the values of cunning, and intense competition. Ade spoke for a growingly skeptical American wit, one that most readily found the stuff of laughter in the hardness of urban knowledge, in the cost of folly and the presumed hollowness of triumph. That he spoke to a lasting mood is suggested by the publication in 1961 of a selection of his writing edited by Jean Shepherd and entitled, *The America of George Ade*.

In 1916, while Ade was still at the height of his popularity, a book of mordant mock letters was published entitled, *You Know Me Al*, and written by a recent graduate from the sporting pages of *The Chicago Tribune*, Ring Lardner. Born in 1885 and raised in the neighboring state of Michigan, Lardner had drifted to Chicago as a newspaperman and would, after a time, move on to New York. The influence of George Ade, and Lardner's growing knowledge of the city, was to lead to his own humorous writing.

To begin with, his field was limited, confined to the world of professional baseball and its foibles. In his first book, Lardner posed as his central character one Jack Keefe, in baseball terms, "a busher," a player from the minor leagues who has been called up for a trial with one of the major teams but whose unconquerable stupidity and uncritical lust for fame and money makes his effort an absurdity. He is, in American slang terms, an ignoramus, a loud-mouth, and at least a little bit of a crook. Lardner's book was made up of letters that Jack supposedly wrote to his friend, Al, recounting his adventures and misadventures in an ignorant language, misspelled, badly constructed, and unconsciously revealing his own venality. When he cannot take advantage of his athletic prospects, he turns to a little financial cheating against his wife:

Now Al you know I am not ma'ing no kick on spending a little money for a present for my wife but I had allready boughten her a rist watch for $15 and a rist watch was just what she wanted. I was willing to give her the ring if she had not of wanted the rist watch more than the ring but when I give her the ring I kept the rist watch and did not tell her nothing about it.

Jack's dreary scheming was the product of a kind of exposé humor that would provide Lardner's staple resource whether he was writing about the limitations of ball player, or, as he was to do in his later stories, about the American everyman.

Though a selection of his work has been reprinted in *The Portable Ring Lardner*, his humor was of and by the earlier twentieth century, that decade and frame of mind we called "the twenties." H. L. Mencken's writing in the Baltimore *Sun* and in *The Smart Set* magazine had introduced his own virulent satire against what he called the American "boob," a slang term for the average citizen suggesting his hopeless foolishness, self-assertion, and ignorance of himself and of his world. He had been the perennial butt of George Ade's "Fables in Slang" and was also to dominate in Lardner's humor. Lardner would write much about various kinds of sports figures, be they professionals or pretentious amateurs cheating and blundering their way through games of golf, but as time went on he would move out, as it were, into the world that gathered around sport and supported it from its own limited imagination and its ignorance of the real nature of whatever allured it.

His parade of ball players and their audience, of rural clowns and urban buffoons, like the foolishness and low cunning paraded through George Ade's fables, finally make Lardner too predictable and dreary reading, though the work of both men was also given sharp point by a caustic sense of reality.

Lardner was to leave Chicago early. As with many newspapermen of his generation, his Chicago success led to better paying work in New York. During the 1920's, however, one figure remained in Chicago, Keith Preston, who in his writing for both the *Tribune* and the *Daily News* was to carry the history of Chicago humor into a final phase. He was both like his predecessors and unlike them. He had been born in Chicago, had his schooling in the city and ultimately took a doctorate in classical studies from The University of Chicago.

Preston practiced little ridicule; rather, in the words of Christopher Morley, who wrote the introduction to Preston's selected writings, *Pot Shots from Pegasus*, he was "parodist, punster, satirist and wit." Both his verse and his prose were marked by elegance and a Horatian deftness of control. Preston wrote for the informed and selective reader, and was conservative or even a little snobbish in his fun. He was gently suspicious of the still untried possibilities of radio, for example. "Improved communication makes it easier for us to misunderstand one another," he remarked. "That putting the human family into a single bed will guarantee harmony of feeling is not borne out by small scale experiments." And one of his verses declared his own attitude toward foolishness (what, in slang, he called "piffle") and toward pretence (in slang "bull"):

> Some sigh for gales of laughter
>   Some whistle for a wheeze;
> I merely aim to riffle
>   Your risibilities.
>
> I like to prod the piffle
>   With which the press is full;
> Or, like the banderillo,
>   Pin ribbons on the bull.

His fondness for the familiar and unpretentious was given expression in a comment on astronomy:

Prof. Michelson announces that the star Antares, in the constellation Scorpio, has a diameter of 420,000,000 miles, and, again, as happens every time Prof. Michelson takes the waist measure of a star, our editorial brethren are overwhelmed with humiliation at the smallness of little old earth. For our part, it troubles us not at all. Earth is a poor thing, perhaps, but our own! And, at that, it seems a deal too big for us to manage. A filip for gaseous Antares, and Betelgeuse, the big bloat! Let us set our house in order and have done with cosmic Babbittry!

Preston's ease of manner and his confidence in quiet good sense stood at an opposite pole from the sardonic direction represented by Ring Lardner, and between the two of them they may have suggested a splitting up of humor, Chicago style: on the one hand, an almost too ready complaisance; on the other, a heavily caustic ridicule. Whatever the differences, it may have seemed that later humorists might seek a combination of their gifts in humor's most significant and durable achievement, a willingness to face the frailties of human nature along with an ability to stand off from them and suggest their true measure in a comprehending laughter.

"If Only Mencken Were Alive . . ."

Louis D. Rubin, Jr.

At regular intervals the public library of the city of Baltimore, Maryland, issues a delightful little periodical entitled *Menckeniana*, in which the editors, in addition to publishing short articles about the late Henry Louis Mencken, attempt to keep track of all the references made to Mencken in public print the country over. Many of these latter are from newspaper editorials and columns, and they are apt to involve something to the effect that "if only H. L. Mencken were alive and writing today. . . ." What they mean is that the assorted confusion, chicanery, and apocalypse of the American scene is badly in need of someone to proclaim the humbug as humbug and to recognize and shoot holes in all the knaves and idiots.

Alas, there is no Mencken. He is gone for good. Furthermore, if his counterpart were to appear before us today and take up the vigil of the master where he left off, he wouldn't be able to get away with it for very long. For the conditions that made a Mencken possible and plausible back in the 1920's, when he was in his public heyday, simply do not exist any more. Nor do the conditions obtain that in the decade of the 1910's permitted him to achieve preeminence as a critic of literature and champion of the bold moderns who opened up American fiction to the insights of the twentieth century. Mencken was of a specific time and place, and when the time ended and the place took on a different look, he was out of it. What most of those who lament his absence today

217

forget is that Mencken ceased to perform his now-legendary function as Lord High Executioner of American Poltroonery several decades before he suffered the stroke that ended his literary career in 1949. The vintage Menckeniana that everyone quotes and longs to have duplicated today was almost all composed in the days of Presidents Wilson, Harding, and Coolidge. By Herbert Hoover's time he wasn't able to bring it off nearly so well, and the Roosevelt years were definitely not for him. Wisely, he realized it soon enough, and turned to other and more fruitful pursuits.

The milieu that Mencken required in order to perform his rituals properly is described with notable accuracy in his classic survey of the national scene entitled "On Being an American," published in 1922. Having established the fact of his oneness of viewpoint with the young American intellectuals who were departing for Paris and the Left Bank in such numbers during those years, he noted that, unlike them, he was staying on, and gladly. The explanation for his failure to decamp, he said, lay in his own personal happiness, and in the United States of the 1920's he was very happy, for

To be happy (reducing the thing to its essentials) I must be:

a. Well-fed, unhounded by sordid cares, at ease in Zion.
b. Full of a comfortable feeling of superiority to the masses of my fellow-men.
c. Delicately and unceasingly amused according to my taste.

It is my contention that, if this definition be accepted, there is no country on the face of the earth wherein a man roughly constituted as I am—a man of my general weaknesses, vanities, appetites, prejudices, and aversions—can be so happy, or even one-half so happy, as he can be in these free and independent states.

Surely the 1920's were such a time for him. The difficulties he had encountered during the period when the United States of America was involved in the First World War were over. His strong anti-British sentiments, his only moderately concealed pan-Germanism, which had caused him much embarrassment, even harassment, and had temporarily undermined his standing and popularity—not only did these no longer constitute a handicap once the war was done and patriotic zeal abated, but indeed they now proved to be a positive benefit. For when it became obvious, as it soon did, that the millennium that the Great War for Civilization was to usher in was not notably closer to arrival in 1920 than in 1914, and that America's attempt to "save the world for democracy" had fallen just a mite short of its target, then what happened was that the citizenry of the Republic began having second thoughts, and became a bit disgusted over the whole enterprise. It was evident that Western Europe was as mixed up as ever, if not more so. The dream of international cooperation in a League of Nations that would bring about political and social stability wasn't going to work out, and part of the reason it wasn't was that the United States was still populated by an electorate made up of fallen human beings. Even so, the United States had emerged from the fighting prosperous as never before and, as they say, perched on the top of the pile.

Here, therefore, was a situation that seemed tailor-made to the measurements of Henry Louis Mencken. Whatever others had done, *he* hadn't indulged in the patriotic excess that had made archfiends of all Germans and angels of all true-born Britons. *He* had not joined in the suppression of courses in the German language, the banishment of Friedrich Nietzsche and the like from college and university curricula, the taboo on performing the operas of Richard Wagner and the orchestral works of Richard Strauss, the changing of the name of formal dances from Germans to Cotillions, the persecution of Theodore Dreiser because his biologically determined fiction was written by a man bearing a Teutonic name, and so on. He had stood aloof and contemptuous during the whole period, and the sole concession he had made to the public frenzy was to stop writing about what was good about the Germans and bad about the English. He had little or nothing to repent, therefore, and considerable right to say "I told you so."

Furthermore, now that the war was over and it became apparent that the advent of the perfect world society was going to be indefinitely delayed, the American people looked around for a scapegoat, someone or something upon whom or which the blame for the failure could be placed. First of all, there were the British. *They* had supposedly talked us into getting ourselves involved, persuaded us to identify our interests with theirs, and then had made it clear once the war was done that they were looking out for themselves only. Here Mencken was a positive comfort to have around. For he hated the British, resented their cultural domination, and was eager to get in his licks against them at long last, after several years of having to fight under wraps. Second, there were those who supposedly had led us into the war, and made the whole thing into a mighty crusade on the side of democracy, civilization, and peace for all time to come. Chiefly this had been managed by President Woodrow Wilson, whose speeches had exhorted Americans to rise above their weaknesses and their failings and commit themselves unreservedly to their highest human ideals. H. L. Mencken detested Woodrow Wilson, and he had a deep suspicion of all abstract ideals and unanchored inspirational sentiments.

And Mencken's willingness to light into Wilson and Wilsonians was comforting, too, for another reason. For it was obvious that not only had the twenty-eighth American President believed thoroughly in the cause he had led and the League of Nations he had championed, but he had more or less given his life and health to the advocacy of that cause, and the defeat of his hopes had broken him. He had been, in short, a veritable martyr to his ideals, and the failure of the American people to back him all the way had been a crushing disappointment that was doubtless responsible for the fact that he now lay paralyzed, helpless, and all but dead. The fallen leader, the betrayed father—this Woodrow Wilson was; and his people, those he had led, had done this cruel thing to him, and they knew it and felt shame and remorse because it had been necessary for them to do it. At melancholy moments such as these, it is solace and consolation if someone who knows about such matters will come along and assure one that not only did one do the right thing, but that one couldn't and shouldn't have done anything else—and that the old man was a hypocritical bastard anyway, who was doing it all for selfish reasons and deserved everything that he got. This, too, H. L. Mencken was able and willing to say and to believe. Thus, when Mencken wrote prose about the conduct of the late war to the effect that

All the idiotic nonsense emitted by Dr. Wilson and company was simply icing on the cake. Most of it was abandoned as soon as the bullets began to fly, and the rest consisted simply of meaningless words—the idiotic babbling of a Presbyterian evangelist turned prophet and seer. . . .

and,

What the London *Times* says today, about Ukrainian politics, the revolt in India, a change of ministry in Italy, the character of the King of Norway, the oil situation in Mesopotamia, will be said week after next by the *Times* of New York, and a month or two later by all the other American newspapers. . . .

and,

Most of the essential policies of Dr. Wilson between 1914 and 1920—when the realistic English, finding him no longer useful, incontinently dismissed him—were, to all intents and purposes, those of a British colonial premier. He went into the Peace Conference willing to yield everything to English interests, and he came home with a treaty that was so extravagantly English that it fell an easy prey to the anti-English minority, ever alert for the makings of a bugaboo to scare the plain people. . . .

When he said this, and more besides, and said it with wit and eloquence, the American reading public ate it up.

But of course this is not all there was to it—far from that. The 1920's were made to order for Mencken for other and better reasons. The decade was one of great urban prosperity and popular pleasure-taking, and what Mencken said was, Go to it, and stop feeling so sheepish about enjoying yourself. It was a decade of increasing cosmopolitanism and sophistication, and that involved learning how to put aside any lingering Puritanical scruples that might inhibit full realization and enjoyment, and Mencken could demonstrate how simplistic and hypocritical such scruples were. It was a decade when the cities and city ways invaded the countryside and, with the help of the Model-T Ford and the radio and cinema and the mass magazines, displaced the agrarian isolation that had largely prevailed since the days of the Founding Fathers, and Mencken could pen lines such as:

There, where the cows low through the still night, and the jug of Peruna stands behind the stove, and bathing begins, as at Biarritz, with the vernal equinox—there is the reservoir of all the nonsensical legislation which now makes the United States a buffoon among the great nations.

And he could declare of William Jennings Bryan, the idol of the corn belt, that "what animated him from end to end of his grotesque career was simply ambition—the ambition of a common man to get his hand upon the collar of his superiors, or, failing that, to get his thumb into their eyes." And refer to the leading religious faiths of the American hinterlands as "Baptist and Methodist barbarism." And insist that "it was among country Methodists, practitioners of a theology degraded almost to the level of voodooism, that Prohibition was invented, and it was by country Methodists, nine-tenths of them actual followers of the plow, that it was fastened upon the rest of us, to the damage of our bank accounts, our dignity and our ease."

The politics of the 1920's—Harding and Coolidge and the Herbert Hoover-Al Smith election of 1928—were such as positively to demand the satirical talents of a Mencken. For the politics were venal, low in content and Fustian in oratorical expression, concerned with issues other than of major significance, and more than usually devoid of ideals and ideology. It was as if the progressivism and the "New Freedom" of the 1910's had exhausted for a space the capacity of the American electorate to deal in genuine reform, and upright citizens were weary of the consideration of moral issues. Nobody of importance was disposed or encouraged to isolate and attack the underlying and unsolved economic and social problems that would once again surface in the wake of the Great Depression; the prevalent disposition was to let well enough alone and to concern oneself with less fundamental matters. The issues that interested voters most in the 1920's—prohibition, the Ku Klux Klan, the Anti-Saloon League, taxation, immigration, the bonus, the tariff —and the terms on which such issues were being dealt with, were uninspiring and sordid, and what was desired by persons of some taste and culture was someone who could ridicule the entire business, point out the crassness, and encourage one to wash his hands of the whole mess and think about more pleasant things. This was precisely what H. L. Mencken was able and willing to do. Repeatedly and in great good humor he blasted the politicians and politics of both national parties. "If any genuinely honest and altruistic politician had come to the surface in America in my time I'd have heard of him," he wrote, "for I have always frequented newspaper offices, and in a newspaper office the news of such a marvel would cause a dreadful tumult. I can recall no such tumult." And, "The only way to success in American public life lies in flattering and kowtowing to the mob. A candidate for office, even the highest, must either adopt its current manias *en bloc*, or convince it hypocritically that he has done so, while cherishing reservations *in petto*." And, in a noted definition that summed up for himself and his readers the results of the presidential election of 1924,

Democracy is that system of government under which the people, having 35,717,342 native-born adult whites to choose from, including thousands who are handsome and many who are wise, pick out a Coolidge to be head of the State. It is as if a hungry man, set before a banquet prepared by master cooks and covering a table an acre in area, should turn his back upon the feast and stay his stomach by catching and eating flies.

What the reader of Mencken could be encouraged to realize was that the situation was hopeless but not serious—the electorate was quite beyond reform, the cultural, political, and social life of the republic was incredibly vulgar, and no thinking man could hope to discover much Truth, Beauty and Goodness in it. The way to take it was to laugh at it, to sit back and enjoy the stupendous carnival of buncombe, and to cultivate one's own private garden of aesthetic and gastronomic delights. And he was so good at pointing the way. One after another his volumes of *Prejudices* appeared, offering document after document of comic genius. He laughed at the yokels, reprimanded the wayward press, exposed the hypocrisy of reformers, dismasted the politicians, poked fun at the unworldly intellectuals, chided pedantic academics, flayed the latter-day Puritans of the Bible Belt, decried bigots, fakes, and confidence artists of all sorts. He traveled to Dayton, Tennessee, for the Scopes Anti-Evolution Trial, and he had a field day at the assembled ignorance and humbuggery. He never missed a national political convention, and he was in his glory as the hot air gusted and the hack politicos posed and preened. No writer, not even his friend Sinclair Lewis, delighted more in the incongruity and madness of the

American scene, and no one had a greater flair for identifying and citing the minute particularities of its zaniness. He had a gift for the concrete example, the specified vulgarity, the tangible image. He singled out individuals and institutions and events, proclaimed their oddity in splendid hyperbole, then clinched his argument by more hyperbole. His forte was the loaded simile, the wickedly absurd metaphor, the hilarious rhetorical question:

It is impossible to fit any reasonable concept of the soldierly into the familiar proceedings of the [American] Legion. Its members conduct themselves like a gang of Methodist vice-crusaders on the loose, or a Southern lynching party.

Or,

One thinks of Dr. Woodrow Wilson's biography of George Washington as one of the strangest of the world's books. Washington: the first, and also perhaps the last American gentleman. Wilson: the self-bamboozled Presbyterian, the right-thinker, the great moral statesman, the perfect model of the Christian cad. It is as if the Rev. Billy Sunday should do a biography of Charles Darwin—almost as if Dr. Wilson himself should dedicate his senility to a life of the Chevalier Bayard, or the Cid, or Christ. . . .

Or,

I am in favor of free competition in all human enterprises, and to the utmost limits. I admire successful scoundrels, and I shrink from Socialists as I shrink from Methodists.

His role, in those days, was essentially negative—the demolition of the rotten, the half-baked, the hypocritical, the petty. If he blasted some targets that didn't deserve it, if he let his numerous personal vendettas color some of his judgments, that was all right. What was most needed was someone to label the fools as fools and the idiots as imbeciles, and no one was better at that than Mencken —just as in the 1910's no one was better or more useful than Mencken in clearing away the falseness, artificiality, squeamishness and prudery that were blocking the coming into being of an American literature that could image the true nature of the national experience.

Yet to say that he was valuably negative and usefully destructive will not quite cover it, either—for there was much, both by inference and explicitly, that was positive and creative to him, too. He championed the beautiful, entertained the ideas and insights of European civilization seriously and applied them to the recalcitrant American scene, valued honesty and praised it, gave needed support to science and knowledge and to fairness and decency, while gleefully nailing the superstitious, the naive, the vicious, the tricky, the bigoted who fought such enlightenment. "Needless to say," he wrote of the humorist George Ade, "a moralist stands behind the comedian. He would teach; he even grows indignant. . . . Up to a certain point it is all laughter, but after that there is a flash of the knife, a show of teeth." He might have been writing of himself as well. Up to a point, anyway.

He was, to repeat, happily at ease in Zion, because he could feel that the resident foolishness and stupidity didn't personally affect him and could not, and that laughing about it was all the defense possible or necessary. The real trouble, the portentous and ominous signs that lay behind the carnival of the 1920's, he did not recognize and did not want to recognize. The fact that the American business prosperity did not extend beyond the cities into the countryside and that its financial underpinnings were fearfully shaky did not occur to him. Nor did the fact that Western Europe was in bad economic and social shape, that ugly things were happening in Germany and that Italy had already turned to a strong man to keep the trains running on time and the Bolsheviks suppressed, that England and France were showing signs of incipient exhaustion—to the significance of all this and to much besides he was oblivious, along with most of his fellow countrymen. And when on an October day in 1929 the stock market collapsed and factories began shutting down and the businesses folded and the banks failed and the United States of America went spiraling down from the good times of the 1920's into the worst economic depression in its history, he could not understand what had happened. His world—the Zion which he was so conspicuously at ease in and which so ceaselessly had amused him and to whose low-life he could feel so superior, *without it mattering* (which is a very important proviso)—fell away from around him like the walls and the roof of a frame bungalow in the path of a cyclone, and left him all by himself.

His day—as public disturber of the peace and flailer of the boo-boisie, at least—was done. No longer might one view the farmer as "no hero at all, and no priest, and no altruist, but simply a tedious fraud and ignoramus, a cheap rogue and hypocrite, the eternal Jack of the human pack" who "deserves all that he suffers under our economic system, and more"—not when he was ragged and starving. No longer might one characterize American democracy merely as "the domination of unreflective and timorous men, moved in vast herds by mob emotions," and advocate government by an elite—not when in Germany the Hitler Youth was learning to march in formation and burn synagogues, and selected socialists were being shot by the rightist opposition in other countries, and in Spain and elsewhere the mass killing was starting. Not only were America and the rest of the world in a seemingly hopeless mess, but it was clearly serious and it clearly *mattered*.

What H. L. Mencken did then, or at any rate tried to do, was to insist that it wasn't so. He shut his ears and eyes to the dreadful evidence, simply refused to admit its existence. He denied that there was a crisis, he declined to recognize the financial chaos and economic misery, he proclaimed the reports of Nazi savagery greatly exaggerated and would not concede any true difference between the Germany he had admired back before the First World War and the Germany of Adolf Hitler. "The real issue in this campaign," he wrote, incredibly, of the Roosevelt-Hoover election of 1932, with the banks failing and the breadlines forming and the mortgages being foreclosed all about him, "is something else again. Unless I greatly err, that issue is Prohibition." And when Roosevelt won in a landslide and the New Deal went to work to revive the nation's broken-down economy, his mild tolerance of Franklin Roosevelt changed to a bitter hatred such as eclipsed even his rage against Woodrow Wilson. For the first time in all his years of covering politics, he lost his sense of humor, and what had been the style of matchlessly witty abuse now turned to sour, sullen viciousness. Even when the barbarity of Nazism began to be unmistakably apparent, and the Wehrmacht's preparations for another world war obvious, he would not concede that this time it was different, and that his beloved German people were desperately and dangerously sick. He had always liked Jews and enjoyed their company;

but now his Jewish friends could not go along with his refusal to accept the seriousness and the ugliness of Nazi Germany, and when he tried to make out that all the alarm over Hitler was a tempest in a teapot, some friendships of long standing ended.

What he did in those years was the best thing he could have done, given his talents and his limitations. He gave up the editorship of the *American Mercury,* and effectively removed himself from the national scene as a commentator on the condition of the nation and the world. For the Baltimore *Sun* he continued his political correspondence, but his main creative efforts went into his ground-breaking work on the American language and on what turned out to be three magnificently humorous and tender volumes of autobiography. He left the contemporary scene and went back to the Baltimore of his childhood, his family, his early years, his beginnings as a newspaperman in the 1900's—and in his three *Days* books produced some of the finest nostalgia, witty, sly, gentle, affectionate, ever written by an American. On November 11, 1948, he suffered a crippling stroke, and though he made a partial recovery, he was unable to read or to write. He could, though, make simple editorial judgments on unpublished material he had written, and could select and organize his papers. For a little more than eight years this man whose entire adult life had been devoted to the written word lingered, with amazing good humor, in a world about which he could no longer write a word, until on January 29, 1956, he died.

He left behind him a shelfload of books which contain some of the richest and most incisive humorous commentary on American life and letters ever written. At his best he was matchless—and not once or twice but scores of times. The collected essays, articles, and set pieces that make up the *Prejudices* volumes constitute, all in all, a literary legacy of remarkable luster. His role in the national letters was invaluable. To historians of American literature his work of the period from 1908 to 1923 is what matters most. During those years, writing almost exclusively as a literary critic, he was a one-man wrecking crew in the task of clearing away the outmoded, imprisoning superstructure of the Genteel Tradition of polite Victorian ideality that was blocking the making of modern American literature, and in championing the bold innovators who wanted to write openly and honestly about their experience. The social historians, however, are more concerned with the Mencken of the 1920's, when as editor of *The American Mercury* he was, as the New York *Times* declared, "the most powerful private citizen in America." Bidding farewell then to the criticism of literature, he took for his province the whole American scene, and for a decade staged a virtuoso performance of dazzling and uproarious brilliance, chronicling the doings of his countrymen with a wit and a joyousness that even today, a half-century afterward when the specific occasions have long since ended and the personalities are mostly only dim memories, can still evoke unfettered merriment. For the student of humor, the devotee of the incongruous and the absurd, almost the entire body of his work, from beginning to end, is a rich mine of resources. Much of it, to be sure, is dated now; no writer who made such brilliant use of the topical and the specific could fail to lose some of his zest once the occasion has passed. How, for example, to translate for today's audience the compacted wit contained in this sentence about the late Nicholas Murray Butler: "Moreover, he is a member of the American Academy himself, elected as a wet to succeed Edgar Allan Poe"? To savor that remark one has to know who Butler was, what the American Academy of Arts and Letters was and was not during the early 1920's, and what being a "wet" meant. But all in all, though much is taken, much remains, and there is a great deal of Mencken that does not date—enough to win him a permanent place in the pantheon of American comic art.

He is, I am convinced, a misunderstood figure—or not so much misunderstood as not understood at all. Because he wrote so dazzlingly of the texture of American life, and because he insisted that the surface was what mattered, critics and historians have tended to take him at his word, and not sought to look behind the facade he projected. But what he wrote about Mark Twain ought not to be overlooked: "Nothing could be more unsound than the Mark Legend—the legend of the lighthearted and kindly old clown. . . . The real Mark was a man haunted to the point of distraction by the endless and meaningless tragedy of existence —a man whose thoughts turned to it constantly, in season and out of season." H. L. Mencken was no Mark Twain; he did not know himself as Clemens did. He did not look inside. But all the same, there are certain things that ought not to go unexamined. Can, for example, that desperate refusal to admit after 1929 that the world had changed be attributed merely to obtuseness, to an invincible hedonism? Or was it that the man could not bear to think about it, could not dare admit to himself that his world really was the desperate, inexplicable thing he said that all great novelists showed? That the Germany of his family background and his father's allegiance really was the Germany of Adolf Hitler? That helpless people were suffering, and that nothing could be done to stop it?

What is the significance of that buried reference in his papers, which Carl Bode mentions in his biography, to a time, back before his father died and he was dutifully laboring in the family cigar factory, that H. L. Mencken strongly contemplated suicide? Why are the three volumes of his autobiography so very external, so completely devoid of any of the pain and travail of growing up? Why did this youth of obvious literary talent and strong intellectual leanings elect not to go to college, but to join his father's business—only to quit the day after his father's death? What did what must have been the searing experience of the First World War and his several years of obloquy and unpopularity mean to this young writer who so enjoyed the limelight and so hungered for fame? How much of his rage against Woodrow Wilson, and later Franklin Roosevelt, is the anger of a son for a self-righteous father figure? What of this warm-blooded, affectionate, sociable man who did not marry until the age of fifty, five years after his mother died? And what did it mean, growing up in the Baltimore that he loved and never left, not even during his years as editor of the *Smart Set* and the *Mercury*, to be a German-American, when the society, the power, the higher education, even much of the official culture of the city were so strongly in the hands of the old Anglo-American establishment? Nobody seems to have inquired into any of these matters. We have taken this very complex and very formidable man entirely on the terms he set forth.

What kind of a man was H. L. Mencken? What made him tick? The biographies and critical studies don't say. Of all our important literary figures he has been the most taken for granted, the least investigated. Nowhere, in the sublimely amused Mencken that most of the printed accounts of his life and times project, is that young man who could write to another young man, Theodore Dreiser, in the year 1911, that *Jennie Gerhardt* "comes upon me with great force. It touches my own experience of life in a hundred places; it preaches (or perhaps I had better say exhibits) a philosophy of life that seems to me to be sound; altogether I get a powerful effect of reality, stark and unashamed. It is drab and gloomy, but so is the struggle for existence. It is without humor, but so are the jests of the great comedian who shoots at our heels and makes us do our grotesque dancing." That is not the picture of his experience that we get in his autobiography. Ought we, therefore, to take his version of his life at its face value?

Everything that we know of humorists tells us that they laugh at the incongruities and absurdities of the *comedie humaine* because they cannot bear to do otherwise. Was it different with Mencken?

Not for the Old Lady in Dubuque

Gerald Weales

When the *New Yorker* was young, it could still laugh at itself. During its first year, Corey Ford contributed a series, "The Making of a Magazine," which presumably took the reader behind the scenes and showed him how Eustace Tilley managed to get the whole thing together. The joke, which was more characteristic than it was funny, was that the tone of the pieces was primly professional while the events described ranged from the purely amateur to the serenely absurd. In the early days, each anniversary number led off with an item in "The Talk of the Town" congratulating the magazine on still being alive; in 1927 (February 19), the note said, somewhat wryly, "We may even, in the next twelve months, develop a Righteous Cause or two and become Important." Not that an occasion was needed for a self-deprecating plug. In "A Reader's Tribute" in the issue of September 11, 1926, Elmer Davis compared the *New Yorker* favorably with "Uncle Cyrus Curtis's weekly." "What with the editorial page and Hergesheimer's stories," Davis explained, the *Saturday Evening Post* had become so heavy that it was not as useful as the *New Yorker* for killing mosquitoes: "the loathsome insects can always hear it coming in time to get out of the way." In one case —a Ralph Barton cartoon—an inside joke had serious implications about what the magazine wanted to be, what it was and what it would become. The cartoon appeared in the issue for December 12, 1925, when the magazine was less than a year old. It shows

231

an attractive matron, wearing a typical short dress of the period; she appears to be dancing and, in the process, kicking over a cocktail shaker and toppling the cigarette out of her elegantly long holder. The caption: "Disturbing Effect of the Spirit of Christmas on the Old Lady in Dubuque, As Revealed in a Christmas Card Received by The New Yorker from That Worthy Dame." The reference, of course, is to the prospectus that Harold Ross wrote when the *New Yorker* was still in the making. Its most famous proclamation was that "The New Yorker will be the magazine which is not edited for the old lady in Dubuque." Ross wanted "a magazine avowedly published for a metropolitan audience," and, particularly in the early days, it was as relentlessly provincial as it had promised to be, mainly concerning itself with the minutiae of New York City life. Yet, as the Barton cartoon suggested, there was not that great a distance between the old lady in Dubuque and the boys and girls from Salt Lake City, Columbus, Ohio, and Mount Vernon, New York, who put out their insular journal. Within a few years, the best of the *New Yorker* contributors—first the humorists, then the short-story writers— found a following far beyond the Hudson River.

"I reflect that not everyone has little pieces published in magazines," wrote E. B. White in a "little piece" about the dangers of not wearing a hat. "*Almost* everyone does, but not everyone" ("No Hat," November 27, 1926). The first few years of the *New Yorker* show how right E. B. White was. Not only do those writers who became identified with the *New Yorker* appear —White, James Thurber, Robert Benchley, Dorothy Parker, John O'Hara, Frank Sullivan—but there are frequent contributions from men like Elmer Davis and Gilbert Seldes, who went on to do other kinds of writing in other places. Actors as different as Leslie Howard and Groucho Marx turn up, being funny, or trying to be, and there are comic pieces from Ernest Hemingway, Upton Sinclair, F. Scott Fitzgerald. What's more, Hemingway's is genuinely amusing ("My Own Life," February 12, 1927). The "little piece," the "casual," to borrow one of Ross's words, was not exactly a *New Yorker* invention. *Judge*, which Harold Ross edited for a while, and the old *Life*, and even *College Humor* and *Vanity Fair*, in their very different ways, had their versions of the "little piece." The minuscule piece, one might say, for some of the contributions in *Life* and *Judge* ran for no more than a paragraph or two, but then neither did some of the early offerings in the *New Yorker*. Ross's magazine finally turned its back on its nearest relatives, but not until it had borrowed the best of their writers and cartoonists, and an occasional idea as well.

As these other magazines faded away and the *New Yorker* solidified its position, the brief, humorous essay began to be identified as "*New Yorker* humor." The label is misleading if it is supposed to define with any exactitude a particular kind of prose work, for the range within the "little pieces" is great—from verbal slapstick to philosophic ruefulness. Still, there is a generic sameness within the variations. The types were established very early. The most common device was for the writer to take a recognizable current event as a place to begin and to build on it an intricate framework of fantasy or simple comment. In "The Seed of Revolt" (May 29, 1926), Robert Benchley contemplates the pedestrians' problem in a city beset by new construction, using as his starting point an actual fire on the wooden staging around a construction site; in "How I Became a Subway Excavator" (January 23, 1926), the building of a new subway becomes the excuse for one of Frank Sullivan's characteristic descents—or ascents—into autobiographical lunacy. When the events were of more than local interest—national and international news stories, real or manufactured—the *New Yorker* writers returned to them again and again; thus, in the early years of the magazine there were a great many pieces that grew out of the Lindbergh flight, expeditions to the North Pole, the Halls-Mills case. Calvin Coolidge was the butt of a great many jokes in both the cartoons and the essays. In "Kamp Koolidge Nights" (June 5, 1926), Robert Benchley imagines the President putting on "that property pair of overalls that was used for photographic publicity purposes during the campaign" and telling stories around the campfire: "A reggeler ghost story about th' time up Bostin way when I run inter a hull tribe er strikin' policemen and held 'em at bay, singlehanded." The piece, however, is the usual one based on a news peg, in this case the announcement that the Summer White House would be in the Adirondacks. Unless some such news story triggered the essay, Coolidge's name was likely to appear simply as one of a number of familiar names of the period—Herbert Bayard Swope, William Lyon Phelps, Grover Whalen—which for some reason the writers found funny in the way that radio comedians used to depend on a mention of Brooklyn or Sheboygan to get a laugh. There was obviously a deal of political acumen in the mock election analyses that Frank Sullivan wrote during the Hoover-Smith campaign, and his response to that election was the most partisan essay I can remember seeing in the early *New Yorker* ("Votes from Contented Precincts," December 1, 1928). For the most part, *New Yorker* humor was not political.

Among *New Yorker* writers in search of a subject, the private incident was almost as popular as the public event. E. B. White got an amiable short piece ("Petit Dejeuner," September 18, 1926) out of trying and failing to explain to an uncomprehending French waiter how to serve the shredded wheat he was so delighted at having discovered in a grocery in Paris. James Thurber, working somewhat more broadly, edged into farce in his account of the aftermath of a presailing party ("My Trip Abroad," August 6, 1927). This kind of piece, in the hands of White and Thurber, became a cross between personal anecdote and social comment. On the one hand, then, it shared the characteristics of those perennial pieces that catalogued the difficulties and the indignities which one faced when one went shopping, went abroad, tried to mail a letter, entered a bank, went to or gave a party, rented a summer cottage—the list is endless. Sometimes, in the hands of Robert Benchley or Donald Ogden Stewart, such material was newly funny; more often, even the masters nodded, and anyone leafing through the pages of the old *New Yorker* is likely to shudder and say, oh, no, here comes another embarkation party. On the other hand, the personal incident began to move toward the character sketch, the short story. Although E. B. White can make me believe that he observed a real drunk when he went to see the Lunts in *Caprice* ("Interpretation," April 13, 1929), there is no real reason why the incidents that the humorists used could not be fictional. Certainly, very early in the *New Yorker*'s history writers like Dorothy Parker, Arthur Kober and Marc Connelly began to invent not only the incidents but the voices that described them.

A typical example is Arthur Kober's "Just a Pal" (March 31, 1928). A girl whom the *New Yorker* readers had met in an earlier Kober piece complains about her friend Florrie for whom she will never again do a favor. When Florrie was delayed in the subway on the way home from work, the narrator kindly agreed to go out with Florrie's boyfriend, just to save the waste of a ticket, but when she discovered that the show was at Carnegie Hall ("and, believe me, I saw a lotta foreign element"), she walked out at intermission and came home to tell Florrie how lucky she was to have missed it. She cannot understand either Florrie's tears or her ingratitude. Such sketches were a first step toward what came to be known as the *New Yorker* story.

Either the personal incident or the public event—more often the second—could be approached through parody, and that form became one of the *New Yorker* standards. It has always been an attractive genre to comic writers whether they really tried to imitate the original they were kidding or whether they went for burlesque and buried a recognizable source under a load of grotesque overstatement. The form was particularly popular in the 1920's, both in book-length works and in the comic magazines that preceded the *New Yorker*. Many of the writers who came over to Harold Ross's new magazine brought a reputation for parody with them. Donald Ogden Stewart is a prime example. His first book was *A Parody Outline of History* (1921), in which he recounts events in American history in a variety of styles, ranging from that of James Branch Cabell to that of Thornton W. Burgess; his second book, *Perfect Behavior* (1922), was a burlesque etiquette manual. There are parody elements in many of his *New Yorker* contributions—the practical advice article peeks through "How I Got My Rabbits to Lay" (April 7, 1928) and "How We Made Both Ends Meet in the Middle" (April 28, 1928)—but there were so many parodists in the *New Yorker* pages that Stewart was barely noticeable in the crowd. Parke Cummings turned up with a description of a bridge contest in a competent sports page style ("Clubs Is Trumps," March 13, 1926), and Nunnally Johnson described a bathroom whistler as though he were writing a music review ("Good Clean Fun," May 15, 1926). Most forms of popular journalism and literature were cycled through the parody mill, and, of course, the more serious writers were fair game. One of James Thurber's early contributions to the magazine was "A Visit from Saint Nicholas" (December 24, 1927), a version of Clement Moore's Christmas poem retold "In the Ernest Hemingway Manner." Hemingway's own *New Yorker* piece was ostensibly a parody of Frank Harris's *My Life and Loves*. As a critic, I admit a certain difficulty with the parodists. I admire individual pieces that range from E. B. White's "Worm Turning" (October 1, 1927), a take-off on Alexander Woollcott at his worst —which could be most anytime—to Peter De Vries's parody of Elizabeth Bowen ("Touch and Go," January 26, 1952). Yet, it is not a genre I warm to. Corey Ford's "New Light on the Rothstein Theory" (March 2, 1929), which discusses the traffic problem in scientific terminology, is an efficient, restrained piece that sticks to its initial conception, but, for me, it is dead after one paragraph. On the other hand, Ring Lardner's "Miss Sawyer, Champion" (September 10, 1927), which begins as a parody of tennis reporting and ends somewhere near surrealism, is the kind of comic writing that remains alive although it kills its first parodic impulse as it grows. *New Yorker* writers, depending on whether they wanted to demonstrate their ear or their imagination, vacillated between restraint and exuberance in their use of parody; particularly in the early days, they tended to walk on the wild side.

Although the best of the *New Yorker* humorists developed unmistakable literary personalities and the styles to express them, there is a storehouse of comic devices and verbal tricks which most of them used on occasion. The non sequitur, for instance, and its cousin, the irrelevant aside. Listen to the parenthetic remark in this sentence from Robert Benchley's "Sex Is Out" (December 19, 1925): "According to Dr. Max Hartmann (I used to have a dentist named Dr. Hartmann, but he was a dentist) there is no such thing as absolute sex." Or take this sentence from Ring Lardner's "Miss Sawyer, Champion": "Yesterday's event was attended by the largest crowd of the season, attracted not only because it was the championship final, but also by the fact that the former Miss Stevens's birthplace in Portugal gave the match an international odor." The line almost makes sense, and then one realizes that its spurious plausibility is completely undone by the fact that there is no Miss Stevens anywhere else in the article. There is something so gentle about E. B. White and something so logical about his writing that it takes a second or two to recognize his personal variation on the standard non sequitur in a line like, "Let a man's leg be never so shapely, sooner or later his garters wear out" ("Garter Motif," June 5, 1926).

Repetition is another of the comic devices. The narrator in Dorothy Parker's "Dialogue at Three in the Morning" (February 13, 1926) is a little bit drunk, which might explain her saying, "Trouble with me is, I'm too kind-hearted. That's what everybody always told me. 'Trouble with you is, you're too kind-hearted,' they said." But almost exactly the same line can be found in Frank Sullivan's "How I Became a Subway Excavator," published a month earlier: "The folks, I guess, think I'm more interested in digging that subway than I am in my job. 'You're more interested in that subway than you are in your job,' they tell me." The joke, I assume, lies in the almost confessional tone of the lines, the suggestion that the alteration of a word or two or the movement from indirect to direct address brings with it a new revelation. Another favorite repetition joke can also be found in the work of Frank Sullivan. He has always been obsessive about fashionable names, as his annual holiday poem for the *New Yorker* indicates, but in an early piece, a mock society column ("The Costume Balls," March 13, 1926), his list of celebrities is designed so that certain names keep appearing. The device is not simply comic, as the repetition of any sounds might be, but satiric as well. The implication is that certain figures manage to elbow their way to a real lion's share of public attention. Elmer Davis makes this specific in his use of the joke. In "Now It Can Be Told" (October 16, 1926), an eyewitness gives a list of the famous people on hand the night of the Halls-Mills murders. After mentioning Herbert Bayard Swope six times, she says, "Oh, dear, I've gone and mentioned Mr. Swope twice; but really that is precisely the impression which he makes upon me." Still another variation in the repetition technique is the line that keeps returning like a refrain. In a parody of syndicated columns that peddle exotic New York to local papers ("Metropolitan Nature Fakers,"

July 23, 1927), Nunnally Johnson describes each of his exciting New Yorkers as "a collector of rare first editions and an admirer of Nietzsche." He caps the gag by changing the wording the last time the line appears; his chorus girl "has an excellent collection of rare first editions including one of 'Thus Spake Zarathustra.' " The switcheroo—as they say in show business—may not be all that funny, but Johnson's comic instincts are sound; the correct finish to that kind of refrain is to deny and fulfill the audience expectations at the same time.

Another popular comic device, and one that may have had a deleterious effect on the *New Yorker* at its most serious, is the use of excessive incidental detail. Originally, of course, the detail itself was supposed to be funny. Thus Frank Sullivan introduced a "Mrs. Maud Fetterdetsch, tester of police whistles" into "How I Became a Subway Excavator," and Corey Ford, writing a fictional history of the magazine ("The Anniversary of a Great Magazine," February 20, 1926), turned out this sentence: "In those halcyon days, for example, a stage-line started at the Public Library (destroyed by fire in 1889, owing to a carelessly-tossed cigarette), circled Bryant Park to avoid the construction which had just started, crossed over to Broadway and ran down James G. Blaine, after which it was discontinued." The honorable ancestry of that kind of comic line can be seen in Crabtree's description of a pistol shot in *The School for Scandal:* "the ball struck against a little bronze Shakespeare that stood over the fireplace, grazed out of the window at a right angle, and wounded the postman, who was just coming to the door with a double letter from Northamptonshire." That kind of extended line was not the only, not even the most conventional way of playing with detail; as often as not, a single phrase, a specific name or location would be imbedded in an ordinary sentence. When Corey Ford mentioned "a prominent manufacturer named Meebles" in one of his essays on traffic problems ("How D'You Get What Way?" January 9, 1926), he probably thought the name Meebles funny—which it may be to some people—but the important part of the phrase is the man's occupation which gives a bogus authority to the whole invention. Perhaps a better example can be found in E. B. White's "Interview with a Sparrow" (April 9, 1927): "I stopped a sparrow recently at the Seventy-

second Street entrance to the Park and put the question bluntly."
In this case, the exact location plays against the unspecific "recently" and the whole air of accident—as though he had just happened to meet the sparrow—and gives the fantasy an almost reportorial substance. The *New Yorker's* preoccupation with detail turned finally to the kind of cataloguing which now makes the magazine almost unreadable. I picked up a recent issue (February 12, 1972) and found an item in "The Talk of the Town" which began, "Having been invited by the Brody Corporation, a hydra-headed association of restaurant operators, whose responsibilities include L'Étoile, Gallagher's Steak House, and the Rainbow Room, to drop in at the last of these during . . . ." The sentence went on for another half column. And it was not even meant to be funny. If Frank Sullivan had written it thirty years ago, it would have been funny and a great deal easier to read aloud.

I might have used Corey Ford's description of the stage-line that ran down James G. Blaine as an example of something other than the *New Yorker* absorption in detail. It also represents a kind of conscious overwriting used for comic effect. Sometimes the elaboration comes from the misuse of metaphor, as in this line, also from Corey Ford: "All too late the lily of truth, crushed to earth beneath the heel of Industry, tears the bandage from its eyes to behold the handwriting on the wall" ("The Bleakest Job," May 29, 1926). In time, such lines almost disappeared from the casuals, but they turned up as filler at the bottom of the page in the series of accidentally funny newsbreaks labeled "Block That Metaphor." Oddly enough, the pun, one of the standard forms of comic ornamentation, appeared infrequently in the early days of the *New Yorker*. One of Wolcott Gibbs's first pieces was built around the phrase "neither beer nor there" ("On Working That Line Into the Conversation," February 25, 1928), but it did not really try to inflict the pun on the reader; instead, it was a first-person account of a man's attempt to work the phrase into a conversation and his failure when the occasion arose. It was not until a master punner arrived that the form came into its own in the *New Yorker*. Of all the outrages committed by Peter De Vries, I prefer the response he swears he never made to the woman who said she saw the geese fly south: "Migratious!" ("Compulsion,"

January 17, 1953). The master of ornamentation at the *New Yorker*, at least since the 1930's, has been S. J. Perelman. His rich and scarcely appropriate vocabulary is one reason why his prose is so lush, but a look at a reasonably commonplace sentence of his will show that his effects are also syntactical. He can take the simplest sentence and convert it into a grandiosity by stuffing it with clause upon clause, phrase upon phrase. "Every woman cherishes a dream" is the kind of direct declarative sentence that might be an appropriate opening for a casual, but look what happens to it in S. J. Perelman's hands: "Every woman worth her salt, and even the few unsalted ones I have known, cherishes somewhere in her heart midway between the auricle and the ventricle a lovely, pastel-tinted dream." It may be inappropriate to make my point from "Why Boys Leave Home," a piece that first appeared in *The Saturday Evening Post* (September 23, 1944), but the example is too good to resist; besides it is typical Perelman. There is no more compelling indication of the variety in the *New Yorker* "little piece" than to consider this kind of prose alongside that of E. B. White and James Thurber, who, as the years passed, became increasingly spare in their effects.

Most of the familiar *New Yorker* names have appeared in the examples I have cited, but my attempt to define the genre and the shared literary devices necessarily buries the individual in the group. There is hardly time in a short paper to discuss each of the writers, but let me take a few minutes to comment on some of those who seem to me most characteristic of the magazine and its humor. Since most of them wrote for other publications as well, a few of my examples come from non-*New Yorker* pages, but so mild an impurity should not obscure the general picture. When Donald Ogden Stewart and Nunnally Johnson went off to Hollywood in the early 1930's, they practically ceased to write except for the films. Their identification with the *New Yorker* was necessarily brief, and I doubt that either man's name would occur to anyone who grew up with the magazine in the 1930's and 1940's. Yet Johnson's workmanlike pieces represent the kind of occasional essay that was the magazine's stock-in-trade in the 1920's, and he left behind him at least one magic line. I have still not mastered the implications of a sentence of his that begins, "This fact was brought home, or even worse, early last Thursday morning . . ." ("Good Clean Fun"). Stewart was at his best in the strange historical essays in which he leavened a demented family chronicle with a touch of social comment. In "The President's Son" (December 10, 1927), an illogical extension of Nan Britton's revelations about President Harding, Stewart tells an idyllic tale of the meetings between his mother and an unidentified president —first, at a white elephant sale in New Britain, Connecticut; then, at Grant's Tomb; finally, in a tree during the Johnstown Flood. This kind of invention has its verbal equivalent in lines like, "But daisies, like the cat who bit John D. Rockefeller, Jr., are often 'all too human,' and this year I'm going to tell" ("After Christmas— What?" December 31, 1927). Frank Sullivan worked a similar vein when he first began to write for the *New Yorker*. For instance, in "Three Methods of Acquiring Loam" (May 26, 1928), he converts the sidetrack into the main road. He explains, almost parenthetically, that the British stripped Manhattan of its loam when they evacuated it during the Revolutionary War, which leads him to Luther Burbank and his separation of "hoats" into "two distinct varieties . . . hay and oats." At another point in the same essay, illustrating the way to show your friends that you would like loam as a gift, he writes a conversation which somehow turns into an attempt to pick up a girl on Fifth Avenue and, then, into a musical comedy with a love song which ends incredibly with "They needed a tenor in Heaven so they took Caruso away." One of Sullivan's later inventions is Mr. Arbuthnot, the cliché expert, who appears in a great many dialogue pieces. The character is a treasurehouse of bromidic answers—a testimony to Sullivan's good ear—but the Arbuthnot exchanges are too restrained to show Sullivan at his best. He is most himself at his most irrelevant—for instance, when, apropos of nothing at all, he suddenly says, "Succotash had not yet, however, come into its own" ("Down the Ages with the Social Center," March 6, 1926).

Presumably most of the *New Yorker* humorists began writing in college, but Corey Ford and S. J. Perelman somehow stayed closer to their campus origins. Ford, who had edited the *Jester* at Columbia, went downtown and began to contribute to *Judge*, *Life*, *Vanity Fair* and, as soon as it was founded, the *New Yorker*.

Perelman came down from Brown, where he had edited the *Brown Jug,* to work for *Judge* and to contribute to *Life* among others. It was not until the 1930's that he began to write for the *New Yorker.* The two humorists differ in that Ford worked in a variety of styles, adapting himself to the immediate needs of the situation and the subject; Perelman early adopted a personal style that has hardly changed between the 1920's and the 1970's. What the two men have in common is that the work of both of them seems very strained; it gives off an air of conscious cleverness that harks back to the editorial rooms of the college humor magazines from which they came. It is this quality in Ford's work, I assume, that kept him from building a large following, as so many of the *New Yorker* writers did—this quality, plus an almost complete absence of literary personality. S. J. Perelman, on the other hand, has—or once had—legions of admirers. If I may wax autobiographical, for a moment, I was once among them. In my college days in the late 1940's, when humor magazines were just beginning to die, I was a Perelman enthusiast at a time when I was no more than an admirer of Thurber and White. I now find it very difficult to read a collection like *Keep It Crisp* (1946). When Perelman calls himself "the present troubadour" ("*Whose* Lady Nicotine?") or says that "Mr. Farber recently sat himself down" ("Hell in the Gabardines"), I squirm a little and try to catch a glimpse of the old imagination behind the fancy wordwork. Perelman is probably in better control in most of his pieces than are Donald Ogden Stewart and Frank Sullivan in the essays I applauded earlier, but a controlled outrageousness has its limits. What he lacks, I think, is a genuine wildness.

It is not particularly evident in his first contributions to the *New Yorker,* but Robert Benchley is the comic in this group who developed the firmest personality. That may be because the character he created—the voice in most of his pieces—had a life both on and off the page. He was a busy and successful journalist in 1923 when he went on stage, in the third *Music Box Revue,* and first performed his famous monologue, "The Treasurer's Report." In 1928, the "Report" was filmed and Benchley went on to make more than forty film shorts in which he tried, with a kind of placid desperation, to make something simple seem complicated; during the

1940's, he played variations on his likable bumbler in feature films. The Benchley character was also clearly delineated in the caricature that Gluyas Williams created to illustrate the many Benchley books. More important, of course, is that the character emerges in the short pieces that Benchley continued to write even after he became a movie star—for instance, in the King Features columns collected in *My Ten Years in a Quandary and How They Grew* (1936). The character is a little vain, always willing to strut a few steps before he falls into a real or imaginary manhole. He is a touch ponderous as he tries to explain things, and he is constantly viewing with mild alarm. Embarrassment is almost a disease with him. He is sometimes fictional—working in the planetarium with Mr. MacGregor, the old Navy man—but more often simply an afterimage of the author himself. As I have described him, he is not unlike a great many other comic characters, the little man beset by the intricacies of life, catching whatever transient pleasures he can. There is, however, a dark side to this man. He would never say so directly, but mortality and an unfriendly universe are also after him. This is clear in "My Trouble," in which he wonders "Do all boys of 46 stop breathing when they go to bed?" and in "Duck, Brothers!" in which he is quite certain that "a full-fledged rain of ten-ton flame-balls" is heading directly for him: "I know where I'm not wanted." These pieces are as funny as the lighter ones, but they do have a disquieting undertone, which may indicate that Benchley was a more serious comic writer than he was ever willing to admit.

James Thurber and E. B. White are the two humorists most closely associated with the *New Yorker*. One could almost say that they were created by the magazine, but they in turn helped create it. It was their work that separated the "little piece" from the slapstick of the early days, that let it turn gentle, ruminative, even somber on occasion. E. B. White came to the *New Yorker* first, when it was only a few months old, and, as Marc Connelly once said, "brought the steel and the music to the magazine." In the early days, White did almost everything, from theater reviews to cartoon captions, but it was in the casuals that he established his authority. There is a sentimental side to the man which expresses itself in spongy lyricism and the kind of rue that grows in Dorothy Parker's garden. Most of that sentimentality was happily milked off in the verse that White wrote in the 1920's. In his prose, that quality was contained, became genuine sentiment, expressed an affection for places and people and the time of day that few other writers have been able to equal. White was quite capable of fooling around in the Frank Sullivan manner. In the collection of society notes that he calls "Fin de Saison—Palm Beach" (April 7, 1934), he uses all the familiar devices—funny names, ludicrous juxtaposition, abrupt irrelevancy—and the result is one of the funniest burlesques to come out of the *New Yorker*. Yet that is not the kind of piece which one identifies with E. B. White. The best of his work is in one of two forms, both allied to the short story—the personal anecdote and the parable. He came to the first quite early. In 1925, he made a characteristic piece ("Child's Play," December 19) out of having buttermilk spilled on him in a restaurant. He manipulated the material more obviously than he probably would have in later years, but he clearly established both a sense of the situation and the character of the narrator—qualities which would continue to mark his anecdotal pieces. In the parables, he displays greater range. It is wry intelligence that shows through "The Wings of Orville" (August 8, 1931), in which the sparrow's wife comes to share her husband's crackpot dream; in "The Door" (March 25, 1939), the irony turns frightening as his narrator's world becomes the rat's cage of the behavioral scientist.

It was 1927 when James Thurber first turned up in the pages of the *New Yorker*—with two poems that are of historical interest only. With his next appearance, "An American Romance" (March 5, 1927), the Thurber tone—or one of them—was already established. "Romance" tells the story of a "little man in an overcoat that fitted him badly at the shoulders" who took refuge in a revolving door and would not come out until he had become a public hero. " 'I did it for the wife and children,' he said." That piece and another early one about a man who tries to take a straw hat to the cleaners ("The Psyching of Mr. Rogers," April 27, 1929) have an undertone of pain and panic that weaves all through Thurber's work. It surfaces lightly in "A Note at the End" of *My Life and Hard Times* (1933), and it grows pervasive in Thurber's last years, as *Further Fables for Our Time* (1956) indicates. There are other Thurbers who

have to live with the dark humorist of the *Fables*. There is the
word crank who can be traced from the early series on "Our Own
Modern English Usage" (1929) through the dialect games of "What
Do You Mean It *Was* Brillig?" (January 7, 1939) to the children's
author of *The Wonderful O* (1957). There is the writer who,
beginning with "The Thin Red Leash" in 1927 (August 13), has
described the most unlikely company of dogs in modern letters.
There is the autobiographer of *My Life and Hard Times*, who
went again to his past in *The Thurber Album* (1952) and built
solid memoirs on ground that had already supported some of the
best and funniest comic writing in America. It seems to me that
what all these Thurbers have in common is the writer who insisted
on being rational in the cause of irrationality—at least, insofar as
that word can stand for fantasy, variety, openness, surprise and a
healthy distrust of all rules. That Thurber is implicit in the car-
toonist whose characters hear seals bark, crouch on bookcases,
"come from haunts of coot and hern." He is explicit in *Let Your
Mind Alone* (1937), the mock-serious discussion of popular psychology in which he says, "The undisciplined mind . . . is far
better adapted to the confused world in which we live. . . . This
is, I am afraid, no place for the streamlined mind."

The world is more confused in the 1970's than it was in the
1930's, but today there is apparently not even room for the undisciplined mind. At least, there is no room for the kind of comic
writing that these humorists represent. S. J. Perelman still turns
up in the pages of the *New Yorker*, but he is like a literary Rip
Van Winkle come home to a village that does not recognize him.
The magazine prints occasional casuals by Woody Allen, who out-
Perelmans Perelman, and by Roger Angell, among others, but it
has grown turgid and heavy, it has—as that 1927 note suggested—
developed "a Righteous Cause or two and become Important."
Hardly the home for the "little piece" that E. B. White had in
mind when he contemplated the dangers of going hatless. Nor is
there any other home. In a world in which there are fewer
magazines and in which the remaining ones tend to be very serious
or fakily flashy or aimed at a nongeneral audience, no magazine
editor wants the kind of comic writing that made the *New Yorker*
famous. No newspaper editor, either. Except for a few regional

columnists, the remaining newspaper humorists are almost completely political. Times change, tastes change. The *New Yorker* humorists have gone the way of Mark Twain and Mr. Dooley and Artemus Ward, into the libraries or into oblivion. It is my job as scholar and critic to record the fact, coldly, and pass on. But somehow this sounds like a lament. That may not be inappropriate. Not only has a kind of comic writing disappeared, but an attitude as well. "Quo Vadimus?" (May 24, 1930) is a case in point. In that piece, E. B. White stops a man in East Thirty-fourth Street and asks "Quo vadis?" He chides the man for giving his time and energy to pointless activities that obscure his simple wants, but before the piece ends it turns back on the author, sees him as one with the harried man and justifies the plural of the title. What all these writers share is a sense of complicity. Even when they are not their own subjects, there is an implicit recognition that only a fine line separates the satirist from his target, the humorist from his subject, the teller from the told. They know that all of us are clumsy, confused, vain and mortal, and that we build the wrong monuments to the wrong gods on the wrong quicksand. Perhaps one can no longer know that and still retain a deep affection for imperfect man and his unlikely works.

For all I know, there may no longer be an old lady in Dubuque.

Anodyne for the Village Virus

C. Hugh Holman

In the Middle Western and North Central states the land is vast, the weather vicious with frigid winters and flaming summers, the settlements few and small, and the people lonely. The wind can sweep across a thousand miles to roar against a small town of a thousand citizens and make them huddle together against its fury. The human spirit is put to special tests here, and the people—the children of immigrants from Scandinavia, Germany, and Central Europe as well as the dominant New Englanders whose Puritanism gives a vise-like strength to the primitive culture—feel the weight of weather, of a close community, of confining evangelical religion. There are two sentimental traditions of such small towns, as Sinclair Lewis asserted in *Main Street:* One is that "the American village remains the one sure abode of friendship, honesty, and clean sweet marriageable girls"; the other is that "the significant features of all villages are whiskers, iron dogs upon lawns, gold bricks, checkers, jars of gilded cat-tails, and shrewd comic old men who . . . ejaculate 'Waal, I swan.'" These traditions have little similarity to actual life in the small towns of this vast region.

The Middle West and the West have taken two anodynes against the waste of spirit and the harsh weight of care of which life can consist on the Great Plains. These anodynes are romantic idealization and self-mocking and sardonic laughter. The romantic idealization has elevated the lonely man, almost always on horseback, into a figure of great force, energy, and—above all—freedom. He is the plainsman, the cowboy, the Indian fighter—a man secure in himself and his skills, a creature of epic proportions. From James Fenimore Cooper's *The Prairie* to Jack Schaeffer's *Shane,* he has dominated the land like a demigod and embodied in his ideal self the aspirations of the little men huddling for comfort against the blank and threatening vastness of the land stretching between the Ohio River and the Rocky Mountains.

The other anodyne has been laughter, but it is a comedy at some variance from the exuberance and wildness and high-spirited extravagance of the Southwest. It has smacked more of New England than of Arkansas or Texas. It has more nearly echoed Seba Smith's Major Jack Downing than George Washington Harris's Sut Lovingood. It has stayed closer to actuality than has Southern humor with its wild anecdotes and exuberant actions. It has been more likely to be an essay than a tall tale, an acid comment on human frailty than an hilarious record of absurdity. Of the two main streams of native American humor which Constance Rourke defined, the West has drawn its major resources from the Yankee rather than the Southern stream, and has directed them against the institutions within which the laughers themselves have lived. Western comedy is social and satiric; it is, if not sober, at least serious; and it is deeply ironic in its view of the world. A major target for its attack early became the villages dotted at widely spaced intervals on the vast Middle Western landscape. The dreariness and quiet despair of life in these lonely towns could catch at the throat with a pathos that approached the tragic, as it did in Willa Cather's story "The Sculptor's Funeral" and in Sherwood Anderson's *Winesburg, Ohio.* It could arouse the anger of Hamlin Garland in *Main-Traveled Roads* or Joseph Kirkland in *Zury, The Meanest Man in Spring County* or E. W. Howe in *The Story of a Country Town.* But these towns could be and characteristically were handled with irony tempered with a sense of the comic. Excellent examples of such treatment, in addition to such Mark Twain pieces as "The Man That Corrupted Hadleyburg," are the *Fables in Slang* of George Ade. One of these "Fables," first published in 1900, illustrates the essayistic, "Yankee" manner and the use of the small town as humorous butt. It is "The Fable of the Slim Girl Who Tried to

Keep a Date That Was Never Made," and the first half of it goes like this:

> Once upon a Time there was a slim Girl with a Forehead which was Shiny and Protuberant, like a Bartlett Pear. When asked to put Something in an Autograph Album she invariably wrote the Following, in a tall, dislocated Back-Hand:
>
> > "Life is Real; Life is Earnest,
> > And the Grave is not its Goal."
>
> That's the kind of Girl she was.
>
> In her own Town she had the Name of being a Cold Proposition, but that was because the Primitive Yokels of a One-Night Stand could not Attune Themselves to the Views of one who was troubled with Ideals. Her Soul Panted for the Higher Life.
>
> Alas, the Rube Town in which she Hung Forth was given over to Croquet, Mush and Milk Sociables, a lodge of Elks, and two married Preachers who doctored for the Tonsilitis. So What could the Poor Girl do?
>
> In all the Country around there was not a Man who came up to her Plans and Specifications for a Husband. Neither was there any Man who had any time for Her. So she led a lonely Life, dreaming of the One—the Ideal. He was a big and pensive Literary Man, wearing a Prince Albert coat, a neat Derby Hat and godlike Whiskers. When He came he would enfold Her in his Arms and whisper Emerson's Essays to her.
>
> But the Party failed to show up.

Could her name have been Carol Kennicott and the name of the town be Gopher Prairie?

One of the most mordant attacks on village life and the way in which it stultifies and poisons the individual came with Edgar Lee Masters' *The Spoon River Anthology* in 1915, a collection of poems supposedly spoken by the dead who lie in the Spoon River cemetery, and describing their lives of frustration, despair, constraint, and suffering. These poems in a flat, effective, and strangely powerful free verse, together comprise a picture of life in a small town. Many of them are grim and dark; all are marked by irony that, although never happy, is often bitterly comic, as in Hod Putt's speech:

> Here I lie close to the grave
> Of Old Bill Piersol,

Who grew rich trading with the Indians, and who
Afterwards took the bankrupt law
And emerged from it richer than ever.
Myself grown tired of toil and poverty
And beholding how Old Bill and others grew in wealth,
Robbed a traveler one night near Proctor's Grove,
Killing him unwittingly while doing so,
For the which I was tried and hanged.
That was my way of going into bankruptcy.
Now we who took the bankrupt law in our respective ways
Sleep peacefully side by side.

Masters' Spoon River is grimly comic and its dead speak a series of dark judgments framed in formal, almost legalistic language.

Ring Lardner was a humorist, where Masters actually was not. Their views of the Middle Western small towns were remarkably alike, but there the similarity stopped, for Lardner was a superb master of the spoken language and he created a long line of characters whose idiom was recorded with great precision, while the frequently vain and empty man behind the words stood forth sharply revealed. Lardner had a wild, delightful, manic quality that could erupt into nonsensical laughter, as in one of his parody plays, "I Gaspiri," in which two strangers meet and this dialogue ensues:

FIRST STRANGER: Where was you born?
SECOND STRANGER: Out of wedlock.
FIRST STRANGER: That's mighty pretty country around there.

This wild play with words mixed together in inspired illogic although they sound as though they should make sense was Lardner's particular gift, and he used it with great skill in his hundreds of parodies. He took the lines:

Night and day under the hide of me
There's an Oh, such a hungry yearning, burning inside of me,

from Cole Porter's song, "Night and Day" which he declared shows up W. S. "Gilbert himself as a seventh-rate Gertrude Stein," and ran seven insane variations on them, including:

Night and day under the bark of me
There's an Oh, such a mob of microbes making a park of me,

and

Night and day under my tegument
There's a voice telling me I'm he, the good little egg you meant.

In the early part of his career, this language gift was employed in drawing comic pictures of small-town people. His first collection of stories, *You Know Me Al* (1916), is a series of letters written by a baseball player Jack Keefe to his best friend. These letters capture perfectly the half-literate Middle Western speech of the protagonist, who is gullible, stupid, conceited, and totally ignoble. Hilariously funny, the tales can almost sicken the reader with their picture of human depravity. Lardner followed this book with many others, among the best being *Gullible's Travels*, in which Mr. Gullible recounts in the exact language of his Middle-Western world the tortures of a vacation trip that he and his wife make. Mr. Gullible's account is filled with the illogic of average speech, with non sequiturs, and with such perfect uses of zeugma as "After supper we said good-bye to the night clerk and twenty-two bucks." This use of a cliché-laden vernacular was his primary means of showing up, without comment, the mindlessness, cunning, and selfishness of the average American. Perhaps his supreme picture of the Middle-Western small town is in "Haircut," a monologue by a barber Whitey, who tells the story of Jim Kendall, his cruelty to his wife and children, and his death, without ever understanding the meaning of what he is telling. It fits perfectly George Whicher's description of Lardner's specialty as being "his ability to report with seeming unconsciousness the appalling mediocrity and vanity of the middle-class soul." As Lardner's career developed, he moved further and further from the provincial life which he began by depicting with precise ironic truth and he wrote more and more about the world of suburbanites and of life on Long Island, in New York City, and in Florida, but he never lost his skill with language, his comic sense of incongruity, or his pessimistic despair.

Sinclair Lewis, America's first Nobel laureate in literature, was the summation and epitome of the satiric and comic reaction to what he labeled the "Village Virus." Indeed, the Nobel citation read: "The 1930 Nobel Prize in Literature is awarded to Sinclair Lewis for his powerful and vivid art of description and his ability to use wit and humor in the creation of original characters." A native of Sauk Centre, Minnesota, Lewis was educated at Oberlin College and Yale University. In the 1920's he turned his attention back to the country of his childhood and adolescence and produced five novels that, despite a number of obvious weaknesses, seem to have a secure place in our national literature. These novels are *Main Street*, a satiric portrait of a small town huddled on the Great Plains; *Babbitt*, a portrait of a representative businessman in a typical small city in the Middle West; *Arrowsmith*, a portrait of the scientist as saint, of a physician pursuing truth with unselfish and absolute commitment, and an attack on the society that tries to inhibit and pervert his search; *Elmer Gantry*, a savagely comic portrait of a dishonest and insincere minister and of the world in which he works; and *Dodsworth*, a mellower satire, this time of Americans seeking culture in Europe. He was to produce ten more novels before his death in 1951, but none of them had the energy, vitality, and originality of the five that established his fame and, in fact, said just about all that he had to say of a world that he both loved and mocked for its painful inadequacies. Yet most of the novels published after *Dodsworth* remained grounded in the life of the Middle West, were couched in the language of the earlier works, and maintained many of the same attitudes, although mellowed by time, of his earlier years.

Lewis was originally taken as a realist, partly because his great power of mimicry gave an apparent authenticity to the speech of his characters and partly because the massive research which he did in getting the surface details of the daily lives of his people precisely right cast an air of great accuracy over the world he represented. But Sinclair Lewis was really a satirist and a humorist, and in his use of the devices and methods of the satirist and humorist lie both his greatest strengths and his chief weaknesses.

As a humorist he belongs clearly in the tradition of Yankee humor, that of the shrewd and knowing peddler or the crackerbox philosopher. For the most important person in Lewis's best work is Lewis himself. It is he who sees with great clarity, describes with deflating directness, mocks, sneers at, condemns. Everywhere in his novels—and particularly in *Main Street* and *Babbitt*—the reader is listening to the narrator-novelist and indeed is being invited to share with him his sense of the incongruity and falseness of the world being described. Thus the novels become extended comic and satiric essays, with narrative exempla to illustrate and underscore the points. The most common posture of the narrator is that of detached observer and sardonic critic. The characters are seen from the outside, their words checked against their deeds, their actions presented mockingly. When we enter their thoughts, it is seldom to explore them as fully realized characters but rather to pinpoint a motive or make ridiculous an aspiration or dream. For example, when Carol Kennicott, in *Main Street*, is putting out plants in a park near the railroad station, Lewis says: "Passengers looking from trains saw her as a village woman of fading prettiness, incorruptible virtue, and no abnormalities . . . and all the while she saw herself running garlanded through the streets of Babylon." Certainly the interior glimpse is not intended to make an exploration of psychological depths but to deflate and to mock. The original plan of *Babbitt* was that it should represent a typical day in the life of a typical businessman. That plan still survives in the first seven chapters, one-fourth of the total book, and it is only after this eventless and typical day that the casual plot of Babbitt's futile efforts at rebellion get underway. Lewis's statement about Elmer Gantry is not unusual: "He had been sitting with a Bible and an evening paper in his lap, reading one of them." Nor is the description of Gantry praying in the pulpit of his church: "He turned to include the choir, and for the first time he saw that there was a new singer, a girl with charming ankles and lively eyes, with whom he would certainly have to become well acquainted. But the thought was so swift that it did not interrupt the paean of his prayer." No, Lewis is not drawing extended psychographs of people; he is exhibiting specimens as though they were insects in a display case, and when he penetrates their skin it is primarily to make them squirm.

This narrator is superior to his subjects. In the five big novels he presents only two characters who are treated with full sympathy, Martin Arrowsmith and Sam Dodsworth, and one, Carol Kennicott of *Main Street*, whom he likes but frequently mocks. The superiority he feels toward his people is based on his greater knowledge and his distance from them but, most important of all, it is based on his moral sense. To find the standard against which to measure these people in establishing this judgment of their morality, Lewis looks toward the past. He finds it in the sturdy pioneers, whom he often celebrates. *Main Street* begins: "On a hill by the Mississippi where Chippewas camped two generations ago. . . ." And it goes on to say, "The days of pioneering, of lassies in sunbonnets, and bears killed with axes in piney clearings, are deader now than Camelot; and a rebellious girl is the spirit of that bewildered empire called the American Middlewest." *Arrowsmith* opens with the protagonist's great-grandmother, as a girl of fourteen, driving a wagon in the Ohio wilderness in the face of great adversity. It is what the towns and cities, the practices of business and the conventions of so-called polite society do to these pioneer virtues that Lewis is attacking, and it is the individualism and rugged independence which the pioneers exemplify to him whose passing he laments. It is little wonder that that most antisocial of American individualists, Henry David Thoreau, should have been one of his ideals.

This narrator is brash and even outrageous in his style. He flings at his satiric target not merely the customary satiric methods, but he brightens and sharpens his writing with vigorous metaphors. In *Elmer Gantry* he describes the workers in the "Charity Organization Society" as being "as efficient and as tender as vermin-exterminators," and he says of a saloon that "it had the delicacy of a mining camp minus its vigor." In *Main Street* he says that the people at a party "sat up with gaiety as with a corpse." He declares of Terwillinger College, "You would not be likely to mistake Terwillinger College for an Old Folks' Home, because on the campus is a large rock painted with class numerals." Sometimes he writes scenes that are clearly boisterous comedy, such as this one about Elmer Gantry: "Elmer's eloquence increased like an August pumpkin. He went into the woods to practise. Once a small boy came up behind him, standing on a stump in a clearing, and upon being greeted with 'I denounce the abominations of your lascivious and voluptuous, uh, abominations,' he fled yelping, and never again was the same care-free youth."

Lewis is a satirist above all other things. While satire is often comic, its object it not to evoke mere laughter but laughter for a corrective purpose. It always has a target, an object which it attacks, such as pretense, falsity, deception, arrogance; and this target is held up to ridicule by the satirist's unmasking it. The satirist's vision is ultimately that of the cold-eyed realist, who penetrates shams and pretenses to reveal the truth. The simplest kind of satire is invective—that is, forthright and abusive language directed against a target so that it makes a sudden revelation of a damaging truth. Another kind of direct satire is exaggeration, by which the good characteristics are reduced and the evil or ridiculous ones are increased. Indirect satire whereby characters render themselves ridiculous by their actions and their speech is more subtle. Lewis as a satirist is usually direct and blunt. His favorite devices are invective and caricature, and in his role of unabashed and self-conscious narrator he can apply these methods directly.

His invective can be devastating. He wrote of small-town ladies as "creamy-skinned fair women, smeared with grease and chalk, gorgeous in the skins of beasts and the bloody feathers of slain birds, playing bridge with puffy pink-nailed jeweled fingers, women who after much expenditure of labor and bad temper still grotesquely resemble their own flatulent lap-dogs." He described a group of small-town citizens as a "Sunday-afternoon mob staring at monkeys in the Zoo, poking fingers and making faces and giggling at the resentment of the more dignified race." He described Gantry as being like his watch, "large, thick, shiny, with a near-gold case," and declared, "He was born to be a senator. He never said anything important, and he always said it sonorously." College teachers were, he said, "spending the rest of their lives reading fifteenth-hand opinions, taking pleasant naps, and drooling out to yawning students the anemic and wordy bookishness which they called learning." Of a Mrs. Bogart, a Good Influence, he wrote,

Mrs. Bogart was not the acid type of Good Influence. She was the soft, damp, fat, sighing, indigestive, clinging, melancholy, depressingly hopeful kind. There are in every large chicken-yard a number of old and indignant hens who resemble Mrs. Bogart, and when they are served at Sunday noon dinner, as fricasseed chicken with thick dumplings, they keep up the resemblance.

Of course, this kind of invective leads very directly to caricature, in which the bad is exaggerated and the good reduced. For example Carol in *Main Street* went calling on Mrs. Lyman Cass, and Lewis wrote that she

pounced on . . . the hook-nosed consort of the owner of the floor-mill. Mrs. Cass's parlor belonged to the crammed-Victorian school. . . . It was furnished on two principles: First, everything must resemble something else. A rocker had a back like a lyre, a near-leather seat imitating tufted cloth, and arms like Scotch Presbyterian lions; with knobs, scrolls, shields, and spear-points on unexpected portions of the chair. The second principle of the crammed-Victorian school was that every inch of the interior must be filled with useless objects.

Lewis then gives a detailed and hilarious listing of the contents of the parlor. The intention and the result is caricature.

Another kind of exaggeration results from a literal-minded reductio ad absurdum, as in the assertion that "the Maker of a universe with stars a hundred thousand light-years apart was interested, furious, and very personal about it if a small boy played baseball on Sunday afternoon." Lewis is a master of this kind of literal statement for satiric ends, as in "In the spring of '18 he was one of the most courageous defenders of the Midwest against the imminent invasion of the Germans." Carol Kennicott observes, "The respectability of the Gopher Prairies . . . is reinforced by vows of poverty and chastity in the matter of knowledge. Except for a half dozen in each town the citizens are proud of that achievement of ignorance which it is so easy to come by." In examining what religious training gave Gantry, Lewis said,

Sunday School text cards! True, they were chiefly a medium of gambling, but as Elmer usually won the game (he was the first boy in Paris to own a genuine pair of loaded dice) he had plenty of them in his gallery, and they gave him a taste for gaudy robes, for marble columns and the purple-broidered palaces of kings, which was later to be of value in quickly habituating himself to the more decorative homes of vice.

One of the qualities of Lewis's work that is difficult to describe or analyze is the way in which he can take the speech of his people, weave it into a monologue or an address, and make of it a severe indictment of the speaker, and yet appear at no point to be exaggerating the normal talk of such men. For example, this monologue from *Babbitt:*

Every small American town is trying to get population and modern ideals. And darn if a lot of 'em don't put it across! Somebody starts panning a rube crossroads, telling how he was there in 1900 and it consisted of one muddy street, count 'em, one, and nine hundred human clams. Well, you go back there in 1920, and you find pavements and a swell little hotel and a first-class ladies' ready-to-wear shop—real perfection, in fact! You don't want to just look at what these small towns are, you want to look at what they're aiming to become, and they all got an ambition that in the long run is going to make 'em the finest spots on earth—they all want to be just like Zenith!

As Edgar Johnson has observed, "Burlesque there is in Lewis, but when we try to put a finger on it, in Babbitt's speech before the Real Estate Board, Luke Dawson's opinions on labor unions, or 'Old Jud's' Y.M.C.A. evangelism, it is embarrassingly apt to melt away and turn into realism. Mainly it is a matter of proportion rather than detail."

Some of Lewis's satire results from extravagant exaggeration with a perfectly straight face. An example is the section on "Weeks" in Chapter XXI of *Arrowsmith:*

If an aggressive, wide-awake, live-wire, and go-ahead church or chamber of commerce or charity desires to improve itself, which means to get more money, it calls in those few energetic spirits who run any city, and proclaims a Week. This consists of one month of committee meetings, a hundred columns of praise for the organization in the public prints, and finally a day or two on which athletic persons flatter inappreciative audiences in churches or cinema theaters, and the prettiest girls in town have the pleasure of being allowed to talk to male strangers on the street corners, apropos of giving them extremely undecorative tags in exchange for the smallest sums which those strangers think they must pay if they are to be considered gentlemen.

Lewis holds the Middle Western world up to Juvenalian laughter, points with unmistakable directness to its weaknesses and errors, and, as satirists have always done, seems to hope that seeing itself in the steel mirror of his description will make it repent and improve. Sometimes what he has to say is blunt and direct. In *Main Street* he declares of the small town:

> It is an unimaginatively standardized background, a sluggishness of speech and manners, a rigid ruling of the spirit by the desire to appear respectable. It is contentment . . . the contentment of the quiet dead, who are scornful of the living for their restless walking. It is negation canonized as the one positive virtue. It is the prohibition of happiness. It is slavery self-sought and self-defended. It is dullness made God.
>
> A savorless people, gulping tasteless food, and sitting afterward, coatless, and thoughtless, in rocking-chairs prickly with inane decorations, listening to mechanical music, saying mechanical things about the excellence of Ford automobiles, and viewing themselves as the greatest race in the world.

Here the outrage and anger are not masked, the comic cushion is not present. The point of view that leads the narrator through his long attack on the people of the books is present in red-faced anger. But such direct statement is unusual in Lewis.

Even at his most solemn moments, wit and the comic spirit usually cloak his rage. In a statement that is almost a declaration of faith for Lewis, he describes Martin Arrowsmith as preaching to himself "the loyalty of dissent, the faith of being very doubtful, the gospel of not bawling gospels, the wisdom of admitting the probable ignorance of one's self and of everybody else, and the energetic acceleration of a Movement for going very slow." In that series of witty paradoxes on a most serious subject Lewis is very much himself. If the paradox undercuts a little the seriousness of the portrait of Martin Arrowsmith, it enhances the role that Lewis the narrator wants to play. If his form is nearer essay than fiction, if his laughter is more embittered and angry than exuberant or outgoing, if his view of men and institutions is that of Juvenal and not Horace—that is merely another way of saying that he is of the Middle West and its towns and Main Streets, and while satiric laughter is an anodyne for what he feels there, he wants it to be more than an analgesic; he wants it to be a specific for the disease that causes the pain. If, as Mark Schorer has said, "he gave us a vigorous, perhaps a unique thrust into the imagination of ourselves," he intended the thrust to be therapeutic. If it has not been, then we are the poorer for its failure.

Light Verse in America

Morris Bishop

It is easier to say what Light Verse is not than what it is. It is not poetry, in the high, pure, and proper sense; for poetry is an effort to discover truth and to reveal it in beauty, while Light Verse has no such lofty pretensions. It looks with suspicion on those who claim divine inspiration; it brings sublimity down to earth; it laughs at sin and wickedness and reduces them to mere misdemeanors. Dante makes the point; there is no comedy in his *Paradiso;* but there is plenty of slapstick farce in two canti of his *Inferno.* These canti are properly light verse, which can flourish even in hell.

"The aim of poetry, or Heavy Verse," I wrote years ago, "is to seek understanding in forms of beauty. The aim of light verse is to promote misunderstanding in beauty's cast-off clothes. But even misunderstanding is a kind of understanding; it is an analysis, an observation of truth, which sneaks around truth from the rear, which uncovers the lath and plaster of beauty's hinder parts."

A definition of light verse must embrace two quite different things. There is, first, light verse proper, which is a variation, a mockery, even a parody, of serious poetry. It treats serious things trivially, and trivial things seriously. It looks like the real thing, displaying strictness of form and elevation of style. But then it suddenly lets you down with a bump, and reveals not only the deliberate falsity of its structure, but also, very often, the falsity of the thing it imitates.

That is light verse proper. Light verse improper might better be called popular verse, as it often is. It is the simple, upsurging poetry

259

of the unlettered, such as ballads, love-songs, country jests set to music, hillbilly songs, lowlife comicalities and tragicalities. Much popular verse charms by its emotion and naïveté. But the naïveté is often false-naïve, for nothing is easier to imitate than the artless effusions of simple poets driven by a crude poetic frenzy, or *furor poeticus*. Sometimes it is hard to tell if the naïveté is genuine or false. Here is an old example of this ambiguity:

> Mr. Finney had a turnip,
>   And it grew behind the barn;
> And it grew and it grew,
>   And that turnip did no harm.
>
> There it grew and it grew
>   Till it could grow no longer;
> Then his daughter Lizzie picked it
>   And put it in the cellar.
>
> There it lay and it lay
>   Till it began to rot;
> And his daughter Susie took it
>   And put it in the pot.
>
> And they boiled it and they boiled it
>   As long as they were able;
> And then his daughters took it
>   And put it on the table.
>
> Mr. Finney and his wife
>   They sat them down to sup;
> And they ate and they ate,
>   And they ate that turnip up.

Not everyone would agree with my classing light verse under two heads, as proper and improper. W. H. Auden defines light verse as that which has for "its subject-matter the everyday social life of its period or the experiences of the poet as an ordinary human being." But this definition seems to me so broad that it would include half of the western world's stock of poetry, from Homer and Horace to Robert Frost.

Let us not, however, become entangled in definition. Let us rather take a quick look at the history of light verse in America. That history is brief and obscure, for much popular verse lies below the literary level, even the level of print. In the eighteenth century songs and ballads, such as "Yankee Doodle," were composed by anonymous bards, but most of these compositions survive, if at all, only in collections of folklore. At the same time sophisticated light verse, or light verse proper, began to appear—political satires and mockeries of men in the public eye, and celebrations of comic incidents in war and peace. Their appeal today is only to the antiquarian taste.

In the early nineteenth century, with the spreading of culture and literary awareness, light verse came into its own. It was composed, even, at the desk of John Quincy Adams, sixth President of the United States. Adams is usually pictured and described as a grim, sour-faced, frost-bitten New Englander. But no such character could have written "To Sally," a melodious imitation of Horace's *Integer vitae, scelerisque purus.* I quote the first two stanzas:

> The man in righteousness arrayed,
>   A pure and blameless liver,
> Needs not the keen Toledo blade
>   Nor venom-freighted quiver.
> What though he wind his toilsome way
>   O'er regions wild and weary—
> Through Zara's burning desert stray,
>   Or Asia's jungles dreary:
>
> What though he plow the billowy deep
>   By lunar light, or solar,
> Meet the resistless Simoom's sweep,
>   Or iceberg circumpolar!
> In bog or quagmire deep and dank
>   His foot shall never settle,

    He mounts the summit of Mont Blanc
        Or Popocatepetl.

And the conclusion—

    Oh! place me where the solar beam
        Has scorched all verdure vernal;
    Or on the polar verge extreme,
        Blocked up with ice eternal—
    Still shall my voice's tender lays
        Of love remain unbroken;
    And still my charming Sally praise,
        Sweet smiling and sweet spoken.

That is very good for a President, indeed, very good for anyone.
With such models, light verse became an acceptable and accepted
diversion. But a diversion only, proper for after-dinner recitation
and for a gentleman's hours of ease. It is true that James Russell
Lowell expressed in dialect verse the political views of abolitionist
New England; but Lowell was an exception, as good poets are
always exceptions. More typical was Oliver Wendell Holmes, the
versatile Boston physician, essayist, and novelist, who could always
be depended on for a humorous ode for celebrations and com-
memorations. Most of them are too long for quotation. In the
nineteenth century people had more time and patience to listen
than they do today; people liked to linger over their jokes. But
Holmes could strike out the unforgettable line, like this couplet
from a more or less tragic ballad:

    Down fell that pretty innocent, as falls a snow-white lamb;
    Her hair drooped round her pallid cheeks, like seaweed on
        a clam.

As the century rolled on, as the American world gained sophistication, light verse too became sophisticated. This was the heyday
of society verse, *vers de société*, elegant trifling for a genteel audience. Its practitioners favored long stories in lilting rhythms, reporting, typically, the amorous addresses of young gentlemen

whose only errors were those of etiquette. One of the best representatives of this courtly fooling was John Godfrey Saxe. He is
usually too diffuse for our impatient taste, but he could by necessity
be brief, as in his "Too Candid by Half":

> As Tom and his wife were discoursing one day
> Of their several faults in a bantering way,
>   Said she: "Though my wit you disparage,
> I'm sure, my dear husband, our friends will attest
> This much, at the least—that my judgment is best."
>   Quoth Tom, "So they said at our marriage."

The obverse of society verse is dialect verse, deriving its comic
effect from the efforts of the uneducated or the ill-educated to
match the speech habits of the writer—and his reader. Dialect verse
is fundamentally offensive, insulting to minority groups, who are
presented as striving comically to ape their betters. James Russell
Lowell was one of the first to essay dialect; he was followed by a
long line of humorous misspellers and of imitators of dialects—
Negro, Irish, German, Jewish, Italian. They are all gone today, and
no one mourns their disappearance.

At the end of the nineteenth century, with the proliferation of
newspapers and magazines, spreading a literate middle-class culture,
the versifiers, serious and comic, had their great opportunity. Most
of them are forgotten; easy achievement leads easily to oblivion.
Some, however, survive in anthologies. Such was Eugene Field, a
Chicago newspaperman, whose poetic work ranged from broad
comedy to charming sentimentalities for and about children. "A
Piazza Tragedy" may represent the frolicsome broad comedy:

> The beauteous Ethel's father has a
> Newly painted front piazza.
>   He has a
>   Piazza;
> When with tobacco juice 'twas tainted,
> They had the front piazza painted,
>   That tainted
>   Piazza painted.

Algernon called that night, perchance,
Arrayed in comely sealskin pants.
    That night, perchance,
      In gorgeous pants;
Engaging Ethel in a chat,
On the piazza down he sat;
    In chat,
      They sat.

And when an hour or two had passed,
He tried to rise, but oh, stuck fast,
    At last
      Stuck fast!
Fair Ethel shrieked, "It is the paint!"
And fainted in a deadly faint,
    This saint
      Did faint.

Algernon sits there till this day,
He cannot tear himself away;
    Away?
      Nay, nay.
His pants are firm, the paint is dry,
He's nothing else to do but die;
    To die!
      Oh my!

Not so well remembered as Eugene Field, but an amusing confectioner of light verse was Ben King, also a journalist. Here is his engaging "How Often," a mockery, rather than a parody, of Longfellow's "The Bridge":

They stood on the bridge at midnight
    In a park not far from the town;
They stood on the bridge at midnight
    Because they didn't sit down.

The moon rose o'er the city,
　　Behind the dark church spire;
The moon rose o'er the city
　　And kept on rising higher.

How often, oh how often
　　They whispered words so soft;
How often, oh, how often;
　　How often, oh, how oft!

　　With the twentieth century came a joyous outburst of light
verse. The times were ripe; the country was prosperous, cheerful,
even smug; America was in a mood for fun and laughter. Our
serious poets had their hours of humorous ease; Carl Sandburg,
Vachel Lindsay, Robert Frost were very gay, frolicsome fellows,
ready to laugh at others and themselves. They came to the edge,
sometimes over the edge, of light verse. Such, for instance, was
Edwin Arlington Robinson's "Miniver Cheevy":

Miniver Cheevy, child of scorn,
　　Grew lean while he assailed the seasons;
He wept that he was ever born,
　　And he had reasons.

Miniver loved the days of old,
　　When swords were bright and steeds were prancing;
The vision of a warrior bold
　　Would set him dancing.

Miniver sighed for what was not,
　　And dreamed, and rested from his labors;
He dreamed of Thebes and Camelot,
　　And Priam's neighbors.

Miniver mourned the ripe renown
　　That made so many a name so fragrant;
He mourned Romance, now on the town,
　　And Art, a vagrant.

Miniver loved the Medici,
  Albeit he had never seen one;
He would have sinned incessantly
  Could he have been one.

Miniver cursed the commonplace
  And eyed a khaki suit with loathing;
He missed the medieval grace
  Of iron clothing.

Miniver scorned the gold he sought,
  But sore annoyed was he without it;
Miniver thought, and thought, and thought,
  And thought about it.

Miniver Cheevy, born too late,
  Scratched his head and kept on thinking;
Miniver coughed, and called it fate,
  And kept on drinking.

In those happy years of the early twentieth century readers of light and middle-weight verse abounded. The great boom in college enrollments had begun, and a swarm of young graduates, men and women, educated in the humanities, had descended on the cities, seeking their fortunes and having a good time doing so. The newspapers featured daily columns of contributed verse and witty prose, conducted usually by an old newspaper man with a record of publication and with an urge to nurse a brood of fledgling bards. Such a "colyum conductor" was Bert Leston Taylor of the *Chicago Tribune;* and Christopher Morley of the *New York Evening Post;* and, most noteworthily, Franklin P. Adams, or FPA, of the *New York World* and other New York papers. FPA's own taste was for scholarly wit and persiflage, in the Calverley tradition of England; he liked humorous imitations of Horace and exercises in the fixed forms, villanelles, rondeaux, double ballades. He liked also the last-line change of pace, which reverses all that has gone before. Here is a celebrated example, "The Rich Man":

The rich man has his motor-car,
    His country and his town estate.
He smokes a fifty-cent cigar
    And jeers at Fate.

He frivols through the livelong day,
    He knows not Poverty her pinch.
His lot seems light, his heart seems gay,
    He has a cinch.

But though my lamp burns low and dim,
    Though I must slave for livelihood—
Think you that I would change with him?
    You bet I would!

FPA's column was beloved by the young poets and wits of the metropolis. One's first public act of a morning was to buy the paper and turn to the column opposite to the editorial page where FPA ruled, to see if one had "made the column." FPA was mentor as well as editor; he gave the encouragement of publication and personal advice to many young poets, later to be famous. Most notable was Edna St. Vincent Millay. Hardly less so was Dorothy Parker, wittiest of American women. She was in many ways a tragic figure, a feminine New York-Jewish Shropshire Lad. Her light verse is a form of self-revelation, turning to self-castigation expressed in irony. Here is an example—"Bric-à-brac":

Little things that no one needs—
    Little things to joke about—
Little landscapes, done in beads,
    Little morals, woven out,
Little wreaths of gilded grass,
    Little brigs of whittled oak
Bottled painfully in glass;
    These are made by lonely folk.

Lonely folk have lines of days
    Long and faltering and thin;

Therefore—little wax bouquets,
   Prayers cut upon a pin,
Little maps of pinkish lands,
   Little charts of curly seas,
Little plats of linen strands,
   Little verses, such as these.

Or try this—"Unfortunate Coincidence":

By the time you swear you're his,
   Shivering and sighing,
And he vows his passion is
   Infinite, undying—
Lady, make a note of this:
   One of you is lying.

And for a résumé, her own little poem entitled merely "Résumé":

Razors pain you;
Rivers are damp;
Acids stain you;
And drugs cause cramp.
Guns aren't lawful;
Nooses give;
Gas smells awful;
You might as well live.

Dorothy Parker and many others, trained in FPA's informal
school for light poets, found a happy lodgment in the pages of the
New Yorker, founded in 1925. To my grief, I can do no more than
mention some shining names—Samuel Hoffenstein, with his *Poems
in Praise of Practically Nothing*, and David McCord, and Phyllis
McGinley, and Richard Armour. But I cannot overlook E. B.
White, kindly observer of human, and animal, foibles, more given
to the smile than to the laugh. Unforgettable is his "Dog around
the Block":

Dog around the block, sniff,
Hydrant sniffing, corner, grating,

Sniffing, always, starting forward,
Backward, dragging, sniffing backward,
Leash at taut, leash at dangle,
Leash at people's feet entangle—
Sniffing dog, apprised of smellings,
Love of life, and fronts of dwellings,
Meeting enemies,
Loving old acquaintance, sniff,
Sniffing hydrant for reminders
Leg against the wall, raise,
Leaving grating, corner greeting,
Chance for meeting, sniff, meeting,
Meeting, telling, news of smelling,
Nose to tail, tail to nose,
Rigid, careful, pose,
Liking, partly liking, hating,
Then another hydrant, grating,
Leash at taut, leash at dangle,
Tangle, sniff, untangle,
Dog around the block, sniff.

Towering over all was Ogden Nash, unquestioned master of modern American light verse. He died in 1971, and left a void too deep to be filled. He nourished a never-failing stream of wit, a faculty of sharp observation, and an impeccable sense of poetic form. He expanded the resources of English rhyme by admitting far-fetched inventions, never too far-fetched for comprehensibility. He planted in his reader an expectation of rhyme, and then outdid the reader's expectation. His public career began when, a young advertising man in New York City, he amused himself by tapping out his remarkable revelations by teletype to a friend in another office. The astute friend sent one of the poems to the *New Yorker* and altered Ogden Nash's life. The fateful poem was "Spring Comes to Murray Hill":

I sit in an office at 244 Madison Avenue
And say to myself you have a responsible job, havenue?
Why then do you fritter away your time on this doggerel?

If you have a sore throat you can get it fixed by using a
   good goggeral,
If you have a sore foot you can get it fixed by a chirop-
   odist,
And you can get your original sin removed by St. John
   the Bopodist.
Why then should this flocculent lassitude be incurable?
Kansas City, Kansas, proves that even Kansas City needn't
   always be Missourible.
Up up my soul! This inaction is abominable.
Perhaps it is the result of disturbances abdominable.
The Pilgrims settled Massachusetts in 1620 when they
   landed on a stone hummock.
Maybe if they were here now they would settle my
   stomach.
Oh, if I only had the wings of a bird
Instead of being confined on Madison Avenue I could soar
   in a jiffy to Second or Third.

That illustrates Ogden Nash's playful affection for the English
language and his pursuit of rhyme even into regions of poetic
hysteria. But he was much more than an eccentric rhymester. The
best of his poems breathe a suppressed melancholy, which is merely
hinted to the reader, not imposed on him. Here, for instance, is
"The Party":

> Come, Arabella, fetch the cake
> On a dish with silver handles.
> Oh, mercy! Feel the table shake!
> Lucinda, light the candles.
>
> For Mr. Migg is thir-ty,
> Is thir-ty,
> Is thir—ty,
> The years are crawling over him
> Like wee red ants.
> Oh, three times ten is thir-ty,
> Is for-ty,

Is fif—ty,
The further off from England
The nearer is to France.

The little flames they bob and jig,
The dining hall is breezy.
Quick! Puff your candles, Mr. Migg,
The little flames die easy.

For Mr. Migg is for-ty,
Is for-ty,
Is for—ty,
The years are crawling over him
Like wee red ants.
Oh, four times ten is for-ty,
Is fif-ty,
Is six—ty,
And creeping through the icing
The other years advance.

Why, Arabella, here's a ring!
Lucinda, here's a thimble!
For Mr. Migg there's not a thing—
'Tis not, I trust, a symbol!

For Mr. Migg is fif-ty,
Is fif-ty,
Is fif—ty,
The years are crawling over him
Like wee red ants.
Oh, five times ten is fif-ty,
Is six-ty,
Is seven—ty.
Lucinda, take the cake away,
We're going to the dance.

What a temptation it is to continue quoting Ogden Nash till the
studio lights are turned off and all listeners have long since ceased

to listen! Since that may not be, I shall merely quote some of his brief observations on zoology. On the turtle:

> The turtle lives 'twixt plated decks
> Which practically conceal its sex.
> I think it clever of the turtle
> In such a fix to be so fertile.

And the kangaroo:

> O Kangaroo, O Kangaroo,
> Be grateful that you're in the zoo,
> And not transmuted by a boomerang
> To zestful, tasty Kangaroo meringue.

And finally the duck:

> Behold the duck.
> It does not cluck,
> A cluck it lacks.
> It quacks.
> It is especially fond
> Of a puddle or pond.
> When it dines or sups
> It bottoms ups.

We come now to our own times, which are favorable to literary production in many ways, but not in the encouragement of light verse. The practitioners of the art are dead or silent, and no young avatars arise to take their places. One reason for their absence is a simply material one—opportunities for publication of light verse have almost disappeared. Few newspapers have their "Poets' Corners"; the magazines publish light verse only very rarely. Light verse depends for its acceptance on a public trained to read and appreciate serious poetry, a public which can recognize the light versifier's liberties and trickeries. That public has diminished, as most of our contemporary serious poets have abandoned the traditional forms of English versification, including rhyme. Light verse is essentially parasitic; it now finds few nourishing hosts to feed on.

There is another and more fundamental reason for the fading of light verse. The world is sad and apprehensive; it is not readily amused. Our satire is bitterly angry; our comedy is likely to be cruel and obscene. A reversal of values has taken place; the hearty comedy of the past is now dismissed as over-simple, as puerile, while laughter itself seems merely an ugly distortion of face and spirit. Thus our gloom is compounded . . . I have said this before, in a form which I hope you will regard as appropriate—that of light verse:

> I used to laugh at folly,
>   At men's absurdities;
> I found extremely jolly
>   Idiosyncrasies
> Of people wooing money
>   Or following a fad—
> These used to strike me funny;
>   Now they strike me sad.
>
> The trickeries of vandals,
>   Society's pretense,
> And governmental scandals,
>   And office-insolence,
> Vagaries economic,
>   Athletic, dietetic—
> I used to find them comic;
>   Now they seem pathetic.
>
> And yet, the large abstractions,
>   Eternities and Fates,
> Mortality's exactions,
>   The issue that awaits
> The gloomy and the glad,
>   The sorry and the sunny—
> They used to strike me sad;
>   Now they strike me funny.

Cabell and Barth:
Our Comic Athletes

W. L. Godshalk

In *Some of Us: An Essay in Epitaphs* (1930), James Branch Cabell turned a critical eye on the American literary scene of the previous decade, a scene in which he, as author of the multi-volumed "Biography of the Life of Manuel," was a chief actor. Writing specifically of those who had come to artistic maturity in the 'twenties, he observed:

It was their melancholy privilege to see with the eyes of maturity the world's civilization collapse like a popped paper bag. Their juniors yet had time to forget; their elders were well past learning anything. They only had seen with the eyes of maturity poor human nature left naked in every quarter of earth and gibbering in a fashion to embarrass any ape that had heard of Darwin. None of these writers, I suspect, has ever quite recovered from the spectacle; before its terrors some turned away to pessimism and the others to a resolute frivolity, but each one of them saw that there is no cure for being human and not any recipe for human living. That perception was perhaps unavoidable. What has followed, though, is that no one of these writers has peddled any recipe such as archbishops might smile on and pedagogues applaud.

The passage perfectly suggests the emotional climate of the 'twenties, and Cabell's reaction to it. On the surface, such a climate may seem hardly conducive to humor, but Cabell points out that one of the alternatives for a novelist in the 'twenties was what he calls "resolute frivolity," the way of the humorist. And Cabell greeted his crumbling world with exactly this formula. But the

275

resolute frivolity which Cabell vaunts is not simply an alternative to "pessimism," for it is a frivolity which takes pessimism as its base, playing arpeggios upon despair.

Resolute frivolity, then, is a way of dealing with pessimism. Although art can provide no answers, it can teach us how to smile, and even how to laugh, and ultimately how to endure.

Twenty-eight years after the publication of Cabell's essay, John Barth in *The End of the Road* (1958) has his characters, Joe Morgan and Jake Horner, face a similar cultural crisis. For them, no moral imperatives exist; the world of objective values has collapsed. "When you say good-by to objective values," Joe explains, "you really have to flex your muscles and keep your eyes open, because you're on your own. It takes *energy*. . . . Energy's what makes the difference between American pragmatism and French existentialism—where the hell else but in America could you have a cheerful nihilism, for God's sake?" Barth's "cheerful nihilism" is a darkening and deepening of Cabell's "resolute frivolity." But Barth's implied reaction to cultural disintegration is similar to Cabell's. When one's civilization collapses like a popped bag, one greets the devastation not with tears, but with a paradoxical jest—"a cheerful nihilism, for God's sake."

Moreover, Cabell's "resolute frivolity" and Barth's "cheerful nihilism" point to a similarity in artistic approach as well as a similarity in attitude. One might call Cabell and Barth the comic athletes of American fiction. They are the players of literary games. In his essay, "The Literature of Exhaustion," Barth contends that once all the possibilities of an art form have been exhausted, then either a new form must be created, or the artist must ironically turn the exhausted possibilities back upon themselves. The ironic alternative—and this is Barth's own method—is essentially a game, a form of play within old rules. In this verbal playing Cabell is Barth's forebear. "I can play with words rather nicely," says a typical Cabellian hero.

If Barth's *Sot-Weed Factor* ironically proves that the eighteenth-century novel ignored its funeral in 1800, then Cabell's early stories prove that the pseudo-medieval romance was also alive and well at the beginning of our century. But Cabell's handling of this form is even more ironic than Barth's handling of the eighteenth-century novel. Cabell's first illustrator, Howard Pyle, the distinguished defender of Robin Hood's authenticity, firmly believed that the Middle Ages was "the age of faith." Yet he continually found in the pages of Cabell's romances allusions to the lack of both strict morality and faith. Pyle finally decided that he could not in conscience illustrate any more of Cabell's stories. The anecdote tells us something about both Pyle and Cabell. In Cabell's hands, pseudo-medievalism became a vehicle for an ironic attack on pseudo-respectability, and his use of the form became an elaborate game.

Further, Cabell and Barth like to play the game of infinite regression in and out of the fictive and the real, putting their fictions within fictional frameworks which pretend to be "reality." Smilingly they ask, "Where does the fiction begin and the reality end?" In *Lost in the Funhouse*, Barth's anonymous character remarks that "assaults upon the boundary between life and art, reality and dream, were undeniably a staple of his own and his century's literature as they'd been of Shakespeare's and Cervantes's, yet it was a fact that in the corpus of fiction as far as he knew no fictional character had become convinced as had he that he was a character in a work of fiction." But Cabell is again first in the field. In *The Cream of the Jest*, the fictional author, Felix Kennaston, does indeed come to believe that he is a character in a work of fiction, that life itself is a form of Romance, and that God is the master artist. In fact, in this novel, Cabell uses a series of authors: Cabell (or his persona, the "real" author); Harrowby (the putative "real" author who is writing a biography of Kennaston); Kennaston (a fictional best-selling author whose fiction forms part of his own biography); and God (the divine author, who may be either fictional or real, as the reader wishes). Each of these authors apparently feels the need to embody himself within his fiction as a kind of demiurgic character. God embodies himself as Christ in his fiction; Cabell uses Harrowby as a demiurge; Harrowby enters his biography in propria persona; and Kennaston assumes the name and bodily form of Horvendile. Barth also is fond of playing with the same kind of regression, as, for example, in *Giles Goat-Boy*, with its pseudo-editorial apparatus—Publisher's Disclaimer, Cover-Letter to the Editors and Publisher, and Footnote to the Postscript to the Post-tape—which lends a fictional frame to the central fiction. And, as much as Cabell, Barth likes to place himself as demiurge in the middle of the novel's action. The description of Harold Bray with his "round, black-mustachioed countenance" distinctly resembles the picture of Barth himself on the dust jacket of *Giles Goat-Boy*, and Bray's former occupations, psychotherapist and "minor poet," remind us of the doctor in *The End of the Road* and Henry Burlingame (the initials are the same) in *The Sot-Weed Factor*. In a final similarity, both authors like to suggest the diabolic nature of their demiurgic characters. Cabell's favorite demiurge, Horvendile, is anagrammatic for "horned evil," and Burlingame has "the eyes of Eden's serpent." Cabell and Barth seem to be suggesting that creation is not exactly a function of the greatest good, that creation—rather ironically—is made and directed by a diabolic power.

However, I am not trying to imply that the games which Cabell and Barth play are mere exercises in irony. As paradoxical as this assertion may seem, they are playing basically serious games. Johan Huizinga has taught us that the playing of games may be fun—"a free activity"—but play may also be deadly serious. Play promotes, according to Huizinga, "the formation of social groupings." It is a matrix for culture. If this is so, may not the playing of Cabell and Barth be a perhaps unconscious effort to reconstruct the civilization which they see collapsing about them? Possibly. But I would suggest that the games of Cabell and Barth are a conscious way of getting at an intellectual solution to the problems of man in a transitory world. Although Christian theology has always emphasized man's impermanence, the twentieth century has added to that idea the concept of relativity. Formerly we might acknowledge man's physical impermanence while yet believing in his absolute spiritual value. Now we are given to feel that no values are absolute.

Cabell's most well-known novel, *Jurgen*, is basically an exploration of values. After Jurgen has tried a variety of approaches to human value, he is left "inch deep in fine white ashes." In the end, all his pretensions to distinction—esthetic, sexual, and religious—have come to this. But a vision of man's universal unimportance has been vouchsafed to Jurgen earlier in the novel by the brown man with queer feet. The brown man is Pan, whose name Cabell interprets as "all." The confrontation of the egotistical Jurgen with Pan is comic, but the essential meaning of the passage is not: "You would have me believe that men, that all men who have ever lived or shall ever live hereafter, that even I," says Jurgen, "am of no importance!" For Jurgen it is a hard fact to accept, and indeed he does not accept it. "I will not," he tells the brown man, "believe in the insignificance of Jurgen. . . . I seem to detect in myself something which is permanent and rather fine." Face to face with meaninglessness, he asserts his personal worth.

In a similar passage in Barth's *Sot-Weed Factor*, Henry Burlingame and Eben Cooke share a vision of "Blind Nature" howling outside, a vision of universal madness. And Burlingame's solution resembles Jurgen's: "One must needs make and seize his soul, and then cleave fast to't," he tells Eben, "or go babbling in the corner; one must choose his gods and devils on the run, quill his own name upon the universe, and declare, ' 'Tis *I*, and the world stands such-a-way!' One must *assert, assert, assert,* or go screaming mad. What other course remains?" To avoid madness, both Burlingame and Jurgen agree, one must postulate one's importance, even if such a postulate flies in the face of the facts. Perhaps both owe something to Vaihinger's "als ob" philosophy. However, for Cabell and Barth the "as if" solution is at bottom a comic one, presented with irony, for in the contexts of the novels man is in no way important. The problem remains, and will not be solved by a mindless, comic affirmation of human worth.

Since both authors mock man's assertions of his importance in the universe, they are at pains to mock his myths and his history—those elements of our culture which are always handled so humorlessly by the professional theologians and historians. Cabell's *First Gentleman of America* is a fictive history of Don Luis de Velasco, born Nemattanon, a prince of the Ajacan Indians. A shadowy figure in the history books, Nemattanon—if this is indeed his Indian name—was found by a Spanish exploratory force in Northern Virginia; he returned with them for Christian baptism in Mexico City, where he gained the name of Luis de Velasco, traveled to Spain where he met King Philip, came back to the New World, lived in Florida for several years, and finally went home to his own tribe with a group of Spanish priests. After massacring the priests, he led his people inland to avoid Spanish reprisals. This fascinating historical incident has been ignored, Cabell theorizes in *Let Me Lie*, "because it did not involve persons of Teutonic ancestry." It is, of course, a basic American myth that "Anglo-Saxons" were responsible for the exploration and colonization of North America; and it is generally forgotten, Cabell notes, that St. Augustine is older than Jamestown.

Cabell takes the bare bones of Nemattanon's history and turns it into, as his subtitle indicates, "a comedy of conquest." In the novel, there is some doubt about the parentage of Nemattanon: his father is reputedly the god Quetzal, who has set himself up as the chief deity of the Ajacans. But Quetzal is probably—though Cabell never tells us—a disguised Spanish soldier, one Vasco de Lerma, who was forced to flee Mexico after rescuing Cortés from the Indians. The story is recounted by the present Viceroy of Mexico:

Lerma pulled Cortés out of the mud, still upside down, like a cork coming out of a bottle. The rude fellow re-inverted, and he propped upright, like a sack of coals, the great Marquis of the Valley. . . . after he had looked at the mud-covered Marquis, who happened at this instant to have a disturbed crayfish hanging on to his left ear, this Lerma laughed.

As Pedro Menéndez comments, "To laugh was not pardonable." But laughter is indeed the only reasonable way to respond to the antics of Spanish conquest. Later in the narrative, Menéndez, whose son has been sacrificed to a local deity by the Indians of Caloosa, marches against them. But instead of punishing the Caloosans for their sacrificial practices, Menéndez marries the Caloosan princess, Antonia, a part-time prostitute and full-time nymphomaniac, thus committing bigamy, in order, so he seriously claims, to bring the Indians to Christianity. And thus Cabell forces us to take another look at the Spanish conquest of America and to see it for what it was, a comedy of pride and stupidity.

Cabell's Luis de Velasco is the imaginative ancestor of Barth's character, Henry Burlingame III. Like Don Luis, Burlingame is an Indian prince of European ancestry, who has gained all the sophistication Europe has to offer. Further like Don Luis, he returns to his tribe and disappears from history. It is interesting to note that Barth's three Burlingames are almost the only nonhistorical characters in *The Sot-Weed Factor*, and even more interesting to speculate whether or not Barth was directly using the history of Don

Luis for his story of Henry Burlingame III. However that may be, Barth handles American history with the same humor that characterizes Cabell's recreation. The wonderful colony to which Eben Cooke aspires to be poet laureate turns out to be "poor shitten Maryland," and Eben's proposed epic of colonization turns into a satire. Furthermore, Barth contrasts the accepted history—John Smith's *True Relation*, a book which Cabell humorously questions in *Let Me Lie*—with the *Secret Historie* supposedly written by Smith, but actually a Barthian reconstruction.

In his *Secret Historie*, Smith offers a partial description of Maryland as he found it: "It doth in sooth transcend the power of my pen, or of my fancie, to relate the aspect of this place, so forsaken & desolate & ill-appearing withal; a sink-hole it is, all marshie and gone to swamp. . . . It is forsooth Earths uglie fundament, a place not fitt for any English man." Smith himself is a satyr, and the Indians he meets are as sexually depraved as he. Hicktopeake's queen—shades of Cabell's Antonia—welcomes his advances, but demands "first some payment, saying, That she was not wont to bestowe her charms for naught." The noble savage queen, however, does not win in her bargaining with the randy Smith. Like Cabell, Barth turns conquest into comedy. The proud history of a proud people becomes a burlesque, and we must darkly smile at what it *must* really have been like. America was not founded by a race of demigods, but by a species of adventurers, sinners like ourselves. As Cabell notes, a "native Virginian historian . . . discovered intrepidly, without needing any mere evidence to abet him, that, 'no doubt,' every one of the jailbirds transported into the Colony of Virginia, during the period of establishment, had been convicted unjustly." The myth of foundation lives on, but Cabell and Barth smile sardonically at the delusions of national grandeur.

The two authors also use more universal myths in their fiction—the myths of the hero and his apotheosis into godhead. Barth indeed has become known for his ironic recreations of classical epic myth, the "Menelaiad," the "Perseid," and the "Bellerophoniad." The emphasis on "phoni" in the final title perhaps indicates Barth's dominant attitude. Cabell had earlier dealt quite explicitly with the myth of the hero in *The Silver Stallion: A Comedy of Redemption* (1926). The series of stories which makes up this volume is concerned with Dom Manuel's fictive apotheosis into a Christ-figure and the reaction of his "disciples," the Fellowship of the Silver Stallion. Cabell leaves us in no doubt about Dom Manuel and his men: "for there was never . . . a hardier gang of bullies than was this Fellowship of the Silver Stallion in the season that they kept earth noisy with the clashing of their swords and darkened heaven with the smoke of the towns they were sacking." Yet out of this reality grows the myth of Manuel's sainthood as Redeemer of Poictesme and his expected Second Coming. Nor does Cabell underestimate the power of this myth. Manuel's spirit is fetched back to earth to explain the meaning of it all to the sturdy realist, Coth of the Rocks, Jurgen's father:

> For Poictesme has now, as every land must have, its faith and its legend, to lead men more nobly and more valorously than ever any living man may do. I, who was strong, had not the strength to beget this legend: . . . it has been created by the folly of a woman [Manuel's wife] and the wild babble of a frightened child [Jurgen]; and it will endure.

Mundus vult decipi: the world desires to be deceived. Although strong men like Coth will never delight in the fantasies of myth, these fantasies do have their function as exemplary tales leading men to more noble actions.

Barth deals at length with the myth of heroism in *Giles Goat-Boy*. Initially Giles is convinced that he is a "grand tutor," a prophet-hero, and the novel traces the multiple vicissitudes of his education and his progress toward enlightenment, for him a relative point of view. He finally comes to believe that all distinctions are fruitless. However, his wife, Anastasia, has developed a "great nagging faith" that Giles is a legitimate Grand Tutor, and she has invented "Gilesianism"—a new religion—which, she feels, "will cure the student body's ills." Their putative son (Giles has his doubts about the father) will, according to Anastasia, "establish 'the New Curriculum' on every campus in the University." As in *The Silver Stallion*, the object of adulation realizes that his status as religious hero is a by-product of his wife's imaginative faith.

In his short story, "Night-Sea Journey," Barth returns to the concept of the hero and puts his ironic monologue in the mouth (so to speak) of a sperm navigating the dark vaginal passage toward the egg. In the beginning we learn that the sperm has "imagined night-sea journeying to be a positively heroic enterprise." But one of his fellow sperm develops a skeptical attitude toward the business of heroic endeavor and suggests that "the genuine heroes . . . were the suicides, and the hero of heroes would be the swimmer who, in the very presence of the Other [i.e., the egg], refused Her proffered 'immortality' and thus put an end to at least one cycle of catastrophes." The speaker seems to accept this cynical stance, but, perhaps driven by his own life-force, ends the story chanting, "Love! Love! Love!"—as he prepares to unite with the egg and lose his identity as a sperm. The chant has been read by some as a positive affirmation of the power of love, but surely in the skeptical context, such an affirmation—like that of Jurgen or Burlingame—is ambiguous. Love is merely another delusion to live by and the sperm's final affirmation is comic.

In sum, Cabell and Barth both seem to suggest that the intellectual "recipe for human living" is a comic acceptance of reality followed by a stoical resignation. At the conclusion of *Jurgen*, the eponymous hero returns to his home and his ill-natured wife. At the end of *The Sot-Weed Factor*, Eben and his sister retire to the family plantation and comparative solitude. Although the innocent may cling to myths and ambitions, the experienced must take an urbanely negative point of view in which nothing matters very much.

Nevertheless, there is an emotional difference between Cabell's "resolute frivolity" and Barth's "cheerful nihilism." Though Cabell may laugh at our need for myth, he sees the possibility that myths may be culturally valuable. Barth treats myth with a similar irony, but seems to see no possibility of a positive effect in the acceptance of illusions. In *The End of the Road*, Jake Horner finds mythotherapy, which involves the acceptance of a mythic role, to be worse than useless; it leads only to death. The loss of hope is certainly a recurring idea in Cabell's artistic universe, but his world is far less hopeless than the world of John Barth, where, ultimately, nothing is of value.

The Humor of
Tobacco Road

Robert D. Jacobs

In the year 1930 a young man named Erskine Caldwell, a native of the state of Georgia, declared to himself that he would never be satisfied as a writer until he had written a full-length novel about the tenant farmers and sharecroppers he had known during his boyhood in East Georgia. His motivation, as he described it, was compassion: "I could not become accustomed to the sight of children's stomachs bloated from hunger and seeing the ill and aged too weak to walk to the fields to search for something to eat," but nothing he wrote on paper, he said, "succeeded in conveying the full meaning of the poverty and hopelessness and degradation" he had observed. The novel that he wanted to write and did write was called *Tobacco Road*, the title coming from the back country trails made by rolling hogsheads of tobacco leaf from the high East Georgia farms down to the Savannah River for shipment to the factories. *Tobacco Road*, published in 1932, was not an immediate success. Total sales that first year were only a few thousand copies, but when this and some of Caldwell's later novels were published in inexpensive paper-back editions the sales went into the millions.

What can account for this tremendous popularity of books chiefly about scarcely human creatures lost in the rural background of an increasingly industrialized, urbanized society? Upon reading *Tobacco Road* one might be inclined to see it as an attempt to give a realistic account of unfortunate people so dehumanized that one can scarcely feel compassion for their plight. One might

think that the book should be tragic instead of comic. But tragedy
centers upon characters that have the sensibility to comprehend
their own predicament, and by such a measure *Tobacco Road* is no
tragedy. Yet in view of the appalling things that happen in the
novel, do we dare call it a comedy? Is it comic when a man is so
hungry that he steals raw turnips from his son-in-law while that
young man is openly engaged in sexual intercourse with his wife's
sister? Is it comic when an aged mother, unwelcome at the family
table, is forced to eat what she can gather from the fields and
woods? Is it comic when a member of this degraded family runs
his automobile into a Negro's farm wagon and leaves the dying
man under the weight of the overturned wagon? From these events
it would seem that what we have in *Tobacco Road* is an accumulation of horrors that will match even William Faulkner's *Sanctuary*,
published one year earlier than *Tobacco Road*. Why, then, can we
call this a comic novel and consider these monstrous people as
comic characters?

There are a number of possible answers to this question, but I
will elaborate only one. Erskine Caldwell's writings, whatever
their social motivation, are in a tradition of American humor that
reaches back over a century to the humorous tales of that region
once called the Southwest, a region which included Georgia,
Alabama, Tennessee, Mississippi, Kentucky, Louisiana and Arkansas. It was in 1836 that an eminent gentleman, a distinguished judge
and educator named Augustus Baldwin Longstreet, published a
collection of stories about backwoodsmen in Georgia. The book
was entitled *Georgia Scenes,* and these scenes contain horrors
enough, although they are intended to be comic. There are fights
between backwoodsmen, who claw and bite each other like animals.
Ears and noses are bitten off, and stalwart young men are maimed
for life in imbecilic brawls. Are these stories really humorous? Yes,
because the backwoodsmen who participate in the violence and
brutality do not view themselves tragically. To them violence and
brutality are the norms of existence and they live accordingly.
They can be treated in the comic vein because they are made to
seem incapable of the pity and fear of ordinary human beings. It is
difficult to feel compassion for those who regard the loss of an eye
or a nose a trifling price to pay for the prestige of being a frontier

champion. It is possible to view such people humorously because to them a bloody fight is entertainment, and a victory in such a fight means local fame and admiration. In the frontier tradition of the old Southwest even the loser avoids pathos by the way he loses. If he has fought a good fight, he has his share of admiration. Violence, then, belongs to the tradition of frontier humor as it was established in the United States. The tradition was partly oral, and the feats of strength and qualities of savagery eventually reached the level of mythic exaggeration. One does not feel compassion for an earth spirit, because all norms of human emotion are absent to him. He is grotesque, insensible to pain and unconscious of affliction. Thus when these tales of violence and derring-do were written down and published, the audience that read them thought of the American backwoodsmen much as a medieval audience might have thought of elves, gnomes, and trolls. One can laugh when a goblin loses an arm or a leg, for he can always grow another.

Erskine Caldwell, then, inherited a literary tradition based at least partly on folk humor. This enabled him to write of the poor farmer of the backwoods as if he were devoid of all normal responses. Jeeter Lester, the hill man of *Tobacco Road*, seems incapable of any recognizable human response in any situation that should be productive of compassion, grief, or even anger. When his daughter Ellie May, whose face is deformed by a split upper lip, makes a sexual assault upon his son-in-law, Lov, Jeeter Lester's reaction is merely delight that the distraction enables him to steal Lov's bag of raw turnips. No one in the Lester family exhibits any normative sexual inhibitions. Whenever sexual intercourse is in prospect, all members of the Lester family, even including the aged, starving grandmother, gather to watch. They climb ladders to peer into bedroom windows when the sex act takes place indoors. They group themselves around the participants if it takes place in the fields or bushes. They are devoid of modesty, shame, and family feeling. The only emotion that Jeeter Lester is given to qualify him as a member of the human race is his agrarian desire to work the land, to raise cotton in his barren fields.

Henri Bergson has written that "a remarkable instinct . . . impels the comic poet, once he has elaborated his central character, to cause other characters, displaying the same general traits, to revolve as satellites round him." So it is with Erskine Caldwell's comic characters. The traits of Jeeter Lester are reflected in his sons and daughters. All are enormously interested in sexuality, either to participate or to observe. They worship an automobile to the point of idolatry. None display any family feeling for brother, sister, father, mother, son or daughter. With the exception of Jeeter Lester's farming instinct, which seems spurious in the context of his general shiftlessness, the attitude of any character is predictable, once one has learned the general traits of Lester himself. Their responses are mechanical, another source of the comic according to Henri Bergson. The comical in human action derives, in part, from the unthinking, automatic quality of a response, or a kind of machine-like indifference when an emotional reaction is called for. Although this lack of a response in certain situations is too gruesome to be called comic, in others it invites laughter. Thus we are shocked when Jeeter Lester actually forgets that his dying mother is lying on the ground unattended, but we are amused when he busies himself pumping up an automobile tire while his young daughter is actually seducing his son-in-law in full view of the family and passing Negroes. We are amused by the automatic quality of the responses of Jeeter and his son Dude when a new automobile is purchased. Jeeter shouts with joy as the automobile appears, and his moronic son, Dude, blows the horn constantly with machine-like regularity, although there are no other cars to be warned out of the way. These people respond like automatons to given stimuli, but like robots they fail to respond to situations that demand compassion or grief.

No doubt Erskine Caldwell has drawn these degenerates with the social purpose of dramatizing the dehumanization that takes place when a class of people are unable to find a place in society. The American critic Robert Cantwell found a good metaphor for this dehumanization when he wrote that the Lesters were "morally disembodied. They floated away from the world of normal reactions as if they had conquered some moral gravitational force." It seems very strange that Caldwell, who sympathized with the poor white farmers of the South, should make them into grotesque monsters. Yet if we compare Jeeter Lester with the comic characters created by the humorists of the old Southwest, we can see that he is following a well-established comic tradition.

The poor white of the South had been described in comic terms ever since the eighteenth-century Virginia gentleman, William Byrd II, gave an account of the poor whites he encountered on a surveying trip to North Carolina. Lazy, improvident, amoral, these "lubbers," as Byrd called them, were no more worthy of compassion than a herd of wild pigs, wallowing in the sun. This same contempt of the gentleman for the degenerate poor white may be seen in Judge Augustus Baldwin Longstreet's account of a Georgia back-woodsman named Ransy Sniffle. Writing in the 1830's, Judge Longstreet described Ransy as

a sprout . . . who, in his earlier days, had fed copiously upon red clay and blackberries. This diet had given to Ransy a complexion that a corpse would have disdained to own, and an abdominal rotundity that was quite unprepossessing. Long spells of the fever and ague, too, in Ransy's youth, had conspired with clay and blackberries to throw him quite out of the order of nature. His shoulders were fleshless and elevated; his head large and flat; his neck slim and translucent; and his arms, hands, fingers, and feet, were lengthened out of all proportion to the rest of his frame.

One *should* feel pity for Ransy Sniffle, but pity for a grotesque wood-sprite is an inappropriate reaction.

With Judge Longstreet's tale, the prototype of the Southern poor white was established for literary purposes. The poor white was called a "cracker," a "wool-hat," or a "dirt-eater" by the more prosperous whites, and he was called "po' white trash" by the Southern Negroes. He reappears again and again in comic literature. In the comic masterpieces of George Washington Harris, a nineteenth-century Southern writer, the comic hero is named Sut Lovingood, and he is described as a "queer looking, long legged, short bodied, small headed, white haired, hog eyed" young man whose chief delights are playing practical jokes, sometimes cruel jokes, and seducing the frontier girls. Sexual amorality appears as comedy in the writings of George Washington Harris just as it does in the writings of Erskine Caldwell. The "cracker" type reappears again and again, significantly in Mark Twain's account in *Huckleberry Finn* of the shiftless loafers in an Arkansas village. These degenerates sat around all day, principally occupied with chewing tobacco and spitting. As for their amusement, Twain writes, "There couldn't anything wake them up all over, and make them happy all over, like a dog-fight—unless it might be putting turpentine on a stray dog and setting fire to him, or tying a tin pan to his tail and see him run himself to death." So even in the works of Mark Twain, who normally exhibited compassion for the poor and oppressed, the Southern poor white appears to be lazy, shiftless, brutal, and sadistic. By and large the comic literature dealing with the Southern poor whites has depicted them as completely amoral, in one way or another. Thus when the great William Faulkner wants to create a character to symbolize the ruthless, amoral, commercial spirit, it is not surprising that he chooses him from the class of poor whites. Faulkner's Flem Snopes, though set in the comic context of a novel called *The Hamlet*, is also too horrible a representation to arouse laughter, for he is a soulless commercial man, devoid even of the sexual appetite that at least qualifies Caldwell's characters for the animal kingdom, if not the human race.

We should be prepared then, when we read Erskine Caldwell's novels about the Southern poor whites, to find characters that conform in a number of ways to the prototypes developed by the Southwestern humorists of the past. We can expect violence, rampant sexuality, simplistic motivations, and unusual or even abnormal responses. Most of the characters will be illiterate, but they may have a flair for coarse, earthy eloquence when moved to speech by their chief interests: sex, food, a new automobile, or, in Jeeter Lester's case, a frustrated desire to cultivate the land. They will live in dilapidated cabins out in the infertile hills, where nothing will grow without fertilizer except pine trees and stunted oaks. Most of the children—the Lesters had seventeen children, twelve of whom are alive at the time of the novel—will go to the towns to work in the mills; but those who remain on the land will be unbelievably improvident. If money is obtained, it will be spent frivolously. If by some miracle a new automobile is purchased, it will be destroyed in a week by careless handling. Family affection is almost nonexistent. The children who escape from the pine barrens and become prosperous in the city avoid their backwoods parents and feel nothing for them but shame and contempt. Brothers lust after brothers' wives, and sisters seduce their sisters' husbands. Fathers will sell adolescent daughters into marriage and will voice eloquent sexual admiration for their son's wives. In fact, Robert Cantwell has written that these characters are actually fearsome because they will do absolutely anything. None of the inhibitions operative in a civilized community restrain the actions of Jeeter Lester and his strange sons and daughters.

What then, does go on in *Tobacco Road?* As the novel opens, we find Lov Bensey, who has married Jeeter Lester's twelve-year-old daughter Pearl, trudging wearily toward the Lester cabin carrying a bag of raw turnips he has walked seven and a half miles to purchase. The Lesters have been watching his slow approach for half an hour. Lov has come to complain to Jeeter that Pearl will neither sleep with him nor talk to him, but the starving Lesters have eyes only for the bag of turnips. The entire first episode of the novel concerns Jeeter's efforts to steal the turnips and Lov's efforts to prevent him. Jeeter is eloquent in voicing his desire for the turnips, raising his voice in rural hyperbole and comic profanity as he blames God and nature for the fact that he has no turnips himself:

> By God and by Jesus, Lov, all the damn-blasted turnips I raised this year is wormy. And I ain't had a good turnip since a year ago this spring. All my turnips has got them damn-blasted green-gutted worms in them, Lov. What God made turnip-worms for, I can't make out. It appears to me like He just naturally has got it in good and heavy for a poor man.

Then, with a comic reversal of his blasphemous attitude toward God, Jeeter indicates that Divine Providence, rather than his own efforts, will save the situation:

> God is got it in good and heavy for the poor. But I ain't complaining, Lov. I say, "The Good Lord knows best about turnips." Some of these days He'll bust loose with a heap of bounty and all us poor folks will have all we want to eat and plenty to clothe us with.

This eloquence fails to move Jeeter's son-in-law, who calmly sits and eats a large turnip while the starving Lesters look on hungrily.

Soon, however, Jeeter's harelipped daughter, Ellie May, tries to attract Lov's attention. Sitting on the hard white sand of the yard, she begins to slide toward Lov, arousing this unbrotherly comment from her brother Dude:

> Ellie May's acting like your old hound used to do when he got the itch. Look at her scrape her bottom on the sand. That old hound used to make the same kind of sound Ellie May's making, too. It sounds just like a little pig squealing, don't it?

Thus the girl's sexual desire is reduced to the animal level and becomes a comic action. It is an ancient humorous device, familiar since the *fabliaux*, the bawdy tales told in the Middle Ages. When people behave like subhuman creatures, we may be appalled, but if no harm is done, the reaction is usually laughter.

Eventually Ellie May, her actions reported in comic metaphor by her brother Dude, succeeds in arousing Lov's sexual ardor and Jeeter takes advantage of the distraction by stealing the bag of turnips. Meanwhile Ellie May, assisted vigorously by her mother and grandmother, has thrown Lov to the ground. It is a virtual rape, and all members of the family have assisted in one way or another. The grotesqueness of the situation is enhanced by the fact that Dude, Ellie May's brother, sits idly by attempting to make casual conversation with Lov while Ellie May has her hapless brother-in-law engaged in sexual intercourse. After the act is over, Dude sits on a stump idly watching red wood ants crawl over the naked body of his exhausted sister. Meanwhile Jeeter Lester has run off into the woods with the bag of turnips. Dude follows him, but has to take some turnips from his father by force. Finally Jeeter returns to the cabin with the remainder of the turnips. The three smallest ones he tosses on the floor to his old mother, whom he hates because she has lived so long. The turnip episode has occupied four and a half of the novel's nineteen chapters and it sets the pattern for the grotesque actions that follow.

In the succeeding chapters we see the sixteen-year-old Dude married to Bessie, who is more than twice his age. Bessie, a self-styled woman preacher, lusts after the moronic boy and secures his consent by buying a new automobile with her late husband's insurance money. Bessie, like Ellie May, has a strange appearance. She was born with no bone in her nose, and her nostrils look like holes on the flat surface of her face. Bessie and Dude go for a wedding trip to a nearby town and spend the night in a cheap hotel, where Bessie is tricked into sleeping with every unattached male on the premises. It is a joyous night for her.

Terrible things happen later in the novel. Dude runs his new automobile into a farm wagon driven by a Negro and drives callously away while the Negro lies dying under the overturned wagon. The family is equally unconcerned when Dude backs the car over the body of his aged grandmother. The family let her lie there in her own blood; and Jeeter, her son, after forgetting her for a while, reacts in this unbelievable way when Lov asks if the old woman is dead: "She ain't stiff yet, but I don't reckon she'll live. You help me tote her out in the field and I'll dig a ditch to put her in."

Finally, it is Jeeter's turn to die. The old cabin catches fire while Jeeter and his wife Ada are asleep. It burns to the ground with both of them in it. Dude regrets the death of his parents no more than he had the death of his grandmother; and the novel ends with Dude driving his car and blowing the horn with mechanical regularity, as it was his habit to do. His final words are that he thinks he will grow a crop of cotton, "like Pa was always talking about doing," but from what we have seen of the Lesters, Dude will no more plant the cotton than Jeeter had done. He will drive the car until it will no longer move, and then he will sit in his cabin waiting for something to happen.

What, finally, can we say about humor like this? As a social novel intended to arouse compassion for the plight of the Southern poor white, *Tobacco Road* must be considered a failure. The Lesters are too degenerate for the reader to believe in, and one must make at least a marginal identification with distress in order to respond to it. Yet as a comic novel, *Tobacco Road* has had enormous popular success. The name of the character Jeeter Lester has entered the American language to signify the Southern poor white, even though the character himself does not bear much resemblance to the class he has been chosen to typify. What Caldwell has done with Jeeter Lester is to create a character myth for the twentieth century, just as George Washington Harris did with Sut Lovingood in the nineteenth. Ragged, forlorn, but irresistibly comic, Jeeter Lester is like some fabled beast-man out of folklore or backwoods legend. Caldwell's comic imagination overpowers his social conscience and produces, not a man, but a grotesque demon of the Southern hills. The novelist never surpassed this, his first novel, for in it he created a myth.

The Harlem Renaissance

Blyden Jackson

The Harlem Renaissance may easily be dated. It extended through the 1920's, with some continuation into the early 1930's. And it *should* be called the *Harlem* Renaissance. The artists who contributed to it did come from all over the United States and—in the case of one or two—from the islands of the sea. Yet Harlem became for all of them much more than a port of call. Harlem signified, moreover, the nature of their bond. Their Harlem was the capital of the "New Negro." It was so that *they* named him. And their Renaissance was their expression of his meaning and his might.

Harlem in the 1920's was different from Harlem in the 1970's. In the first place, it was smaller. Its southern boundary was effectively 125th Street, fifteen blocks north of Central Park and far north of Lower Manhattan's famous skyline. Its northwest province was Sugar Hill, the southern boundary of which was 145th. The "Sugar" had reference to money and the higher up on Sugar Hill a Negro lived the better off he was supposed to be. For Harlem had bourgeois values in the 1920's. It was the mecca of migrants, the biggest and brightest spot in a Promised Land for eager pilgrims who had come north, in very American Cinderella terms, to improve their way of life. To sense the condition of Harlem as it appears in the literature of the last twenty years or so is, therefore, not to know Harlem of the Harlem Renaissance. It is, as a matter of fact, to live in an almost incredibly dissimilar world. In Renaissance Harlem the two main arteries were the immediately parallel north-

and-south avenues, Lenox and Seventh. On Seventh Avenue, before the Lafayette Theater, stood a tree called The Tree of Hope. Theatrical people congregated under, and around, it, especially if they were out of work, for a pleasant legend said that none of them could linger long within the tree's circumference of shade without good luck. Now the tree has been chopped down. It would no longer represent a prevailing Harlem mood.

In the Harlem Renaissance the tree did represent a dominant mood. An optimistic view of life pervaded Harlem then. That was the whole idea of the New Negro, the notion that a bad past was virtually over and that a new day was genuinely beginning to take its place. A comic spirit much akin to Shakespeare's in *Twelfth Night,* that of an Illyrian spring, did possess the Harlem of the Renaissance and, indeed, all Harlemites were then somewhat Elizabethan. Today, of course, it may be wrong to say so, for today nothing black should ever be white, and vice versa, but some of the same bold and gusty exhilarated spirits which have been attributed to Shakespeare's groundlings, as to his contemporaries of wealth and title, flourished in the Harlem Renaissance. It was a time for joy. Felice is the name of the teasing, loving, caramel-colored cocotte whom black Jake Brown finds and loses, and then finally finds again, in Claude McKay's novel, *Home to Harlem.* Felice could have been the name of every golden-limbed chorine in *Shuffle Along,* the Negro musical show—the best, perhaps, that ever was—which did as much as any single event to usher in the Harlem Renaissance. Bourgeois as was the Renaissance, it was yet critical of white folks. They had money-making too much on their minds and their prim puritan souls shrank from the pleasure of the flesh. So, although Harlem treasured Sugar Hill, it still also went stomping at the Savoy or it chased innumerable Felices at its house-rent parties or it simply filled its streets, where one black woman made a fortune selling pigsfeet, with life and sound and often raucous laughter.

Lyric poetry early caught the tone and movement of the Renaissance. The best-known Negro poet before the Renaissance had been Paul Laurence Dunbar, who versified with marked adeptness in both a purported black plantation dialect and in standard English. Neither the black Dunbar nor the white sufficed for the

Renaissance. The black Dunbar, even with his surreptitious adjustments, was basically comic in a distasteful tradition. The white Dunbar was often "dicty," a term that Negroes used in scorn for the aping of white respectability. Some of the Renaissance lyric appeared, however, near the beginning of the Renaissance in *Cane*, Jean Toomer's book in which, to quote Arna Bontemps, "poetry and prose were whipped together in a kind of frappé." In *Cane* the "New Negro" first, defended his American folk past and, then, summoned to sharp inquisition the Nordicized inhibition, by sadly corrupted Negroes, of basic human instincts. Lyricists feel. Comedians think. And Toomer was too exclusively lyric for the comic imagination to play a lively role in *Cane*. But at least one Renaissance lyricist, Langston Hughes, mixed his expressions of emotion with notable comic comment. Indeed, the two volumes of poetry which Hughes assembled and published during his Renaissance years bear for the student of comedy interesting titles: *The Weary Blues* and *Fine Clothes to the Jew*. Where *Cane* is most memorable in its genre painting of the agrarian South and broods over nature as much, if not more, than man, *The Weary Blues* and *Fine Clothes to the Jew* are urban-centered and their chief focus is upon people in social situations. Comedy, that is, inheres in their very selection of material. The title poem of *The Weary Blues* presents a jazz pianist who plays and sings in a Negro bistro on Lenox Avenue "by the pale dull pallor of an old gas light." *Fine Clothes to the Jew* contains its sardonic hint that the time can come when an improvident high stepper may fall on evil days. For the "Jew," of course, to whom fine clothes are taken, operates a pawn shop. Both *The Weary Blues* and *Fine Clothes to the Jew* proceed, then, from comic impulse. Indeed, a ready eye for human foible may well have been Langston Hughes's greatest artistic gift. Curiously enough, however (if it should be curious), this very gift seemed to make him esteem and sympathize with people not less, but more. There was a congenial warmth about Hughes. His laughter did not pillory a victim. It only surrounded its target with mirth that was affectionate and full of understanding even while it took full note of mankind's general tendency to err. If no writer of the Renaissance matched Toomer as a metaphysician of the human condition, none other, in great probability, was quite as free of gall and gloom, quite as much the true, disinterested comedian, even with his penchant for irony, as Hughes. Between these two, Toomer and Hughes, were set the limits of the comic spirit for the Renaissance. Toomer affected the mind of God, yet surfeited himself on sense-impressions. Hughes was every man's brother beneath the skin. Yet to read Hughes is to pass from one exercise of clinical analysis to another. It is, despite the constancy of Hughes' love affair with people, and his disarming mien, an intellectual's odyssey.

There were, of course, poets in the Renaissance other than Toomer and Hughes. Countee Cullen, Claude McKay, Arna Bontemps, James Weldon Johnson (by the 1920's an elder statesman of black letters), the much too ignored Anne Spencer, Frank Horne, who would have a famous niece, Gwendolyn Bennett, Helene Johnson, Waring Cuney, Sterling Brown and Melvin Tolson, along with a small host of lesser lights, all wrote poetry during that exciting time. Brown and Tolson, incidentally, as poets, had to delay until the Renaissance had run its course before taking the steps which ultimately defined their careers. Even so, it was not in poetry that the comic spirit of the Renaissance found its most hospitable place of residence. As a matter of fact, aside from Hughes, and isolated examples, like James Weldon Johnson's "St. Peter Relates an Incident" or the trifles by Countee Cullen written (he said) by his cat, fun, unless it is rather dark and heavy-handed irony—the kind of laughter mixed with pain wherein the pain outdoes the laughter—tends not to exist in Renaissance poetry. The Renaissance doctrine of joy, that is, received its more conspicuous formulations in Renaissance prose rather than in verse. We have already alluded to *Home to Harlem*, a novel by Claude McKay. It was in the novel that Renaissance comedy found its purest and most vigorous expression. The writers of the Renaissance did not really leave an abundant corpus of literature behind them. In the *amount* they did, compared with the interest they have inspired, it is almost as if they, or someone, has created an illusion. And so the very paucity of their poetry may, at least in part, account for the relative lack of fun within it. They had so much to say, so much to expose and attack, especially in derogation of American color caste, so much to emphasize in which the joke (always a bad one) was on them, that to expect their slender outpouring of verse not to be notably monomaniac is, it may easily be arguable, to expect of them, under their circumstances, a conceivably impossible measure of achievement and yet restraint. A novel, however, is a more commodious vehicle than an ode or sonnet. In a novel, to paraphrase a justly famous observation by Henry Fielding, the action can be extended and comprehensive, containing a large circle of incidents and introducing a great variety of characters. It was, therefore, in the novel that the writers of the Renaissance, when they did choose to be sportive, gave their sense of the incongruous freest rein. And, although it can never be maintained that all of the novelists of the Renaissance were capable of easy laughter, some were. Among those some were Hughes, Cullen and McKay, as well as Rudolph Fisher, Wallace Thurman and George Schuyler.

"Easy laughter" is here used as a convenient term. All Negro literature is suffused with an uneasy laughter, the wry reaction of the ironist. We have already noted its presence in Renaissance poetry. Readers of the novels of Jessie Fauset, Nella Larsen and Walter White may well become aware of its presence in Renaissance fiction. And, if it is everywhere in Negro literature, it can hardly be expected to be absent from the fiction of Hughes, Cullen, McKay, Fisher, Thurman or Schuyler. Nor is it. Nevertheless, these six were more playful than Fauset, Larsen and White, much less solemn about the enterprises of living and being black, and their capacity for jest did make of them preeminently the comic spirits of the Renaissance. If it were possible to range them in a line proceeding toward the pole where the comic spirit would be purest, at least in terms of what might well be called laughter for sheer laughter's sake, probably Thurman, the satirist would be at one end, farthest from the pole, and Cullen, with his one novel, *One Way to Heaven*, and Hughes, in *Not Without Laughter*, at the other.

Thurman died young. He came out of the west to Harlem, for he was born in Utah and schooled in California. "A strangely brilliant black boy," is the way Hughes spoke of him and added that he was a "fellow . . . who liked to drink gin; but *didn't* like to drink gin; who liked being a Negro, but felt it a great handicap; who adored bohemianism, but thought it wrong to be a bohemian."

His first novel, *The Blacker the Berry*, derives its title from an old Negro saying, "The blacker the berry, the sweeter the juice." Its thematic sarcasm requires, therefore, that its heroine be very black, as she is, and that she should suffer the tortures of the damned, both from other blacks and from herself, because she is not "light." Thurman's other novel, *Infants of the Spring*, of which he was sole author (he collaborated with a white associate, Abraham L. Furman, in the novel, *Intern*) derives its title from Shakespeare's *Hamlet:* "The canker galls the infants of the spring/too oft before the buttons be disclos'd." For his own satisfaction Thurman had coined the term "Niggeratti" in reference to his colleagues in the Renaissance, and *Infants of the Spring* satirizes the bohemian element, the "canker," in "Niggeratti" conduct. Hence, in neither *The Blacker the Berry* nor *Infants of the Spring* can Thurman be absolved of an acid touch in his use of the comic imagination. Moreover, like Thurman in both the novels named above, Schuyler, in the novel, *Black No More*, invokes his comic muse principally for the ends of satire, and of satire with a venomous edge. A Negro chemist devises a chemical process which will turn Negroes white. On this farcical ingenuity *Black No More* depends for its whole effect. In addition, the blacks turned white, a distressed nation eventually discovers, are even whiter than the original whites. With all Negroes disappearing, the end of *Black No More* discovers an America in which a new premium has been placed on tanning. Everyone wants to be white, but no one wants to be too white. Schuyler is not an accomplished novelist. But nothing he can do can overcome the hilarity inseparable from the mere mechanics of the basic absurdity in *Black No More*.

There is, however, in both Thurman and Schuyler a tendency toward burlesque. *Infants of the Spring*, indeed, is all burlesque. Why else concoct a term like Niggeratti? Moreover, both Thurman and Schuyler display a fondness in their burlesque, if not a fiendish glee, for making game not only of everyone, but especially of persons and personalities who might well be thought of as much like them. As a matter of fact, it is largely this very fondness—or, rather, the manner in which they indulge it—that probably prevents Thurman and Schuyler from rising to the highest levels of comic invention and achievement. The picture, for instance, of Dr.

Shakespeare Agammemnon Beard in *Black No More* does provoke laughter. This Beard must be, as anyone who knows Negroes can see, W. E. B. DuBois, and the justice of much of the caricature, despite the savagery, can hardly be denied. DuBois-Beard did go to Harvard. He did dress in a certain unlikely way and have an eye for a pretty face and a well-turned ankle. He could be something of an ass and cad, and he was undoubtedly not the most modest, nor the least devious, nor the most forgiving of men. But Schuyler's lampoon of DuBois, as of the other butts of his wit in *Black No More*, reveals as much about Schuyler as about those at whom he sneers. Schuyler is too caustic and too defensive for his own good.

Significant characters, as might well be expected, do abound in Renaissance fiction. The participants in the Renaissance were decidedly, among other things, a coterie, and coteries would not be coteries if they did not preen, or try to preen, themselves, before an audience of those not so favored as to be in their own charmed circle of a superior breed. So, the principals of *The Blacker the Berry* must be gathered at a party where the guests are Renaissance celebrities in very thin disguise. So, *Infants of the Spring* is all *roman à clef*. So, Marcus Garvey is no more kindly treated, nor overlooked, nor exempt from almost scurrilous ridicule, in *Black No More* than DuBois. So, too, the General Improvement Association of Rudolph Fisher's *The Walls of Jericho* is obviously the National Association for the Advancement of Colored People, its annual costume ball an occasion for the novel's author to burlesque both types and specific individuals of his acquaintance and the *salon* of Constancia Brandon in *One Way to Heaven* as full of transparent masquerades of real people as any single episode in any of the fiction of Thurman, or Schuyler, or any other novelist of the Renaissance. But Fisher and Cullen are not quite so self-defensive in their burlesque as Thurman and Schuyler. They are often equally as clumsy, if not clumsier. Yet *The Walls of Jericho* and *One Way to Heaven* are happier books than *The Blacker the Berry* and *Black No More*. The world of the first two books, despite the loss, in one novel, of a house and, in the other, of a life, is sunnier. The humor there is happier. And so is the burlesque.

Critics of the Harlem Renaissance may some day agree that the

finest comic character in the fiction of the Renaissance is Little
Augie, the jockey, of Arna Bontemps's *God Sends Sunday*. Certainly
as the Negro past recedes into the distance and the legends grow
of St. Louis women and diamond rings, of sporting life and
traveling men, and of the regrettable distortions of human aspiration
of which these all, to some degree, bespeak, Little Augie seems
increasingly a triumph of poetic vision. He had, indeed, at least
something of a mate in Sam Lucas of *One Way to Heaven*. Both
are high-water marks in the fiction of the Harlem Renaissance.
Both are comic characters, not tragic. Both exploit and truly represent the inner essence of stories in which the comic vein runs
deep.

Even so, it is almost surely in the novel *Not Without Laughter*,
by Langston Hughes, a family chronicle, not in the accounts of
men who, perforce, come and go, that the comedy of the Renaissance arrives at its apogee. Families endure. Three generations—
Aunt Hager, her daughters, and her middle daughter's son—are
represented in *Not Without Laughter*. These generations form,
clearly, a family, a Negro family in a white world. There can be
nothing more comic, certainly not the satiric inversions of *The
Blacker the Berry*, nor the farce of *Black No More*, nor the burlesque of *Infants of the Spring*, nor even the apparition of Little
Augie retreating from his world of bright lights and big spenders
to the new West, nor even the final gallantry of Sam Lucas, playing
his role of the sweet cheat, for someone else's benefit, in the very
hour of his certain death. For Aunt Hager and her children and one
of her children's children are the whole human comedy incarnate.
Nothing is funnier than man—puny, insignificant man—pitting himself in utter seriousness against the universe. This is the incongruity
of all incongruities. And it is even funnier when it is accepted not
in fear and trembling, but with some devil-may-care exuberance
on the part of the challenger about the final outcome. Like the
shadow of a magnitude, the shape and substance of this comedy
of comedies appears in the plan, and the execution, of *Not Without
Laughter*. It is Aunt Hager's family—poor, humble, alley-dwelling
Negroes—against a whole socio-politico-economic system that despises, as it expects to overwhelm, them. The system obviously
should win. But Goliath should have whipped David. And so

Hager's grandson, as he walks with his mother, one of Hager's daughters, down a Chicago street in the closing scene of *Not Without Laughter*, is, indeed, as funny as the shepherd boy. He is laughable, too, in his dreams. But he is, thus, also Everyman in Everyman's finest comic guise. And he is, thus, also the comic spirit of the Harlem Renaissance in its most attractive mold.

Faulkner's Humor

Robert D. Jacobs

In *The Hamlet,* William Faulkner's first novel of the Snopes trilogy, Pat Stamper, peerless horse trader, inserts a bicycle valve in a bony horse's skin, pumps him up, dyes the horse's hair, and sells him back to Ab Snopes, from whom he had just purchased the worthless beast. Thus William Faulkner employs one of the most common situations to be found in the tradition of folk humor—the trickster tricked—for Ab Snopes had deliberately tried to trick Stamper in the first place. If we wanted to trace the lineage of this episode, we would have to go back to 1836, when Augustus Baldwin Longstreet's *Georgia Scenes* was published. Longstreet's tale, "The Horse Swap," was based on an equivalent situation, with two unscrupulous rogues vying with each other in the gentle art of horse trading.

In Faulkner's last novel, *The Reivers,* chicanery involving a horse is again a source of fun. A fast but reluctant racehorse becomes so fond of sardines that he sweeps gloriously to the finish line ahead of a rival because his temporary trainer motivates him with his favorite food. In Faulkner's third novel of the Snopes trilogy, *The Mansion,* V. K. Ratliff, a shrewd and witty *eiron,* eliminates Clarence Snopes as a candidate for Congress by persuading two little boys to brush the Snopes trousers with bush branches saturated with dog urine. When all of the dogs in the vicinity stand in line to urinate on Snopes's legs, the candidate flees ignominiously; and Will Varner, political boss of the rednecks,

305

orders Snopes out of the race, because, as he said, "I aint going to have Beat Two and Frenchman's Bend represented by nobody that ere a son-a-bitching dog that happens by cant tell from a fence post."

Obviously, then, much of Faulkner's humor is folk comedy: it resembles the tall tales told around campfires or on the porches of country stores. A masculine humor, frequently bawdy, sometimes cruel, it is nearly always based on some kind of trickery. Normally the victims of the trickster deserve what they get. Frenchman's Bend, the "hamlet" of Faulkner's first Snopes novel, is very much like the frontier communities of the nineteenth century that were the setting of the tales of J. J. Hooper, Joseph G. Baldwin, and George Washington Harris; and Faulkner's humorous techniques often parallel those of the nineteenth-century humorists. To be able to surpass others in strength, skill, or cunning was necessary for survival on the frontier, and the heroes of that society performed feats, according to the humorists, that were almost superhuman. Davy Crockett could "grin" a squirrel down out of a tree or trade the same coonskin over and over for whiskey by the simple expedient of stealing the coonskin back whenever the cunning Yankee who sold the whiskey turned away. Faulkner's Boon Hogganbeck could kill a giant bear with a hunting knife, and his Flem Snopes could outwit the Devil himself. When Crockett, real-life character but also hero of many nineteenth-century comic tales, cheats the Yankee Trader, he has clearly surpassed a master rogue. This is a feat to win him total admiration from the people of the community. Faulkner's rogues do not always excite admiration, but some of them are as cunning as Davy Crockett and the Yankee Trader combined.

The Hamlet, a genuine folk comedy in spite of the grimness of some of the episodes, is composed, so Olga Vickery writes, of tales of love and tales of trade. It is in the tales of trade that Faulkner gives full expression to the kind of humor he inherited from the writers of the old Southwest. The new prince of rogues is neither a Yankee Trader nor a powerful backwoodsman of the Davy Crockett stripe. Instead he is a short, squat, gray-skinned man, with a broad, expressionless face ornamented by a small parrot's-beak nose and eyes the color of stagnant water. None of the endearing qualities that were present in even the most outrageous characters of Southwestern humor can be found in Flem Snopes. George Washington Harris's Sut Lovingood, who perpetrates dangerous, sometimes fatal tricks on his fellow countrymen, is entitled to a measure of approval because he tricks those who deserve to be tricked, the pompous and the morally rigid, the skinflints and the fools. Flem Snopes, in contrast, has no sense of humor. His trickery, always for financial gain, is employed in this novel on the poor and sometimes the helpless people of the French-man's Bend community as well as on would-be rogues like Jody Varner and worthy opponents like V. K. Ratliff. Sut Lovingood exhibits an amusing strain of country bawdiness, tirelessly trying to persuade the nubile maids of the backwoods to roll in the hay with him. Flem Snopes is as immune to sexual feeling as he is to any other emotion. He feels no love, no hate, no compassion, no anger. Faulkner has deliberately dehumanized this character. He is a grotesque like Dickens's Uriah Heep, yet far less vulnerable. We can see him properly only in the role of the commercial spirit: he is a symbol of trade. Mechanical and grotesque as he is, in *The Hamlet* Flem is never quite ridiculous and never quite humorous in himself. His habit of chewing tobacco until the "suption" is out of it, then later chewing gum because it is cheaper, and later still chewing air because it costs nothing at all, would be laughable in another character, but in Flem it is somehow sinister. He is like some great, devouring insect, with his jaws always working.

Precisely because he possesses no recognizable human qualities, Flem is demonic rather than comic, and one critic has argued that his creator, William Faulkner, was afraid of what his character represented, the passionless commercial spirit, and made him look ridiculous as a kind of psychic defense. According to Lewis Lawson, this is the technique of *meiosis*, by which we verbally diminish that which we are afraid of. Flem, scarcely five feet tall, is not the Devil; he is more than a match for the Devil. In the tall tale narrated by Ratliff, Flem goes to hell and legally cheats the Devil out of the infernal kingdom, because the soul he had given to the Devil in exchange for favors could not be located, not even in the tiny matchbox where the Devil thought it was confined. In Stephen Vincent Benet's "The Devil and Daniel Webster" the great

orator defeats Satan through sheer power of expression, but Flem
Snopes rarely talks. He wins because he is invulnerable to any
passion. He has no weakness, and normally he is within the letter
of the law. As Robert Penn Warren has said, the "humor in Faulkner's work is never exploited for its own sake. It is regularly used as
an index, as a lead, to other effects." Flem Snopes, then, represents
Faulkner's indictment of what Thomas Wolfe called "single selfishness and compulsive greed."

A genuinely comic character in *The Hamlet* is V. K. Ratliff,
who possesses some of the external characteristics of the Yankee
Trader—he is shrewd and he travels the countryside selling sewing
machines—but who is human, fallible, and attractive as a person.
He is a keen observer of human nature and his trades are never
made at the expense of the ignorant and the helpless. When he
enters the lists against Flem Snopes, we enjoy—or perhaps fear—the
spectacle of the shrewdest of human beings contending against
the commercial spirit incarnate. Ratliff ultimately loses, because he
is human. He falls for one of the oldest tricks in the American
tradition of trickery, acquiring a tumble-down old mansion because
he had seen Flem secretly digging for buried treasure on the premises. The "salted" gold mine was a standard device by which
Western rogues sold worthless claims to the tenderfoot in the
mining country. Flem "salts" the old Frenchman's place with some
silver dollars and capitalizes on the greed which is present even in
Ratliff, who together with two poor farmers purchases the old place
from Flem to dig for the supposed buried treasure.

Normally in *The Hamlet* the people are tricked because of what
Faulkner seems to think is a universal flaw in human nature, the
desire to get something for nothing. The Snopeses gain a foothold
in Frenchman's Bend when Jody Varner, son of the rich patriarch
of the community, thinks he can trick Ab Snopes, Flem's father,
into working a cotton crop for nothing. He has to hire Flem as a
clerk in the Varner store because he is afraid that Ab, who is a
reputed barn burner, will burn down some of the Varner property.
Flem's rise in the community is at the expense of the people. They
borrow money from him at exorbitant interest rates and they purchase the wild horses he brings from Texas because they are an
apparent bargain at five dollars a head; but the horses are untamable

and everyone loses except Flem. As a Snopes relative says, cackling
in glee, "By God! You can't beat him!"

Faulkner goes beyond the antecedent Southwestern humor as he
depicts symbolically the results of Snopesism. Old Varner's daughter, Eula, described lyrically as if she were Helen of Troy, Lilith,
Semiramis, and Proserpina blended into one glorious incarnation of
sexual desire, is made pregnant by Hoake McCarron, a wild young
man who was brave enough to take what all men wanted. Eula,
surely symbolic of the rich, lovely earth itself, was traded to Flem
Snopes. Varner gave Flem the old Frenchman's place as Eula's
dowry, a sharp bargain, for the place was deemed worthless. Flem's
acquisition of the earth goddess, already fertilized by another,
represents the tragedy of the land in modern times; it was destined
to be owned by tradesmen who could neither plant it nor cherish it.

Percy Adams calls the Eula-Flem episode "epic burlesque," a
parallel to the tale of Helen of Troy. Young Helen was ravished
by Theseus (Hoake McCarron) and then married to Menelaus
(Flem Snopes), only in later years becoming the paramour of Paris
(Manfred de Spain, in *The Town*). Faulkner uses the technique of
mythic enlargement copiously in *The Hamlet*. Eula is more splendid than anything in life, Flem more despicable; and the result of
this technique is to create a sense of the inscrutability of fate oper-
ating even in the high jinks of country bumpkins. Eula is no Helen,
except in her irresistible attraction; certainly Flem Snopes is no
Menelaus (he is more like the Pluto who takes Proserpina to his
own dark dominion), but by allowing us to hear the reverberation
of these mighty names through the cotton patches and tenant
shacks of rural Mississippi Faulkner gives his grim comedy a cosmic
dimension. This is not merely Frenchman's Bend; it is the world.

Humor of character and of situation does not exhaust the comic
potential of *The Hamlet*. Faulkner makes use of Rabelaisian bawdiness, irony, satire, macabre effects, in fact almost every identifiable
kind of humor. One of the most startling episodes portrays the
love of a Snopes idiot for a cow. It is described mock-heroically,
in rhetoric that would be appropriate for one of the great loves of
legend, that of Tristram for Isolde, or, more directly, that of Zeus
for Io. Yet the whole extravagant episode is given its rude comic
dimension when I. O. (does this name reflect the myth?) Snopes

proclaims that "The Snopes name has done held its head up too long in this country to have no such reproaches against it like stock-diddling." The cow loses her dimension as Io when Jack Houston, her owner, catches the idiot in *flagrante delicto* and shouts at her, "Git on home, you damn whore!" Gross comedy with a powerful satiric thrust mingles with pathos when later we find that Lump Snopes, another member of that ubiquitous tribe, has been selling tickets to the loafers to watch through a gap in the stable wall the idiot performing sexually with the cow. Only Ratliff, the shrewd humanitarian, is outraged enough to attack this aspect of Snopesism, the willingness to do anything, no matter how despicable, that will make money.

Verbal humor is present in abundance, ranging from the obscene to the witty. When Jody Varner learns that his unmarried sister Eula is pregnant, he rages at his father for immediate punitive action against the seducer. Old Will Varner's pungent reply diminishes the event from the potentially tragic to the inconsequential: "Hell and damnation, all this hullabaloo and uproar because one confounded running bitch finally foxed herself. What did you expect—that she would spend the rest of her life just running water through it?" The wit is usually from the lips of V. K. Ratliff, and it reflects his cynical but good-humored tolerance of the flaws of human nature: "I've heard laziness called bad luck so much that maybe it is."

Humor is also present in the given names of the Snopes clan. In *The Hamlet* appear Admiral Dewey Snopes, Colonel Sartoris Snopes, Launcelot Snopes, Mink Snopes, Saint Elmo Snopes, and Wallstreet Panic Snopes. Montgomery Ward Snopes arrives on the scene in *The Town*, and Watkins Products Snopes makes his appearance in *The Mansion*. It has been reported that Faulkner and his good friend Phil Stone used to spend hours thinking up outrageous new names for the Snopeses. "Dollar Cotton" Snopes was invented but never made his appearance; but twin boys, named after the notorious "red-neck" politicians of Mississippi, Vardaman and Bilbo, were sired by I. O. Snopes, the platitudinous sometime schoolteacher of Frenchman's Bend. There is no apparent humor in these last two names except to those familiar with Mississippi politics during the first third of the twentieth century. The tenant farmer class often named children after their current political heroes. Bilbo was once called by *Time* magazine the worst man in the United States Senate, and the national reputation of Vardaman, an earlier figure, was little better. Giving these names to Snopes children is an ironic indication of the type of voter that gave the redneck politician his power, and we are not surprised when a Snopes politician appears on the scene. Clarence Egglestone (this second name his own elegant invention) Snopes showed up first in *Sanctuary*, where he distinguished himself by peeking through keyholes in Miss Reba's whorehouse. Successful in being elected to state office, he eventually ran for Congress, only to be eliminated from the race by Ratliff's successful trick in making him the equivalent of a canine lamppost.

Although most of Faulkner's humor is concentrated in the Snopes trilogy, he showed from his very first novel that he was just as interested in comic effects as in tragic. *Soldiers' Pay*, his first novel, exhibits a character named Januarius Jones who was more satyr than man. Here Faulkner uses somewhat crudely a comic technique that was to become effective in *The Hamlet*, the technique of blending the mythic with the local. Jones, a fat college instructor, is in his local aspect merely an effetely literary young man who parades his sophistication; in his mythic extension Jones is the goat god, lust incarnate: "Jones' eyes were clear and yellow, obscene and old in sin as a goat's." The comedy, literary and contrived, centers on Jones's repeated frustration as he follows his goatish inclinations among the maids of the community. *Mosquitoes*, Faulkner's second novel, is a satiric comedy about the artists (and their sycophants) of the French Quarter in New Orleans. One of the characters, Mr. Talliaferro, who, like Jones, spends his time in futile efforts at seduction, is a Faulknerian version of T. S. Eliot's J. Alfred Prufrock, a timid little man more at home among women than men but totally unsuccessful in his sexual enterprises. Notably in *Mosquitoes*, however, appears Faulkner's first tall tale, an account of a descendant of Andrew Jackson who lived in the swamps so long that he developed fish-like attributes. He became half shark, half man, herded fish for his living, and was a terror in the water off swimming beaches, where he enjoyed himself with the exposed legs of female bathers.

When Faulkner first engaged with the subject of Yoknapataw-
pha County, his mode was to be chiefly tragic. There is little
comedy in *The Sound and the Fury*, and though the materials of
As I Lay Dying lend themselves to comic treatment, the humor is
macabre. For many readers there is little laughter in the total effect
of this novel, although some of the scenes are hilarious. *Sartoris* has
occasional comic relief, but the tone is serious. In 1931, however,
Faulkner proved in *Sanctuary* that he could juxtapose the broadly
laughable to the terrible without destroying either effect. Nothing
in Faulkner is funnier than the account of Virgil Snopes and Fonzo
Winbush coming from Jefferson, Mississippi, to Memphis, Tennessee, to attend barber college. The two bumpkins are looking for
an inexpensive place to live; they mistake Miss Reba's brothel for a
boardinghouse and think the prostitutes are Miss Reba's multitudi-
nous daughters. Absurdly, they spend a considerable amount of
time actually looking for a brothel, oblivious to the fact that they
are living in one. One of the functions of the comic episodes in
Sanctuary is to serve as relief from the horror of murder, rape, and
lynching; but they are also thematic. Faulkner provides us with
two castes of characters, one drawn from the "best" people in the
state of Mississippi, as represented by Temple Drake and Gowan
Stevens, the other drawn from the red-necks, prostitutes, bootleggers, and gangsters. Ironically, each class apes the mores of the
other. Gowan Stevens, a student at the University of Virginia,
drinks like a Memphis wino and abandons Temple in the hideout
of the bootleggers. Temple, a coed at the University of Mississippi,
finds her proper metier in Miss Reba's whorehouse. Daughter of a
Mississippi judge, she is more sexually depraved than the whores
around her and scandalizes Miss Reba herself, who believes in certain proprieties of behavior. In contrast, the denizens of the under-
world ape respectability. Miss Reba has guests and politely gives a
tea, except that she serves gin. A "respectable funeral" is arranged
for the gangster Red, slain by the chief bootlegger and gang boss,
Popeye. It appears in this novel that Faulkner cynically equates
the best and the worst of society. The best people may be drunkards
and sluts; the representatives of religion and social order instigate
a lynching; and the daughter of a judge, far worse than the ex-
whore, Ruby Goodwin, lies on the witness stand and dooms an

innocent man to a lynching. Thus the comedy of *Sanctuary* serves a satiric purpose in Faulkner's indictment of contemporary life.

Humor is present in Faulkner's *Light in August,* but the tone is predominantly tragic until the very end of the novel. The author has counterpointed two themes, one tragic, the other comic; but the comic theme is almost submerged, in effect, at least, by the tale of Joe Christmas, whose savage life is the result of race relations in the South. In contrast, the tale of Lena Grove is folk comedy, as the simple young girl from Alabama, whose very name invites an extension into nature myth, seeks the wandering satyr who impregnated her. Fortune favors her and she finds Byron Bunch, the good Everyman of the folk, who will follow her peregrination over the land until she is willing to stay and fulfill her natural function of peopling the earth. That the novel ends on a comic note is prognostive of the later Faulkner, who increasingly tended to find tolerance and understanding for even the most malicious of the human race.

By 1941, with the publication of *The Hamlet,* the Mississippi novelist had modified the tone of his novels from the predominantly tragic to the predominantly comic. This novel, first of the Snopes trilogy, is grim enough in a number of its episodes, but its characters and situations are chiefly in the comic mode. The sequel to *The Hamlet, The Town,* published sixteen years later, reveals a new Faulkner, one who has gained such tolerance for human frailty that he is willing to humanize his great symbol of avarice, Flem Snopes.

In *The Hamlet* Faulkner employed with superlative skill his technique of making country bumpkins into mythic figures by exaggerating their physical or mental characteristics. In this novel Eula Varner was not merely a nubile country girl: "Olympus-tall," with a beautiful, queenly face, she towered over the squat figure of Flem Snopes as Aphrodite towered over the crippled Hephaestus, her unworthy husband. In *The Town,* however, Eula is diminished to a mere mortal, carrying on an affair of nearly two decades with Manfred de Spain, who, unlike Hoake McCarron, the wandering Pan who impregnated Eula in *The Hamlet,* is limited by a place, a position, and a defined character. De Spain is an "invincible" bachelor of a recognizable type; he is mayor of the town and president of a local bank; he drives a red E.M.F. roadster and carries on a silly rivalry, adolescent in its prankishness, with Gavin Stevens over the favors of Eula Varner Snopes. The comedy sometimes descends to crude horseplay, as De Spain sends a gift to Gavin Stevens consisting in part of two flowers tied with a used contraceptive (with the implication that it had been used on Eula). Most of the substance of *The Town* is devoted to this unequal rivalry, and to the efforts of Ratliff and Gavin Stevens to combat Snopesism. Increasingly Flem Snopes himself is depicted not as a monster of avarice but as a clever country bumpkin whose prime motivation is to achieve upward social mobility, to become respectable. This he does by driving out, one by one, the more disreputable of the Snopes clan who had followed him to prey on the town of Jefferson. Flem's trickery now is at the expense of his own depraved relatives, as he plots to become a solid citizen. Perhaps the most humorous episode in *The Town* is Faulkner's recapitulation of a tale published years earlier, "Centaur in Brass," in which even the redoubtable Flem is outmaneuvered by two Negro employees in the town power plant, whom he attempted to make unwitting confederates in his scheme to steal the brass fittings from the steam generator and sell them for scrap metal.

Except for episodes that were previously published as separate tales, Faulkner's method in *The Town* and its sequel, *The Mansion*, tends toward the realistic instead of the fantastic. Comedy, being traditionally based on the foibles of human nature within a social context, normally has a realistic texture. At least sophisticated comedy does. Folk comedy, particularly that type known in America as the "tall tale," is frequently marked by fantastic events. Faulkner in his two later novels of the Snopes trilogy uses fewer tall tales, but when they do appear, we see that he has lost none of his inventiveness. The last episode of *The Town*, coming appropriately as comic relief after the sad account of Eula Varner Snopes's suicide, is a tale of four horrific children, sired by ex-bank clerk Byron Snopes (who had stolen some money from De Spain's bank and disappeared into the West) on a Jicarilla Apache squaw in Mexico. The story of the "things," too terrible to be children, is told by Charles Mallison, one of Faulkner's delightful boy taletellers who bear a family resemblance to Huckleberry Finn in their probity, insight into human nature, and capacity for outwitting their elders. One of the "things"—Charles never knows which—has a switchblade knife that appears magically at the first hint of danger, and even the local Snopeses are unable to cope with the young savages. Their first notorious escapade is to steal, no one knows how, the pampered and expensive Pekingese of wealthy Mrs. Widrington. The children eat the dog, it is assumed, for all that is found of him is a small pile of bones by the ashes of a cooking fire. Young Clarence Snopes (the infamous politician of *Sanctuary* and *The Mansion*) takes over the four savage Snopes children and claims he is going to train them to "hunt in a pack," that they would be better on a trail than a pack of dogs; but it is not many days before Clarence is heard screaming out in the woods and the men find him "tied to a blackjack sapling with something less than a cord of wood stacked around him jest beginning to burn good." Creatures that are half-Apache, half-Snopes are too much for Jefferson, and the now "respectable" Flem sends the little savages back to Byron Snopes in El Paso. Thus in the final episodes of *The Town* Faulkner blends the macabre with the comic in the tradition of American frontier humor, wherein violence and even cruelty were made part of the fun.

The Mansion, the concluding novel of the Snopes trilogy, is less than a comic masterpiece. Faulkner fails when he ceases to mine the vein of folk humor and fantasy and attempts to exploit contemporary society for comic effects. Even the tried and true V. K. Ratliff becomes tiresome as he journeys to New York with the garrulous Gavin Stevens and buys two seventy-five-dollar neckties from Allanovna. We learn that Ratliff's mysterious initials stand for Vladimir Kyrilytch, and an attempt is made to gain some comic effect from his sensitivity to his given names. Much of the book is a recapitulation of the Snopes history through Ratliff's voice, but the later voice of Ratliff sometimes lacks the rich folk idiom it had in *The Hamlet*. He has grown self-conscious about his use of the vernacular, and Faulkner quite tediously shows him attempting to correct his grammar. No one had a more accurate ear for the cadences and coinages of the vernacular than William Faulkner; but Ratliff's speech in *The Mansion*, as he recapitulates the whole story of Eula Varner and Flem Snopes, features characteristic Faulknerian rhetoric along with the folk idiom: "So the whole idea might be what you would call a kind of last desperate instinctive hereditary expedient waiting handy for ever young feller (or old one either) faced wth some form of man-trouble over his gal." Evidently Ratliff had absorbed some of Gavin Stevens' grandiloquent vocabulary, and the tendency of his speech in this final appearance is toward tedium rather than wit. He becomes a countrified version of Gavin, who is at times the most tedious of Faulkner's characters.

The most genuinely humorous episode of *The Mansion* has already been referred to: it is the tale (published separately as a short story) of the elimination of Clarence Egglestone Snopes from the race for Congress. Ratliff's account has the flavor of one of Mark Twain's animal stories as he describes a dog lifting his leg in the "dog thicket" after sniffing the odor of his predecessor and declaring, in dog talk, "I be dawg if here aint that old bobtail Bluetick from up at Wyott's Crossing. What you reckon he's doing away down here?" After Clarence Snopes's trousers had been anointed with dog urine, the "standing-room-only customers [the dogs] strung out behind him like the knots in a kite's tail until he got inside the car . . . the dogs was travelling on three legs, being already loaded and cocked and aimed you might say." Once more it appears that Faulkner's most effective humor is folk comedy in the form of a tall tale, either involving animals or depicting animal-like behavior in human beings.

The Reivers, Faulkner's final book, is perhaps his most hilarious, for it is nearly all comedy. In fact, it almost requires tragedy for relief. The redoubtable Boon Hogganbeck, the powerful, simple-minded, half-Indian who performed the superhuman feat of killing Old Ben, the great bear, in *Go Down, Moses*, is brought into the town of Jefferson and becomes one of the principals in a tale replete with trickery, ribaldry, and relatively harmless violence. Faulkner has no axes to grind in this, his last book, and the result, though not a great novel, is great fun. The tale is told by Lucius Priest as a reminiscence by an old man of a great adventure when he was eleven years old, when he, Boon Hogganbeck, and black Ned took without permission his grandfather's automobile, one of the two in town (it was 1905), and made an epic journey to Memphis (eighty miles away) to Miss Reba's whorehouse. There Boon fell in love with a gentle and ladylike whore and pulverized his rival, the brutal

Butch. Black Ned in a masterful and involved scheme swapped the automobile for a stolen racehorse, induced the reluctant thoroughbred to win a race by teaching him to like sardines and then enticing him to run wherever Ned stood waiting with the sardines in his pocket, finally recovered the automobile and returned the racehorse to his owner without penalty. The whole scheme was devised to rescue Bobo (Ned's cousin) from his own foolishness (Bobo had stolen the horse) and reinstate him in his job with the horse's owner. The star-crossed lovers, Boon and Everbe, the gentle whore, are united in matrimony and the delightful novel ends appropriately as the boy Lucius enters Boon's house and sees in a cradle a remarkably ugly infant. "His name is Lucius Priest Hogganbeck," Everbe tells him. These are the last words of the novel.

Faulkner's best comic effects from his first book to his last were derived from the two most ancient sources of humor in the Western world, sex and avarice. Goatishness was the character trait made fun of in *Soldiers' Pay*, and sex lay behind the humor even in that savage satire, *Sanctuary*, where the impotent demon, Popeye Vitelli, hung onto the bed post and whinneyed like a horse as the robust young gangster, Red, serviced the failed debutante, Temple Drake. Sex was again the source of humor in the antebellum tale, "Was," in *Go Down, Moses*, where bachelors Uncle Buck and Uncle Buddy, who shut up their slaves at night, are outwitted first by a rutting young black and then by a man-hunting spinster whose success ensures the perpetuation of the McCaslin line. Avarice makes its appearance also in *Go Down, Moses* when Lucas Beauchamp, the dignified black patriarch of *Intruder in the Dust*, appears in a comic role by spending his nights looking for gold with a divining machine instead of resting his ancient bones at home. By the time the Snopes tribe appears on the center of Faulkner's stage, avarice is the predominant human flaw to receive comic treatment. Flem Snopes is Faulkner's miser, more sinister and threatening than Molière's, but sexual comedy is not neglected as the goatish bumpkins of Frenchman's Bend bleat and scamper after the gorgeous mammalian flesh of Eula Varner. Sexual comedy is primary in *The Town*, when Gavin Stevens and Manfred de Spain brawl like schoolboys over the favors of the diminished but still portentous Eula Varner Snopes. Finally, in *The Reivers* sex and avarice are featured in almost equal measure, but the avaricious rogue has been reduced to the dimension of a vicious child. It is an undersized Arkansas boy, Otis, who bargains for pennies and commits his paramount act of greed by stealing black Minnie's cherished gold tooth while she sleeps. The sexual comedy in this novel is soft, almost sentimental, as uncouth Boon loses his animal ferocity under the ministering affection of the gentle whore, Everbe. None of the tooth-grinding lust that Faulkner depicted so savagely in *Sanctuary* violates the generally benevolent ambience of *The Reivers*, even though the scene is often that same whorehouse that provided "sanctuary" for the ironically presented temple of Southern Womanhood, Temple Drake. Instead of making a whore out of a lady, as he did in *Sanctuary*, Faulkner in this last novel makes a lady out of a whore.

It appears that in his last two novels Faulkner's comedy has lost its satiric edge. His miser, Flem Snopes, was murdered almost gratuitously in *The Mansion*, long after he had been turned from an incarnation of Mammon into the country boy who made good. It is a measure of Faulkner's final reconciliation to human frailty that the most apt exemplars of Snopesism we can find in *The Reivers* are a country farmer who plows mudholes in the Memphis road so that he can use his mule team to pull out mired automobiles for a fee, and a depraved little boy, Otis—Ned calls him "Whistle-britches—whose greatest feat is to steal the gold tooth from a sleeping Negro maid in a whorehouse. It's all good fun, but for great satiric comedy, with a Swiftian bite and Rabelaisian pungency, we must still turn back to *The Hamlet*, surely one of the great comic creations of our time. In it Faulkner proved himself a master of the comic mode, as *Absalom, Absalom!* had proved him a master of the tragic.

Eudora Welty's Comic Imagination

Seymour L. Gross

Eudora Welty is a southern writer whom some specialists of the literature of the South consider second only to her fellow Mississippian, William Faulkner, as a writer of fiction. This is an astonishingly high evaluation considering how relatively little she has published. Since her first story in 1936, Miss Welty has produced only four collections of short stories and five novels. But almost everything she has written has been greeted with critical enthusiasm and acclaim. She has received more awards and prizes for her fiction than she has written books. Katherine Anne Porter, Robert Penn Warren, and William Faulkner have all expressed admiration for her works.

Miss Welty's uniform excellence is such that anything of hers that one picks up is worth reading; but reading one of her stories is often little preparation for reading another. For very few American writers have her command over such a wide variety of tones, styles, and narrative techniques. Her inventiveness is seemingly inexhaustible. She has given us, for example, the hilarious monologue of a half-crazy Southern woman's fight with her family in "Why I Live at the P.O." and the hauntingly beautiful emergence of passion in a deaf-mute in "First Love"; the wild account of the effects of a nutty saint on his town in *The Ponder Heart* and the tragic aloneness of the "Death of a Travelling Salesman"; the surrealistic suggestiveness of "The Purple Hat" and the starkly realistic portrait of a young man caught in the guilt of his past in

"Keela, the Outcast Indian Maiden"; the blistering attack on man-destroying women in "Petrified Man" and the "golden moments" imbedded in the screaming vulgarity of the Italian-Americans in "Going to Naples." And one could go on and on—indeed, should go on and on—if one is to do justice to Miss Welty's stunning virtuosity.

In one of her essays, Miss Welty approvingly quotes from *Macbeth* what might well stand as the signpost to her fictional world—"Security/Is Mortal's chiefest enemy." "In fact," she goes on to say, "when we think in terms of the spirit, which are the terms of writing, is there a concept more stupefying than security?" "Security," as Miss Welty uses the term, is characteristic of those writers whose work is so shaped by their ideas that they produce a body of work, the outline of which is predictably and unmistakably their own. Miss Welty's fictional world, in contrast, is difficult to encircle precisely because whatever personal beliefs and ideas she may privately hold, they exercise little influence on her fiction. She seemingly has no social or philosophical arguments to advance—which of course is not the same thing as saying that she ignores the ways in which social assumptions and ethical commitments shape the lives of her characters. Miss Welty faces the world, as she has implied on several occasions, as a lyric poet—life comes to her as music rather than as lesson. And the music she "hears," in her own words, "is endlessly new, mysterious, alluring." "Life *is* strange," she has told us. "Stories hardly make it more so . . . they make it more believable, more inevitably so." Her fiction, in short, authenticates the mystery and multiplicity of experience. It does not try to command it into shape.

Generally speaking, in her noncomic stories Miss Welty confronts experience with an almost incredible sensitivity to the mysterious uniqueness of each individual life. In those of her works in which the mode is primarily comic—which is our concern here—what predominates is her hospitality to the diversity and energy and magical surprises of the human carnival. When her vision is comic, it is dazzled by the transformation of identities, the mischievous eruptions of nature and natural impulse, the ways in which "the pure wish to live" breaks free of the forces which would inhibit its spontaneity. So it is that feeble-minded Lily Daw slides out from under the thumbs of the Baptist ladies who would protect her from herself, and Powerhouse in the story of that name improvises a jazz history of his own identity which defies all attempts to place him as a "nigger musician." Old Mr. Marble-hall—whom Natchez has dismissed with a "Why look twice at him?"—has two wives and two sons and wakes in the night with his heart thumping wildly at the precious thought "that if people knew about his double life, they'd die." King MacLain of *The Golden Apples*, a fascinating combination of satyr-god and rabbit, amorously triumphs over the sobriety and decorum of Morgana with his golden children, "known and unknown." Uncle Daniel Ponder makes a shambles of the medical, religious, judicial, and social institutions which try to stem the overflow of his generous heart and make him measure up to accepted standards. And Jack Renfro, in *Losing Battles*, good-humoredly but decisively evades all attempts, even that of his loving and beloved wife, to save him from the consequences of his irrepressible hospitality to come what may.

As these examples illustrate, Miss Welty's comedy, with few exceptions, is celebrative not critical. She does not, as do, say, Twain, Sinclair Lewis, or Ring Lardner, try to correct society by exposing its hypocrisies and stupidities. She simply shows it as fighting a losing battle with the diverse, vital, and indeterminate reality which is life. As such, she belongs in the American Transcendentalist comic tradition, some of whose great moments are Emerson's early essays, Whitman's *Song of Myself*, Thoreau's *Walden*, and Ralph Ellison's *Invisible Man*. Like these great testaments to diversity and freedom, Miss Welty's comedies know that men are not contained between their hats and their boots, that nature not society is decisive, and that although there will always be, as Ellison says, "gangs" which will try "putting the world in a straitjacket, its definition is possibility."

The Robber Bridegroom, Miss Welty's first novel, reveals in the bold outline of fantasy the essential qualities of her comic imagination. It is a minor masterpiece in a form all its own—a delightful crossing of the European fairy tale with the fabulous folklore of the American frontier. Evil stepmother, beautiful princess, and disguised prince mix freely with Indian captivities, infamous outlaws such as the Harpe brothers, and one of the great liars of American folk history, Mike Fink. But what is really fabulous in *The Robber Bridegroom* is not so much its talking heads, its days-long fist fights, its incredible tricks and adventures. It is rather the fabulous nature of reality which these all point to— the "whirling . . . dance we had never suspected lay in our limbs."

The plot of *The Robber Bridegroom* involves the kidnapping of Rosamond Musgrove by a disguised bandit of the forest and her father Clement's attempts to find and capture the man who first robbed her of her clothes and then returned to rob a willing Rosamond "of that which he had left her the day before." To help him, Clement enlists the aid of Jamie Lockhart, a respectable young man who had earlier saved his life, promising him his daughter if he succeeds. But Jamie *is* the robber bridegroom, so Jamie has only agreed to find himself and win the girl he already has. When Clement brings Jamie home to dinner, Rosamond (who moves between forest and plantation as she pleases) does not recognize him, nor he her, though they have been lovers in the forest. They do not recognize each other because they have known each other only in a single way—as kidnapped beauty and dark lover; here "he was too clean and she was too dirty" for recognition. Pressed by her stepmother to penetrate her lover's disguise, Rosamond removes the berry stain from his face while he is sleeping. In doing so she disenchants their relationship; now he is only Jamie Lockhart and she is only "Clement Musgrove's silly daughter." Jamie leaves her, but Rosamond suddenly feeling the stirring of "a fresh piece of news" within her—she is pregnant—goes in search of him. When she finds him, they marry.

The theme of the novel is the liberating discovery of multiple identity. Each of the main characters is in some way double. Clement Musgrove is wanderer and planter; Rosamond is as beautiful as truth "but when she opened her mouth in answer to a question, lies would fall out like diamonds and pearls." And Jamie is of course respectable citizen and romantic bandit. All three succeed—which in a fairy tale is appropriately measured by happiness-ever-after—because each comes to an acknowledgement and understanding of doubleness. Clement, in pursuit of his daughter's ravisher, suddenly perceives the ambiguity of his intention. "If being a bandit were his breadth and scope, I should find him and kill him for sure," he thinks to himself. "But since in addition he loves my daughter, he must be not the one man, but two, and I should be afraid of killing the second. For all things are double, and this should keep us from taking liberties with the outside world, and acting too quickly to finish things off." Rosamond intuits the truth that "all things are double" from the "news" from her belly: she is carrying twins. And Jamie finally understands that whether bandit or merchant, the true "hero" is he who has "the power to look both ways and to see a thing from all sides." The marriage which closes the novel celebrates this comic enlargement of vision: a double Rosamond is united to a double Jamie to produce a pair of twins in that "marvelous city" of New Orleans where "Beauty and vice and every delight possible to the soul and body stood hospitably, and usually together. . . ."

Salome, the evil stepmother, is the enemy to the presiding vision of variety and novelty which the novel celebrates. Narrow, calculating, and tyrannical, her ugliness is the outward sign of her resistance to everything that is free, open, and therefore beautiful. She rejects the multiplicity of human nature because she rejects the promiscuous energy of nature itself, as the manner of her death makes clear. Captured by the Indians, she screams at them until they put their fingers in their ears. Summoning what for them is the highest authority, the Indians tell her that "It is the command of the sun itself . . . that you be still." But to their horror, Salome contemptuously dismisses the sun as "a weak thing . . . like all the rest of life," and announces that *she* has the power to command *it* to be still. Outraged at her blasphemy, they order her to dance until either she or the sun stops. She dances till she falls over "stone dead" and "the sun went on as well as ever."

The impulse to limit and control embodied in Salome is in contrast to the actions of Goat, whose name immediately associates him with the carefree joy of fertility rites, and reminds us of King MacLain who "butted like a goat" against the walls of life in his "pure wish to live" and of the "profane" Don McInnis, in "Asphodel," who appears "naked as an old goat" to the three old maids on the day after the funeral of his Salome-like wife, Miss Sabina. Goat is so named, the narrator tells us, "because he could butt his way out the door when his mother locked him in and . . .

butt his way in when she locked him out. . . . Anything he found
penned up he would let out, including himself. . . . He would
let anything out of a trap, if he had to tear its leg off to do it."
Goat represents those irrepressible forces of freedom in the natural
world, the romping insolence of growing things, which the main
characters enact in the human. He is the only character in the
novel who never suffers capture. Amoral and unruly as the world
of nature itself, Goat takes life as he takes it. When, for example,
he comes upon a weeping Rosamond who tells him, "Oh I have
lost my husband, and he has lost me, and we are both tied up to
be killed in the morning," Goat responds with "Then cry on, for I
never expect to hear a better reason." Although he never makes
moral judgments, all his actions conspire toward freedom; he is
forever untying people. And it is Goat, after all, who frees Big
Harp's head from the box, passes it off as the robber bridegroom's,
and thus makes possible Jamie's escape and the happy ending.

The collision of the social impulse toward order and control
with the natural spirit of spontaneity and freedom—Salome versus
Goat—takes a variety of forms and achieves a variety of comic
effects in Miss Welty. The frequently anthologized "Petrified
Man" is actually unusual for Miss Welty, unusual because there
is nothing, or almost nothing, of the force of nature to stand in
mischievous opposition to the forces of constriction. We are totally
locked, so to speak, into the vulgar, life-denying artificiality of the
beauty parlor. There being no goat figure in the story to upset the
posture of these terrible ladies, Miss Welty is compelled to bring
the full weight of her satiric scorn on those who seemingly carry
the day. These women, it becomes clear, apparently in the process
of making themselves more desirable, actually hate and emasculate
their men—petrify them—because they hate nature. Leota's first
remark to the little boy who has been left to play in the beauty
parlor—"mustn't bother nice ladies"—takes on significance when
we realize that these "nice ladies" look upon pregnancy as something dirty and shameful done to them by men who should be
making money, not babies. The beating of the boy with which the
story ends—"From everywhere ladies began to gather round to
watch the paddling"—is a ritualistic summary of the punishing blows
these women have always rained upon their men for their sexual

unruliness. Yet, somehow, the last words belong to Billy Boy. Kicking himself free of "the wild-haired women," he flings back at them a remark both magnificently irrelevant and pointedly apt— "If you're so smart, why ain't you rich?"

It is much more customary for Miss Welty, who has little of the malice needed for unrelieved satire, to treat the exponents of rationality and decorum with tolerant amusement, being content to let them tangle themselves up in the very nets they try to cast over experience. This is handled in a special way in the justly famous "Why I Live at the P.O." The postmistress of the second smallest post office in Mississippi is a devotee of reason and what she calls "the facts of life"; and she tells us her story in order to justify her decision to move away from her bizarre and bouncing family and into the post office where, she says, "It's ideal"—"I've got everything cater-cornered the way I like it." But the effect of her self-justifying monologue is the reverse of what she intends. It reveals instead her frustration, exasperation, and isolation—"There are always people who will quit buying stamps just to get on the right side of Pappa-Daddy." The empty post office is a neatly ordered but diminished alternative to the zany goings-on in the family house.

In "Lily Daw and the Three Ladies," Miss Welty contemplates the minister's wife, the widow in everlasting black, and the spinster postmistress, with a humor commensurate to their bumbling efforts to control Lily Daw, a pretty retarded girl in Victory, Mississippi. The three have made it their chief concern in life to see to it that Lily is clothed, housed, and taught the Baptist "Lord's teachings." As the story opens, their efforts in the service of respectability are about to be rewarded: Lily has been accepted into the Ellisville Institute for the Feeble-Minded. "She'll be tickled to death," they tell themselves. But when they find Lily, dressed only in a petticoat with a zinnia in her mouth, she announces that she is going to marry a man in a red coat who "took little sticks and went *ping-pong! ding-dong*" at the carnival the night before. "The xylophone player!" shrieks the minister's wife. "Tell me, Lily—just yes or no— are you the same as you were?" the widow hysterically inquires. Aimee, the spinster, nearly faints. Almost beside themselves with anxiety at the thought of Lily wandering the community with a knowledge of sex—they are sure the xylophonist "was after Lily's body alone"—they bribe her into going to Ellisville by promising her a cake, a gold-lettered Bible, a toy bank and a brassiere—the last particularly useful since "What would they think if she ran all over Ellisville . . . looking like a Fiji?" Then, incredibly, the xylophone player shows up—short, deaf, drowned in shaving lotion—ready to get married. Bewildered almost to the point of panic, the ladies change direction: they are going to make an honest woman of Lily. An impossible marriage is going to take place in spite of all that is reasonable in this world. Life—just simply that—has gotten away from the ladies—and the band breaks out in the "Independence March," the crowd cheers, "and a straw hat was thrown into the telephone wires."

An even more unsettling fate awaits Judge Moody in *Losing Battles*. Because he does not understand the ritual comedy of the fight between Jack, the exuberant darling of the Renfro clan, and Curley, the penny-pinching and lecherous storekeeper-politician, he sends Jack to jail for "aggravated battery" as a "lesson to the rest" that there must be respect for the law and those who have been "raised to office." This decision, ultimately, involves the judge, his wife, and, preeminently, their car—one of the great nonhuman "characters" in American literature—in a series of hilarious misadventures too complicated for summary. After two days with Jack (who has escaped jail a day before he was to be released) and the rest of the wild clan, the judge is dirtier, wearier, more battered and more bemused than he has ever before been in his life. About to depart for Ludlow where they come from, Mrs. Moody tells the judge that when the Presbyterians back home see him, "They'll say it's lucky you had me along to vouch for who you are." Actually, he will never again be quite what he was.

But nowhere in Miss Welty does the comic spirit make such a shambles of the assumptions of society as in *The Ponder Heart*. Here it literally kills with kindness and tickles to death. This is the story of good-as-gold Uncle Daniel Ponder as told by his niece, Edna Earle, a knowing and tough-minded woman with more of an appreciation for the comedy of life than she lets on. Uncle Daniel's problem—but it is really society's problem—is that his heart is so full of love for the world that it spills over in the socially unsettling form of giving things away—food, clothes, cattle, land, trips to Memphis, a pick-up truck, a hotel, "even his own cemetery lot, but they wouldn't accept it." Grandpa, Daniel's father, who believed that "people exist in the realm of reason" and who "was of the old school, and wanted people to measure up," dies trying with Daniel. When Grandpa finds out that Daniel passed out ice cream cones to the line of dancers at the fair—no one had suspected that Daniel had an interest in sex—he has a heart attack; when he recovers, he decides he had better "fork up a good wife" for his son. The choice is Miss Teacake Magee who sings "Work, for the Night Is Coming" at the Baptist church. But the "marriage," in Edna's words, "didn't hold out." Although neither Daniel nor Teacake will say one word about why, the implication is pretty clear that Teacake didn't take to Daniel's own brand of "hymn"— Play, for the Day Is Here. When Daniel gives Edna the hotel, Grandpa decides to become "strict." He wears out two preachers praying over Daniel and then sends him to the lunatic asylum. But one day when Grandpa returns to the asylum with Daniel after taking him to town to vote, Daniel innocently gets Grandpa locked up and he himself returns to town in Grandpa's car. And that's the end of the asylum. Next Daniel falls in love with Bonnie Dee Peacock, a doll-sized girl with a brain to match. Bonnie Dee agrees to marry Daniel on *trial*, Daniel accepts, and that's the end of Grandpa—he has his final heart attack. After almost six years of putting down payments on everything in sight and keeping Daniel away lest he be there "giving things away as quick as she could get them in the door," Bonnie Dee decides the trial has failed. Uncle Daniel is so unhappy that Edna bribes Bonnie Dee back. But at their reunion in a lightning storm, Bonnie dies. After what is surely the funniest funeral in literature, Mrs. Peacock, who looks like "a row of pigs," brings a charge of murder against Uncle Daniel. What happened was that in trying to distract Bonnie Dee from her terror at the lightning, Uncle Daniel tickled her to death—her heart couldn't take the laughter. But this the court will never know, for at a critical moment in the proceedings, Uncle Daniel throws the whole judicial process into turmoil by passing out the money he has drawn from the bank that morning. And that's the end of the trial.

I have been concerned here with some of the more joyful manifestations of Miss Welty's comic imagination. They do not, of course, tell her whole story. Sometimes, as in "A Piece of News," the comic conditions for expanding a pinched life are all there, but the character sadly fails to rise to them. Sometimes, as in *The Golden Apples*, the comic is so closely joined to the tragic that, as the presiding moral intelligence in the final story realizes, they are "unrecognizable one from the other . . . making moments double upon themselves, and in the doubling double again. . . ." And sometimes the vision is so purely on those passions which separate and defeat that there is no place for the comic to gain a foothold. Miss Welty knows what chaos is. But that knowledge has never threatened to overwhelm her work because she knows, too, that despite the world's substantial weight—its pain and sadness—human nature has an astonishing capacity for dancing free.

Jewish Humor

Allen Guttmann

Although it may seem odd to say so, there really is no such thing as "Jewish humor." If the term refers to some form of humor which has been characteristic of Jews from the time of Moses to the day of Moshe Dayan, then clearly the term has no referent at all. There *is*, on the other hand, a kind of humor which is common to the great Yiddish writers of the nineteenth century and to many Jewish-American authors in the twentieth century. This kind of humor is not, however, the result of Judaism as a religion and cannot be traced to the experiences of Biblical Jews. This kind of humor is rather the product of the social situation of East-European Jews as a minority which maintained a precarious existence within the larger culture of Christendom.

Another way to make this point is to say, quite simply, that the greatest of all Jewish books, the Old Testament, is scarcely typified by elements of comedy. In contrast to the *Odyssey* or even to the *Iliad*, the Old Testament is a very solemn book. It has moments of grandeur and epic sweep; it has—in the Book of Job— one of the great tragic dramas of world literature, but it has little that we can call humorous. Laughter is not the usual response. Of course, we can *imagine* comic moments. How did the citizens of Jericho look when Joshua's men blew their trumpets and brought the walls tumbling down? How did Joseph behave when Potiphar's wife tried to seduce him? The authors of the Old Testament ignore the comic potentialities.

329

Ironically, the present generation of Jewish writers in America is quick to take irreverent advantage of this almost humorless book. Paul Goodman, for instance, has written a play entitled *Jonah: A Biblical Comedy with Jewish Jokes Culled Far and Wide*. In the play, Goodman relies on the humor of incongruity. He has the Biblical prophet speak in the dialect of Brooklyn. When the Angel of God appears to Jonah and requests that he go to the people of Nineveh, Jonah answers with sarcastic intonations: "To *Nineveh!* I should go to Nineveh? *There* I'll be popular! A prophet they need, you should pardon the expression, like a pain in the arm." Had Goodman published his play in 1965 rather than in 1945, he might have avoided the euphemism of "a pain in the arm" and thus come even closer to authentic Brooklyn humor.

Goodman's comedy at the expense of Jonah is an especially useful example for my purposes. Not only does Goodman in his play suggest some of the comic possibilities that the ancient authors chose to leave unrealized; he also exemplifies the note of self-mockery which is one important element of Jewish humor.

But what exactly is this Jewish humor bequeathed to us by the East-European Jews? It is, as I said, a product of the social situation of a minority group within a hostile majority. To be more precise, it is the result of a proud people acutely sensitive of their lowly social status. The Jews of Eastern Europe considered themselves the Chosen People set apart from all others by their unique role as the transmitters of God's message. From them, or from their brethren scattered about the world in the Diaspora or dispersion of the Jews, was to come the Messiah. But religious pride coexisted with political, economic, and social deprivation. The Chosen People of God were also the despised people of the Polish or Russian village. The Jew of Eastern Europe used humor as a way to mediate the chasm between his spiritual claims and his material situation. As his faith in his own religion waned, as skepticism became increasingly common, the contrast between the hope and the reality became more and more ironic. A famous story serves well as an illustration. The mythical town of Chelm, located somewhere in Eastern Europe, is isolated from the world by mountains on every side. The villagers feared that the Messiah might return and miss them. Therefore, they asked one of the town's beggars to watch from a tower built upon a mountain top. When he saw the Messiah, he was to shout and catch his attention and alert the rest of the village. The beggar, however, complained about the pay that was offered him. "But consider," replied the village elders, "the pay is low but the work is steady." The work is steady because the skeptical Jews of Chelm doubt the millennium which they pray for. The Messiah may come but he is not likely to come soon. In the meantime, let us go about our business as best we can.

When the hopes of the wise seem foolish, then the foolishness of simple men can be seen as a kind of shrewdness. The reverse of the anecdote I have just told is the famous story, "Gimpel the Fool," by Isaac Bashevis Singer, the greatest twentieth-century Yiddish writer. Gimpel is a dweller in the village of Frampol. He is the butt of the town's jokers. Because of his gullibility, he is married off to a slovenly woman who already has one illegitimate child and is seventeen weeks pregnant with another. She beats poor Gimpel and refuses to let him sleep with her. She betrays him with other men and denies her guilt even when Gimpel discovers her in bed with her lover. Gimpel decides that faith is better than doubt: "All Frampol," he says, "refreshed its spirits because of my trouble and grief. However, I resolved that I would always believe what I was told. What's the good of *not* believing? Today it's your wife you don't believe; tomorrow it's God Himself you won't take stock in." Gimpel outlives his wife and looks forward to his own death: "When the time comes I will go joyfully. Whatever may be there, it will be real, without complication, without ridicule, without deception. God be praised; there even Gimpel cannot be deceived." The elders of the village of Chelm are not all that different from Gimpel the Fool. Like him, they make an effort not to doubt and not to lose hope. They are more realistic than he is, but whether they are better off is quite another question.

There is a special term for characters like Gimpel the Fool. They are referred to as schlemiels. The term schlemiel has a disputed etymology, but its contemporary significance is clear enough. The schlemiel is someone whose luck is always bad. But the Jews are a people whose luck has very often been bad—whose fate has, in fact, often been persecution. The catastrophes of the

1930's and 1940's were the worst in Jewish history, but they were not the first. No wonder then that Jewish humor has the schlemiel as one of its central figures. And no wonder that the portrait is sometimes a sympathetic one, as in Singer's story of Gimpel the Fool. The East-European Jew who scorned the victim of ill fortune was all too likely to be caught himself in some luckless situation over which he had no control. In the face of disaster, the comic response was to shrug's one's shoulders and sigh, "So what else is new?" It is all very well to dream of David defying Goliath and Samson slaughtering the Philistines, but the Jews of Eastern Europe were in no position to defy the Cossacks of Czar Nicholas.* Once I was asked, "Are you ever so happy you have to cry?" "No," I answered, "but sometimes I feel so wretched that I have to laugh." Humor has always been one defense, until even humor proved inadequate in the Holocaust of the 1940's.

When the Jews of Eastern Europe began to migrate in large numbers to the United States, it was natural that they brought their humor with them. The Portuguese and German Jews, who began to arrive in the New World as early as the seventeenth century, had adapted themselves extremely well to the conditions of American life and were very largely assimilated into American society when the East-European Jews began to immigrate in the 1880's. The Jews of Austria, Poland, and Russia came in much larger numbers and in much poorer circumstances than their predecessors from Holland, Germany, and France. Although their exodus to the promised land of America saved them from the threat of physical extermination in the form of a *pogrom*, they nonetheless had ample reason to employ their self-mocking humor. Success in the United States was less elusive than the Millennium, but the gap between the dream and the reality was still there; the bridge of Jewish humor was still necessary.

Elements of Jewish humor can be found in the work of Abraham Cahan, a Yiddish-language journalist who is today best remembered for his long novel, *The Rise of David Levinsky*, published in 1917. More popular as a writer and more devoted to the comic mode was

* The Jews of the State of Israel have, on the other hand, played the role of David defeating Goliath. Israeli humor is, predictably, very different from the sort I've been discussing.

Montague Glass, who won an audience with a pair of characters named Potash and Perlmutter. Glass was by no means a great writer, but one can hear in his dialogue the typical accents of the Jewish humorist. When Abraham Potash, a petty capitalist, dissolves his partnership with Pincus Vesell, exclaims, "I got my stomach full with Pincus Vesell already, and if Andrew Carnegie would come to me and tell me he wants to go with me as partners together in the cloak and suit business, I would say 'No,' so sick and tired of partners I am." To the reader, who may have been a struggling ghetto businessman, the very notion of partnership with Carnegie was laughable. The multimillionaire industrialist and philanthropist was about as likely to approach Abraham Potash as the Messiah was to arrive at the gates of the village of Chelm.

Although William Dean Howells was very receptive to the work of Abraham Cahan, Jewish writers did not really win general acceptance from American readers until after the Second World War. From 1945 to the present, however, Jewish writers have tended to dominate the literary scene. Saul Bellow, Norman Mailer, Bernard Malamud, and Philip Roth are all among the most widely respected of contemporary novelists. And their books are read by every literate person, not just by Jews. It is, moreover, important to recognize that all of them have written comic novels.* They have done more than merely to popularize a kind of Jewish humor. They have made it an element in literature of the highest order.

Bernard Malamud's fiction is full of schlemiels of one type or another. His novel, *A New Life* (1961), has for its protagonist a hapless professor who manages to be surprised while nakedly making love in a barn with a moderately attractive and extremely stupid waitress. Malamud's stories, especially those collected in *Pictures of Fidelman: An Exhibition* (1969), are a rich source of humor. Fidelman, for instance, manages to stumble his schlemiel-like way through an absurd series of Italian adventures. Attempting to make love to a beautiful Italian girl, he becomes ludicrously overexcited. She cries out, "Enough of antipasto," and reaches for

---

* The most popular comic novel of the era was probably Leonard Q. Ross's *The Education of Hyman Kaplan*, the very title of which invites invidious comparison to one of the most famous of American autobiographies, *The Education of Henry Adams*.

his genitals. He is overwrought and has a premature orgasm, where-
upon she says, "Pig, beast, onanist," and kicks him out of bed.

The most interesting of the American schlemiels is the creation
of Saul Bellow rather than of Bernard Malamud. (Bellow, inci-
dently, is the American translator of Singer's story, "Gimpel the
Fool.") Moses Herzog, the somewhat autobiographical hero of the
novel *Herzog* (1964), characterizes himself as a poor, suffering
fool, but he is considerably more than that. Like Gimpel, Moses
Herzog is a luckless cuckold, but he is also a learned scholar with
an international reputation. He is the accomplished lover of a
number of remarkable women. It is, in fact, the contrast between
his intellectual ability and his physical passions which leads to the
self-ironic musings of this extraordinarily self-aware protagonist.
Herzog thinks of his physical lust as a duck-like noise that rises
from his depths. At the end of the novel, he gazes at beautiful
Ramona and feels the same helpless response: "She pretended,"
writes Bellow, "to look for something in her purse because her
cheek quivered. The perfume of her shoulders reached his nostrils.
And, as almost always, he heard the deep, the cosmic, the idiotic
masculine response—*quack*. The progenitive, the lustful quacking
in the depths. *Quack, Quack.*" When Moses Herzog settles for
that half a loaf which realists claim is better than none, he shares
something of the stoic resignation of Gimpel the Fool, who settled
for even less than half a loaf.

Moses Herzog may be the most complex and interesting of
American schlemiels, but Alexander Portnoy is easily the most
absurd. He is the psychically distraught caricature of the Jewish
boy dominated and finally destroyed by his mother's excessive love.
Philip Roth sends him stumbling from humiliation to humiliation.
While an adolescent, he masturbates compulsively and in the most
unlikely ways. When he arrives at statutory (but not psychological) manhood, he attempts to flee the remnants of his Jewish
identity; he tries to make love to girls of impeccable Puritan
ancestry. The final humiliation comes when he visits Israel and is
sexually attracted by a healthy young girl. "Naomi," he exclaims
to his analyst back in New York, "The Jewish Pumpkin, the
Heroine, that hardy, red-headed, freckled, ideological hunk of a

girl!" Naomi is a veteran of the Israeli army and the member of a dedicated commune on the Syrian border. She symbolizes all womanhood that is not Mrs. Portnoy. In a marvelously comic scene, Portnoy tries to seduce her. She rejects him and his self-depreciative Jewish humor, which she derisively calls "ghetto humor." When Portnoy fails to persuade her, he tries to rape her, only to discover that she is nearly as strong as he is. At length he overpowers her and shouts, "Down, down with these patriotic khaki shorts, spread your chops, blood of my blood, unlock your fortressy thighs, open wide that messianic Jewish hole! Make ready, Naomi. . . . !" And then, having reached the verge of success, he is sexually impotent. She is understandably annoyed. When he suggests oral-genital intercourse, she flattens him with one powerful kick. He is, as he well realizes, the most pathetic of schlemiels, a grotesquely parodied version of the comic figures of nineteenth-century Yiddish fiction.

But contemporary Jewish-American literature is also influenced by *American* literature of the nineteenth and twentieth centuries. Norman Mailer, for instance, is far more influenced by Melville, Hemingway, and Faulkner than by any past or present Jewish author. Saul Bellow's novel, *Henderson the Rain King* (1959), is full of allusions to American authors. Philip Roth's Portnoy suffers the classic difficulties of the schlemiel, but his wild exaggerations are very much in the American tradition of Mark Twain and frontier humor. While the comic spirit in England cultivated irony and understatement, American humorists of the nineteenth century developed a boastful style full of outrageous overstatements and outlandish imagery. The extraordinary material success of American Jews brought with it a tendency to emulate American speech as well as the patterns of American capitalism. One result of this linguistic assimilation is an outspoken pride whose accents any American can quickly recognize. A well-known joke parodies this attitude, this boastfulness: "Help, help!" cries the distraught woman on the beach, "my son, *Dr.* Irving Diamond, is drowning." The ultimate parody of the Jewish mother's pride in her son, the doctor, is Philip Roth's version in *Portnoy's Complaint*. Portnoy tells his analyst what his mother told him about what Seymour Schmuck's mother told her:

. . . I met his mother on the street today, and she told me that Seymour is now the biggest brain surgeon in the entire Western Hemisphere. He owns six different split-level ranch-type houses made all of fieldstone in Livingston, and belongs to the boards of eleven synagogues, all brand-new and designed by Marc Kugel, and last year with his wife and his two little daughters, who are so beautiful that they are already under [a film] contract to Metro, and so brilliant that they should be in college—he took them all to Europe for an eighty-million-dollar tour of seven thousand countries, some of them you never even heard of, that they made them just to honor Seymour, and on top of that, he's so important . . . that in every single city in Europe that they visited he was asked by the mayor himself to stop and do an impossible operation on a brain in hospitals that they also built for him right on the spot. . . .

Exaggeration is one characteristic of American humor. Obscenity has come to be another. It may well be that folk humor is always obscene, but it has only been in the years since 1945 that censorship has ended for the kind of sexual and scatological literature that Mark Twain wrote and published privately.

A mild example of this new freedom in comic literature can be seen in Bernard Malamud's account of the painter Fidelman. I noted above how unfortunate Fidelman failed in his attempt to make love to beautiful Annamaria Oliovino. Malamud goes on, in the story entitled "Still Life," to give the schlemiel a second chance. Having painted Annamaria as the Virgin Mary, Fidelman dresses as a priest and paints a portrait of himself with a cross. Annamaria now thinks differently and makes herself physically available: Malamud's final sentence is witty in its metaphoric play: "Pumping slowly he nailed her to her cross."

Norman Mailer's obscenity is much less mild. His gift for extravaganzas of colorful off-color rhetoric was vividly displayed in his most recent novel, *Why Are We in Vietnam?* (1967). The novel must be a translator's nightmare. The most obscene kind of slang predominates and the slang appears in a swift flow of puns, verbal play, insinuation, and obscure allusion to the artifacts of contemporary American life. To follow Mailer's disk-jockey narrator through his comic romp, it is not enough to be an American *au courant* with the world of the mass media; it is also necessary to be a participant in or a student of the youth culture.

What is most interesting about Mailer's humor, however, is its intentional Americanness. In a book published just after the novel appeared, Mailer commented on what he had done in *Why Are We in Vietnam?* Referring to himself in the third person, he wrote,

Mailer never felt more like an American than when he was naturally obscene—all the gifts of the American language came out in the happy play of obscenity upon concept, which enabled one to go back to concept again. . . . Yeah, that was Mailer's America. If he was going to love something in the country, he would love that. So after years of keeping obscene language off to one corner of his work . . . he had come back to obscenity again in the last year—he had kicked goodbye in his novel . . . to the old literary corset of good taste, letting the sense of language play on obscenity as freely as it wished, so discovering that everything he knew about the American language (with its incommensurable resources) went flying in and out of the line of his prose with the happiest beating of wings—it was the first time his style seemed at once very American to him and very literary in the best way. . . .

One need scarcely add that the almost bombastic obscenity of Mailer's marvelously absurd novel is a total contrast to the Jewish humor of his East-European ancestors.

Although it makes a certain kind of sense to stop with Mailer, whose novel provides the contrast I have mentioned, I prefer to double back to another kind of humor found in Philip Roth. In addition to the Jewish humor of *Portnoy's Complaint* and the satiric obscenities of his recent attack on President Nixon in the book entitled *Our Gang* (1971), Roth rivals Saul Bellow as a master of subtle irony. My favorite example is his short story, "The Conversion of the Jews."

The young hero of the story, Ozzie Freedman, has difficulties with the rabbi who attempts to teach him Judaism. Ozzie continually asks the devastatingly simple question: why, he wonders, do Jews claim to be the Chosen People when the Declaration of Independence asserts that all men are created equal? The questions annoy Rabbi Binder. Ozzie queries him about the Jewish rejection of the Doctrine of the Virgin Birth; if God can do anything, asks Ozzie, why cannot he allow a woman to conceive without sexual intercourse? Embarrassed, Rabbi Binder loses his temper and strikes Ozzie, who runs up to the roof of the school building. He locks the door behind him and threatens to jump from the ledge overlooking the street. When the Rabbi and Ozzie's mother plead with him from below, "Don't be a martyr!," the other children misunderstand and urge him to defy authority, "Be a Martin, be a Martin. . . ." Ozzie is neither a martyr nor a Martin. Firemen arrive with a net to catch him, but before he leaps he becomes the teacher of his teachers:

> "Rabbi?"
> "Yes, Oscar."
> "Rabbi Binder, do you believe in God."
> "Yes."
> "Do you believe God can do Anything?" Ozzie leaned his head out into the darkness. "Anything?"
> "Oscar, I think—"
> "Tell me you believe God can do Anything."
> There was a second's hesitation. Then: "God can do Anything."
> "Tell me you believe God can make a child without intercourse."
> "He can."
> "Tell me!"
> "God," Rabbi Binder admitted, "can make a child without intercourse."

Having accomplished his purpose, having instructed his elders never to hit anyone about God, Ozzie says he can come down. In Roth's words, "And he did, right into the center of the yellow net that glowed in the evening's edge like an overgrown halo." The halo is doubtless a symbolic one. The moral of the fable is clear enough—not that the Virgin Mary conceived without intercourse but rather that no one should hit anyone else "about God." The humor is subtle; whether or not it is Jewish is difficult to determine, but difficult determinations are, after all, what provides the literary critic with steady work.

Southerners in the City: Flannery O'Connor and Walker Percy

Walter Sullivan

Walker Percy and Flannery O'Connor share in many ways a common background. Both were born in the Southern part of the United States, both were Roman Catholics in a region that is largely Protestant, both were concerned with that most prevalent of all themes in modern literature—the alienation of contemporary man. But Percy is older than Miss O'Connor would be—he was born in 1916 and she in 1925—and he came to the business of writing at a later age. Trained as a scientist, he practiced medicine until he was striken by tuberculosis, and his first novel was not published until he was forty-five. Flannery O'Connor, who never considered being anything but a writer, produced two novels and over two dozen short stories and died when she was thirty-nine years old.

The Moviegoer is Mr. Percy's most widely read work, and typically, it is about a young man's effort to grasp reality and thereby to overcome his existential malaise. Only once, when he lay wounded on a Korean battlefield, has Jack Bolling felt that he was fully alive. When he is back home in New Orleans, living in the middle-class suburb of Gentilly and working at the ordinary job of selling stocks and bonds, his sense of the reality of life begins to fade. The images that he sees on the television tube and on the cinema screen achieve for him an authenticity that his own experience lacks. "Other people," he says, ". . . treasure memorable moments in their lives: the time one climbed the Parthenon at sunrise, the summer night one met a lonely girl in Central Park. . . .

339

What I remember is the time John Wayne killed three men with a
carbine as he was falling to the dusty street in *Stagecoach,* and the
time the kitten found Orson Welles in the doorway in *The Third
Man.*"

The difference between Bolling and the other characters in the
novel is that he knows the truth about himself. Or more than this:
that he is willing to continue the search for identity and for meaning in his own existence while most of those around him have made
a separate peace. Aunt Emily, the sister of Bolling's dead father,
lives by the formulas of the past. She believes in inherited virtue,
in good manners and tough moral fiber and she deplores having
been forced by history to endure a century that makes a hero of the
common man. She is an anachronism and she knows it, but being
old herself, she counts on an adherence to the old ways to see her
through. Her husband Jules survives simply in the detachment that
his wealth affords him. He allows himself to be insulated from the
agonies of life by the luxury of his house, the competence of his
wife, the faithfulness of his servants. Even the black butler Mercer
makes an accommodation with reality by assuming various roles:
he is servile or arrogant, stupidly indifferent or intellectually committed according to his own mood and the demands of the occasion.

For Bolling's mother, who has married again since the death of
Jack's father and borne many children by her second husband,
domesticity is a way to avoid life's confrontations. "By the surest
of instincts," Bolling tells us, "she steers clear of all that is excep-
tional or 'stimulating.' Any event or idea which does not fall
within the household regimen, she stamps at once with her own
brand of the familiar." Of his half brothers and sisters, only Lonnie,
afflicted by cerebral palsy and deeply religious, responds to Bolling's
search for the real. Lonnie too is a moviegoer and the ability that
he shares with Jack to discover the authentic within the make-
believe is apparently the first step toward a full grasp of life.

All of this seems very serious and indeed is and becomes more so
as Bolling attempts to develop his relationship with his Aunt's step-
daughter Kate. A sincere effort to deal with reality has damaged
Kate psychologically and in this respect, she is a typical Walker
Percy character, a figure that recurs in his work again and again.
He seems to be telling us that we risk grave disorientation if we

attempt to engage life directly. Our alternatives are to embrace the physical suffering that fate has sent us as Lonnie does, or like Jack to make the search along oblique lines: that is, in moviegoing and in the pursuit of women.

Pursuit is the key word here, for Bolling is singularly inept at the art of seduction. He conceives of himself as a cinema hero, as Tony Curtis or Rory Calhoun. And when, on the way to the beach with a girl, a minor motor accident brings new but endurable grief to his old war wound, his delight knows no bounds.

O Tony. O Rory. You never had it so good with direction. Nor even you Bill Holden, my noble Will. O ye morning stars together. Farewell forever, malaise. Farewell and good luck, green Ford and old Ohioan. May you live in Tampa happily and forever.

And yet there are fellows I know who would have been sorry it happened, who would have had no thought for anything but their damned MG. Blessed MG.

This sequence in the novel assumes a kind of double focus. As the beautiful girl whom he desires extravagantly ministers to his slight injury, cradling his shoulder in her hands, giving him aspirin and whisky, the fictional character Bolling indulges in a further fiction: he plays a scene within a scene. Here may be discovered Walker Percy's comic method at its best. The moviegoer does not know who or what he is. He is trying to find out. But both he and we know what he is not, and he amuses us by playing his false role in which he is continually ineffectual. He is not a great lover. The girls do not go to bed with him. The charades that he devises, though promising at the outset, devolve quickly into tentative gestures. Nothing is accomplished by this foolish play-acting; nothing is solved.

Yet, if we are to believe Percy, the vast majority of us are moviegoers. His book takes place during the Mardi Gras season when in New Orleans all the procedures of living are given over to show. There are balls with make-believe kings and queens, parades in which people costumed as creatures of myth and fantasy ride on floats of strange design. It is all play—from the *krewes* who plan and sponsor the individual celebrations to the masked tourists who watch from the curb. Even on Ash Wednesday, even among the

minor characters, life remains a role to be filled. The Negro whom
Bolling watches go into the church attended mostly by white
people and emerge later with a smudge on his forehead is comical in
his uncertainty. Is he here for business reasons? Or because of his
need for social equality? Or because he believes?

The solution to all this, Percy's move toward reconciliation,
which is the true and final aim of comedy, is not surprising to a
generation well read in existentialism, but it works well enough.
Bolling turns to the nervous and insecure Kate, and when she demands his physical love, he is hardly able to give it to her. This is
a comic reversal, since as we have seen in the early sections of the
novel, Bolling has believed that reality might be found in the excita-
tions of the flesh. Finally he must trust Kate and care for her and
she must trust him. Which is to say they must accomplish in their
relationship with each other that most difficult of affections: each
must care for the other deeply enough to grant him his freedom. Or
in the case of Jack and Kate, for him to force her freedom upon her.

In the final scene of the book, Jack sends Kate alone into the
city to perform a simple errand. He insists that she go, but with
equal fervor, he insists that all still will be well should she fail. It
is the trying that counts. And the faith he has in her that she can
live within her own strength. And her trust in him that he would
not set her to a task that is beyond her energies. But this is not all,
for Walker Percy is a Catholic, and the death of Lonnie endows
the conclusion of the book with a Christian dimension. Throughout
his life, Lonnie has offered his suffering to the glory of God. He
has embraced it as a means toward gaining for himself a better
disposition. His fortitude displayed both in his living and in his
dying supports his younger brothers and sisters in their own
searches for freedom and meaning and simple security in a harsh
and alien world.

II

"A Good Man Is Hard to Find" is probably the most widely read
of Flannery O'Connor's short stories and in its superrealism and
extraordinary use of violence it is typical of much of her work. A
family of six, on vacation, wreck their automobile, fall into the
hands of escaped convicts, and are murdered one by one. On the

surface, the motivation for these killings is slight: the grandmother, who is the protagonist of the story, has identified the leader of the gang—the self-proclaimed Misfit who acknowledges that he is a criminal, but who cannot match the crimes he has committed with the punishments that he has been required to undergo.

Motivation in O'Connor's work is seldom conventional. She believed that her fiction derived much of its character from what she called a "reasonable use of the unreasonable," which means that she searched continually for the good and evil that lurk in the depths of the human soul. At the end of "A Good Man Is Hard to Find," the Misfit sets forth in blunt terms one of the oldest of our metaphysical dilemmas. If Jesus truly performed miracles, if He raised the dead and were Himself resurrected, then there is nothing to do but follow His teachings. But the Misfit does not know that this happened. He was not there. Consequently, he cannot believe and he has decided to live his own life the best way he can—"by killing somebody or burning down his house or doing some other meanness to him. No pleasure but meanness," the Misfit says.

"Why you're one of my babies," the grandmother declares just before the Misfit kills her. "You are one of my own children." This gesture, according to Miss O'Connor, is the key to the story. The old lady "realizes, even in her limited way, that she is responsible for the man before her and joined to him by ties of kinship which have their roots deep in the mystery she has been merely prattling about so far." We are urged to hope that this act of recognition by the grandmother will plant the mustard seed of faith in the Misfit's heart.

Thus for Miss O'Connor and for those readers who are willing to interpret her according to her own standards, the reconciliation is effected in the midst of bloodshed. The humor comes from dialogue and from characterization. The mother in the story has "a face . . . as broad and innocent as a cabbage . . . tied around with a green headkerchief that had two points on the top like rabbit's ears." Unknown to her son, the grandmother brings the cat along on the journey, for she fears it might accidentally turn on one of the gas burners and asphyxiate itself if it is left alone. After the automobile has turned over, the children are delighted to have had an accident, but disappointed that no one has been killed. Even the last line of this grim narrative generates its own humorous irony. The Misfit, having caused the deaths of half a dozen people, asserts that there is "no real pleasure in life."

Miss O'Connor established the tone that her work was to assume in this early story, and she was able to develop her gift for the comic and the grotesque in the longer narratives that she wrote later in her career. *The Violent Bear It Away*, which takes its title from the twelfth verse of the eleventh chapter of St. Matthew, begins with one of O'Connor's favorite situations—an old man and a boy who live together and depend on each other, but who argue continuously, half in anger, half in mutual affection. The elder Tarwater is a self-proclaimed prophet and he intends to pass his gift and the responsibility for work that he may have left undone on to the boy. Young Tarwater finds the prospect scarcely attractive. He is appalled by the old man's notion of heaven which is to sit eternally on the banks of the Jordan River eating fish that have been miraculously multiplied. Nor does he willingly accept his first duty as a prophet which will be to bury the old man when he dies.

The old man has constructed a casket for himself, but he has grown too fat to fit comfortably inside it.

> "It's too much of you for the box," Tarwater said. "I'll have to sit on the lid to press you down or wait until you rot a little."
> "Don't wait," old Tarwater had said. "Listen. If it ain't feasible to use the box when the time comes, if you can't lift it or whatever, just get me in the hole but I want it deep. . . . You can roll me to it if nothing else. I'll roll. Get two boards and set them down the steps and start me rolling and dig where I stop and don't roll me over into it until it's deep enough. Prop me with some bricks so I won't roll into it and don't let the dogs nudge me over the edge before it's finished. You better pen up the dogs," he said.

This incredible passage, which continues in the same vein for several pages, is a consummate challenge to our ordinary attitude toward dying and much of its humor is a result of this disparity. By presenting death as a natural and even desirable experience, it furthers Miss O'Connor's general effort to bring spiritual enlightenment to a largely faithless world. As things turn out, young Tarwater does not bury his great uncle; he gets drunk and burns the house down instead. But as he learns later, the body does get buried in spite of his defection, just as against his will the mission the old man imposes on him is accomplished in a most bizarre and unforeseen way.

Tarwater has been commanded to baptize his mentally defective cousin and around this proposed sacrament the conflicts of the novel expand. Within himself Tarwater is divided, pulled one way by the remembered admonitions of old Tarwater, drawn the other by the temptations of the demonic voice which speaks inside his mind. And there is the opposition of Rayber, father of the idiot Bishop, who is a modern man, a proper child of the age of scientific materialism and a familiar type in Flannery O'Connor's work. Symbolically, Rayber is deaf: he can hear only with the aid of a device that causes Tarwater to wonder whether his head works by electricity. Rayber believes in no transcendent reality, he considers Bishop to be simply a mistake of nature and he lives according to the psychological theories in which he is trained.

This is to say that under the Cartesian rubric which separates the head from the heart and denies the human senses their proper place in our lives, Rayber's existence becomes a struggle against his affectionate instincts. Believing in love in general, knowing its power in the abstract, Rayber nonetheless must be on guard against "love without reason, love for something futureless, love that appeared to exist only to be itself, imperious and all demanding, the kind that would cause him to make a fool of himself in an instant." He must keep a tight hold on his emotions, submitting only to those mild affections that seem likely to bring about some change in the world, to achieve some end.

Because he was caught unaware by love, Rayber failed in an effort to drown Bishop. One glance at the familiar face struggling beneath the water was enough to make Rayber release his grip and stand on the beach terrified, an apparently grief-stricken father until Bishop began to breathe normally again. But Tarwater is driven by a different compulsion. He knows nothing of the scientific method: he is indifferent to the meanings of measurements and test scores; the struggle of which he is a part is between universal forces and he acts for reasons that he does not understand.

Tarwater's life in the city is marked by contradictions. After the death of his great uncle, he has come voluntarily to live with Rayber and Bishop. But he will not shed his country costume and put on the new clothes Rayber has bought him. He refuses offers of friendship, declines to be grateful for favors done him, and in spite of his repeated repudiations of the religion that the old man taught him, he attends a fundamentalist service where he listens to a little girl preach the gospel of Christ. "I only gone to spit on it," he tells Rayber.

"I'm not so sure of that," Rayber replies.

In the climactic scene of the book, Tarwater succeeds in drowning Bishop. He hopes by this act to be freed from the strong and unaccountable urge to fulfill the mission that his great uncle imposed upon him. But the result is the opposite of what he expects. As he pushes the idiot boy's head beneath the water, he speaks the words of baptism and the sacrament is complete. His denials, to a truck driver who gives him a ride, to a homosexual who later assaults him can change nothing. The rite has been completed.

What all this means, how what is clearly intended to be murder may issue into sanctity, can be explained only in terms of Flannery O'Connor's sense of total reality. She lived and worked completely within what Etienne Gilson calls the "enchanted universe" of Christian doctrine. This meant first of all that she saw man as a fallen creature whose flawed nature prevents his achieving on this earth the full dimensions of the good. "Most of us," she said, "have learned to be dispassionate about evil, to look it in the face and find, as often as not, our own grinning reflections with which we do not argue, but good is another matter. Few have stared at that long enough to accept the fact that its face too is grotesque, that in us the good is something under construction."

It is easier for us to recognize the mask of the devil than to comprehend the workings of grace. We identify immediately the disembodied voice that speaks to Tarwater and the tramp with the unhealthy face who proclaims a specious freedom and the young man with the strange smell and the violet eyes who drugs Tarwater with bad whisky and commits sodomy upon him and steals his hat for a souvenir. The representatives of the good are less flamboyant: the Negroes who bury old Tarwater; the child evangelist; the woman at the crossroads store who reprimands the boy for having failed to respect his great uncle's corpse.

When Tarwater awakens from his drugged sleep, he burns the vegetation in the area where he was assaulted. In fire, violence and purification are encompassed in a single image. After the burning of the corrupted woods, the peace of nature reasserts itself: birds sing in the soft air; the growing corn whispers and waves in the wind; Tarwater looks at the old man's grave in the cooling twilight. He discovers that regardless of his own desires, he has been called to be a prophet. Throughout the novel he has endured a physical hunger which no amount or kind of food has satisfied. He knows now that what he hungers for are the symbolic loaves and fishes, and he sees that he will be driven by this unfulfilled desire as long as he remains on this side of the grave. So he leaves for the city "to warn the children of God of the terrible speed of mercy."

III

Walker Percy was born in the city, and though he lives now in a small town in Louisiana, his work is oriented to the urban centers of America, to New York and New Orleans and densely populated points in between. I mean by this that even when his plots take him into rural areas, the reader is aware that the voices which are doing the speaking are city voices and that the intelligence which informs the novel's creation is in tune with the issues and opinions of the day. The same was not true of Flannery O'Connor: she lived on a farm in Georgia where she raised peafowl and grew flowers and where her mother supervised the daily milking of a herd of cows. I do not mean to exaggerate the importance of the environment in which the artist lives and works and from which he draws his backgrounds. But comedy is frequently a product of an iconoclastic view and it is not always easy to be an iconoclast in an American city.

Percy's humor is splendidly done. When, in *The Last Gentleman*, one of his characters takes a drug which turns his skin black and then falls into difficulty in a white neighborhood, we laugh, but we also have a sense of *déjà vu*. We have seen it all before on the television news and in the *New York Times*, and we know what our intellectual and emotional responses ought to be. On the other hand, bulls running loose in rural communities, fat country women who claim to be faith healers, Bible salesmen who carry contraceptives in their sample cases are fresh images which demand fresh attention from us. But the main differences between Walker Percy and Flannery O'Connor are temperamental and philosophical, as the story in which the Bible salesman appears illustrates very well.

The main character of "Good Country People" is a girl named Hulga who has a Ph.D. in philosophy. She is a tireless student of the existentialists and she believes what she reads. But in the course of the story she is betrayed first by her long-suppressed affections and later by the Bible salesman who steals her wooden leg. Abandoning her in the barn loft where ostensibly he has taken her for romantic purposes, the Bible salesman scoffs at Hulga in farewell.

> "I've gotten lots of interesting things," he said. "One time I got a woman's glass eye this way. And you needn't think you'll catch me because Pointer ain't really my name. I use a different name at every house I call at and don't stay nowhere long. And I'll tell you another thing, Hulga," he said, using the name as if he didn't think much of it, "you ain't so smart. I been believing in nothing ever since I was born!"

Percy takes our alienation and our doubts and our loneliness with high seriousness, and it is a part of his great talent that he can find life amusing and hopeful in spite of contemporary agonies and doubts. He speaks to us with a voice that is amusing and comforting and extremely gifted. But Flannery O'Connor's genius for comedy and reconciliation was unique in her time.

Black America and
the Mask of Comedy

Richard K. Barksdale

Since his enforced migration to America from the shores of West Africa, beginning in the seventeenth century, the Black American, both as slave and freedman, has had to resort to many strategies of offense and defense in order to cope with the manipulative devices and subtle depredations of a powerful white majority. At times he has used the strategy of angry physical confrontation and revolt in an attempt to wrest some vestiges of power out of the hands of the white man. Almost always such an offensive strategy has had the net ultimate result of crystallizing the defensive fears of a somewhat paranoid white majority. Both the Nat Turner revolt of 1831 in Southampton County, Virginia, and the Black ghetto riots in America's large cities in the late sixties inspired a fear of the Black presence which hardened racial attitudes and increased racial distrust. In neither instance did a powerless Black minority gain power or achieve any radical alteration in its relationship to a powerful white majority. Following Turner's revolt the Black remained a slave until emancipated by force of arms in a bloody Civil War thirty years later; following the big urban riots, the majority of America's Blacks have remained entrapped in ghetto areas where they continue to suffer various kinds of social, political, and economic discrimination. Black anger still exists and finds some outlet in the activities of activist groups like the Black Panthers and in the literature of racial confrontation of some young Black writers like Don L. Lee, Sonia Sanchez, and Nikki Giovanni.

349

Generally, however, today's Black leadership is searching for more subtle offensive strategies which will not have the self-destructive fury of the big-city Black ghetto riot but rather will achieve some transfer of political or economic power to the Black masses.

In the meantime, the Black man continues to place his stress on a wide variety of defensive and offensive strategies which the racial encounters of the centuries have taught him are necessary for survival. During the period of his enslavement, his primary defensive strategy was one of accommodation to, and suffering endurance of, the rule of the overseer's whip. During this time he was fortified by the Christian hope that "trouble would not last always" and that earth's pain would be compensated by heaven's joys. Admittedly, there were many who, like Frederick Douglass, Moses Roper, Henry Bibb, Lewis and Milton Clarke, and William Craft, refused to accommodate or endure and escaped to freedom. Others who resisted the cruelties of slavery comprise the nameless thousands who, throughout the centuries, suffered an early death at the hands of slavemaster or slavemistress or overseer. After Emancipation the chief proponent of a formula for accommodation and survival through economic self-help and political uninvolvement was Booker T. Washington. Today it is still debated whether his defensive strategy, broadened somewhat but not substantially changed from the accommodationism of slavery, was effective or necessary. To most Blacks it is remembered as a degrading and racially demeaning kind of capitulation to the white power structure, which can be dismissed as Uncle Tomism, a term developed from the dominant attitude expressed by Harriet Beecher Stowe's principal character in *Uncle Tom's Cabin* (1852). Some Blacks today, however, view Washington's emphasis on economic self-help as a necessary first step toward Black separatism and racial self-sufficiency.

Two other strategies of racial confrontation have had both the survival value of an effective defensive strategy and the psychological inspiration and lift of a good offensive strategy. One, the recent movement led by the Reverend Martin Luther King, Jr., sought through nonviolence and Christian charity to convert the white majority to the cause of racial integration. The moral idealism of the movement broke the back of legal racial segregation in the American South and almost converted the rest of America to the cause of racial charity and understanding. And, although the movement's inspired leader was assassinated in 1968, America as a Christian nation still remembers how close it came to a full implementation of the moral and social truths of Christianity.

The second strategy, having both defensive value and the kind of racial gratification found in a subtle but effective offensive strategy, is the use of comic ridicule. Actually, the Black man's use of comic ridicule is as old as the Black man's presence in America. During slavery it was an effective means of counterbalancing the self-demeaning accommodationism demanded by the powerful white majority. So there was hidden Black laughter in songs and ballads and stories in which the white slaveholder was subtly ridiculed. These songs and ballads and stories were part of a rich, oral folk tradition which the Black man had brought with him from Africa. Not only were there the bestiaries or Brer Rabbit and Buh Bear stories in which Brer Rabbit, symbolizing the powerless slave, always outtricked Buh Bear and the other animals who represented the white power structure; but there were also broadly circulated tales in which the "Marsa" was manipulated or humiliated or ridiculed. One story, "Swapping Dreams," pits a Master Jim Turner against a witty slave named Ike. The Master had had a seemingly disturbing dream about a "Nigger Heaven" in which the streets were strewn with garbage and filled with ragged and dirty Blacks who lived in torn-down houses. To this Ike replied that he "sho musta et de same t'ing . . . 'cause Ah dreamed Ah went up ter de white man's paradise." There, he went on, the streets "wuz all ob gol' an silvah" and there were "putty pearly pearly gates" and "lots o' milk an' honey"—but "dey wuzn't uh soul in de whole place." Stories like these in which the Black slave donned the mask of comic ridicule effected no broad shifts in the power relationships between master and slave, but they were excellent psychological compensation for the cruel physical and mental harassments of physical enslavement. Thus they provided the spiritual stabilization of a good defensive strategy and the emotional lift of a good offensive strategy.

After Emancipation many of these stories continued to circulate. Indeed, Freedom gave the storyteller more opportunity for narrative elaboration and embellishment. The conversion of the many stories about John, the witty slave, into a continuous story about "High John the Conqueror" is a case in point. During slavery times there had circulated many separate stories about John who performed with high comic heroism in ridiculing his master or engaging in hazardous but successful competition with other slaves in order to outwit and ridicule their masters. In "High John the Conqueror," as the story developed in a time of continued folk enrichment during the late nineteenth and early twentieth centuries, the John incidents were linked together and given a beginning, a middle, and an end. At the end, John's master asks John to drown him in a gunny sack in an effort to make some money, and John quietly complies with his master's last request.

In this context some notice should be made of the fact that with Freedom and Emancipation a creative Black literature which had had its beginnings in the eighteenth century began to expand, and a corps of known and identifiable authors emerged. Many of these poetized and fictionalized or editorialized in protest over the Black man's lot as a freedman in America; others wrote escapist literature and hence avoided the problems of race. But one author, Charles Chesnutt, drew many of his short story plots from Black folk literature ("The Goophered Grapevine" and "The Conjure Woman" are examples), and at least one of his stories—"The Passing of Grandison"—is in the tradition of comic ridicule, so effectively communicated through the Black man's folk literature. Chesnutt's account of how Grandison, an apparently loyal slave, carefully plots his escape and effectively ridicules both young and old masters is related with disciplined narrative control and suspense. The net effect of the story is comic in the best sense of the word, for Grandison's departure to freedom provides a full psychological and moral release in a story dominated by slavery's distrust, fear, and suspicion.

In the twentieth century the major Black writers have devoted most of their literary energies to works of social and moral protest over the Black man's lot in America. Much of Langston Hughes's poetry, all of Richard Wright's fiction, and all of the poetry of contemporary young Black poets like Don L. Lee fall into this category. In a sense, their literature is part of the Black man's offensive strategy in race relations. A second but related emphasis in twentieth century Black literature has been the glorification and celebration of the Black life style and the affirmation of the beauty of Blackness. The novels of Claude McKay—*Home to Harlem, Banjo,* and *Banana Bottom*—celebrate the Black life style and extol the primitive vigor of Blackness. This is also true of the Harlem detective fiction of Chester Himes, although his novels provide only swift, panoramic glimpses of Black life styles in the urban ghetto. Behind this emphasis on the beauty of Blackness is the growing importance of the concept of *négritude,* a world-unifying creed of Blackness first formulated by Senghor of Sénégal, Césaire of Martinique, and Damas of French Guiana in the Paris of the late 1930's. It should also be noted in this context that the concept of *négritude* received considerable reinforcement from the French intellectual establishment, largely through Jean-Paul Sartre's 1948 essay, "Orphée Noir," which served as an introduction to Senghor's anthology of African and West Indian poetry. The principal thrust of Sartre's essay is that the cultural and artistic emphasis on Blackness is an excellent defensive strategy for Blacks in their continuing struggle with the world-wide white power structure.

Fortunately, these two major emphases in contemporary Black literature have not precluded some concurrent developments in a literature of comic ridicule. Admittedly, in a time of continuing racial tumult and confusion, it is difficult for a Black writer sensitive to racial problems to muster the disciplined detachment and objectivity demanded by the comic mode. Generally, novelists and dramatists can do this, since a certain amount of objectivity is essential for success in their respective crafts. By the same measure, poets who generally write out of the immediacy of their emotions and private fancies usually do not write with detached objectivity. For this reason, contemporary Black writers most noted for their use of comic ridicule of white characters are the two novelists, James Baldwin and Ralph Ellison, and the playwright Douglas Turner Ward.

Of James Baldwin's several novels—*Go Tell It on the Mountain, Giovanni's Room, Tell Me How Long the Train's Been Gone, Another Country*—at least the last three named present characters who are involved in interracial love affairs. However, only in Ida's characterization in *Another Country* is there comic intensity as she relates to her two white lovers, Vivaldo Moore and Steve Ellis. Actually her relationship with her white lovers is on a somewhat confused love-hate continuum, characteristic of Black-white relations in urban America. Vivaldo is kind, understanding, and fully worthy of her love; but white America must pay for the way it took her brother Rufus's soul, talent, and body. So Ida says to white America:

You don't have any experience in paying your dues and it's going to be rough on you, baby, when the deal goes down. There's lots of back dues to be collected, and I know damn well you haven't got a penny saved.

But sex looms large in this novel, and Baldwin has his Black heroine focus her comic ridicule on white America's sexual inadequacy. On one occasion she speaks to Vivaldo in a tone of unrefined raillery:

Can't none of you white boys help it. Every damn one of your sad-assed white chicks think . . . they don't piss nothing but ginger ale, and if it wasn't for the spooks wouldn't a damn one of you . . . *ever* get laid. That's *right*. You are a fucked-up group of people. You hear me? A fucked-up group of people.

And of white sex Ida comments:

I used to watch them wriggle and listen to them grunt, and, God, they were so solemn about it, sweating yellow pigs, and so vain . . . and I wasn't touched at all. . . . Oh yes, I found out all about white people, *that's* what they were like, alone, where only a black girl could see them. . . .

At the end of the novel, Ida, somewhat purged of her comic disdain of the white world, finds true love with Vivaldo. Nevertheless, even though assured of Vivaldo's love and companionship, Baldwin's Black heroine retains her broad comic view that the world of white America is "just one big whorehouse" in which everyone must "pay his dues" for services rendered.

The odyssey of the hero in Ralph Ellison's *Invisible Man* mirrors the pain, frustration, and psychological victimization not only of the American Black man but the massive failures of twentieth-century man. The great appeal of this novel is that the antiheroic exploits of the central character are supported by incidents and anecdotes that reinforce his sardonic conclusion that life is better spent hiding in womb-like seclusion than participating in "the struggle that nought availeth." One of the more interesting incidents that help the hero to arrive at this conclusion is the Trueblood incident which occurs in the second section of the hero's odyssey— the section relating his college experiences with the infamous Dr. Bledsoe. The Trueblood incident stands out because it pits a Black man of truth against a white man of wealth in an essentially comic confrontation. The Black man is a peasant, living so far back in time and history that he occupies a cabin actually built in slave times. In his circumstances and expectations Trueblood is a century removed from Dr. Bledsoe, the Black college president, and two centuries removed from Mr. Norton, the white Yankee college trustee.

As the narrative unfolds, the hero, who is an innocent but emotionally involved observer (actually he is chauffeuring Mr. Norton around the college environs, at Dr. Bledsoe's request) is most unwilling to have the white patron and the Black peasant meet. Somehow, he feels that this would be an accident with unfortunate consequences. In a sense, the novelist aids the reader in preparing for the psychological implications of the encounter of patron and peasant. First, we are told that Norton has had a daughter, now deceased, of whom he was inordinately fond and whose premature death left him paralyzed by a grief which was still with him. Early in their ride, Norton somewhat emotionally displays the picture of his deceased daughter to his chauffeur; she is a person of surpassing beauty, and Ellison's hero is quick to understand the college trustee's grief. On this occasion, however, there is a significant omission of any mention of the girl's mother or of Mr. Norton's wife. Second, we are told that Trueblood has been guilty of the ancient but heinous crime of incest with his daughter—the crime that drove Oedipus to scratch out his eyes and Elektra to bemoan her fate. Trueblood even wears the stigmata of his guilt—a festering axe wound on one side of his face, placed there by an angry wife when the horrible deed was discovered.

Although Norton, the white patron, is fully aware of the Black peasant's crime, his disturbed chauffeur is unable to dissuade him from introducing himself to Trueblood in order to hear the latter's story. When they shake hands across the centuries of time and circumstance, the comedy begins. The Black peasant, whose roots are in an earthy primitive past, relates in naïvely copious detail how in a dream he had done his terrible deed. The white patron listens with an eye-riveted fascination, for he, too, had once had such a dream which intense Freudian fears forced him to repress; and his stigmata is an infinite regret that sears his soul.

The Trueblood incident, then, in *Invisible Man* is comic because it confronts a Black man who has nothing but his truth with a white man who has everything but his truth. The listener who cannot but hear and the speaker who cannot but speak remind one of the confrontation in Coleridge's *Rime of the Ancient Mariner*. There are one or two singular differences, however. First, Trueblood, whose very name indicates that he is, perforce, a truth-speaker, has committed a crime far more heinous in Western culture than slaying an albatross. Second, Mr. Norton, the enraptured listener, is emphatically involved in the story; for driven by ancient desires and longings, he had pondered the deed which Trueblood had accomplished. The net result of the incident is comic ridicule of a white man's civilization which places a greater emphasis on repression and suppression than on expression and fulfillment. Moreover, the social inversion that places a Black man's primitive deed stage-center in the somewhat whitened, antiseptic world of the middle-class Black college is also comic—just as comic as Norton's unrestrained and eager participation in the incident and his silent adoration of Trueblood's sexual heroism.

Comic ridicule of white America is much less subtle and indirect in Douglas Turner Ward's two plays, *Day of Absence* and *Happy Ending*. In fact, the dramatic purpose in each play is to ridicule white America's racial mores. *Day of Absence* is a blatantly farcical treatment of a racial event in the small-town, rural South; and *Happy Ending* examines comic ridicule of a white family in a Northern urban setting. In both plays the racial content is purposely exaggerated and overstated; truths are illuminated about Black-white relationships, but these are blown up and flashed on a screen much larger than life-size.

The plot of *Day of Absence* may be briefly summarized. On a routinely hot, lazy summer morning in a small town in the American South, it is discovered that all of the "Nigras" have vanished. As a consequence, many essential services—baby care and nursing, garbage disposal, all cleaning chores, maid service everywhere—have been left undone. Soon a situation of crisis-like proportions develops in the small town, and a frantic official search begins to locate the hiding place of the "Nigras." In the meantime, it is discovered that even some who passed for white and were actually Black all the time had left with the "Nigras." This is most poignantly revealed in the case of Mr. Woodfence who, as the mayor's son-in-law and assistant, has actually been a Black man, spying on white folks in high places. The town's most unusual dilemma quickly becomes an exciting news item on national television, and all the nation begins to fear that what has begun in this small town will spread nationwide or at least to all of the small towns of the American Southland. If either happens, a national crisis will assuredly be at hand.

As excitement and neurotic civil tension mount in the small town so adversely affected by a total withdrawal of Black menial labor, the mayor of the little community promptly assumes a leadership role in an attempt to redress the situation. In so doing, he quickly becomes a caricature of the loud-mouthed Southern politician blown up to farcical levels. At one point he is momentarily comforted by the realization that some "Nigras" might be found in the Black wing of the hospital or in the Black section of the city jail. Assuredly, these will tell where the others went, for, historically, Blacks had always informed on other Blacks. But it is quickly discovered that the Blacks in the hospital are all in a mystifying coma and that the automatic cell-block door will not open in the Black section of the jail. So both of these avenues of solution are mysteriously closed. By midday of the "Day of Absence" the situation has grown desperate. Says the community's major industrialist:

Half the day is gone already, Henry. On behalf of the factory owners of this town, you've got to bail us out! Seventy-five percent of all production is paralyzed. With the Nigra absent, men are waiting for machines to be cleaned, floors to be swept, crates lifted, equipment delivered and bathrooms deodorized. Why, restrooms and toilets are so filthy until they not only cannot be sat in, but it's virtually impossible to get within hailing distance because of the stench.

Moreover, a businessman complains that "the absence of handymen, porters, sweepers, stockmovers, deliverers and miscellaneous dirty-work doers" has paralyzed the entire marketing process. Then, too, "a plethora of unsanitary household disasters" looms forth threateningly—things like food poisoning, "severe indegistitis, chronic diarrhea, advanced diaper chafings"—largely because of the absence of Black cooks and maids. The "Day of Absence" closes with the harassed community on the verge of a collective nervous breakdown. Long-established traditions are in danger; the social order of whites over Blacks is about to become meaningless; the prospect of no more "Nigras" to patronize, resent, insult, or lynch is a shattering prospect to this community. Then, the next day, as silently as they vanished, the "Nigras" return; and what had been a "sick" town on the "Day of Absence" becomes once again a "healthy" community.

After the manner of good and well-plotted farce, *Day of Absence* relates a highly improbable event; but it is, nevertheless, extremely effective comic ridicule. Under the pattern of ludicrous episodes, certain racial truths are forcibly stated about the Black man's economic and social status. He works at the lowest economic scale and lives on the lowest social level. And yet, the ironic question is implied, why is one so abused by white America yet so needed by white America? Possibly, Ike, the witty slave in the folktale "Swapping Dreams" had an explanation if not an answer when he described how empty of inhabitants was the white man's heaven.

Ward's second play of comic ridicule, *Happy Ending*, has a somewhat different thrust. The locale is not the small-town South but the urban North. The principal characters are two sisters who work as maids for a wealthy white suburban family and the somewhat sophisticated, middle-class nephew of the sisters. He has been to college and bitterly resents the fact that both of his aunts work in service. At the beginning of the play's action both of the aunts are crying uncontrollably because the family for whom they have been working is about to be dissolved by divorce. This is too much for the college-bred nephew, who, using considerable revolutionary rhetoric, upbraids his aunts for crying over a subservient maid's position. In his thinking, all of them could well convert this event into the beginning of a long-awaited and long-needed economic, political, and social revolution against white domination over Blacks in America. Then an overwhelming truth begins to emerge. The aunts have been stealing all kinds of consumer goodies—shoes, food, clothing—from their employer for years; the ending of their employment means the end of the thievery; and it is for this grievous state of affairs that they weep. When the once scornful nephew hears the truth about the heroic thievery on such a massive scale by the aunts, and begins to understand that whatever material affluence enjoyed by him is attributable to their efforts, he too raises a cry of lamentation and grief. All understand that another maids' position would never afford the spacious opportunity for such in-depth thievery; it takes years of careful planning and a certain kind of employer to reach that kind of maid-mistress relationship. There must be just the right amount of trust, craft, guile and mutual admiration for a stealing maid to be successful with a gracious and kind employer. The important thing is that the maid who steals must not feel guilty and the mistress or employer must not be suspicious. After such experienced comments on the need and nature of Black domestic thievery, word is received by the two aunts that the planned divorce that would have dissolved the family for whom they work is cancelled. Accordingly, they can return to their stealing and what had appeared to be an unmitigated tragedy now has a "happy ending."

Underneath the farcical humor of Ward's play there lies the comic truth that, given the social and economic and political inequities on the American racial scene, the Black man in his ghetto has the right to steal to redress the racial balance. Inevitably, the playwright's "truth" is in direct opposition to sacred American "truths" about the sanctity of personal property and the need for honesty in social and economic transactions. But, as Chesnutt's Grandison learned and used as a basis for the action which he eventually took, there are at least two sets of truths—one Black and one white. Indeed, in multiracial America, as the phenomenal success of the Italian Mafia proves, there may be many kinds of truths governing social and economic transactions.

As indicated initially in this discussion, the Black man's comic ridicule of white America in his literature is an offensive-defensive strategy in race relations that causes no radical alteration in the power relationships between a Black minority and a white majority.

The Black man still remains relatively powerless and the white man relatively powerful. But comic revelation of social sin and immorality provides America's citizenry with the opportunity for the kind of therapeutic laughter that can help to heal the long-festering wound of racism.

The Mode of "Black Humor" *

Brom Weber

The late Edmund Wilson was one of the most influential of American literary critics. Though generally sympathetic to humor and the unconventional in art, in 1954 he bitterly charged that the humorous writings of a virtually unknown nineteeth-century American writer were unadulterated poison. The occasion was the publication of a collection of George Washington Harris's Sut Lovingood sketches in a volume edited by me. Wilson's *New Yorker* review granted that Harris had "real literary merit." Nevertheless, it condemned Harris for his allegedly "crude and brutal humor." Without mentioning black humor by name, Wilson was denouncing Harris for being one of this nation's early black humorists.

By 1964, ten years after Wilson's outburst, the seriocomic tradition of George Washington Harris had reappeared vigorously in a pack of important novels. Vladimir Nabokov's *Lolita*, William Gaddis's *The Recognitions*, Thomas Berger's *Crazy in Berlin*, James Purdy's *Malcolm*, William Burroughs' *The Naked Lunch*, J. P. Donleavy's *The Ginger Man*, and Terry Southern's *The Magic Christian* were published before the 1950's were over. In their grimly comic wake followed even more powerful works of black humor which startled yet pleased the American public in the early 1960's: Joseph Heller's *Catch-22*, Ken Kesey's *One Flew Over the Cuckoo's Nest*, Thomas Pynchon's *V.*, Walker Percy's *The Moviegoer*, John Barth's *The Sot-Weed Factor*, John Hawkes's

* The term "black humor" as used herein has nothing to do with race.

The Lime-Twig, and Bruce Jay Friedman's *Stern*. Some of these black humorists are now regarded as among the leading American novelists of our time, successors to the previously dominant generation of Sherwood Anderson, Ernest Hemingway, William Faulkner, and F. Scott Fitzgerald.

When Edmund Wilson attacked black humor, he applied a perspective which others also may believe appropriate. Black humor disturbs because it is not necessarily nor always light-hearted, funny, amusing, laughter-arousing. Furthermore, black humor seems to have little respect for the values and patterns of thought, feeling, and behavior that have kept Anglo-American culture stable and effective, have provided a basis of equilibrium for society and the individual. Black humor violates sacred and secular taboos alike without restraint or compunction. It discovers cause for laughter in what has generally been regarded as too serious for frivolity: the death of men, the disintegration of social institutions, mental and physical disease, deformity, suffering, anguish, privation, and terror. For anyone steeped in the dominant tradition of Anglo-American culture, which since the eighteenth century has believed that humor is intrinsically good-natured, trivial, and kindly, the unpredictable, topsy-turvy, often hostile and sadistic character of black humor may well appear to be perverse and intolerable.

As we shall see later when considering the background of black humor in American literature, especially since World War I, neither in its general temper nor in many of its particulars is black humor a newcomer on the American scene. Admittedly, it has played a subordinate role and frequently been neglected, but its practitioners have been among our greatest writers. Before exploring these matters in greater detail, however, one must cope with an issue that has tended to raise confusion about the subject of literary black humor and its continued right to its traditional name.

Ever since the late 1960's, sociopolitical developments in American life have made it difficult for us to continue using the term "black humor" without a sense of confusion. We are not always certain to what the term refers. This was not always the case. In American culture, as in many other cultures, the color white has tended to represent the sacred, the innocent, the pure and the good. On the other hand, an antithetical set of associations has clustered around the color black: the diabolic, the unknown, the irrational, the inhuman, the corrupt and the bad. There is no denying that black humor as a categorical term entered the literary idiom in order to designate, and often strongly to depreciate, a literature which resembled traditional humor yet seemed alien to the latter's spirit and almost to subvert it. Viewed objectively, then, whatever racism is implicit in the use of blackness to denote unpalatability or unwholesomeness may well be implicit in the traditional term "black humor" itself.

Certainly an impressive argument can be made for the abandonment of the literary term. Indeed, those Americans who were once given the appellation "Negro" have made a start toward that end. Their mounting ethnic pride and search for identity has led them to invest blackness with many of the positive elements that once were exclusively properties assigned to whiteness. Thus, by an accelerated evolutionary process, black humor is for some people an ethnic designation that coexists as a phrase alongside such new linguistic coinages as "Black Power," "Black Studies," "Black Politics," and "Black Is Beautiful."

Let me illustrate briefly the tendency to claim for a particular ethnic phenomenon the name of that which had begun as a general literary phenomenon participated in freely by Americans of all ethnic backgrounds and skin colors. Two collections of writings identified as traditional black humor appeared in the 1960's: *Black Humor* in 1965 and *The World of Black Humor* in 1967, edited by Bruce Jay Friedman and Douglas M. Davis respectively. Only two among the contributors to these volumes were known Afro-Americans or Blacks. On the other hand, an anthology entitled *Black Humor*, published in 1972, features works by black writers only. This new collection, with few exceptions, contains no writing that warrants assignment to the category of literary black humor as the term had been conceived of less than ten years ago by editors Friedman and Davis.

The future of the ethnically centered phrase "black humor" in the world of politics and society is uncertain. It already may have served its practical purpose in that arena and thus soon be abandoned like so many other political slogans. In the world of literature, one may hope, the phrase will not disappear at all. Sensitive to language as they are, many writers might well believe that political censorship of the literary phrase foreshadowed social censorship of the old-time black humor and they would hesitate to express it. One may be sure that some writers will persist. For example, Philip Roth, originally deeply rooted in the Henry James school of psychological analysis and aesthetic formalism, became a forthright black humorist with *Portnoy's Complaint* in 1969 and *Our Gang* in 1972. Established black humorists such as Walker Percy, Thomas Berger, John Barth, Kurt Vonnegut, and William Burroughs seem unable to create in any other mode of vision. In any case, the responsibility of critics is to be sympathetically aware of the impulses animating writers as well as to evaluate them scrupulously. For that reason, accordingly, and also because black humor under that very title has had a lengthy and significant record of achievement in American and other cultures, it seems proper now and in the future to use the term "black humor" with its traditional literary references intact.

The term "black humor" should not be subject to revision of meaning by Americans, furthermore, because it happens not to have originated in the United States, and neither does it describe a mode of vision and expression uniquely limited to American culture. Black humor is a linguistic importation from France which, despite its colonialism, has long provided a hospitable, nonracist environment for those of African ancestry, one in which sensitive, frustrated black Americans such as Richard Wright and James Baldwin have lived with satisfaction. *L'humour noir*, which in English translation becomes black humor, functioned as a central doctrine of French surrealism almost from its inception in the 1920's. Surrealism recognized that black humor transcends race and nation. When André Breton, theorist and leader of French surrealism, compiled his *Anthologie de l'humour noir* in 1940, he included therefore not only such French exemplars as the Marquis de Sade, Count de Lautréamont, Arthur Rimbaud, Alfred Jarry, and Jacques Vaché, but also such prototypical English black humorists as Jonathan Swift, Thomas De Quincey, and Lewis Carroll.

The heterogeneity of the writers whom André Breton dubbed black humorists strongly indicates the extraordinary variability of black humor's form and content. Sade, who extolled sexual and psychological brutality . . . Rimbaud, who sought to abandon logic and language . . . Lautréamont, who revelled in nightmare . . . Jarry, who scatologically mocked and parodied middle-class culture while drinking himself to death . . . Swift, who relentlessly scorned most of mankind . . . Carroll, who wove intricate patterns of fantasy and nonsense . . . Vaché, the Dadaist who asserted that humor was "a sense of the theatrical and joyless futility of everything" and proved it with his blackly humorous suicide that involved the concurrent murder of a friend—Breton linked these conglomerate writers under the generic title of black humorist by profoundly fusing and expanding concepts of humor developed in Hegel's philosophy and Freud's psychoanalytic theories.

Breton's surrealist theory of humor rationalized the disgust with established society and its stabilizing culture, as well as the consequent individualistic breaches of sociocultural taboo, which to a considerable extent are prominent in black humor. Humor, he believed, was a means whereby one defended the inner self against the constraints of the human condition, physical and psychological as well as social. Humor enabled one to transcend the trivial reality in which man is imprisoned by logic, reason, and subjective emotion, freeing him to achieve union with the objective metaphysical Absolute. Detached by humor from the determinism of the material world and from the culturally determined self, man's dark unconscious could express its metaphysical yearnings and intuitions in the form of untrammelled dream, fantasy, and non-sense. Hence black humor.

The indignant laughter of the black humorist, Breton went on to say, animated more men and resounded most vibrantly in periods of great stress engendered by crises such as war or the demoralization of Europe in the 1920's. But it was manifest always, even though minimally, for a few men heard constantly the grinding noises of a crumbling world, were subject to numerous fears, doubted the reality of fact and object. Black humor's blackness, then, derives from its rejection of morality and other human codes ensuring earthly pattern and order, from its readiness to joke about the horror, violence, injustice, and death that rouses its indignation, from its avoidance of sentimentality by means of emotional coolness, and from its predilection for surprise and shock.

André Breton's theoretical system, though probably unknown to most contemporary American black humorists and not applicable without modification to each of them in particular, is nevertheless a generally illuminating key to the motivations, attitudes, and direction of black humor in the 1960's. Breton lived in New York City from 1941 to 1946, a refugee from World War II and fascism. However, it is dubious that his presence did much to advance the understanding and progress of black humor in the United States. Indeed, surrealism, and the dadaism from which it stemmed, had reached the country well before Breton's arrival. The surrealist magazine *View*, for example, had been founded by 1940, the same year in which the annual *New Directions* devoted several hundred pages to European surrealist writing in English translation. Much earlier yet, in 1913, Francis Picabia and Marcel Duchamp had acquainted avant-garde artists in the New York area with the nihilistic rudiments of what a few years later would be known as dadaism in Europe. Many young American writers thereafter became directly familiar with dadaism and surrealism by virtue of residence in France, Germany, and Switzerland in the 1920's. Those who did not cross the Atlantic read dadaist and surrealist literature in little magazines such as *Little Review, Broom,* and *transition,* some of which had been founded by Americans and were published in Europe.

Of all the young American avant-garde writers influenced by the dadaist-surrealist ferment in the 1920's, only one—Nathanael West—managed the feat of creating an extended work of black humor. His extraordinarily good first novel, *The Dream Life of Balso Snell,* appeared in a limited edition in 1931. Despite its stylistic and intellectual brilliance, little attention was given it until the 1950's. Only three hundred copies were made available for sale in the United States, yet I still was able to purchase a copy at list price in the mid-1940's at the bookstore of Moss and Kamin, West's publishers: a whole shelf of unsold copies of the elegantly printed work reposed in neglect in the shop. Despite the great depression and World War II, not all Americans were ready for West's kind of sardonic, scatological, mocking, parodistic assault upon the elements of American civilization, of Western civilization as a whole. His anti-hero Balso Snell undertakes a fantastic journey through the steamy bowels of the Trojan horse. During its course, West questioned and turned upside-down not only the cultural values and patterns of tradition, but also those of the intellectual and artistic vanguard which opposed them. The satire, cool detachment, joking, grotesque characters, wild situations, paradox, morbidity, and wit of *The Dream Life of Balso Snell* were whipped up into a sardonic dark comedy which West admirably sustained in three other novels —*Miss Lonelyhearts, A Cool Million,* and *The Day of the Locust*— completed before his untimely death in 1941.

That West was proud of his membership in the clan of black humorists is evident in an anonymous third-person advertisement he wrote for the publishers of *Balso Snell.* "English humor has always prided itself on being good-natured and in the best of taste," he observed. "This fact makes it difficult to compare N. W. West with other comic writers, as he is vicious, mean, ugly, obscene and insane." Though he acknowledged the similarity of *Balso Snell* to Lewis Carroll's tales of Alice's fantastic adventures, West emphasized more strongly his affinity with French black humorists: "In his use of the violently disassociated, the dehumanized marvelous, the deliberately criminal and imbecilic, he [West] is much like Guillaume Apollinaire, Jarry, Ribemont-Dessaignes, Raymond Roussel, and certain of the surréalistes."

Like most of his American contemporaries in the literary avant-garde of the 1920's and 1930's, Nathanael West consciously sought new artistic and intellectual stimulus from European rather than American sources. A few Americans did not. William Carlos Williams praised the pessimistic, pre-Spenglerian poetry of Edgar Allan Poe. Hart Crane embraced the dark psychophysical mysteries of the sea which Herman Melville had delineated. But they were part of a tiny minority. On the whole, young writers regarded the American literary record as one dominated by superficiality and emptiness, by a vapid contentment with things as they were that discouraged probe and experiment.

William Dean Howells, the novelist-critic who had begun his career in the 1860's and was still alive in 1920, symbolized for them the fossilized state of the American arts. Forgotten were his successful championship of literary realism, his laudable introduction to the United States of nineteenth-century masters from Russia, Italy, and France. American literature from its start, the avant-gardists angrily insisted, had been heading for the dead end epitomized by Howells's famous advice that the American writer should portray the smiling aspects of the national life instead of those which writhed hidden away on its dark underside.

Howells's penchant for happy comedy that softened tragedy represents the profound streak of optimism in the American character. It has been one of the sustaining factors in the national experience ever since English Puritans and other refugees from European reality first landed on this continent. However, high hopes of creating a spiritual and material paradise on earth have often been frustrated. So it was in the American beginning. Aspiration clashed with the uncontrollable, dream with fact. The Puritan temper was compelled to reconcile incompatibles. Its zealous religious faith was balanced with gloomy foreboding. By 1676, the Puritan poet-satirist Benjamin Tompson typically mourned the moral and social decline of a culture merely fifty years old, satirizing church, government, and men alike for failing to uphold the norms and patterns that had made life free and happy in the past. It was equally in order for Tompson to poke fun at Boston women and Harvard academics, intermingling his gayety with lines and scenes of deeply somber tone. A more toughly humorous mood than Howells displayed had been part of the American scene long before the twentieth century.

Puritan culture merits special attention because many contemporary black humorists believe that Puritanism banished love, life, and laughter from North America. It would be more accurate to say that Puritans did their best to come to realistic grips with the limitations inherent in the human condition. Furthermore, they actually cherished humor and applied its liberating, restorative spirit to aspects of daily existence that, like war and death, were embittering. The Reverend Richard Bernard declared in 1626, for example, that "there is a kind of smiling and joyful laughter, for anything I know, which may stand with sober gravity, and with the best man's piety." In 1707, the Reverend Benjamin Colman devoted three sermons to the improvement of humor, eager to reveal that in the eyes of nature, God, and Christianity humor was beautiful and essential.

Mirth [he wrote] "is some loose or relaxation to the labouring Mind or Body. . . . 'Tis design'd by nature to chear and revive us thro' all the toils and troubles of life. . . . That by no means must they [Puritans] seem to place any thing of Religion in being *Dull and heavy, sad and disconsolate, sour and morose*. Not only does religion *Allow* but *Obliges* unto chearfulness with Sobriety: It gives the most reason for it, and is serv'd by it: None have that *License*, and in none is it so Decent and Comely as in them that are good.

Puritan dominance of American culture ended long before the eighteenth century was over. Some elements of its legacy have not been satisfactory. But it did provide a model for emulation in its blending of grim experience and disappointment with idealistic hope in an amalgam permeated by humor. The model was not always emulated. Indeed, in the United States as in other nations, black humor—at least until the 1960's—has been an underground murmur surfacing only upon occasion. But these occasions have been impressive in a qualitative sense, as we have come increasingly to understand during the past thirty or so years of careful re-examination of American literary culture.

Profuse historical evidence of black humor's long presence can be found in an anthology of American humor that I edited in 1962, the first collection of its kind to encompass the whole body of American humorous literature from the seventeenth century through the 1950's. Two guidelines established to facilitate editorial selection of entries in the book are pertinent, for they were derived from an objective reading and rereading of fiction, poetry, and non-fictional prose without concern for prior categorization of the literature as either humorous or nonhumorous. First, many serious, post-Puritan writers not customarily considered humorous were in fact darkly seriocomic in intention and result. Second, the view that humor focuses only upon trivia and merely provides frivolous amusement is contradicted by the writings of numerous distinguished American authors.

Some outstanding examples of the literature upon which the guidelines were based are the macabre chapter from Nathaniel Hawthorne's *The House of the Seven Gables*, that brutally ridicules Judge Pyncheon's corpse and laughs at the doom of his materialistic values and plans; the cold-blooded, satirical account of a young sailor's legalized surgical murder by a dehumanized, bureaucratic naval doctor in Herman Melville's *White-Jacket;* and Ambrose Bierce's hilariously ghoulish "Oil of Dog," in which an upholder of bourgeois ideals calmly relates how commercial enterprise led his parents first to boil dogs, then children and adults, and finally themselves in order to manufacture oil for medicinal preparations. This brief listing of black humor can be expanded with selections from Benjamin Franklin, Washington Irving, Edgar Allan Poe, Mark Twain, Stephan Crane, Edith Wharton, Sherwood Anderson, Robert Frost, F. Scott Fitzgerald, William Faulkner, and Ernest Hemingway, to name only a few of the better-known writers who preceded Nathanael West as deliberate practitioners of black humor.

Black humor leaped into prominence in the ten years between 1955 and 1965, as if it never before had existed in American literature. Indeed, it not only capitalized upon historical ignorance, but often—as in Thomas Pynchon's *V.* and John Barth's *The Sot-Weed Factor*—repudiated the notion that history was relevant to the present. Black humor proved extraordinarily congenial to our now-centered culture. At its best, black humor helped some readers to cope with the omnipresence of potential nuclear destruction, with the massive bureaucratization of social institutions and relations, with the individual's helplessness under the power of material objects and invisible forces, with the nerve-racking manner in which all things ceaselessly and rapidly changed, with the terror and death of hot and cold wars that seemed to have fastened themselves like parasites upon human existence. The saving therapy of laughter was highly beneficial as always.

Despite its initial astonishing success, however, black humor soon experienced a precipitate decline in quality and prestige from which only a few of its writers—Walker Percy and Thomas Berger pre-eminently—have escaped. Some—William Gaddis, Joseph Heller, Terry Southern—have not been published for several years and may have stopped writing altogether. The recent fiction of Bruce Jay Friedman, J. P. Donleavy, and William Burroughs has been repetitious and uninspired, truly dull. Kurt Vonnegut's apparent upward flight from the juvenile realm of science fiction ironically returned him full-circle in *Slaughterhouse-Five* to the

exhausted sentimentality and moral-intellectual banality of the counter cultural adolescent. Dark laughter's coolness had been institutionalized into a mechanized, totalitarian disregard of the mundane but important concerns of existential human experience. Culture-fatigue had been succeeded by nihilistic emptiness in which even the creation of black humor had no meaning, so that John Barth devoted himself to demonstrating that writing has no function and silence is preferable. The suicidal example of nightclub comic Lenny Bruce hovered ghost-like over the once promising scene.

Not all black humorists, fortunately, underwent the self-destruction which their apocalyptic spirits had wished in vain upon the rest of the world. Thomas Berger's *Vital Parts* and Walker Percy's *Love in the Ruins*, novels published in 1970 and 1971 respectively, are works in the great black humor tradition of Hawthorne, Melville, Faulkner. Both Berger and Percy have managed to extricate themselves from the morass of intellectual and moral void into which their lesser brethren sank. With the complexity of minds directly attuned to the disintegrating powers of nightmare and chaos, they search for positive alternatives that will provide a rallying center. Berger and Percy have avoided the temptation inherent in black humor to imitate disorder, to parody the incoherence of reality by slipping unself-consciously into literary incoherence. It is a pleasure to note that Thomas Berger and Walker Percy are as hilariously comic and laughter-evoking in their works as black humor traditionally has been. These writers reassure us that black humor will not disappear from American literature.

"Anti-Fiction" in American Humor

William Harmon

Since Gertrude Stein's *The Autobiography of Alice B. Toklas* is not the autobiography of Alice B. Toklas, our terminology is challenged to say exactly what it is. It might be what Miss Toklas's autobiography might look like if its subject were not herself but Miss Stein—a plausible concoction, but still a concoction. Such fabulation, common in the literature of the forty years that have elapsed since Miss Stein's book, belongs in the ragged category of "anti-fiction" or the "anti-novel" that is emerging as one of the most engaging manifestations of American humor.

Miss Stein's anti-novel is not what it seems: such play between appearance and reality is a typical subject for comedy. The comic resolution of "The Ugly Duckling," for example, is generated by one's realization that the threat (of ugliness and its consequent suffering) posed by appearances is canceled by the reality of the creature's not being a duckling at all. This sort of conclusion is possible when audience and artist share a context in which both can be reasonably sure that they know the difference between appearance and reality, name and nature. Such comedies, potentiated by the harmonious reconciliation of appearance and reality, are ordinarily presented "straight." They are just told, and they do not seem to be so conscious of themselves as fictions that any strain is felt between the fact that the very form of the story is an "appearance" and the fact that the subject of the story is "reality." A straight story, with the reader free (because conditioned) to suspend all sorts of doubt and disbelief, is commonly an integrated, simple, unambiguous, third-person account whose narrator is transparent and, as often as not, anonymous.

Virtually from the beginning, however, fiction—because it must remain, after all, fiction—begets its own opposite in the forms of parody, self-parody, and anti-fiction. Epic provokes mock-epic and burlesque; Richardson's grand *Pamela* breeds Fielding's grand *Shamela;* the Gothic novel is answered by Jane Austen's *Northanger Abbey.* Any fiction, it seems, depends on the temporary abdication of some quality of the reader's mind that demands eventual restoration in some countervailing fiction, as when a poet like Milton or Browning commonly produces poems in complementary pairs. A fiction can even contain its own anti-self, its own built-in self-correction—scarcely a new phenomenon in the novel, because it is conspicuously present as early as Sterne's *Tristram Shandy*, perhaps the greatest anti-novel ever written. With similar sophistication, a complex fiction can be fabricated out of two or more subordinate degrees of fiction. *Wuthering Heights*, for example, is presented as Lockwood's "diary," which contains Nelly Dean's "narrative" of the events of the inner story, which itself contains such lesser concoctions as letters and lies. Dickens's *Bleak House*, to take another example, is presented by two narrators with distinctly different attitudes and voices—the one anonymous, omniscient, present-tense, aloof; the other (Esther Summerson) limited, past-tense, involved, and evidently unaware of the other narrator with whom she alternates in the telling of the story.

When a man telling a joke self-consciously realizes that he is doing a bad job and stops to apologize, his apology is such a countervailing concoction that in effect he is telling two stories at once. I call this sort of effect "sophisticated," but that does not mean that it is anything new. It is present, implicitly or explicitly, in any fiction; and its recent emergence as a most salient literary phenomenon should not be construed—as it seems to have been construed by a crowd of apocalypse-mongers—as a sign of the death of fiction or anything like that. An anti-novel is as much a novel as an antibody is a body. Even with such clumsy terminology, however, one may still suggest a few features of the anti-novel.

Probably the first thing that happens to a story that realizes that it is a story is that it ceases to be a strictly coherent story. Once the integrity of the fictional membrane ruptures, the plot disintegrates into fragments—episodes thematically connected but not necessarily ordered. Let me again call on Gertrude Stein, a great writer of anti-fictions and a great American humorist. Lecturing in 1935, she conceded that there would always be a place for a "story," in newspapers, nonfiction, and ordinary novels, but that the most serious works of modern fiction deal instead with "making portraits." "A thing you all know," she said, "is that in the three novels written in this generation that are the important things written in this generation, there is, in none of them a story. There is none in Proust in The Making of Americans or in Ulysses." Now, one may object to these particular terms and judgments, but one ought to see that in a significant number of recent fictions—by Nabokov, Salinger, Barth, Pynchon, Donleavy, Barthelme, Mailer—there is patently some sort of "fiction" but not very much to satisfy an old-fashioned ordinary concept of "story." And what there may be in the way of a "story" is almost certain to be an ironic parody of some pre-existing contour of romance, travel, detection, or revenge.

Once the shaping principle of a fiction ceases to be its story, many things can take place. The size and shape of the fiction go haywire, and it becomes difficult (as in the case of *The Autobiography of Alice B. Toklas*) to say what is a novel and what is not. The recent squall of interest in the "non-fiction novel" concentrated on Capote's *In Cold Blood* but could just as workably apply to Mailer's *Armies of the Night* (which alternates between "history-as-novel" and "novel-as-history" until the ordinary meanings are quite reversed), Styron's *The Confessions of Nat Turner*, Rexroth's autobiography (which, flatly autobiographical as it is, calls itself *An Autobiographical Novel*), John McPhee's *Levels of the Game*, Hemingway's *A Moveable Feast* (which, the author says, "may be regarded as fiction" on the chance "that such a book of fiction may throw some light on what has been written as fact") and *Green Hills of Africa* (which tries "to see whether the shape of a country and the pattern of a month's action can, if truly presented, compete with a work of the imagination"), Cummings' *The Enormous Room* and *Eimi*, and even *The Education of Henry*

Adams. Recognizing that telling "the truth, the whole truth, and nothing but the truth" is impossible, we might cry out, "What is *not* fiction?" Very well. Everything is fiction, then: a version of the world that each creature, conditioned by its own faculties, makes up as it goes on, hoping that the concoction harmonizes at some points with a real world beyond the reach of its perceptions. But some fictions are clearly more fictional or fictitious than others, and it may be that the falsest fiction is the one that tries to deny itself.

Novels, fascinated by the strife between fact and fancy, work toward fact and seem to regret their own state as fiction. At the same time, other kinds of concoction, even less dignified, invite reading as though they were novels. Al Capp, for instance, has suggested in an interview that his comic strip "Li'l Abner" ought to be read as a novel—a very long novel, to be sure, a novel with plenty of pictures, but still a novel. And such "news-magazines" as *Time* and *Newsweek* contain so much of fabrication, invention, concoction, distortion, advertisement, rhetoric, propaganda, and stylish prose that we might as well read *them* as novels, quite like a comic strip: enormous, didactic, illustrated, serial sermons—the Dickens of the day.

Fiction sick of itself as fiction can be expected to prevail in such an age as this one, morbidly sensitive, particularly in America, to tricky appearances and sham. The typical heroes of such fictions—Hemingway's and Salinger's most thoroughly—display a pitiful awareness of the insincerity of others and of their own potential hypocrisy as narrators. As their first token of attempted sincerity, they jettison the wholeness of a shapely plot. *The Sun Also Rises* and *The Catcher in the Rye* do not satisfy the reader by a plot with a resolving *dénouement* (and, as Holden Caulfield says, "all that David Copperfield kind of crap," or, as Buddy Glass says in a later work by Salinger, "what that old Chekhov-baiting noise Somerset Maugham calls a Beginning, a Middle, and an End"); they satisfy rather by maintaining their own integrity, however painful or precarious, as reliable instruments for sensing and recording the things of this world, themselves included.

If such honest-seeming disintegration of the well-made plot is the first token of what I am calling "fiction sick of itself as fiction," the second kind of dissolution takes the form of mistrust of the all-knowing narrator. In his place, the humorists of anti-fiction put a poor but honest working man who clumsily but winningly does his self-conscious best to piece a comedy together. (Needless to say, I have been using "humor" and "comedy" all along in broad senses that may include hilarity but do not preclude the most profound seriousness; Jake Barnes and Holden Caulfield are not clowns, but they are comedians, in a way, and there are passages in their books that can make you laugh.)

The characters at the centers of most modern comedies are victims, and in most such works the narrator is practically as much a victim as any of his characters. With figures incapable of controlling their destinies, with plots dissolving into atomized mosaics of episodes, the narrator is correspondingly unable to manage his chores. This comedy of incompetent narration, a feature of most anti-novels, is particularly salient in first-person fictions in which the narrator (commonly a man of letters of some such marginal sort as journalist or academic) is conscious of himself as a story-teller. In Humbert Humbert's "confession" that constitutes the bulk of Nabokov's *Lolita*, for example, the narrator says in the third paragraph, "You can always count on a murderer for a fancy prose style," and continues to police himself—"if you can still stand my style"—throughout. Alfred Appel, Jr., has pointed out that some of Humbert's excesses and errors—such as his confusion of "peritoneum" and "perineum"—have been corrected in later editions lest the narrator's foolishness be mistaken for the novelist's. A kindred sort of mismanaged narration is found even in *The Sun Also Rises*, where the physical impotence of the narrator, Jake Barnes, is mirrored by a kind of literary impotence. A journalist, he seems conscious of his own limits as a storyteller, a consciousness most evident in a passage in the tenth chapter: "I went to the Ayuntamiento and found the old gentleman who subscribes for the bullfight tickets for me every year, and he had gotten the money I sent him from Paris and renewed my subscriptions, so that was all set. He was the archivist, and all the archives of the town were in his office. That has nothing to do with the story."

One of this narrator's problems is the conduct of his life, and, in the passage just quoted, he describes the preparations he had

carefully made for a holiday. He is a man who describes and
explains, who attends to small details, partly for their own sake and
partly to keep his mind off the larger problems. The sentence, "That
has nothing to do with the story," adds another dimension to his
pain by disclosing his excessively self-conscious monitoring of the
details of what he is doing on the page. Here, with the mask of
able narrator slipping down to reveal the desperate features of a
damned but stubborn man, the storyteller begins to sound like one
of Beckett's clowns, unable to go on but going on, coming as close
as a modern artist can come to realizing all at once man's triple
nature as glory, as jest, as riddle. In much the same way, the mask
slips down even in that highly self-assured narrative, Gertrude
Stein's *The Making of Americans*, when the storyteller's voice says,
"I am altogether a discouraged one. I am just now altogether a
discouraged one. I am going on describing men and women." And
she goes on going on, until later, in a lecture called "The Gradual
Making of The Making of Americans," she could go on to add,
with splendidly irrational confidence, "I was sure that in a kind
of a way the enigma of the universe could in this way be solved.
That after all description is explanation, and if I went on and on
and on enough I could describe every individual human being that
could possibly exist. I did proceed to do as much as I could."

These extraordinary fictions, less about the world than about
themselves, comment on their own progress or lack of it, usually
in a mocking way, with the narrator typically finding himself a
first-person participant whose status as a discouraged victim is
reflected by his status as an unstable storyteller. Needless to say,
the projection of such a fiction requires extreme aptitude in the
storyteller's art; otherwise, the fictions would be unbearably boring.
In a striking surrealist display of narrative self-consciousness,
Donald Barthelme's *Snow White*—arguably a parody of Disney's
travesty of the fairy tale—stops to address the reader directly with
fifteen questions, such as "Do you like the story so far?" and "Is
there too much *blague* in the narration?"

Comic anti-fictions concentrate on the conduct of the act of
writing in itself. The achievement of the telling itself represents a
victory of articulation over diffidence, and the existence of the
work itself represents the consummation of the comedy. However

discouraged or defeated the narrators of *The Making of Americans,* *The Sun Also Rises,* or *The Catcher in the Rye* may seem, they have at least accomplished one positive thing. The book itself, conscious of itself as an artifact, betokens some relief from victimization. The deed of writing, the act of finishing something with the tools of a trade, is the end of the comedy.

At an extreme limit of self-consciousness, some narrators are not only aware of themselves as storytellers in a vague sense but in a precise sense as people who are using paper. The narrator of *The Making of Americans* says, "Bear it in your mind my reader, but truly I never feel it that there ever can be for me any such a creature, no it is this scribbled and dirty and lined paper that is really to be to me always my receiver . . . ." In a cognate passage in the only fiction he has published in the last thirteen years, the epistolary story "Hapworth 16, 1924," Salinger gives us Seymour Glass at the age of seven writing an enormous letter to his parents. The letter concludes with some requests in behalf of Seymour's five-year-old brother, Buddy, who is already a writer:

Also, lest I forget, Buddy requests that you be sure to send him some of those very big tablets, quite without lines, for his haunting stories. Absolutely do not send him the kind with lines, such as I am using up for this day of pleasant communication, as he despises them. . . . As well as not sending him any more tablets with lines for his stories, also absolutely do not send him any tablets with very flimsy paper, such as onion skin, as he merely drops this kind in the garbage can. . . . Also worth keeping in mind, it is this chap's leonine devotion to his literary implements, I give you my word of honor, that will be the eventual cause of his utter release, with honor and happiness, from this enchanting vale of tears, laughter, redeeming human love, affection, and courtesy.

Getting the thing done—not achieving some worldly or spiritual success but just in finishing the writing job itself—marks the end of *The Autobiography of Alice B. Toklas:* "About six weeks ago Gertrude Stein said, it does not look to me as if you were ever going to write that autobiography. You know what I am going to do. I am going to write it for you. I am going to write it as simply as Defoe did the autobiography of Robinson Crusoe. And she has and this is it." And it is it: an accomplished thing.

We have noted already the syndrome of the "nervous narrator" in *The Catcher in the Rye*, the strain between the distrust of insincerity and the awareness of the necessarily fictional concoction. But Holden Caulfield has survived the conflict at least long enough to get his writing written: "I'm sorry I told so many people about it. About all I know is, I sort of *miss* everybody I told about. . . . It's funny. Don't ever tell anybody anything. If you do, you start missing everybody."

The most extreme case of such nervous narration is the last of Salinger's stories to appear in book form, "Seymour—An Introduction." With outlandish self-consciousness, Buddy Glass opens up with two lengthy epigraphs (from Kafka and Kierkegaard) about the unavoidable insincerity and hypocrisy in the act of writing. "The actors by their presence always convince me, to my horror, that most of what I've written about them until now is false. . . ." "It is (to describe it figuratively) as if an author were to make a slip of the pen, and as if this clerical error became conscious of being such. . . ." Buddy tries to describe his late brother Seymour, a poet and suicide, but the final attitude seems to be that any such description is impossible but that the effort itself acts as radical therapy for the narrator himself. At the end he addresses the reader ("I'm finished with this. Or, rather, it's finished with me") and, in the last sentence, addresses himself ("Just go to bed, now. Quickly. Quickly and slowly"). Much of this—the paradox of pace, the extreme self-consciousness, the concentration on the Glass family—sounds like an address to the reader in *The Making of Americans:* "And so listen while I tell you all about us, and wait while I hasten slowly forwards, and love, please, this history of this decent family's progress."

The "American" works of Vladimir Nabokov resemble Salinger's: ironic, clownishly obsessive, ostensibly incompetent stories of love, somehow bent and perverted, told in fantastic formats correspondingly bent and perverted. As with the anti-fictions of Stein and Salinger, the reader cannot be quite certain what it is he is reading. Titles, subtitles, prefaces, notes, footnotes, afterwords, and such aids abound; the more they abound, the less the reader really knows. *Lolita* is Humbert Humbert's "confession," with a foreword by an "editor" pointing out the educational value of the story and an afterword by the "author" denying any meaning but "aesthetic bliss" in the creation of another world. *Pale Fire* is a terrific contraption so rigged as to baffle analysis: a long poem in rather mannered couplets accompanied by an insane critical apparatus that makes a mess of the poem and a mockery of scholarship. In *Lolita* and *Pale Fire*, as in *Ada*, the world of art retreats further and further from any other world into "unreal estate" that becomes unrealer and unrealer. *Ada* reconstructs the whole world and all its history, with the existence of our Earth a matter of vexed speculation.

The work of Nabokov suggests another dimension of anti-fiction that I have not yet said much about: the decay of language corresponding to the decay of plot and narration. As with so many American comedians—Thurber and Salinger among them—Nabokov backs off from concern with the world into a kindred but impotent concern for various games and languages that may symbolize the world. The reader's last view of Seymour in "Seymour —An Introduction" is of him in his role as a spectacular player of certain childhood games; the reader's ultimate realization of Nabokov and his creatures is of them as players of a game, an artificial world, like a language. *Ada* backwards remains *Ada*; at an angle, it is *Ardor*. But all these interactions are among words *as words* much more than words as tools of perception and communication. In Salinger's "A Perfect Day for Bananafish" a little girl transforms "Seymour Glass" into "see more glass," as though a glass were reflecting itself reflecting itself reflecting itself. Humbert's vision of "therapist" as "the rapist" is as touching as it is amusing, but here again the most prominent aspect of language is as a reflector of language. The concentric spheres of "closed" anti-fictions echo each other: the story is about a story and the language becomes ingrown.

At the end of some such process of linguistic disintegration, nothing remains but a scattered alphabet, the comedian reduced to the letter *c*. *V.* is the title of a novel published ten years ago by the American writer Thomas Pynchon, then in his middle-twenties. *V.:* just that—a capital letter "V" followed by a period. The title page of *V.* may remind the reader of another book and its presentation of a young man's thoughts as he considers the enigma of the universe, "ineluctable modality." In *Ulysses*, as Stephen Daedalus walks along Sandymount Strand, he remembers a youthful scheme: "Books you were going to write with letters for titles. Have you read his F? O yes, but I prefer Q. Yes, but W is wonderful. O yes, W"—books about what Stephen calls the "signatures of all things." Experience at this level is a serial mosaic of jots ("jot" is the Englished *iota*, the smallest letter of the Greek alphabet), and making sense of them, reading the signatures, constitutes the quest of human life, parodied in *V.* by Herbert Stencil's pursuit of the meaning of evil realized in one repeating shape: "As spread thighs are to the libertine, flights of migratory birds to the ornithologist, the working part of his tool bit to the production machinist, so was the letter V to young Stencil." His pursuit leads nowhere; despite his fantastic series of adventures all around the world and back into certain recesses of history, Stencil remains as much a "human yoyo" as Benny Profane, the clownish Everyman of *V.*

This theme—the simultaneous necessity and futility of the search for the meaning of evil—makes *V.* an inversion and parody of *The Scarlet Letter*, another book about the nature of evil, figured forth time after time in a single symbol. The ambiguity of wrongdoing generates a complex novel that could be called *A.*, after all, and its great *A*—stitched onto Hester's clothing, burnt somehow into Arthur's bosom, even writ large across the night sky—stands for anything and finally for the ineluctably enigmatic mystery of everything: Adulteress, Angel, Able, All.

If the shape of *V.* is a redundant row of yoyoing V's, the shape of Pynchon's second novel, *The Crying of Lot 49*, is an equally futile circle. The reader begins with the hermetic title and ends with the words, "the crying of lot 49"—"crying" being a term from auctioneering and "lot 49" a particular batch of objects up for sale. The story of Mrs. Oedipa Maas's quest for the meaning of a legacy dwells, even more than *V.*, on mythic figurations of destructive self-closure: Oedipus, Narcissus, Echo. And—almost as with the numerological figures that buttress the religious art of the Middle Ages and the Renaissance—myth in *The Crying of Lot 49* is buttressed by mathematics, not in headily ascending patterns of three or four or golden sections, but by self-limiting patterns of frustrated numerals, repeating or redundant. The end of Oedipa's quest is as empty as the end of Stencil's, and the she finally glimpses a universe compressed into an America of no vocabulary but ones and zeroes, something and nothing, arranged in mindless patterns that alternately suggest a centuries-old conspiracy of waste and death or a mindless muddle. "For it was now like walking along matrices of a great digital computer, the zeroes and ones twinned above, hanging like balanced mobiles right and left, ahead, thick, maybe endless." She tries, without success, to sort out the meaning of the characters she has encountered. In the passage that follows, attend to the recurrence of "or" and do not ask who the people or things are:

Behind the hieroglyphic streets there would either be a transcendent meaning, or only the earth. . . . Tremaine the Swastika Salesman's reprieve from holocaust was either an injustice, or the absence of wind; the bones of the GI's at the bottom of Lake Inverarity were there either for a reason that mattered to the world, or for skin divers and cigarette smokers. Ones and zeroes. . . . Either Oedipa [was] in the orbiting ecstasy of a true paranoia, or a real Tristero. For there was either some Tristero beyond the appearance of the legacy America, or there was just America and if there was just America then it seemed the only way she could continue, and manage to be at all relevant to it, was as an alien, unfurrowed, assumed full circle into some paranoia.

Doctor Johnson dismissed "Lycidas" as over-concocted: "Where there is leisure for fiction there is little grief." If that is so, and if the world around us, particularly this "legacy America," calls for a very heavy debt of grief indeed, what can be said for ordinary fiction?

In the first place, it is still thriving. The art of the novel continues to be practiced today as it has been practiced for almost three hundred years, with writers of all sorts—Philip Roth, Peter De-Vries, Calder Willingham, Saul Bellow, Bernard Malamud, John Updike, William Styron, Ken Kesey—offering fictions that embody an intelligible theme in some formal arrangement of coherent actions involving fully realized characters, all told in a suitable style from an appropriate point of view.

But alongside the ordinary fictions, the typical comic affirmations of human dignity—books like *One Flew over the Cuckoo's Nest* and *Mr. Sammler's Planet*—there thrives as well a large body of extraordinary, atypical fictions that may before long become the norm: things we call "anti-novels." The careers of a good number of modern writers have moved in this direction, with Roth in *Portnoy's Complaint* doing away with "story" and falling back on the double format of the joke and the psychoanalytic confession, or with Mailer in *Why Are We in Vietnam?* falling back on the taped stream of chatter of a disc jockey. Such first-person fictions, as I have suggested, risk the danger of going too far (as Salinger and Nabokov may have done) in so retreating into private worlds of incommunicado fictions that their work either appears incomprehensible or stops appearing at all. There is an equivalent danger in third-person anti-fictions, like those of John Barth, who, in recent works, has become "lost in the funhouse" of rendering fictions that contain fictions and so on and on and on until the reader finds himself trying to fight his way out of nests of six or seven sets of quotation marks around one speech.

They can't go on. They go on. Joseph Heller's *Catch-22*, perhaps the funniest of our anti-novels, goes on by abundantly, almost jubilantly, displaying the absurd contradictions of war, commerce, politics, logic, biology, machinery. J. P. Donleavy's *The Ginger Man* and *The Beastly Beatitudes of Balthazar B* go on—shifting between first person and third person, past and present, poetry and prose—to rig the inventive survival of a fundamentally humane man against the alien world. These writers go on giving us figures—such anti-heroes as Heller's Yossarian and Donleavy's Sebastian Dangerfield—who, in spite of much grief, do go on, are still talking.

"The Barber Kept on Shaving": The Two Perspectives of American Humor

Louis D. Rubin, Jr.

"Our humor needs to be democratized," Representative Samuel S. "Sunset" Cox of Ohio in 1876 wrote in a book entitled *Why We Laugh*. "Our genteel laughter needs crossing with that of hearty toil." (A Congressman the author of a study of humor? What could be more amusing than that?) The truth is, however, that the essence of American humor lies in what has been made out of just that division that Cox sees as a disadvantage. The recommendation that a blending, a combining of the genteel and the vulgar mode is what American humor requires is tantamount to the suggestion that American humor give up its most distinctive characteristic: which is, the incompatibility of the vulgar and the genteel viewpoints within a single society. What is funny about most American humor is that the two perspectives *can't* and *won't* be united. Each persists in making the other look ridiculous, and usually that is what is funny.

The remark by Sunset Cox is loaded on the side of the vernacular viewpoint. Genteel laughter is not democratic: i.e., to be truly democratic, laughter should not be genteel. The language of toil is the language of democracy: i.e., the language of educated folk is not. In Henry Watterson's Preface to *Oddities in Southern Life and Character* (1882), a collection of "frontier humor" pieces, something of the same assumption is made. The literary humor of America, Marse Henry informs us, "is full of imitation: our anecdotes are our own, the outgivings of a nature, habit of thought, and

385

mode of existence whimsically real." Literature, it is obvious, is not only less authentically American than humorous anecdotes, but also less faithful to "real" life. For anecdotal humor, "although for the most part of a low order," is "yet essentially representative and picturesque." To be properly and characteristically American, therefore, is to cherish low life, from the perspective of its greater fidelity to reality, and to suspect whatever is Literary of being imitative and less genuinely American.

There can be little doubt that this perspective—the vernacular perspective, set forth in opposition to the cultural, the literary—is the approved American mode of humor. The characteristic comic situation in American humorous writing is that in which cultural and social pretension are made to appear ridiculous and artificial. The bias is all on the side of the practical, the factual. Thoreau's *Walden*, a book that we are always being assured has a great deal more humor in it than is usually realized by unsuspecting readers, is full of this attitude.

Which would have advanced the most at the end of a month [he asks]—the boy who had made his own jackknife from the ore which he had dug and smelted, reading as much as would be necessary for this,—or the boy who had attended the lectures on metallurgy at the Institute in the meanwhile, and had received a Rogers' penknife from his father? Which would be most likely to cut his fingers? . . . To my astonishment I was informed on leaving college that I had studied navigation!—why, if I had taken one turn down the harbor I should have known more about it.

At the end of each of those two propositions he clinches the argument for the practical by making a supposedly witty, down-to-earth observation weighted in favor of the practical as opposed to the theoretical and couched in everyday metaphor: "to cut his finger," "taken one turn down the harbor." He thus reduces the argument to the absurd, since one does not study metallurgy in order to avoid cutting oneself with a knife, nor is the object of the art of navigation that of taking a turn down Boston harbor. But that is no matter; it was never Henry Thoreau's objective to be logical, only convincing. The superior version of reality afforded by the practical, the "common sense" of the matter, is made to triumph over the theoretical and the academic.

Just how this bias works in American popular literature can be illustrated by a poem by the distinguished American verifier and editor James T. Fields, entitled "The Owl-Critic." (Fields is also author of "The Captain's Daughter, or, the Ballad of the Tempest," with its immortal lines, " 'We are lost!' the Captain shouted,/As he staggered down the stairs.") "The Owl-Critic" describes the young intellectual who comes into a barber shop and observes an owl on a perch. "Who stuffed that white owl?" he asks. He then proceeds to tell what is wrong with the way the owl is stuffed, and informs the barber of· his impeccable credentials for rendering such a judgment.

> "I make no apology;
> I've learned owl-eology
> I've passed days and nights in a hundred collections,
> And cannot be blinded to any deflections
> Arising from unskillful fingers that fail
> To stuff a bird right, from his beak to his tail.
> Mister Brown! Mister Brown!
> Do take that bird down,
> Or you'll soon be the laughing-stock all over town!"
> And the barber kept on shaving.

The speaker goes on to tell in detail what is unnatural about the way the owl is roosting. The position of his claws, legs, bill, and neck, are "against all bird-laws," since

> "Anatomy teaches,
> Ornithology preaches,
> An owl has a toe
> That can't turn out so!"

The young man has "made the white owl my study for years." The glass eyes used by the taxidermist are so unnatural that "They'd make Audubon scream" and "John Burroughs laugh." And so on, for a number of stanzas, each ending with the refrain "And the barber kept on shaving." In the penultimate stanza, of course, the

owl gets down off his perch, walks around, and hoots at the young
man, as if to say,

> "Your learning's at fault *this* time, anyway;
> Don't waste it again on a live bird, I pray.
> I'm an owl; you're another. Sir Critic, good day!"
> And the barber kept on shaving.

What Fields's poem does is to assert for purposes of humor the
proposition that book-learning—education, courses in ornithology,
etc.—is so unrealistic as to be unable to distinguish between a live
and a dead owl, and also that the "knowledge" that is afforded by
advance study fails to describe real life actuality. The young scholar
possesses a detailed knowledge of why the owl is unnaturally
stuffed, and why it is therefore not a decent job of taxidermy. He
is brashly confident in his knowledge. But even though his book-
learning "proves" that the owl is poorly stuffed, it turns out that
the owl is not merely lifelike, but alive.

The hero of the poem is the barber; he has no college education,
has never studied ornithology, has never been taught to make the
detailed observation of the various parts of the anatomy of an owl,
but he knows the one essential fact—that the owl is not dead.
(Presumably he has to clean up after him.) While the young
Platonist expatiates on the details of poor taxidermy, the barber,
good Aristotelian that he is, says nothing and keeps right
on shaving. The educated, cultivated young man has "knowledge."
He can therefore theorize from it eloquently. The barber, the
cherished vernacular figure, needs no theory, for he possesses the
fact, which is all that matters. Here, put forth with the deck stacked
for purposes of humor, is the clash of the two modes for apprehending reality: the genteel—theoretical, learned, cultivated; and
the vernacular—pragmatic, common-sensical, realistic. There is no
question of which mode is superior: the vernacular fact has got
to triumph convincingly, from the way the thing has been set up,
and the humor lies in its complete undercutting of the learned
and theoretical.

We see the same technique for humor being used, in rather

heavy-handed fashion, in an early novel, William Gilmore Simms's *The Yemassee* (1835). A group of Carolina settlers are besieged inside a blockhouse, and men are needed to go out and cut down some stakes that might enable the Indian attackers to come close enough to the walls to set it on fire. Among the settlers is one Dr. Nichols, a surgeon who is given to elaborate speechmaking. He is eminently ready to give up his life, he says, for his country. But when volunteers are called for, he demurs.

"I can't use the axe," cried Nichols, hurriedly. "It's not my instrument. Sword or pistol for me. In their exercise I give way to no man, and in their use I ask for no leader. But I am neither woodman nor blacksmith."

"And this is your way of dying for the good of the people?" said the smith contemptuously.

"I am willing even now—I say it again, as I have before said, and as now I solemnly repeat it. But I must die for them after my own fashion, and under proper circumstances. With sword in hand crossing the perilous breach—with weapon befitting the use of a noble gentleman, I am ready; but I know not any rule in patriotism that would require me to perish for my country with the broad-axe of a wood-chopper, the cleaver of a butcher, or the sledge of a blacksmith in my hands."

"Well, I'm no soldier," retorted the smith; "but I think a man, to be really willing to die for his country, shouldn't be too nice as to which way he does it. . . ."

And so on. The learned doctor, master of dramatic rhetoric and patriotic theory, expostulates and speechifies; the blacksmith takes up an axe and goes out to do the job. The windy demagogue, who has probably read *Henry IV* and learned a thing or two from it, uses his bluster to avoid risking his life; the blacksmith has no theory of democracy and of country, but he knows how to wield an axe, and he does it. The implication seems to be, in *The Yemassee* if not always in the Simms novels, that learning, rhetoric, polished peroration, and so forth, like the use of the more formal implements of warfare such as the sword and the pistol, are ways of fending off reality, which is something to be dealt with in plain talk and with axes.

Is the doctor merely a learned man who is a humbug, or is he a humbug *because* he is a learned man? One is not certain, but what is obvious is that the humor is based on the exposure of the windy demagogue's patriotic theory and educated speechifying by the plain blacksmith's vernacular fidelity to the facts. From the vernacular perspective, deeds, not words, are what are real, and the uncultured blacksmith goes out and does the axe work. So much for a college education.

The American humorist who rang the changes on this kind of comedy, of course, is Mark Twain. Sam Clemens was not raised in Dens of Culture such as Boston or New York or Philadelphia, where Taste was imported from England and Europe. He did not attend college; a riverboat was his Yale College and his Harvard. He came to the wealthy, refined East by way of the Rocky Mountains, and so he was in touch with Real Life, not some fancy Theory of what it was. Even his friend William Dean Howells, who though born in the Midwest had made it big in Boston and was the nation's leading literary man, could see that. He had, he said in his memorial to his friend, known numerous literary men: "Emerson, Longfellow, Lowell, Holmes—I knew them all and all the rest of our sages, poets, seers, critics, humorists; they were like one another and like other literary men; but Clemens was sole, incomparable, the Lincoln of our literature." (He did not mention his other dear friend, Henry James; whatever James was, he was no Lincoln, of course—he had never split a rail or an infinitive in his life—but was he too just like all the others?)

Every one of Mark Twain's major books is based squarely on the clash of cultural modes. *The Innocents Abroad* goes at it most obviously of all. A common-sensical middle-class American visits the repositories of culture, tradition, history and religion in France, Italy and the Near East. He finds the paintwork on the "Last Supper" far inferior to that of freshly painted copies. He composes a mock theatre bill for a gladiatorial performance at the Coliseum— "Unparalleled Attraction! New Properties! New Lines! New Gladiators!"—then reviews the performance after the manner of a contemporary theatrical notice. He swiftly becomes tired of the almost uniform expressions of misery on the faces of the various saints painted by the Italian masters. He compares Lake Como and the Dead Sea to Lake Tahoe, and both of these fabled bodies of water are found wanting. He pays a visit to the grave of Adam:

The tomb of Adam! How touching it was, here in a land of strangers, far away from home, and friends, and all who cared for me, thus to discover the grave of a blood relation. True, a distant one, but still a relation. The unerring instinct of nature thrilled its recognition. The fountain of my filial affection was stirred to its profoundest depths, and I gave way to tumultuous emotion. I leaned upon a pillar and burst into tears. I deem it no shame to have wept over the grave of my poor dead relative. . . . Noble old man—he did not live to see me—he did not live to see his child. And I—I—alas, I did not' live to see *him*. Weighed down by sorrow and disappointment, he died before I was born—six thousand brief summers before I was born. But let us try to bear it with fortitude. Let us trust that he is better off, where he is. Let us take comfort in the thought that his loss is our eternal gain.

Such burlesquing of sentimentality and of all such relic hunting is based directly on the opposition of the vernacular and the genteel attitudes, and the ridicule is possible because of the superior fidelity of the vernacular viewpoint to everyday experience. The exaggerated emotion, the poetic effusion—"the fountain of my filial affection was stirred to its profoundest depths"—is so inappropriate in the face of the evident and obvious absurdity of the fact itself that we have to laugh at the incongruity. The experience of viewing the sacred scenes in the Holy Land is spoiled because of the pettiness of the tourists, the avarice of the resident Arabs, and the obvious implausibility of the Christian legend when examined from the vernacular common sense perspective. When the pilgrims reach the River Jordan and go joyfully wading in singing "On Jordan's stormy banks I stand," only to find the water "so fearfully cold that they were obliged to stop singing and scamper out again," the superior reality of the facts—cold water is cold water, whether in the Jordan or the Schuylkill—destroys the attempt to assume the reverential religious attitude toward the experience, and humor results.

In Mark Twain's best work, *Adventures of Huckleberry Finn,* the same trick of incongruity is used again and again for purposes of humor. One need only consider the difference between Melville's use of Shakespearean syntax and diction in the great scenes with Captain Ahab in *Moby-Dick,* and Mark Twain's depiction of the Duke and the Dauphin throwing together snippets from various Shakespearean quotations into a travesty of the "To Be or Not

to Be" soliloquy, to realize the difference in levels of discourse in
the two novels. What in Melville's novel is the diction for high
tragedy becomes in Clemens's hands the stuff of mocking comedy,
in which the pretense and the self-conscious poeticism of the
Shakespearean soliloquy are made ridiculous by the vernacular
perspective from which Huck Finn and the reader view them. An
instant's ridicule, a moment's exposure to the irony of the vernacular viewpoint, and the language of Shakespearean tragedy is ruined
for purposes of describing everyday middle-class experience. What
Clemens is stacking the deck against is Culture—which in his skillful
hands is made into something artificial and rarefied, an affectation
that is portrayed as divorced from "real life." This is very much
a manifestation of the great American tradition of anti-intellectual-
ism, the suspicion of conceptualized thought as falsifying experience—even though one's political and social values are based on
precisely such abstract concepts, as formulated in the Declaration
of Independence and the Constitution.

Nothing so amuses and exasperates Clemens as the spectacle of
Americans in Europe affecting to be Europeanized, and he is
savage in his parodying of them. Clearly in so behaving Clemens
is in part satirizing an aspect of himself—what he fears is that he
shall be caught, as it were, with a copy of Shakespeare's sonnets
in his hand, by a fellow American of the middle class who will
instantly proclaim him a sissy. The rage with which Tom Sawyer
pummels the "model boy" of St. Petersburg, whose "cap was a
dainty thing," who was dressed in a "close-buttoned blue cloth
roundabout" and wore "a necktie, a bright bit of ribbon," and
whose "citified air . . . ate into Tom's vitals," is part of the same
impulse which compels the traveler of *Innocents Abroad* to satirize
the affectations of Americans living abroad and scoff at the
monuments of culture in the museums of France and Italy. *The
Adventures of Tom Sawyer* represents, among other things, the
author's urgent insistence that whatever he was, he was a bad boy,
not a good one, who played tricks in school, and suffered at church,
and sat around discussing politics with low types like Huckleberry
Finn.

In *Huckleberry Finn* even Tom Sawyer proves to be too genteel,
too addicted to Culture and book learning to suit Mark Twain,

and so he transfers his persona to Huck. Tom insists on viewing a Sunday school picnic as a caravanserai of Spanish merchants and rich Arabs who are camping in Cave Hollow with two hundred elephants and six hundred camels and a thousand mules laden with diamonds, with a guard of four hundred soldiers. Huck goes along, but "it warn't anything but a Sunday school picnic, and only a primer class at that." And at the end, when they are digging a tunnel into the cabin where Jim is imprisoned, Tom calls for the job to be accomplished with case knives, because who ever heard of a prisoner having mere picks and shovels? It then turns out that to excavate the tunnel with case knives would take too many years, so Tom comes up with a solution: "We got to dig him out with the picks, and *let on* it's case-knives." Huck agrees with him enthusiastically, so Tom goes to work. "Gimme a case-knife," he tells Huck. But when Huck hands him one, he flings it down. "Gimme a *case-knife*," he insists. Finally even Huck catches on, finds him a pickaxe, and the job is eventually done. There is no question where the truth lies: If Tom wants to pretend that a pick axe is a case-knife because in storybook rescues pick axes are not available to prisoners, it is all right with Huck, but he knows that a pick axe is a pick axe and that such jobs are done best with pick axes. So does Mark Twain, and so does his audience, for they too believe in the fact, and suspect imaginative pretense as being designed to obscure or gild it, or—as in the case of Simms's Dr. Nichols—to avoid it entirely.

But while Clemens's use of the clash of modes is in the great tradition of red-blooded American humor, the exploding of pretense, it is not the only way to approach the humorous chasm between the real and the ideal in American life. Almost from the beginning of American history there has been another comic tradition, which goes at its job from the opposite perspective. What this approach finds amusing is the inadequacy of the everyday, the ordinary, for it measures the raw fact from the standpoint of genuine culture and absolute value. It assumes that the mere fact of something is not what is important; what is crucial is what one can make of the fact. It is all very well to ridicule the traditional values of culture, knowledge, taste, ethics, but what is to be substituted in their place, if life is to rise above the level of mere getting and spending? What is wrong with the genteel tradition in arts and letters is not that it is overly civilized, but rather that it is not civilized enough. It is false, sentimental, pretentious—because it is not sufficiently imaginative, sufficiently knowing, sufficiently beautiful. Thus Henry James, whom Mark Twain never liked, surveys the artistic taste of the American public in the early 1900s: ". . . the public so placidly uncritical that the whitest thread of the deceptive stitch never makes it blink, and sentimental at once with such inveteracy and such simplicity that, finding everything everywhere perfectly splendid, it fairly goes upon its knees to be humbuggingly humbugged. It proves ever, by the ironic measure, quite incalculably young."

The humor of the Old Southwest, of course, is made up, in part at least, out of this viewpoint. For while a "frontier" humorist such as A. B. Longstreet has a lurking respect for the vitality and realism of the vernacular characters of the unformed society of the frontier, he is also appalled by the crudeness, the brutality, the sheer animality of a style of life in which culture, refinement, moral and ethical standards are lacking, and much of his satire is devoted to pointing out their absence. Before him, William Byrd II registered the same reaction in reporting on the sloth and the squalor of colonial Lubberland. And this is precisely the perspective assumed by Nathaniel Hawthorne in his "Custom House" sketch, preceding *The Scarlet Letter,* as in his humorous description of a permanent Inspector of Customs:

It was marvellous to observe how the ghosts of by gone meals were continually rising up before him; not in anger or retribution, but as if grateful for his former appreciation, and seeking to reduplicate an endless series of enjoyment, at once shadowy and sensual. A tenderloin of beef, a hind-quarter of veal, a spare-rib of pork, a particular chicken, or a remarkably praiseworthy turkey, which had perhaps adorned his board in the days of the elder Adams, would be remembered; while all the subsequent experience of our race, and all the events that brightened or darkened his individual career, had gone over him with as little permanent effect as the passing breeze. The chief tragic event of the old man's life, so far as I could judge, was his mishap with a certain goose, which lived and died some twenty or forty years ago; a goose of most promising figure, but which, at table, proved so inveterately tough that the carving-knife would make no impression on its carcass; and it could only be divided with an axe and handsaw.

What is being undercut is not the cultural ideal, but the fact. Observe what a soulless, mindless specimen of fallen humanity this ordinary American is, Hawthorne is saying. And in the tale that follows, by implication he contrasts the slothful inhabitants of tolerant nineteenth-century Salem with the intolerant folk of Puritan Boston two centuries earlier, for whom morality and ethics are real and vital, and who, unlike their descendant of two centuries later, are alive and capable of a genuinely tragic apprehension of reality.

Henry James possessed a similar suspicion of the red-blooded vernacular perspective, but what concerned him was less the crudeness of American low-life than the falseness and sentimentality of the middle-class American's attempt to acquire Culture and Value as if they were purchasable commodities. This, he felt, was at least as unpalatable as the reliance upon the mere unvarnished fact itself, if not indeed more so. As he wrote of Lady Barberina, "It was not in the least of American barbarism that she was afraid. Her dread was all of American civilization." The genteel tradition, for James, was sentimental, thin, false; it was based on an unthinking, quantitative apeing of real culture. It was thus just as myopic, as little concerned with genuine imagination and value, and every bit as dollar-minded as the crude materialism it affected to despise.

The humor in the early sections of *Daisy Miller*—James's humor almost always comes in the earlier portions of his books, before he settles down to work—is based on the invincible crudeness and provinciality of the middle-class American making the tour of Europe, as for example Daisy's mother on the subject of the Castle of Chillon:

"We've been thinking ever so much about going," she pursued, "but it seems as if we couldn't. Of course Daisy, she wants to go round. But there's a lady here—I don't know her name—she says she shouldn't think we'd want to go to see castles *here*; she would think we'd want to wait till we got to Italy. It seems as if there would be so many there," continued Mrs. Miller, with an air of increasing confidence. "Of course we only want to see the principal ones. We visited several in England," she presently added.

Here ridicule is directed not at the out-of-date plumbing or the lack of paint in castles, nor yet at Americans who feign ecstacy at the site of Byron's famous poem, as Clemens would doubtless have chosen to do if he had written it. Rather, it is at the failure of the wife of the businessman Ezra B. Miller of Schenectady, N.Y., to comprehend the history and the beauty of Chillon, at her philistinism in dealing with European culture as a purchasable commodity. It is the cultural barbarity of Mrs. Miller that James is satirizing. The "great American joke," in other words, is turned around. The dominion of the vernacular fact falls before the assertion of the cultural ideal.

James's most famous "joke" is the business about the unmentionable article of manufacture that constitutes the basis of the Newsome fortune, in *The Ambassadors*. Maria Gostrey is curious to know what it is, but Lambert Strether will not tell her. It is his little joke. He assures her that it is nothing improper: "Unmentionable? Oh no, we constantly talk of it; we are quite familiar and brazen about it. Only, as a small, trivial, rather ridiculous object of the commonest domestic use, it's rather wanting in—what shall I say? Well, dignity, or the least approach to distinction. Just here, therefore, with everything about us so grand—!" Miss Gostrey presses her friend—" 'Clothes-pins? Saleratus? Shoe-polish?' "—but Strether will not reveal the secret. And so that we will not get sidetracked ourselves, the authorial persona informs us that "he, in the sequel, never *was* to tell her," and that ultimately the fact that she didn't know "converted itself into a positive cultivation of ignorance. In ignorance she could humor her fancy, and that proved a useful freedom. She could treat the little nameless object as indeed unnamable—she could make their abstention enormously definite. . . ." Thus Strether's—and James's—insistence upon not naming the article, upon withholding the fact, is made into a humorous affirmation of the supremacy of the imagination over "real life." If we knew what specific article of common use lay behind the Newsome fortune, then the affirmation of the need to live one's life fully while one is able, which is the theme of the novel, would have been weakened. For the existence of that fact— say, for example, a knowledge that the Newsome fortune, and what is possible for Chad Newsome to become, is based on the manufacture of corset stays—would act to discount and to undercut the ideal that Strether posits and Chad proves incapable of apprehending. What we must not say of Strether's choice is, "Yes, but after all, waists are waists, and corsets are necessary to keep them in line, and if Chad doesn't go home and see that they are manufactured, someone else will have to do it . . . ." To prevent this, James cleverly and deliciously leaves the specific article unnamed, and while like Maria Gostrey we are entitled to suspect the worst, the fact that we don't know exactly what it is helps to preserve Strether's advice to Chad from seeming to be precious or unrealistic. By refusing to name the article, James substitutes mystery for fact, and so reinforces his central thesis that not things, but what one can make of them, is the essence of civilized experience. The humor in this instance, arising out of the disproportion between the piqued curiosity of Maria Gostrey and the agreed-upon triviality of the unknown item of manufacture, is the classic American joke—but so dealt with that the ordinariness of the vernacular item, not the excess or affectation of the speculation as to its identity, is what is satirized.

Yet oddly enough, Henry James, not Mark Twain, is the one who seems always to wind up "defending" the American imagination; and Mark Twain, not James, usually ends up declaring it a snare and a delusion. At the conclusion of *Daisy Miller*, when the American girl has died of an infection caused by exposure to the unhealthy night air of the Colosseum (i.e., mosquitoes), it is the expatriate Winterbourne who realizes that he has been too long away from America to appreciate his compatriot's directness and innocence, and so will waste his remaining years in triviality and hedonistic purposelessness. And Lambert Strether of *The Ambassadors*, once he has learned what the Europeans have to tell him about living, proves superior to them all, for Strether has learned how to ground his moral sense in real life, which is a very different thing from abandoning it altogether. So the effete, precious Henry James winds up as the literary patriot. Though his version of the Great American Joke is weighted on the side of the inadequacy of the fact in the face of the ideal, it always turns out that the American ideal, at its best, *is* grounded in human fact, and so it is the superior version of reality. However much James may apprehend and appreciate European culture, he seems finally to find it morally deficient. Clemens, by contrast, though he pokes fun at traditional culture and genteel refinement, ended up denying the supposedly superior reality of that world of common-sense fact that he tried to anchor his values in, and proclaiming, in "The Mysterious Stranger," that "you are but a *thought*—a vagrant thought, a useless thought, a homeless thought, wandering forlorn among the empty eternities!" The great American joke, in short, turns out to be on good old, common-sensical, red-blooded Samuel L. Clemens.

One might think that as America grew more sophisticated and more cosmopolitan in its tastes in the twentieth century, and as the frontier ceased to be a fact of American life, the humor would move around more and more to the Jamesian perspective—would, that is, learn to discount the raw fact rather than the imaginative ideal. But what has happened is that both perspectives have retained their ardent adherents. We might consider, for example, the so-called "melting pot" school of humor, which chronicles the throes of assimilation of minority groups into the general American culture. Among the better examples of such humor are the Hyman Kaplan stories that Leonard Q. Ross was writing in the 1930's and 1940's, describing the attempts of a teacher in the adult beginner's class in English in New York to reconcile the experience of his immigrant charges with the customs and attitudes of American life. The teacher, Mr. Parkhill, is presumably an Anglo-Saxon Protestant American, with the proper training and culture. He presides over a class of ladies and gentlemen named Gidwitz, Trabish, Wilkomirski, Mitnick, Pomeranz, Caravello, Matsoukas, Moskowitz, and in particular one Hyman K*A*P*L*A*N, whose zeal for knowledge is the terror of Mr. Parkhill and the delight of some of his fellow students. In one such story, "Christopher K*A*P*L*A*N," Mr. Parkhill introduces his class to the news that October 12 is Columbus's Birthday. Unfortunately for him it also turns out to be Mr. Kaplan's birthday, and so Mr. Kaplan not only defends Columbus with enthusiasm, but will countenance no mistreatment of his idol. He is especially irate over the behavior of Ferdinand and Isabella, and their stinginess in dealing with Columbus:

Mr. Kaplan paused to let the drama sink home. "Vell, in *vat kind boats* Columbiss made the vunderful voyitch?" Mr. Kaplan's eyes narrowed. "I esk—*in vat kind boats?* Leetle, teentsy sheeps! Chizz boxes! Boats full of likks. Boats full doit, joims, vater commink in! *Som* boats for discoverink America! An' det's vy I'm sayink '*Shame* on you, Foidinand an' Isabel!'" Mr. Kaplan's eyes flashed. "Couldn't dey give a man like Columbiss batter transportation?"

This causes tumult in the class. Mr. Plonsky, who understands the problem, says sarcastically, "Maybe dey should builded in 1492 a S. S. Quinn Marie?" Mr. Parkhill attempts to mediate between the extremes, but Mr. Kaplan will have no excuses. Christopher Columbus deserved the best and he didn't get it. At the close, "Mr. Parkhill felt that General Discussion had not been a complete success this evening. If only Columbus had discovered America on October eleventh; if only Hyman Kaplan had been born on October thirteenth."

The humor is genteel, but the joke is on the ideality. Mr. Parkhill represents culture, tradition, sophistication. Mr. Kaplan is the vernacular perspective incarnate. What is talk of historical differences and changed conditions to him? A ship is a ship. Our sympathies may be with the weary and badgered English teacher, but our hearts are with the vigorous, colloquial Hyman Kaplan, for whatever his lack of historical sense, his world is so much more convincing and closer to experience than that of Mr. Parkhill's learning that it carries us along with it.

Or to consider a more formidable literary example, we might think of a work such as John Barth's *The Sot-Weed Factor*. This elaborate and hilarious work of comic genius is based on the imaginary doings of one Ebenezer Cooke in seventeenth-century America. Barth chose his hero from the real life Hudibrastic satirist Ebenezer Cooke, whose poem "The Sotweed Factor" was a witty castigation of the barbarity of life in colonial Maryland. But where Cooke's poem was done from the same perspective as Byrd's *History of the Dividing Line*, and makes sport of the shortcomings of New

World civilization, Barth reverses the approach. He portrays Eben Cooke, both in England and in Maryland, as a callow, idealistic youth who is constantly insulted and injured by the realities of the vulgar world. There is also a tremendous amount of spoofing of history and historians, and parodying of older writings. The author, having done a formidable job of research into seventeenth-century history and pornography, uses his knowledge to suggest, much as James Branch Cabell did before him in the novels of Poictesme and Mark Twain before that in *A Connecticut Yankee*, that the citizens of bygone times were every bit as mortal and fallible as those of today. One of Barth's best touches has to do with the purported inside story of the famous encounter between Captain John Smith and Pocahontas. Burlesquing the prose of a colonial travel journal, he tells what actually happened in Powhatan's lodge when the Indian maiden interceded to save the English captain's life. The story is, like much of *The Sot-Weed Factor*, very funny and very dirty. The humor resides in the irreverence toward history and the introduction of a great deal of vulgar sexual detail into the hitherto chaste accounts of the colonial past. Once sex is permitted to rear its ugly head, the traditional attitudes toward the brave Captain Smith and the tender-hearted Indian maiden are upset. The historical legend, the patriotic respect for the heroic virtues of the immoderate past, falls before the triumphant reality of the vulgar fact.

Yet the contrasting viewpoint is very much a part of our humor, too. One thinks, for example, of Ring Lardner, whose mastery of the flatness of the common idiom of Middle America was employed to savagely satirical advantage in his stories of barbers, ballplayers, businessmen, prizefighters, songwriters, chauffeurs, drugstore clerks, and the like. Here is a paragraph from a letter, written to a man in New York by a girl in Chicago, in which she tells of a visit from her sister:

Well, Sis and I have been on the "go" ever since she arrived as I took yesterday and today off so I could show her the "sights" though she says she would be perfectly satisfied to just sit in the apartment and listen to me "rattle on." Am afraid I am a great talker, Mr. Lewis, but Sis says it is as good as a show to hear me talk as I tell things in such a different way as I cannot help from seeing the humorous side of everything and she says she never gets tired of listening to me, but of course she is my sister and thinks the world of me, but she really does laugh like she enjoyed my craziness.

In the letterwriter's pathetic effort to tell her correspondent of her supreme charm without seeming to, and in the general banality and flatness of her writing, Lardner is portraying cultural starvation, the absence of taste and discrimination, the tediousness and the materialism of the "ordinary" citizen. What the lady wants is a man, and she goes about it doggedly and unimaginatively, with her every attempt to seem coquettish made so painfully obvious that whatever sympathy one might otherwise have for her is undercut by her own dreary self-seeking. As for the man, he toys with her while he is still loose in New York and anxious for his prospects, but once he begins to make his way in the Big Town he drops her without further ado. Here the clash of modes is used by Lardner to demonstrate the tawdriness and venality of the vernacular culture; the humor lies in the incongruity between what the girl is pretending to be and what she so clearly is. What she is pretending to be is civilized. There is so appalling a gulf between the good, the true and the beautiful on one side, and the crass values and limited imaginative capabilities of the letterwriter on the other, that one would feel shame for the human race if the comparisons were not being made so amusingly.

We will find a similar approach in the humor of H. L. Mencken, the professional scourge of middle-class American standards of the 1910's and 1920's. Mencken came into American life as a literary critic, a champion of European ideas and sophisticated standards in combat with the bloodless ideality of the waning genteel tradition. By the 1920's he had branched out into social and political criticism, and in the pages of his magazine *The American Mercury* he led a vigorous campaign against hypocrisy, prohibition and William Jennings Bryan. Here is the earlier Mencken, writing about the deficiencies of American dramatic reviewing in the 1910's:

. . . consider Clayton Hamilton, M.A., vice-president of the National Institute of Arts and Letters. Here are the tests he proposes for dramatic critics, *i.e.*, for gentlemen chiefly employed in reviewing such characteristic American compositions as the Ziegfield Follies, "Up in Mabel's Room," "Ben-Hur" and "The Witching Hour":

1. Have you ever stood bareheaded in the nave of Amiens?
2. Have you ever climbed to the Acropolis by moonlight?
3. Have you ever walked with whispers into the hushed presence of the Frari Madonna of Bellini?

What could more brilliantly evoke an image of the eternal Miss Birch, blue veil flying and Baedeker in hand, plodding along faithfully through the interminable corridors and catacombs of the Louvre, the while bands are playing across the river, and young bucks in three-gallon hats are sparking the gals, and the Jews and harlots uphold the traditions of French *big leef* at Longchamps, and American deacons are frisked and debauched up on martyrs' hill?

At first glance this might appear to be spoken in favor of the vernacular, colloquial perspective—the "fact"—rather than the other side, since Mencken is obviously opposing the notion of ideality and the pose-striking of high culture. But what he is really doing is just the opposite. He is calling for a criticism—and a literature—that can deal genuinely with truth and beauty, without the artificial attitudinizing of polite culture. The "fact" that Mencken is scoffing at is the fact of Clayton Hamilton, M.A., and the genteel tradition; and the concrete metaphors of "real life" that he is citing to illustrate what genteel literature leaves out are really only hypothetical examples, made to stand for an approach to life and literature that will not attempt to find real value and real meaning. Mencken's great skill as a humorous crusader for truth and beauty lies in his artful ability to seize upon and manipulate the concrete detail. He selects Clayton Hamilton, M.A., and he cites several fatuously idealistic pronouncements. He makes Hamilton stand for what is false about the genteel tradition. Then he proposes some other supposedly concrete details, which are in reality only hypothetical examples, and points out the incongruity between the genteel tradition's artificial, bloodless aesthetic and the flesh-and-blood real world that a truly imaginative literature would seek to image. The vision of the Paris scene, the bands across the river, the gourmets and gourmands at the restaurant, the frisking and debauching of puritans by the wickedness of Paris, is made to stand for the reality that is missing from the literature of the genteel tradition. It is American critical standards, not the cultural ideal, that are being attacked.

For Mencken's ideal is a literature that can encompass the true emotional range of American life, and his "fact" is Clayton Hamilton, Bliss Carman, James Whitcomb Riley, and the bloodless sentimentality that passed for the national literature in *Harper's*, *Scribner's*, *The Century*, and the other "cultural" repositories of the day. To deal with H. L. Mencken as an idealist may seem sacrilege, for no one was more devoted to the specific documentation of the American scene. Yet when we get down to what Mencken wants, as distinct from what he is against, it is the cultural ideal that he has in mind, as when he says of Dreiser's early novels that "they get below the drama that is of the moment and reveal the greater drama that is without end. They arouse those deep and lasting emotions which grow out of the recognition of elemental and universal tragedy. His aim is not merely to tell a tale; his aim is to show the vast ebb and flow of forces which sway and condition human destiny. . . . The one thing he seeks to do is to stir, to awaken, to move." Against this cultural objective he posits the fact of genteel American taste in the arts. "The central trouble with America," he says, "is conformity, timorousness, lack of enterprise and audacity. A nation of third-rate men, a land offering hospitality only to fourth-rate artists."

This is a very different business from Mark Twain complaining about Americans in Europe taking on phoney Continental airs. What Twain was saying is that Culture is artificial, while the vernacular fact is real. Mencken, by contrast, is on the side of the High Culture, and is attacking the fact of American "culture" because it is not really elevated enough. He wants Beethoven, not Victor Herbert; Dreiser, not Henry Sydnor Harrison. His great comic talent for ridiculing American middle-class cultural standards by making them seem vague and idealistic, while reinforcing his own cultural ideal by using specific, albeit hypothetical, examples, tends to disguise the fact that he is right there on the side of Henry James, so far as his perspective on the conflicting claims of the ideal and the actual goes. It is not the importation of alien European cultural attitudes into a virtuously democratic American society that frets him; he is concerned for the promulgation of genuine cultural values. His wickedly humorous recourse, therefore, is to make fun of the democratic actuality and to show the incongruity between it and the cultural ideal.

To examine American comic writing from colonial times down to the present is to see how the writers have arrayed themselves on one side or the other in the clash of cultural modes, and have used the humor of incongruity to satirize and ridicule the opposing viewpoint. Of course this approach is not peculiar to America, for in a sense all comedy is built upon the discrepancy between the real and the ideal. But in America the matter has always been imbued with a special bread-and-butter relevance. The very nature of an open, democratic society, founded upon abstract principles involving the theoretical equality of all men, has given continuing urgency to the clash of cultural modes. The dichotomy—and that is what it is, since it involves not only division but contradiction— has tended to turn up in every realm of the national experience: political, social, cultural, economic, ethnic, even linguistic. If the role of comedy is to dramatize the conflict between the ideal and the actual, then American society has provided a veritable Civil War of the emotions for use as subject matter.

Each successive political and social crisis affords material for a restatement of the problem all over again. Much of our public and private attention during the last several decades, for example, has gone into the civil rights struggle, and this has offered a mine of opportunities along the comic line. Ralph Ellison's Invisible Man, for example, is determinedly seduced by a zealous white female liberal, who urges him to "beat me, daddy, you big black bruiser. Hurry up, knock me down!" He picks up a lipstick and in red letters across her belly, he writes:

SYBIL, YOU WERE RAPED
BY
SANTA CLAUS
SURPRISE

Ellison uses ridicule to make a telling comment on racial stereotyping and the discrepancy between theory and actuality. The young lady believes herself so emancipated, so free from prejudice, so enlightened, and yet the human being she sees before her is just as surely a stereotype as any minstrel show Mister Bones. But the Invisible Man finally realizes that if he is invisible to others as a man, so is everyone else. Like any other great comic artist, Ellison turns the joke back upon the jokester, questions the very nature of the real and the illusion, and makes the audience examine its own assumptions about where the truth actually lies. "Who knows but that, on the lower frequencies, I speak for you?" his protagonist asks in conclusion. Nothing could be more characteristic of American humor.

Was Miguel Cervantes an American? If not, why not?

About the Contributors

Louis D. Rubin, Jr., is professor of English at the University of North Carolina at Chapel Hill. A native of Charleston, South Carolina, he has written or edited sixteen books, most of them on Southern history and literature, including a novel, *The Golden Weather*.

Richard K. Barksdale, professor of English at the University of Illinois at Urbana-Champaign, was born in Winchester, Massachusetts. He is author of numerous articles on English literature and on Afro-American literature, and coeditor with Kenneth Kinnamon of an anthology, *Black Writers of America*.

Morris Bishop, professor emeritus of romance languages at Cornell University, is both a noted scholar in French, Spanish and Italian literature and the author of three often-quoted collections of light verse. He is a native of Willard, N.Y., and a former president of the Modern Language Association of America.

Hennig Cohen is professor of English at the University of Pennsylvania. A native of Darlington, South Carolina, he was formerly executive secretary of the American Studies Association and editor of *American Quarterly*, and is now chairman of the editorial board of that publication. He has edited numerous books on American literature.

George Core, former senior editor of the University of Georgia Press, is now editor of the *Sewanee Review*. A native of Lexington, Kentucky, he has taught at Davidson College, Vanderbilt University, and the University of North Carolina at Chapel Hill. He has written extensively on American literature and has edited four books in that field.

James M. Cox, professor of English at Dartmouth College, is a native of Independence, Virginia. He has written on numerous

American writers, and his most recent book is *Mark Twain: The Fate of Humor*. He is on leave from his teaching duties in 1972–1973 as a Guggenheim Fellow.

Bernard Duffey is a native of Cincinnati, Ohio, and grew up in the Cleveland area. He is professor of English at Duke University. He has written extensively on American poetry and is author of a book-length study of the Chicago Renaissance of the early 1900's.

Cecil D. Eby, Jr., professor of American literature at the University of Michigan, has written books on the Spanish Civil War and on American literature. He is a native of Charles Town, West Virginia, and has twice served as Fulbright professor at Spanish universities.

William Leigh Godshalk is a native of Bangor, Pennsylvania, and professor of English at the University of Cincinnati. He received the doctorate from Harvard University and has written extensively on the English Renaissance and on James Branch Cabell. He is editor of *Kalki*, a journal devoted to the work of James Branch Cabell.

Seymour L. Gross, a native of New York City, is Burke O'Neill Professor of American Literature at the University of Detroit. His publications include work on Afro-American literature, Nathaniel Hawthorne and Herman Melville.

Allen Guttmann is professor of English and American Studies at Amherst College. He has written books on America and the Spanish Civil War, the Conservative Tradition in America, and the Jewish Writer in America. He is a native of Chicago, Illinois.

William Harmon is associate professor of English and chairman of the Department of English at the University of North Carolina at Chapel Hill. A native of Concord, North Carolina, he is a poet whose first collection, *Treasury Holiday*, was published in 1970. A second volume, *Legion: Civic Choruses*, appeared in the spring of 1973.

C. Carroll Hollis is a native of Needham, Massachusetts, and is professor of English at the University of North Carolina at Chapel Hill. A specialist in Walt Whitman and nineteenth-century American culture, he has written numerous articles on American writers.

C. Hugh Holman, Kenan Professor of English at the University of North Carolina at Chapel Hill, is a native of Cross Anchor, South Carolina. Among his numerous books are studies of Thomas Wolfe, Southern literature, John P. Marquand, and others. The University of Georgia Press has recently published his *The Roots of Southern Writing.*

Blyden Jackson, a native of Louisville, Kentucky, is professor of English at the University of North Carolina at Chapel Hill, and before that was dean of the graduate school at Southern University. He is former president of the College Language Association and an authority on Afro-American Literature.

Robert D. Jacobs is professor of American Literature at Georgia State University. He is a native of Vicksburg, Mississippi. He is author of *Poe: Journalist and Critic* and co-editor of several books on Southern literature.

Lewis Leary, a native of Blauvelt, New York, was professor of English and chairman of the Department of English and Comparative Literature at Columbia University before joining the English faculty at the University of North Carolina at Chapel Hill in 1968. A specialist in colonial American literature, he has written and edited numerous books in that field and on Mark Twain, William Faulkner, Washington Irving, and other subjects.

Jay Martin is professor of English and Comparative Literature at the University of California at Irvine. A native of Newark, New Jersey, he has written books on Conrad Aiken, Robert Lowell, Nathanael West, and a thematic study, *Harvests of Change: American Literature, 1865–1914.*

Lewis P. Simpson is William A. Read Professor of English Literature at the Louisiana State University, Baton Rouge, and co-editor of *The Southern Review*. He is the author of *The Man of Letters in New England and the South* and the editor of books on the literature of the Federalist Period and on Robert Frost. He is a native of Jacksboro, Texas.

Walter Sullivan, a native of Nashville, Tennessee, is professor of English at Vanderbilt University. He is author of two novels, *Sojourn of a Stranger* and *The Long, Long Love*, and a collection of essays on Southern literature, *Death by Melancholy*.

Arlin Turner is editor of *American Literature* and professor of English at Duke University. A native of Texas, he has written extensively on George W. Cable, Nathaniel Hawthorne and other nineteenth-century American authors.

Brom Weber is professor of American studies and founder of the Program in American Studies at the University of California, Davis. He is a native of New York City. His many books include studies of Sherwood Anderson and Hart Crane, editions of Crane, the "Sut Lovingood" stories of G. W. Harris, and American humor, and a study, *Sense and Sensibility in Twentieth-Century Writing*.

Gerald Weales, a native of Connersville, Indiana, is professor of English at the University of Pennsylvania. He has written six books on modern drama as well as a novel, and has edited volumes on drama. He was awarded the George Jean Nathan Award for drama criticism for 1964–1965.

Louis B. Wright recently retired as director of the Folger Shakespeare Library in Washington, D.C. A native of Greenwood County, South Carolina, he has written and edited many books on Colonial American Literature, including the publication, after their rediscovery in the 1930s, of the diaries of William Byrd.

Index

The text of this book was set in Janson Linotype and printed by offset on RUP Offset supplied by Lindenmeyr Paper Corporation, Long Island City, N.Y. Composed, printed and bound by Quinn & Boden Company, Inc., Rahway, N.J.

Index compiled by Roberta Blaché